A SOUTH AFRICAN PERSPECTIVE
ON
THE NEW TESTAMENT

A SOUTH AFRICAN PERSPECTIVE ON THE NEW TESTAMENT

*Essays by South African New Testament Scholars
presented to Bruce Manning Metzger
during his Visit to South Africa in 1985*

EDITED BY

J. H. PETZER AND P. J. HARTIN

LEIDEN — E. J. BRILL — 1986

Financial assistance from the Council for Human Research for the publication of this book is hereby acknowledged. The opinions expressed and conclusions drawn in the articles in this book are those of the authors and in no way of the Council for Human Research.

Financial assistance is also acknowledged from:
Barclays National Bank (Ltd.)
The House of Irrigation (Pty. ltd.)
The Reformed Church Viljoenskroon

BS
2395
.S65
1986

ISBN   90 04 07720 0

PRINTED IN THE NETHERLANDS BY E. J. BRILL

CONTENTS

NEW TESTAMENT METHODOLOGY

THE GOSPELS

THE LETTERS

PREFACE

To attempt to summarise the contribution of Professor Bruce Manning Metzger to the study of the New Testament would be an impossible task. Without doubt he is one of the foremost New Testament text critics whose contribution to this field of study is immeasurable. But, this contribution is not restricted to this field of study alone; it extends to almost every aspect of the New Testament. This fact can be seen very clearly from his bibliography and curriculum vitae, initially printed in the *Festschrift* edited by *Eldon Jay Epp* and *Gordon D. Fee*, which appeared in 1981 at the Clarendon Press, and is updated in this present volume.

For us it is a great privilege and honour to have Professor Metzger as the guest of various South African universities. We felt that the most fitting way to express our gratitude and pleasure towards such an eminent scholar for visiting various universities in South Africa would be by means of a *Festschrift* in his honour, containing essays by some of the leading New Testament scholars in South Africa.

The essays in this present volume cover a wide range of New Testament topics and are not restricted to one area of the study of the New Testament. This may leave the impression that the *Festschrift* lacks homogeneity. However, in not restricting the topics of these essays, a much better view could be given of the present state of New Testament scholarship in South Africa. At the same time one can note the basic issues which are being discussed and studied at the various centres where the New Testament forms an aspect of study in this country.

By presenting this *Festschrift* to Professor Metzger, we express, firstly, our gratitude to him for visiting South Africa, and, secondly that our best wishes accompany him and his wife on their tour of South Africa. Through this personal encounter it is hoped that all will be greatly enriched in their scholarship and investigation of the New Testament. May this volume constantly remind him of the time spent in South Africa.

The editors' responsibilities were restricted to the *technical aspects* of the essays, and the authors, therefore, take total responsibility for the contents. The editors express their gratitude to Dr. Keith Elliott for his valuable suggestions, Mrs. Nardine Bothma for the typing of the manuscript and Mr. Jan Botha for his help in the proofreading of the manuscript.

A special word of gratitude goes to *The Council for Human Research* and *Barclays National Bank Limited*, without whose financial contribution this *Festschrift* would never have appeared in print, and *E. J. Brill* for acceptance of the *Festschrift* for publication.

J. H. Petzer and P. J. Hartin

FOREWORD

Bruce Manning Metzger has already been lauded in various ways by several institutions as a renowned New Testament scholar and an exemplary man of the church. This eulogy from the southern tip of Africa represents a wholehearted identification with the world-wide respect and grateful appreciation that exists for the person, the life and the work of this God-gifted man.

He is known throughout the Christian theological world as a result of his publications, many of which have been translated into different languages and in turn has gained him a large number of student followers.

In South Africa Metzger also attained prominence. Here too it is his publications which have distinguished him among students from our own ranks. Recently this alliance has been considerably strenghtened by the work on the new translation of the Bible into Afrikaans. Directly and indirectly Metzger has made a contribution and theologians in South Africa have once again realised the value and range of his work. His highly esteemed *A textual commentary on the Greek New Testament* provided a unique motivation for the choice of texts for specific editions of the Greek New Testament which were used.

Bruce Metzger is one of the five members of the United Bible Societies' international panel revising the Greek text of the New Testament. All this was indispensable material for the translators, as I also, in all humility experienced.

It is widely known that Metzger is a first-rate, precise and productive student, academic and teacher. The painstakingly neat person, the dignified gentleman enjoys the respect and reverence of his students. Metzger, the gifted, is known among his students as the "walking encyclopaedia". Despite all these things for which he is revered and respected the most important has not been mentioned.

Bruce Metzger is honoured and revered above all for his outstanding academic and professional skill which has not been the actual goal. In everything he maintains a consistent humbleness for which he is particularly revered and which makes him a welcome friend.

We dedicate this volume to the gentle, modest and humble person with great appreciation - to Bruce Metzger! May the world and the church of Christ still have him in health and strength to serve for many years.

T. van der Walt
Principal

Potchefstroom University
for Christian Higher Education

LIST OF ABBREVIATIONS

The following abbreviations occur in the articles:

AnBib   – Analecta Biblica
BETL   – Bibliotheca Ephemeridum Theologicarum Lovaniensum
BH   – Biblia Hebraica
BS   – Bibliotheca Sacra
BT   – Bible Translator
BZ   – Biblische Zeitschrift
CBQ   – Catholic Biblical Quarterly
EQ   – Evangelical Quarterly
ET   – Expository Times
ETL   – Ephemeridum Theologicae Lovaniensis
GNB   – Good News Bible
GNTMT   – Greek New Testament according to the Majority Text
GTT   – Gereformeerd Theologisch Tijdschrift
HThR   – Harvard Theological Review
Interp   – Interpretation
JBL   – Journal of Biblical Literature
JETS   – Journal of the Evangelical Theological Society
JR   – Journal of Religion
JSOT   – Journal for the Study of the Old Testament
JThS   – Journal of Theological Studies
KJV   – King James Version
LXX   – Septuagint
NEB   – New English Bible
NGTT   – Nederduitse Gereformeerde Teologiese Tydskrif
NIV   – New International Version
NT   – Novum Testamentum
NTS   – New Testament Studies
NTSMS   – New Testament Studies Monograph Series
NTSSA   – New Testament Society of South Africa
NTSup   – Novum Testamentum Supplements
NTT   – Nederlands Theologisch Tijdschrift
RB   – Revue Biblique
RQ   – Restoration Quarterly
RSR   – Recherches de Science Religieuse
RSV   – Revised Standard Version
SBL   – Society of Biblical Literature
SJT   – Scottish Journal of Religion
SNTS   – Societas Novi Testamenti Studiorum
Str-B   – Kommentar zum Neuen Testament aus Talmud und Midrasch von H. L. Strack
              & P. Billerbeck
TDNT   – Theological Dictionary of the New Testament
TEV   – Today's English Version
ThD   – Theological Digest
ThLZ   – Theologische Literaturzeitung
ThR   – Theological Revue
ThTO   – Theology Today
TijdsTh   – Tijdschrift voor Theologie
TRE   – Theologische Realenzyklopädie

TS   – *Theological Studies*
TWNT   – *Theologische Wörterbuch zum Neuen Testament*
TynB   – *Tyndale Bulletin*
VG   – *Vigiliae Christianae*
VT   – *Vetus Testamentum*
WTJ   – *Westminster Theological Journal*
ZNW   – *Zeitschrift für die Neutestamentliche Wissenschaft*
ZThK   – *Zeitschrift für Theologie und Kirche*

CURRICULUM VITAE OF BRUCE M. METZGER

BACKGROUND AND EDUCATION

Born: February 9, 1914 at Middleton, Pennsylvania

— A.B., Lebanon Valley College, 1935 (awarded prize in the Bimillennium Horatianum)
— Th.B., Princeton Theological Seminary, 1938 (awarded New Testament Fellowship)
— Th.M., Princeton Theological Seminary, 1939
— M.A., Princeton University, 1940
— Ph.D., Princeton University, 1942 (Greek and Latin Classics)

HONORARY DEGREES

— D.D., Lebanon Valley College, 1951
— L.H.D., Findlay College, 1962
— D.D., University of St. Andrews, 1964
— D.Theol., University of Münster/Westf., 1970
— D.Litt., Potchefstroom University for CHE, 1985

PROFESSIONAL ACTIVITIES

— Teaching Fellow in New Testament, Princeton Theological Seminary, 1938-40
— Ordained to the Christian Ministry, Presbyterian Church, USA, 1939
— Instructor in New Testament, Princeton Theological Seminary, 1940-42; Assistant Professor of New Testament, 1942-48; Associate Professor, 1948-54; Professor of New Testament, 1954-64; George L. Collord Professor of New Testament Language and Literature, 1964-84; Professor Emeritus, 1984
— Visiting Professor, New College for Advanced Christian Studies (Berkeley), 1978
— Visiting Fellow, Wolfson College, Oxford, 1979
— Visiting Professor, North Park Theological Seminary, Chicago, 1984

AWARDS AND HONOURS

— Prizes for books in competitions sponsored by the Christian Research Foundation, 1955, 1962 and 1963

— Honorary Fellow and Corresponding Member, Higher Institutes of Coptic Studies, Cairo, 1955--
— Recipient, Certificate of Distinguished Service in the Preparation of the Revised Standard Version of the Bible with the Apocrypha, National Council of Churches, 1957
— Recipient, Distinguished Alumnus Award, Lebanon Valley College, Alumni Association, 1961
— Corresponding Fellow of the British Academy, 1978--

EDITORIAL RESPONSIBILITIES

— Editorial Secretary, *Theology Today*, 1947-59
— Member, Editorial Council, *New Testament Studies*, Cambridge, 1954-57
— Member, Editorial Committee, *Translators' Greek New Testament*, United Bible Societies, 1956--
— Member, Board of Managers, *Index to Religious Periodical Literature*, 1958-68
— Member, Editorial Committee, *Theology Today*, 1962--
— Member, Board of Editorial Advisors, Project on the Pseudepigrapha, Duke University, 1972--
— Chairman, American Committee on Versions, International Greek New Testament Project, 1950--
— Visiting Lecturer, Seminário Theológico Presbyteriano do Sul, Campinas, Brazil, 1952
— Secretary, Panel of Translators of the Apocrypha, Revised Standard Version, 1952-57
— Secretary, American Textual Criticism Seminar, 1954-56
— Member, Managing Committee, American School of Classical Studies at Athens, 1958-84
— Member, Kuratorium, Vetus Latina Institut, Beuron/Hohenzollern, 1959--
— Member, Wissenschaftlicher Beirat, Institut für neutestamentliche Textforschung, Münster/Westf., 1961--
— Delegate of the Society of Biblical Literature to the American Council of Learned Societies, 1963-67
— Chairman, Committee on Translation, American Bible Society, 1964-70
— Member, Institute for Advanced Study, Princeton, 1964 and 1974
— Scholar-in-Residence, Tyndale House, Cambridge, 1969
— Distinguished Visiting Professor, Fuller Theological Seminary, 1970
— Chairman, American Executive Committee, International Greek New Testament Project, 1970--

— Chairman, New Testament Section, Revised Standard Version Bible Committee, 1971--
— President, Society of Biblical Literature, 1971
— President, Studiorum Novi Testamenti Societas, 1971-72
— President, North American Patristic Society, 1972
— Visiting Fellow, Clare Hall, Cambridge, 1974
— Chairman, Revised Standard Version Bible Committee, 1976--
— Visiting Professor, Gordon-Conwell Theological Seminary, 1978
— Member, Advisory Committee, *Thesaurus Linguae Graecae*, University of California (Irvine), 1972-81
— Member, Scientific Council, *La Concordance de la Bible*, Brepols, Turnhout, Belgium, 1976--
— Member, Advisory Committee, *The Collected Works of Erasmus*, University of Toronto Press, 1977--

ACADEMIC LECTURES

Aberdeen University; Albion College; Albright College; Anderson College; Asbury Theological Seminary; Ashland Theological Seminary; Belhaven College; Bethany Lutheran College; Bethel College; Bethel Theological Seminary (Adolf Olson Memorial Lectures); Boston College (Humanities Lecture); Brigham Young University (twice); Cambridge University; Central Baptist Theological Seminary; Chicago University; Claremont School of Theology (Colwell Lecture); Concordia Senior College (Fort Wayne); Concordia Theological Seminary (Springfield); Concordia Theological Seminary (St. Louis); Dallas Theological Seminary; Detroit University; Durham University; Eastern Baptist Theological Seminary; Eastern Mennonite Theological Seminary; Evangelical Congregational Theological Seminary; Exeter University; Findlay College; Friends Bible College; Glasgow University; Grace College; Haverford College; Houghton College (twice); Institute of Advanced Study; Institute of Classical Studies, University of London; King College (twice); Lebanon Valley College (twice); Leeds University; Lincoln Christian Seminary; Malone College; Miami University (twice); Divinity School, McMaster University; Milligan College; Moore Theological College (Melbourne); New Brunswick Theological Seminary; New College, University of Edinburgh; New Orleans Baptist Theological Seminary; North Park Theological Seminary, Chicago; Northwest Christian College; Oberlin College; Pacific Christian College; Pfeiffer College; Pittsburgh Theological Seminary; Potchefstroom University for Christian Higher Education; Presbyterian Theological College, Aberystwyth; Rand Afrikaans University; Rhodes University; Southwestern Baptist Theological Seminary (three times, including the Day-Higgenbotham

Lectures); St. Andrews University; Shenandoah College; Trinity College (Burlington); Trinity College (Dublin); Trinity University (Willson Lectures); University College, Lampeter (Wales); University of Cape Town; University of Durban-Westville; University of Münster/Westf.; University of Natal; University of the Orange Free State; University of Port Elizabeth; University of Pretoria; University of South Africa; University of Utah; University of the Witwatersrand; Valparaiso University; Wellesley College; Wesley College; Western Theological Seminary; Westminster Theological Seminary; Wheaton College (twice); Winebrenner Theological Seminary; Yale University; University of Zululand.

BIBLIOGRAPHY OF BRUCE M. METZGER

A bibliography of 150 books and articles down to 1979 is included in E. J. Epp & G. D. Fee (eds) 1981. *New Testament Textual Criticism, Its Significance for Exegesis; Essays in Honour of Bruce M. Metzger.* Oxford: Clarendon Press. The following list brings the record up-to-date at the end of 1984.

1979

The Text of the New Testament, Its Transmission, Corruption, and Restoration, Korean translation by Yoo-Choong Kang. Seoul: Pyong Wha-Sa. 350 pp.

Handing down the Bible through the Centuries. *Search* (Dublin) 2, 19-26.

1980

Lexical Aids for Students of New Testament Greek, (British Edition). Oxford: Basil Blackwell. xi + 100 pp.

An Early Protestant Bible Containing the Third Book of the Maccabees, in M. Brect (ed), *Text-Wort-Glaube; Studien zur Überlieferung, Interpretation und Autorisierung biblischer Texte: Kurt Aland gewidmet.* Berlin: Walter de Gruyter, 123-133.

A Rare Latin Bible in Speer Library, *Princeton Seminary Bulletin* N S 3, 71-75.

1981

The Text of the New Testament, Its Transmission, Corruption, and Restoration, Chinese translation by Paul Kong. Taipei: China Evangelical Seminary Press. viii + 292 pp.

The Westcott and Hort Greek New Testament - Yesterday and Today. *Cambridge [University] Review* 20 November 1981, 71-76.

The Revised Standard Version (of the Bible), in L. R. Bailey (ed), *The Word of God, a Guide to English Versions of the Bible.* Atlanta: John Knox Press, 28-44.

1982

An Introduction to the Apocrypha, Korean translation by Young-Jin Min. Seoul: Concordia Press. 256 pp.

1983

General Editor of *The Reader's Digest Bible*; Condensed from the Revised Standard Version Old and New Testaments by the Editors of Reader's Digest Pleasantville: The Reader's Digest Association, 1982. xvi + 799 pp.; British edition, *The Reader's Bible*, with a Foreword by Donald Coggan, London, 1983.

Foreword to *A Concordance to the Apocrypha/Deuterocanonical Books of the Revised Standard Version*. Grand Rapids: Eerdmans.

The New Testament, Its Background, Growth, and Content, Korean translation by Chae Woon Na. Seoul: Korean Christian Literature Publishing Co. 344 pp.

The Fourth Book of Ezra, in J. H. Charlesworth (ed), *The Old Testament Pseudepigrapha*, vol. 1. Garden City: Doubleday, 516-559.

On Making Sense of the Book of Revelation. *Trinity Occasional Papers* (Brisbane) 2, 46-56.

The Prayer that Jesus Taught his Disciples, in P. Rogers (ed), *Sowing the Word, Biblical-Theological Essays*. Dublin: Dominican Publications, 125-134.

The Reader's Digest Bible (with R. C. White Jr). *Princeton Seminary Bulletin* N S 4, 84-87.

1984

Contributed to *The New Testament in Greek: The Gospel According to St. Luke*, Part One, Chapters 1-12. Edited by the American and British Committees of the International Greek New Testament Project. Oxford: Clarendon Press.

The Jehovah's Witnesses and Jesus Christ (A Biblical and Theological Appraisal), translated into Chinese by Shing Chan Leung. Hong Kong: Seed Press. 46 pp.; also translated into Malaysian by Hwa Chien. Pahang: Trinity Annual Conference, Methodist Church.

Bilingualism and Polylingualism in Antiquity, with a Check-List of New Testament MSS written in more than One Language, in *The New Testament Age, Essays in Honor of Bo Reicke*, vol. 2. Macon: Mercer University Press, 327-334.

A Classified Bibliography of the Graeco-Roman Mystery Religions 1924-1973, with a Supplement 1974, in W. Haase (ed), *Aufstieg und*

Niedergang der römischen Welt, II, 17. Band, part 3. Berlin: Walter de Gruyter, 1259-1423.

How well do you know the Apocrypha? *Guideposts* November 1984, 28-31.

TABULA GRATULATORIA

The following scholars could for various reasons not contribute to this volume, but wished to be associated with it by wishing Metzger a pleasant and blessed stay in South Africa:

F. J. Botha — Dept of New Testament, University of Pretoria

J. L. de Villiers — Dept of New Testament, University of Stellenbosch

G. P. V. du Plooy — Dept of Greek, University of Stellenbosch

J. J. Engelbrecht — Dept of New Testament, University of Pretoria

P. A. Geyser — Dept of Divinity, University of the Witwatersrand (emeritus)

E. P. Groenewald — Dept of New Testament, University of Pretoria (emeritus)

H. L. N. Joubert — Dept of Biblical Studies, University of Fort Hare (emeritus)

S. G. Kemp — Dept of Biblical Studies, Potchefstroom University for CHE

C. E. T. Kourie — Dept of New Testament, University of South Africa

M. A. Kruger — Dept of New Testament, Theological School of Hammanskraal

H. R. Lemmer — Dept of Biblical Studies, Academy in Windhoek

S. J. P. K. Riekert — Dept of Greek, University of the Orange Free State

S. W. Theron — Minister in the Dutch Reformed Church, Pretoria

C. J. H. Venter — Minister in the Reformed Church, Stellenbosch

J. L. Venter — Minister in the Reformed Church, Pretoria

T. van der Walt — Principal of the Potchefstroom University for CHE

H. J. B. COMBRINK

THE CHANGING SCENE OF BIBLICAL INTERPRETATION

Much has already been written in recent years about the changing scene in the interpretation of the New Testament, and the Bible as a whole (cf Lategan 1984). Yet it may be fitting to call attention to it again here especially as in the midst of the scholarly community honouring Professor Metzger with this volume, a willingness to respond to the call to venture on different methodological ways became apparent in the course of time (cf besides Louw 1982, some of the issues of *Neotestamentica*, the publication of the *New Testament Society of South Africa*).

There was a time when scholarship championing the cause of rhetorical criticism (Muilenburg 1969), or urging biblical scholars to return to the tested ways of literary criticism 'proper' (Frye 1971, 1979a & b), seemed not to receive the attention of the scholarly community they in fact deserved. At a stage when current New Testament scholarship consisted to a large degree in looking *through* the text itself at the history of the text *behind* it, the judgement of the literary critic Frye sounded harsh but, nevertheless, quite appropriate: "And this is what the methodologies in question yield: not sound literary history, but a mass of speculations and conjectures, a labyrinth of pseudo-historical constructs... they are not recognizable as literary history to one who represents this field in secular scholarship" (Frye 1979b:218).

Since then the scene has changed decisively. New Testament scholarship—or at least an increasing section of it—has been moving through various phases of renewal in methodology, and the debate on these matters has in a certain sense only just started gaining momentum. This is attested by the manner in which these topics feature at the meetings of the *Society of Biblical Literature*, as well as in seminars of the *Studiorum Novi Testamenti Societas*.

Perhaps the single most important characteristic of this phenomenon is the (renewed) awareness of the contribution made by other disciplines and by scholars who are themselves not New Testament exegetes, but whose contributions have played an important role in changing the scene. Especially remarkable is the amount of interest of literary critics in biblical studies (cf also Frye 1982), as well as the enthusiasm with which many exegetes have taken to implementing literary criticism in the 'secular' sense of the word (cf Spencer 1980; Rhoads & Michie 1982;

Culpepper 1983; Kingsbury 1983). Perhaps one could also say that in a certain sense the wheel has turned full circle, and that in many respects biblical research is now back again at certain points of the agenda which were seemingly left behind a while ago, by some scholars at least. And yet everything is not exactly the same as before.

Although the almost exclusive focus on a synchronic approach to texts is clearly one-sided and is to be seen as a reaction to an equally one-sided historical (or rather historicist) approach to texts, it cannot be denied that the concentrated attention—in various forms—on the text, is of the utmost importance. But even in this focusing on the text, one can distinguish between the *message* (signified, content) and the *means* (signifier, expression), being aware, however, that these aspects of a text can never be divided into watertight compartments.

It cannot be denied that even today 'rhetoric' has a negative connotation for many people. Of late a renewed and positive appraisal of the rhetorical features of a text can be detected. This can be traced to the facelift the concept of rhetoric received from Perelman (1979) and others. This is now evident in biblical research too, though not everybody consciously uses the term 'rhetoric' (Kessler 1982; Nida *et al* 1983; cf Dewey 1980). Attention is therefore directed again to the various rhetorical devices and techniques discernible in a text, as well as to the macrolevel and microlevel of rhetorical structures. It is important that in these approaches to the text, even in the case of the synoptic gospels, the text in its final form is taken as the object of research. This emphasis on the *how*, the *means* of the *surface structure* of the text, is perhaps one of the dimensions which did not receive adequate attention at a certain stage of structural research, however interesting or important the concentration on the text as such might have been in this approach.

Before leaving the notion of rhetoric, it should also be pointed out that often an awareness of the rhetorical dimensions of the text is not coupled with an adequate perception of texts functioning as signs having meaning for receptors. This is the one-sidedness of the structural or discourse analysis as practised, at least at a certain stage, by several members of the NTSSA (cf Deist 1979 and Steyn 1984). They failed to reckon with the semiotic dimensions and the function of rhetorical features. Such reckoning entails a sensitivity not only to the textual context (co-text), but also to the communicative and cultural context. To this we shall have to return later.

Besides the renewed attention to the *how* of the text, the *what*, the *message* has also been the object of intensive research. Again it is difficult to separate form and content, but the intense literary critical debate on for example the narrative for the past ten to fifteen years (cf Prince 1982;

Chatman 1980), has definitely contributed to the interpretation of Old and New Testament narratives (cf Alter 1981; Berlin 1983; Rhoads & Michie 1982 and Culpepper 1983). The research in this respect is forwarding the interpretation of gospel narratives by using narrative criticism. In this process some remarkably new and stimulating insights are being brought to light.

One should, however, keep in mind that not everyone talking about narrative in theology is doing it from the same perspective. In the so-called *narrative theology* three approaches are usually distinguished: canonical story, life story and community story. According to Stroup "our real interest is not the literary genre but the hermeneutical process which is the foundation for Christian narrative" (Stroup 1981:96).

Without entering into the merits of doing systematic theology from the perspective of the narrative structure of Christian faith, it should be clear that the new emphasis in biblical studies is directly related to the implementing of literary categories such as point of view, voice, characterization, reported and direct speech and other related matters. Although much has still to be done in these respects, it is obvious that this approach to the *what* of the text promises stimulating and fruitful results.

The interesting thing is now that, just as in the case of the rediscovery of rhetoric, the *function* of narrative in the communication process is also a factor to be reckoned with. In other words, why was the narrative option chosen to communicate the gospel message in the light of the availability of other literary options?

The obvious starting point would be to compare the functioning of Jesus' parables. In this case it is clear that in most instances the parable had a 'jolting function' (Beardslee 1975:308). Even more in general one could say, "Stories move us from where we are to where we could or ought to be" (Luera-Whitmore 1980:91). It should furthermore be realized that really listening to a story is actually the beginning of the telling of another story, the reader's/listener's story as influenced and directed by the story he made his own. But here the interests of pragmatics and the literary interpretation coincide—what is the point of the narrative or the parable? It should be obvious that an answer concerning the pragmatic point cannot be seen in isolation from the textual clues of the narrative as a whole.

Another implication of this renewed attention to biblical narratives from a literary point of view is that the more one learns about the making of the gospel narratives, the more one acquires a 'narrative competence', the capability for "narrating today and in modern verbalization 'stories about God'" (McKnight 1978:109). This implies that research along these lines should inevitably also bear fruit for the way in which biblical narratives function in the preaching and the teaching of the church.

It is evident that narrative research unlocked new and stimulating perspectives in the case of individual biblical stories. But perhaps the biggest benefit from this research is the new perspective on the way in which each one of the individual gospels function as a narrative in its own right. This, of course, has important implications for the interpretation of the individual gospels. And then the effect would not be much different from what the proponents of the so-called narrative theology have in mind. When one really comes to grips with 'God's story' in one of the gospels for example, it is evident that the aim of this narrative is not only a personal identification of the believer with this story with a view to his own 'life story', but also an identification of the reader/hearer with the ongoing story of the people of God, the church of Christ.

Although it has already been suggested more than once in the course of our discussion so far, it is clear that the exclusive attention to 'the text itself', not even accepted by all biblical scholars, did not last so long. Not that this emphasis on the text was an unnecessary luxury when seen against the background of a one-sided preoccupation with the traditions and history of the text. In the world of literary criticism the reaction against the 'New Criticism' exhibits a variety of tendencies (Detweiler 1980). The three key concepts of current literary theory were identified in 1979 as structure, function, and communication. "The historical sequence of the respective booms enjoyed by each of the concepts has a certain element of inevitability, as the links in this chain are the deficiencies of each preceding concept" (Iser 1979:15). In passing it should be added that at present one would, of course, have to add 'deconstruction' to the list too, though not many biblical scholars have yet engaged in this kind of criticism (cf Detweiler 1982).

The latest boom is reader-response criticism or reception theory (cf Holub 1984). But even in this field one can distinguish six different forms of reader-orientated criticism: rhetorical, semiotic and structuralist, phenomenological, subjective and psycho-analytical, sociological and historical, and hermeneutic (Suleiman 1980). In this approach the dialectical process of production and reception of a literary work is emphasized. One may have the impression of complete relativism due to the creative role attributed to the reader. Yet this would not be a valid judgement since it must be remembered that the 'author' is actually a textual strategy and the 'model reader' is in reality a set of felicity conditions (Eco 1979:11; cf Steinmetz 1981:434). Some biblical scholars are already implementing the insights of reception criticism (cf Phillips 1983 and *Neotestamentica* 1984).

Although the role of the reader is to be seen as textually defined, the extratextual context of a text cannot be side-stepped indefinitely. This brings to mind the aim of semioticians like Eco (1976:4) to bridge the dichotomy between semantics and pragmatics. While the structural semiotics in the tradition of de Saussure saw the meaning of an autonomous text as the relation between a signifier and a signified, semioticians following the line of Peirce recognize a relation between the sign and reality as well. One could say that while semantics is the study of meaning in the sense of the interrelation of signs, pragmatics occupies itself with the relation between the sign and the concept, as well as between the sign and the interpreting subject.

The importance of pragmatics for biblical studies is that it underlines again the necessity of dealing with the extra-textual context of the text. Pragmatics recognizes that biblical texts were written, with a view to a specific community in which faith played an important role, a community living in a specific time and setting, determined by specific religious and social sub-codes. Pragmatics therefore deals not only with the specific denotations of the text, but also with the (numerous possible) connotations of a text to be realized according to the competence of the actual readers presupposed by the author (cf Van Wolde 1984:165f). This is what was meant earlier by the remark that in a certain sense the wheel of biblical criticism has turned full circle, although everything is not just as it was before. This is the reason why Barton ventures to classify as a *pragmatic theory of biblical study* the views of 'pre-critical' exegesis "sometimes expressed in (broadly) Barthian circles, that the Bible *becomes* the Word of God when it transforms its hearers as they receive it in faith" (Barton 1984:32).

One should, nevertheless, keep in mind that two variants of pragmatics can be identified. On the one hand, extensional pragmatics deals with the use of signs by existing, real interpreters. This calls for empirical research into the reception of a text by real readers, something obviously very difficult, if viable at all, in the case of the New Testament. On the other hand intensional pragmatics acknowledges the semantic openness of texts, the phenomenon of unlimited semiosis, which then implies the actualization of the interpretative options in the text by the textually implied reader.

It is important that intensional pragmatics deals with the implied or model reader, and not with the empirical, real reader. This does not mean that the extratextual context can be ignored. "Who divorces a text from its context focusing purely on the co-text invariably *supplies* a context for that text, namely the context of his own world, and thus produces underhand eisegesis" (Deist 1983:85). Thus without in any way distracting anything from the valuable emphasis on intrinsic criticism, the extratextual social, cultural and historical dimensions of the communica-

tion situation have to be dealt with. For it is necessary to distinguish between speech acts and speech products, and the pragmatic norms as well
as the pragmatic functions of a speech product are historically determined (cf Seung 1982:113).

As Barton has pointed out, a certain aspect of what biblical critics did
before, could be seen as part of a *pragmatic theory* of biblical interpretation.
It should, however, be also clear that the focus on the use and function of
the text and the effect on the reader is now to be seen within a totally new
theoretical context. Some biblical scholars are already venturing into this
field in an attempt to utilize the results of literary critical research in the
study of the New Testament (cf Frankemölle 1983; Phillips 1983b).

To deal adequately with all the relevant aspects concerned, one needs a
comprehensive textual theory dealing with the mimetic as well as the
communicative dimensions of the text. In this respect the model proposed
by Hernadi (1976) seems to supply the basic components to be dealt with.
It can be supplemented by Eco who accommodates in his model the insights from different theoretical frameworks, including the important
characteristic of both an intensional and an extensional approach
(1979:14). His intensional pragmatic approach to texts can definitely be
of decided value for the interpretation of biblical texts from a pragmatic
point of view.

Together with this renewed attention to the extralinguistic context co-
determining the communication process, one finds the growing
awareness that the sociological factors in this process are to be dealt with
as well. This is not to be done by replacing this historical-philological
method with a new one, or simply by amending it in some ways, but by
completely rethinking and redesigning the method to be used to complete
its task. "This two-fold task focuses on literary matters on the one hand,
and on broadly conceived sociological matters on the other—'broadly
conceived' meaning that the notion of 'sociology' should include in addition to matters usually dealt with by sociological disciplines matters dealt
with by the several disciplines of the field of anthropology" (Petersen
1984:3).

Some basic convictions of proponents of the sociological study of the
New Testament may be mentioned briefly (Best 1983:183f; cf Scroggs
1979/80). Following Berger and Luckmann it is insisted that ideas can
only be understood properly in terms of the social context in which they
originate. Ideas therefore embody a certain social context, but can also be
effective in creating or maintaining one's self-understanding or status.
Furthermore, the distinctiveness of the early Christian church should be
acknowledged. This implies that one should not only be aware of the
danger of modernizing Jesus, but also of modernizing the early church.

In the third place it is realized, as was said above, that 'sociology' should be taken in the broad sense of the word, including a whole set of other disciplines.

It is also important to distinguish between two levels of application of sociological categories to the New Testament. The level of *description* is in line with valuable work done by earlier generations of New Testament scholars. This will remain of great importance in the future too. But the real challenge is to move into the second level, that of *explanation*. With the aid of sociology the aim is here "not merely to describe but also to probe the inner dynamics of the early Christian movement, regarded not as a unique event but as an example of patterns of behaviour which may be widely observed and objectively studied" (Best 1983:185). Interestingly enough, Best insists upon the importance of the faith-dimension in the text of the New Testament precisely for the sake of an accurate sociological analysis, for without that dimension a description of the early Christian movement will be incomplete. After all, it was the Christian faith that was decisive in the shaping of the self-understanding and the social structures of Christianity (Best 1983:192, 194).

This does not mean that there are no problems and pitfalls along this new road for the theologian. As in the case of literary criticism, one will be moving into the more or less unknown area of other disciplines with all the accompanying dangers such as adopting a specific scholar or theory as a favourite, without a really comprehensive and balanced judgement. One must further realize that different sociological models tend to pro duce different results, even in the case of the same texts. In a critical discussion of the sociological analysis of the origin of apocalyptic literature by Paul Hanson, De Villiers (1982:28) identifies certain crucial problems having a reductionist effect on the analysis and its results, without for a moment denying the crucial value of the sociological approach to biblical texts.

It is thus evident that in this respect too biblical interpretation is again experiencing a change of scene. It is, however, interesting that the call for a well-motivated and adequate integration of methods is being taken up by even more scholars. This integration of methods is explicitly stated as his aim by Onuki (1982), who takes his cue from the sociology of knowledge of Berger and Luckmann, as well as from the textual theory of S. J. Schmidt. Although it is probably too early to talk about a consensus in this respect, one may perhaps be permitted to harbour some optimism that New Testament interpretation will benefit decidedly from these efforts.

When one sees the unfolding of the changing scene of biblical interpretation, and especially when one is confronted with the perennial problem of the multiple meaning and interpretation of a text (cf Combrink 1984), it behoves one to be modest about one's own interpretation of the New Testament, without for that reason being daunted in the least from the exciting task lying ahead. It is to honour this combination of exacting scientific research and solid scholarship with profound Christian humility in the life and work of Bruce Metzger, that this contribution is dedicated.

BIBLIOGRAPHY

ALTER, R. 1981. *The art of biblical narrative.* New York: Basic Books.
BARTON, J. 1984. Classifying biblical criticism. *JSOT* 29, 19-35.
BEARDSLEE, W. A. 1975. Narrative form in the New Testament and process theology. *Encounter* 36, 301-15.
BERGER, P. L. & M. LUCKMANN 1967. *The social construction of reality. A treatise in the sociology of knowledge.* New York: Anchor.
BERLIN, A. 1983. *Poetics and interpretation of biblical narrative.* Sheffield: Almond. (Bible and Literature series 9.)
BEST, T. F. 1983. The sociological study of the New Testament: promise and peril of a new discipline. *SJT* 36, 181-194.
CHATMAN, S. 1980. *Story and discourse. Narrative structure in fiction and film.* Ithaca: Cornell University.
COMBRINK, H. J. B. 1984. Multiple meaning and/or interpretation. *Neotestamentica* 18, 26-37.
CULPEPPER, R. A. 1983. *Anatomy of the fourth gospel. A study in literary design.* Philadelphia: Fortress. (Foundations and facets: New Testament.)
DEIST, F. E. 1978. Ope vrae aan die diskoersanalise. *NGTT* 19, 260-71.
DEIST, F. E. 1983. Again: method(s) of exegesis, in J. J. Burden (ed), *Old Testament essays, Volume 1.* Pretoria: Department of Old Testament, University of South Africa, 73-88.
DETWEILER, R. 1980. After the New Criticism: contemporary methods of literary interpretation, in R. A. Spencer (ed), *Orientation by disorientation. Studies in literary criticism and biblical criticism presented in honor of William A. Beardslee.* Pittsburgh: Pickwick, 3-23. (Pittsburgh Theological monograph series.)
DETWEILER, R. 1982. Derrida and biblical studies. *Semeia* 23.
DE VILLIERS, P. G. R. 1982. Renaissance van die sosiologiese teksanalise. *Theologia Evangelica* 15/3, 19-32.
DEWEY, J. 1980. *Markan public debate: literary technique, ring composition and theology in Mark 2:1-3:6.* Chico: Scholars.
ECO, U. 1976. *A theory of semiotics.* Bloomington: Indiana University. (Advances in semiotics.)
ECO, U. 1979. *The role of the reader. Explorations in the semiotics of texts.* London: Hutchinson.
FRANKEMÖLLE, H. 1982. Kommunikatives Handeln in Gleichnissen Jesu. Historisch-kritische und pragmatische Exegese. Eine kritische Sichtung. *NTS* 28, 61-90.
FRANKEMÖLLE, H. 1983. *Biblische Handlungsanweisungen. Beispiele pragmatischer Exegese.* Mainz: Grünewald.
FRYE, N. 1982. *The great code. The Bible and literature.* New York: Harcourt.
FRYE, R. M. 1971. A literary perspective for the criticism of the gospels, in D. G. Miller and D. Y. Hadidian (eds), *Jesus and man's hope II. A perspective book.* Pittsburgh: Pittsburgh Theological Seminary, 193-221.
FRYE, R. M. 1979a. The Jesus of the Gospels. Approaches through narrative structure, in D. Y. Hadidian (ed), *From faith to faith. Essays in honor of Donald G. Miller.* Pittsburgh: Pickwick, 75-89. (Pittsburgh Theological monograph series 31.)
FRYE, R. M. 1979b. Literary criticism and gospel criticism. *ThTo* 36, 207-19.

HERNADI, P. 1976. Literary theory: a compass for critics. *Critical Inquiry* 3, 369-86.
HOLUB, R. C. 1984. *Reception theory. A critical introduction.* London: Methuen. (New accents.)
ISER, W. 1979. The current situation of literary theory. Key concepts and the imaginary. *New Literary History 11*, 1-20.
KESSLER, M. 1982. A methodological setting for rhetorical criticism, in D. J. A. Clines *et al* (eds), *Art and meaning. Rhetoric in biblical narrative.* Sheffield: *JSOT.*
KINGSBURY, J. D. 1983. *The christology of Mark's gospel.* Philadelphia: Fortress.
LATEGAN, B. C. 1984. Current issues in the hermeneutical debate. *Neotestamentica* 18, 1-17.
LOUW, J. P. 1982. *Semantics of New Testament Greek.* Philadelphia: Fortress. (Semeia studies.)
LUERA-WHITMORE, M. W. 1980. *The role of story/storytelling in Christian spiritual formation.* University Microfilms International.
McKNIGHT, E. V. 1978. Generative poetics and New Testament hermeneutics. *Semeia* 10, 107-21.
MUILENBURG, J. 1969. Form criticism and beyond. *JBL* 88, 1-18.
NIDA, E. *et al* 1983. *Style and discourse. With special reference to the text of the New Testament.* Cape Town: Bible Society.
ONUKI, T. 1982. Zur literatursoziologischen Analyse des Johannesevangeliums - auf dem Wege zur Methodenintegration. *Annual of the Japanese Biblical Institute* 8, 162-216.
PERELMAN, C. 1979. *The new rhetoric and the humanities. Essays on rhetoric and its applications.* Dordrecht: Holland.
PETERSEN, N. R. 1984. Towards a literary-sociological method. (Unpublished paper read at universities in South Africa. To be published during 1985 in, *Rediscovering Paul. Philemon and the sociology of Paul's narrative world.* Philadelphia: Fortress.)
PHILLIPS, G. A. 1983a. History and text: The reader in context in Matthew's parable discourse, in K. H. Richards (ed), *Society of Biblical Literature 1983 seminar papers.* Chico: Scholars, 415-37. (*SBL* seminar paper series 22.)
PHILLIPS, G. A. 1983b. "This is a hard saying. Who can be a listener to it?": Creating a reader in John 6. *Semeia* 26, 23-56.
PRINCE, G. 1982. *Narratology. The form and functioning of narrative.* Berlin: Mouton. (Janua Linguarum series maior 108.)
RHOADS, D. & D. MICHIE 1982. *Mark as story. An introduction to the narrative of a gospel.* Philadelphia: Fortress.
SCROGGS, R. 1979/80. The sociological interpretation of the New Testament. The present state of research. *NTS* 26, 164-79.
SEUNG, T. K. 1982. *Semiotics and thematics in hermeneutics.* New York: Columbia University.
SPENCER, R. A. (ed) 1980. *Orientation by disorientation. Studies in literary criticism and biblical criticism presented in honor of William A. Beardslee.* Pittsburgh: Pickwick.
STEINMETZ, H. 1981. Rezeptionsästhetik und Interpretation, in H. Brackert, J. Stückrath & E. Lämmert (hrsg), *Literaturwissenschaft: Grundkurs 2.* Reinbek: Rowohlt, 421-35.
STEYN, J. 1984. Some psycholinguistic factors involved in the discourse analysis of ancient texts. *Theologia Evangelica* 17/2, 51-65.
STROUP, G. W. 1981. *The promise of narrative theology. Recovering the gospel in the Church.* Atlanta: John Knox.
SULEIMAN, S. R. & I. CROSMAN 1980. *The reader in the text. Essays on audience and interpretation.* Princeton: Princeton University.
VAN WOLDE, E. 1984. Semiotiek en haar betekenis voor de theologie. *TijdsTh* 24, 138-67.

J. H. PETZER

THE PAPYRI AND NEW TESTAMENT TEXTUAL CRITICISM CLARITY OR CONFUSION?

It is not necessary to seek evidence to prove the importance of the papyri for New Testament Textual Criticism. The attention which the Chester Beatty and the Martin Bodmer papyri have been receiving since their discovery, is enough proof of this. All of the important papyri which contain more than a mere fragment of the New Testament, have been studied with great curiosity by different scholars from different points of view. The works of Aland (1965, 1965/66), Fee (1968, 1974), Porter (1962, 1967) on the Bodmer papyri and Zuntz (1953) on P46 are, for instance, noteworthy examples. What makes the papyri important, is not the fact that they are written on papyrus rather than on parchment, but the fact that they are dated before the fourth century. These manuscripts supply information from a period of which Westcott and Hort had no Greek evidence. Hort's reconstruction of the history of the text which formed the principle upon which subsequent reconstructions of this history during the first part of the 20th century were based, could thus be re-evaluated in view of the evidence which has emerged from the study of these papyri.

More than two decades have passed since the discovery of the last important papyrus (P75) and the number of articles and monographs with topics related to the papyri, proves that due attention has been given to these manuscripts. However, the stream of literature on the papyri has been weakening since the late seventies and it seems a fair time to recapitulate and ask what influence these manuscripts have had on the development of the methodology of New Testament Textual Criticism during the last part of the century. Did the papyri bring a better understanding of the history of the text, better methods to choose between variants and more confidence that the text we are using is in fact close to the original; or are we no better off than before their discovery?

The History of the Text

Westcott and Hort were really the pioneers in the reconstruction of the history of the text of the Greek New Testament. Although elements of the reconstruction of the textual history were present in the work of their predecessors, these elements had not been integrated into a whole. In Bengel's work, for example, the principle to distinguish between groups of manuscripts was present. He divided the manuscripts into two groups, the Asian and the African. Semler took this a step further by distinguishing three groups, and instead of calling them families, he called them recensions. With this, Semler took Bengel's development a step further, by saying implicitly that these groups of texts were deliberate productions. Griesbach said that the Constantinople group originated from the other two. This represents a further development, as it can be viewed as a suggestion concerning the relationship of these groups. Lachmann took the next very important step by supplying the theory behind the grouping of manuscripts in his genealogical method (cf Metzger 1968: 106-129; Aland & Aland 1982:16-24 for a survey of the development during the 18th and 19th centuries).

It was left, then, to Westcott and Hort to integrate these 'loose' elements of the textual history into a meaningful whole and to give a proper discussion of the history of the text. To do this, they made use of their predecessors' work to a great extent. They based their reconstruction of the history on the grouping of manuscripts (Bengel's principle as worked out by Griesbach and Semler) by distinguishing three basic text-types, the Alexandrian, the Western and the Syrian (cf Martini 1978:288 on the Neutral text). They used Griesbach's theory that the Constantinople text originated from the other two and combined Lachmann's genealogical principle with it to prove that the Syrian text was a late text. A note on Westcott and Hort's usage of the genealogical principle is necessary here. They never used the 'genealogical method proper'. Because of the obvious problems attached to this method (e.g. mixture and the fact that the stemma always results in two branches), they did not apply the genealogical principle to the manuscripts but to the groups (textual families) and this they did with excellent results (cf Westcott & Hort 1974: 39ff). Combining these elements with the textual quality of the two ancient uncials Aleph and B, they produced a text which was meant to be the original New Testament. Their work was presented with such persuasion that it dominated the textual scene well into the 20th century. Although there were attempts to prove them wrong, alternative theories of the history of the text, such as Von Soden's or Streeter's, made use of the same basic aspects as Westcott and Hort: both Streeter and Von Soden identified three main groups (Streeter of course adding the Caesarean text), and made use of the genealogical relationship of these groups in order to reconstruct the history of the text (cf Metzger 1968:139ff, 169ff for a useful summary). It seems that there was some kind of silent agreement among textual scholars that the history of the text ought to be sought in the area of the genealogy of groups of manuscripts.

This tendency seems to have dominated the text-critical scene during the first part of the 20th century. Much attention has been given to the study of Westcott and Hort's families. Studies by the Lakes (1928, 1941), Streeter (1924), both especially on the Ceasarean text, and Von Soden (1902-1910) are especially notable. Though it was agreed that Hort had a too optimistic view of the textual quality of Aleph and B, it seemed to be agreed that the text of the New Testament was transmitted in three basic text-types (Alexandrian, Western and Byzantine) with the possible addition of a fourth (Caesarean). It also seemed common cause to state that the Byzantine text was inferior to the other text-types because of its eclectic and inferior internal value (cf e.g. the handbooks of the early part of the century, such as Nestle 1909:168ff; Vogels 1920:173ff). This fact is also proved by the leading texts published during this period which can almost all be characterized as basically Westcott and Hort. In short, after more or less half a century of intensive research on the history of the text, the basic elements of Westcott and Hort's history of the text seemed justified.

The discovery of the Chester Beatty papyri, especially P45, caused some problems to this point of view. Though mainly Caesarean, the text of this manuscript appeared to be somewhat mixed—as a result of which existing questions about the homogeneity of the Caesarean text had been confirmed: P45 has shown that it is fully justified to distinguish between the so-called pre-Caesarean and, what could be called, the 'Caesarean text proper', with P45 a noteworthy member of the first group (Lake & Lake 1941:7-8; Metzger 1966/67:372-373; Hurtado 1981:88-89). The term 'pre-Caesarean', however, suggests something of the dilemma which originated with the discovery of this manuscript. The consequences of this dilemma had not been fully understood until after the discovery of the Bodmer papyri: pre-Caesarean actually means 'a Caesarean text before the existence of the Caesarean text'. Could it be seen that this nomenclature denoted something of an ancient 'mixed Caesarean text' (whatever this would be taken to mean)—in other words an anachronism? What this actually means is that the pre-Caesarean text is a type of text (not yet a text-type in the technical sense of the word) in which many of the readings of the later Caesarean text could be found. Instead of 'mixed', it would be more accurate to call this pre-Caesarean text the group of manuscripts which could be shown to be the sources of the later Caesarean text. They are in no way Caesarean (cf Hurtado 1981:88-89), but represent manuscripts in which many of the later Caesarean text's readings could be found. This may be the reason why the Caesarean text is today being called a textual process rather than a textual family (Metzger 1966/67:372-373).

The consequences of the rather 'mixed' character of the more ancient P45 had not been noted by textual critics until the discovery of the Bodmer papyri. Attempts to classify these documents as part of the existing text-types, gave rise to the same problems as P45 had given 25 years before. Although they could be classified as mainly Alexandrian, the same signs of mixture were notable in these documents (cf King 1964:56-57; Edwards 1976:211-212; Birdsall 1960:10-11; Klijn 1956/57: 331-332). More or less every single textual critic who attempted to classify these documents was forced to characterize their texts as 'mixed'.

This raised serious doubts about the validity of Westcott and Hort's textual history. Though some scholars (cf Delobel 1977:322-323; Black 1977:120) claimed that the papyri basically substantiated Westcott and Hort's theory, the majority of scholars concluded from the study of the papyri that these manuscripts have shown that Westcott and Hort's theory needed serious revision (cf Aland 1965:346; 1970/71: 1-2; Birdsall 1960:10-11; Klijn 1960/61:161-164). At first sight these two viewpoints seem contradictory. From a closer analysis, however, it is clear that they are not. The former focuses mainly on Westcott and Hort's preference of Aleph and B, in other words, not their textual history as such, but the main substance of their text. In this respect this view is certainly correct: the similarity between the texts of especially B and P75 has strengthened their preference of this uncial. The close links between these two manuscripts had been sufficiently proven by a number of scholars (cf e.g. Fee 1974:24-28; Metzger 1966/67:374; Porter 1962:376) and these links have shown the text of B to be much older than the 4th century, at least as old as the first part of the 2nd century. This is the historical evidence which Westcott and Hort needed to prove that the Alexandrian text is older than the Western (cf Epp 1976:238-242). This, however, need not to be taken as confirmation of Westcott and Hort's reconstruction of the history of the text, since there is much more attached to their reconstruction of the textual history than their preference of Aleph and B. Their preference of these two manuscripts is no more than the result of their reconstruction of the history of the text.

With regard to the relationship of Westcott and Hort's reconstruction of the history of the text and the text of the papyri, the perspective which Aland (and others) had opened on the 'mixed' character of these manuscripts is important, because it was especially Aland who pressed the idea that we cannot speak of 'mixed texts' with regard to the text of the papyri. Such terminology is anachronistic, for it suggests that these pre-fourth century texts are being studied from the point of view of the fourth century and later. In other words, the fact that three or four text-types existed in the fourth century and later, does not necessarily imply that they existed a century or two earlier in the same way (cf e.g. Aland 1967). The 'mixture' in the papyri is really no mixture, because there were no clearly distinguishable text-types prior to the fourth century. Instead of looking at the papyri from the perspective of the text-types, the papyri should be studied as entities on their own and conclusions should be drawn from this study for the existence and nature of the text-types. When this pattern is followed, it becomes clear that the papyri may come from a time when no text-types existed, or when the text-types are not as sharply distinguishable as Westcott and Hort had done. Aland, therefore, started to refer to the 'frühe Text' when referring to the time before the text-types (cf e.g. Aland 1970/71:1-2; Aland & Aland 1982:67-74).

Currently his theory seems to explain the text of the papyri best. Although this theory has obviously demanded a revision of Westcott and Hort's theory, it does not necessarily mean that Westcott and Hort were wrong in their reconstruction of the textual history. It only means that their textual history does not apply to the time from which the papyri came. Their evidence was restricted to the 4th century and later, and they probably did a good job with their reconstruction of the history in and after the fourth century, because their theory still holds for this period. Nobody seems to be able to prove their basic outline of the history after the fourth century wrong. All that the papyri have shown is that this reconstruction does not apply to the 3rd and 2nd centuries.

This is exactly the point where the problems start. Although nobody can deny the demand for a new reconstruction of the textual history, nobody seems to be able to reconstruct such a history. Only Aland seems to be moving in a new direction, though there are still many problems and questions attached to his attempt (cf Aland & Aland 1982:57-81). The problem is clear: enough papyri are available to prove the existing theories not to be applicable to the first few centuries. There are, however, not enough manuscripts from these centuries available to provide enough information for the reconstruction of a new textual history. It is, for instance, only in John 10 and 11 where more than two of these early documents overlap (P45, P66 and P75), while there are only a few chapters in John where two of these manuscripts (P66 and P75) overlap. This is by far not enough material to trace the characteristics of the early text, and without a properly reconstructed textual history, we are, so to speak, back to square one. We can follow the most ancient witnesses, and maybe combine them with the existing reconstructions of the history of the text and choose the Alexandrians with these papyri as our most important manuscripts. There is, however, no way in which we can decide which reading to follow where the papyri differ from each other or where there is no such attestation for a specific variation-unit, except for internal criticism. Because of the lack of a proper textual history, it cannot be decided which of the papyri are the best manuscripts, where more than one is available, or to what extent we should follow the papyri where only one is available.

It is no wonder that fewer and fewer scholars become interested in this branch of the New Testament studies and that there is a sense of frustration among textual critics because of a lack of any real methodological progress (cf e.g. Epp 1974). The recovery of the history of the text is still one of the most important tasks which face the textual critic. The papyri have proven the existing reconstructions to be of little or no value for the pre-fourth century stage, but could not supply enough information regarding these centuries to build a new reconstruction of this history.

Methods of textual criticism

When one looks at the methods which are today being used to edit the text of the New Testament, the confusion in this field of study becomes even clearer. There seems to be no consensus among textual critics in what direction to seek for the text of the New Testament. Three basic methods can as such be identified:
— moderate eclecticism;
— thoroughgoing eclecticism; and
— the majority text method.

Each of these methods gives different results from the other and finally also different texts. The question whether and why these methods are correct or incorrect, is not at stake in this paper. I would rather want to show how they are related to the uncertainty which the papyri have brought to New Testament Textual Criticism.

The first two of these methods, moderate and thoroughgoing eclecticism, are in principle actually the same method, since both are based on the eclectic principle, viz. to work with each variation-unit isolated from the other. Eclectic critics choose from among a set of criteria, those criteria which are applicable in the case of each variation-unit, and by applying these criteria to the given variation-unit, choose one reading from the existing variants (cf Epp 1976: 212). They differ, however, in the 'set of criteria' from which they choose their criteria to be applied in each case of variation (cf Epp 1974: 214 for discussion). The result is that these two kinds of eclecticism actually use two different eclectic methods (method in the sense of the practical step-by-step guide to the solution of textual problems).

Moderate eclecticism is by far the most popular method today. It uses internal as well as external evidence as its 'set of criteria', by assigning the same weight to both kinds of evidence, at least in theory. In practice, however, much more weight is attached to external than internal evidence (Epp 1976:248-249; Fee 1976:197). This is also clear from the *Textual Commentary*, where the reasons for the choices of the committee which edited the UBS-texts are given (cf numerous instances in Metzger 1971). Moderate eclecticism can be viewed as the continuation of the classical method, and more specifically, Westcott and Hort's method. It is more or less a refinement of Westcott and Hort, in which this classical method has been adjusted to fit the modern circumstances (cf Epp 1976:248-249). It developed gradually during the 20th century.

Though based on the same basic principle, thoroughgoing eclecticism differs from moderate eclecticism with regard to the 'set of criteria' from which the criteria, applicable to each variation-unit, are to be taken, because this method only uses internal evidence. Originating in the work of B. Weiss and J. Lagrange, this method is now followed only by Kilpatrick and Elliott (cf e.g. Epp 1976:251-254; Elliott 1968:1-12; 1972:342-343; 1974:349-350; 1978:96 for a discussion of the method).

It is certainly incorrect to see the papyri as the cause of the eclectic method, because the principle of the eclectic method was already present in the work of scholars like Weiss, Lagrange, Vaganey (amongst others) and even Westcott and Hort themselves (cf their 'internal evidence of readings' in Westcott & Hort 1974: 19ff). However, the uncertainty which the papyri brought to the history of the text in the first three centuries, forced textual critics to adopt the eclectic method more and more. The classical method, with its two branches of recension and emendation (cf Metzger 1968: 156-159) became more and more difficult to use, the reason being clear: the core of the classical method lies in recension rather than in emendation, viz. to choose a 'best manuscript' on historical grounds. This has been a fairly easy process since Westcott and Hort, because these two scholars have sufficiently proven the Alexandrian text to be the best. Because of the fact that the papyri, which supplied earlier evidence than the manuscripts of the existing text-types, could not be classified into these textual families, distrust of the method (and results) of the traditional process of recension started to grow. There is, however, not enough historical evidence to replace Westcott and Hort's recension with a new one, while the former had been proven not to be relevant any more. This forced textual critics to pay more attention to the process of emendation, since there were no historical grounds upon which the 'best manuscript' could be chosen any more. The textual history of the first few centuries is so uncertain, that no real historical grounds could be offered to say that P75, for example, is a better manuscript than P45. Since it could not be determined which papyrus has the best text, a method had to be developed by which textual critics could choose between the readings of the papyri where they differ. All that was left was emendation. Placing more emphasis on internal criticism, the readings of the manuscripts are analyzed in order to see which manuscripts offer the most correct readings. The 'best manuscript' is then chosen on the basis of the 'internal quality' of the manuscripts. As such, this manuscript is then followed in the majority of cases in the variation in the text, the exceptions being those instances where clear internal evidence sides with the 'second best' or other 'inferior' manuscripts. Thus, instead of historical evidence, internal evidence now seems to be the basis upon which the best manuscript is chosen. Eclecticism has changed the two processes of the classical method around:

— According to the classical method text-historical (genealogical) evidence is used to choose one manuscript from among the existing manuscripts (recension). This manuscript formed the core of the restored texts, after being corrected by internal and other evidence (emendation).

— According to the eclectic method internal and other evidence are being used to choose a best manuscript and as such this forms the basis of the reconstruction of the history of the text. Theoretically at least, the internal evidence forms the basis of this method.

Although it has been stated by textual critics that the 'cult of the best manuscript' is dead (cf e.g. Elliott 1968:4), this is not entirely true. What is true is that the former way of choosing the best manuscript is dead. The historical grounds for choosing the best manuscript have given way to internal evidence as the basis for choosing the best manuscript.

By pushing this eclectic principle too far, thoroughgoing eclectics discard the history of the text altogether. The reason can only be that they think the history of the text to be so uncertain that it is impossible to base any conclusions upon it. Where Weiss and Lagrange did not discard the history of the text absolutely, the two current thoroughgoing eclectics pay no attention to this kind of evidence, though Kilpatrick sometimes works with the basic elements of the history of the text (cf Epp 1976: 250).

The 'return of the *Textus Receptus*' in modern Textual Criticism is another sign of the current confusion in this discipline. After Westcott and Hort had demolished the claims of the *Textus Receptus* to represent the original text of the New Testament, very few textual critics have given attention to the TR or its text. After Burgon (1883, 1896) it was only in 1956, when Hills (1956) published his defence of the King James Version, that this text received serious attention. Twenty years later new claims for the originality of the text of the *Textus Receptus*, the Byzantine text, were put forward. The most noteworthy scholars in favour of the majority text are Pickering (1978, 1980), Van Bruggen (1976) and especially Hodges (1978a, 1978b, 1980). The result of Hodges' work, which represents a much more scientific and critical approach to the problems of the text of the New Testament than other representatives of this method, has recently been published in the GNTMT (1982) (cf also Fee 1978a, 1978b, 1978/9, 1980; Taylor 1977, 1978 for a discussion). Whether the arguments which are being raised in favour of the majority text by its defenders are right or wrong is not at stake in the present discussion. Enough has been said by scholars like Fee (1978a, 1978b, 1978/9, 1980) to prove these arguments to be troublesome. What this 'rise of the *Textus Receptus*' indicates, however, is the uncertainty toward the history of the text. There is so much confusion in the reconstruction of the history of the text, that it is possible to ignore the text of the papyri and to raise arguments in favour of the majority text. Though the papyri should not take the total blame for the 'revival of the Textus Receptus', they have something to do with it:

— From the recent monographs and articles by these textual critics (cf e.g. Pickering 1980: 31-97) it is clear that they are still trying to prove Westcott and Hort's rejection of the Byzantine text wrong, and rightly so, since it was these two scholars who raised the final arguments against the *Textus Receptus*. The papyri have strengthened the arguments against Westcott and Hort somewhat, because of the questions they raised about the relevance of Westcott and Hort's reconstruction of the history of the text, and as such removed something of the firm basis for ignoring the Byzantine text in the restoration of the text of the New Testament. The fact that no substitute for Westcott and Hort could as yet be supplied, opened the door somewhat for the revival of this approach. It should be noted, however, that the papyri have not really cast doubt upon the rejection of the Byzantine text in Westcott and Hort's theory. This is one part of the theory that still holds good.

— It is commonly accepted today that the papyri contain a number of Byzantine readings (cf e.g. Sturz 1980:68-69). From this it follows that Westcott and Hort may have been too harsh in their total rejection of the Byzantine readings. Because of the fact that the evidence from the papyri is too scanty and too restricted to one place (Egypt) for really meaningful conclusions, it cannot yet be determined to what extent the Byzantine text should be used in recovering the text of the New Testament. This created elbow-room for those textual critics, since there might be some hopes that entirely Byzantine papyri might be discovered in other parts of the world. Such manuscripts, it can be argued, will prove the majority text to be the original.

Epp's words concerning this movement in favour of the majority text are relevant: "I am being factitious only to a limited extent when I ask, if the *textus receptus* can still be defended, albeit in merely a pseudo-scholarly fashion, how much solid progress have we made in textual criticism in the 20th century?" (Epp 1974:405).

It would be unfair to conclude from all that has been said above that the papyri gave birth to these three approaches to the text of the New Testament, since all of them were implicitly part of methods and approaches before the discovery of the papyri. It would not, however, be an overstatement to say that the papyri gave momentum to these methods and brought to light some problems as to the certainty of the texts which have been published recently.

The text of the New Testament

The confusion which the papyri brought to the reconstruction of the history of the text and the method for the restoration of the text of the New Testament, can also be seen in the texts of the New Testament which have recently been published. This is no surprise, since the text is no more than the practical result of the method by which it is edited. When the method is uncertain, it can certainly not be expected of the text to yield any kind of certainty. I shall take the recently published text of the United Bible Societies (UBS 3cor) (published in 1983, cf Aland *et al* 1983) and the new 'Majority Greek New Testament' (GNTMT) (published in 1982, cf Hodges & Farstad 1982) as examples.

Edwards (1977:122) tabulated the 'percentage of certainty' from the ratings of the choices of the committee which edited the third edition of the UBS text (1975):
— A-ratings: 8,7%
— B-ratings: 32,3%
— C-ratings: 48,6%
— D-ratings: 10,4%.

If one distinguishes between the A and the B ratings on the one hand, assigning the broad classification 'certain' to them, and the C and the D ratings on the other, assigning the broad classification 'uncertain' to them, the decision of the committee is still uncertain in more than 59% of the more or less 1,440 variation-units included in the text. From this could not be concluded that the whole of the text is for 60% uncertain, since the great majority of variants are regarding minutiae which have no influence on the contents of the text and which are fairly easily solved. The variation-units given in this text's apparatus are, however, the really meaningful variation, which make a difference to the translation and exegesis of the text. These are, in other words, the variation-units which are really important and which textual criticism really is about. If there is a degree of uncertainty of more or less 60% in the choices in these variation-units, it is surely a legitimate question to ask how certain we really are about the exact words of the original authors. From the apparatus it is further clear that it is mainly the ancient manuscripts which have caused this uncertainty, for the greatest body of C and D ratings consist of variation where the ancients, especially the papyri, are divided in their evidence, or where it is clear that their witness is of no value, and that consequently the reading of the majority text, for instance, should be preferred to the reading of the ancient manuscripts. This is surely enough proof of the uncertainty which is attached even to this text, which could be called the culmination of the results of the eclectic method.

However, even though this uncertainty is attached to this text, it is still very popular, to such an extent that it is regarded by many as the new standard text of the New Testament (cf Aland & Aland 1982:41ff; Baarda 1980:136; Omanson 1983:121-122). The editors of this text, especially Aland, were subjected to much criticism for referring to this text as the new standard text, but Aland is undoubtedly correct in pointing to the fact that it was not the editors who made this text the new standard text, as the Elzeviers had done in the 17th century, but that this characterization of the text originated from its popularity, as is clear from the fact that more of these texts have been sold than any other text (cf Aland 1982:145ff). From this it indeed seems that this text has become the new standard text. Now very few people will argue with the quality of this text, and it is clear that this text is probably the best and closest to the autographs that New Testament Textual Criticism can come today. Notwithstanding this quality of the text it can surely not be accepted as a standard text because of the uncertainty attached to it. Many of its readings might in the future be proven wrong. The fact, however, that it is accepted as a standard text by the scholarly world is a further proof of the current confusion in New Testament Textual Criticism, for a standard text with a 60% degree of uncertainty attached to the important variation in the manuscripts could hardly be called a standard text. The fact that it is accepted as a standard text, however, shows that this discipline has no answer to the problems which face it, and that it could do no better than it has done so far.

A short reference to the GNTMT illustrates this confusion in New Testament Textual Criticism clearly. The GNTMT, edited by Hodges and Farstad, could be called the new 'critical *Textus Receptus*'. This is the first text in three centuries which is based on the late-minuscule text of the New Testament. This text is, however, presented as some kind of an intermediary text, since the method which the editors propose has not been applied in the editing of this text. Only the text of the pericope of the adulteress (Jh 7:53-8:12) and the text of Revelation have been edited by the 'new' genealogical method proposed by Hodges. The problem with the rest of the New Testament is that the editors did not have a full collation, or even an extensive collation, available from which they could construct their stemma, as they had done with the two mentioned parts. Where they could not base their text upon a constructed stemma, they merely counted the manuscripts and published the text which appeared in the majority of the manuscripts. Even this text, thus, is an intermediary text and it is still not certain what the original text of the New Testament should be, according to the Majority text.

Conclusion

It is no overstatement to speak of a confusion in New Testament Textual Criticism today. Although we have much *more* evidence than a century ago, and much more *older* evidence, we seem unable to come to specific conclusions about the text of the New Testament. The papyri seem to have much to do with this confusion, and instead of bringing greater clarity, they have brought greater confusion, because enough papyri have been discovered to prove the older theories, reconstructions of the history of the text, wrong, but there is still not enough evidence to supply new theories. This has led to some kind of a methodological confusion, with the result that our current 'leading' texts are much more uncertain than the texts of a century ago. The only thing that seems to be clearer is the fact that we are forced to make changes and adjustments to long-accepted theories.

The future also does not look very bright. With fewer and fewer scholars interested in this field of study (cf Epp 1979) and the problems of New Testament Textual Criticism becoming greater and greater, it is hard to see that the '20th century interlude'' (cf Epp 1974) will come to an end. What is needed today is not so much a re-interpretation of the existing facts, but rather a new set of facts. Without a new bunch of pre-fourth century manuscripts, preferably not all from Egypt, it is hard to see how the problems of this discipline can be solved, since these problems arose from the lack of material. What we need is not so much a new Westcott and Hort, or a new Bengel—this field of study has very competent scholars to interpret the existing material; they have already done marvellous work with the scanty evidence which is available—but rather a new Tischendorf—someone who could supply a new Aleph. Without new evidence, it is difficult to see how really meaningful progress in the methodology of New Testament Textual Criticism could be made.

BIBLIOGRAPHY

ALAND, K. 1959. The present position of New Testament textual criticism, in K. Aland (ed), *Studia Evangelica* 1. Berlin: Akademie, 717-731.

ALAND, K. 1965. The significance of the papyri in New Testament research, in J. P. Hyatt (ed), *The Bible in modern scholarship*. New York: Abington, 325-346.

ALAND, K. 1965/66. Neue neutestamentliche Papyri II. *NTS* 12, 193-210.

ALAND, K. 1967. Das Neue Testament auf Papyrus, in K. Aland, *Studien zur Überlieferung des Neuen Testaments und seines Textes*. Berlin: Akademie, 91-137.

ALAND, K. 1970/71. Bemerkungen zu den gegenwärtigen Möglichkeiten textkritischer Arbeiten aus Anlass einer Untersuchung zum Cäsarea-Text der Katholischen Briefe. *NTS* 17, 1-9.

ALAND, K. 1982. Ein neuer Textus Receptus für das Griechische Neue Testaments. *NTS* 28, 145-153.

ALAND, K. & B. ALAND 1982. *Der Text des Neuen Testaments*. Deutsche Bibelgesellschaft.

ALAND, K., M. BLACK, C. M. MARTINI, B. M. METZGER & A. WIKGREN (eds) 1983. *The Greek New Testament*. 3. cor ed. United Bible Societies.

BAARDA, Tj. 1980. Auf dem Wege zu einem Standard-Text des Neuen-Testaments? *GTT* 80, 83-137.

BIRDSALL, J. N. 1960. *The Bodmer papyrus of the Gospel of John*. London: Tyndale.

BLACK, M. 1977. The United Bible Societies' Greek New Testament evaluated - a reply. *BT* 28, 116-120.

BURGON, J. W. 1883. *The revision revised*. London: Murray.

BURGON, J. W. 1896. *The traditional text of the Holy Gospels vindicated and established*. London: George Bell.

DELOBEL, J. 1977. The Bodmer papyrus of John. A short survey of the methodological problems. *BETL* 44, 317-323.

EDWARDS, E. J. 1977. On using the textual apparatus of the UBS Greek New Testament. *BT* 28, 121-142.

EDWARDS, S. A. 1976. P75 under the magnifying glass. *NT* 18, 190-212.

ELLIOTT, J. K. 1968. *The Greek text of the Epistles to Timothy and Titus*. Salt Lake City. University of Utah Press. (Studies and Documents 36.)

ELLIOTT, J. K. 1972. Rational criticism and the text of the New Testament. *Theology* 75, 338-343.

ELLIOTT, J. K. 1974. Can we recover the original New Testment? *Theology* 77, 338-353.

ELLIOTT, J. K. 1978. In defence of thoroughgoing eclecticism in New Testament textual criticism. *RQ* 21, 95-115.

EPP, E. J. 1974. The twentieth century interlude in New Testament textual criticism. *JBL* 93, 386-414.

EPP, E. J. 1976. The eclectic method in New Testament textual criticism - solution or sympton? *HThR* 69, 211-257.

EPP, E. J. 1979. New Testament textual criticism in America: requi for a discipline. *JBL* 98, 94-98.

FEE, G. D. 1968. *Papyrus Bodmer II (P66): Its textual relationship and scribal characteristics*. Salt Lake City: University of Utah Press. (Studies and Documents 34.)

FEE, G. D. 1974. P75, P66 and Origen: The myth of early textual recension in Alexandria, in R. N. Longenecker & M. C. Tenney (eds), *New dimensions in New Testament study*. Grand Rapids: Zondervan.

FEE, G. D. 1976. Rigorous or reasoned eclecticism - which? in J. K. Elliott (ed), *Studies in the New Testament text and language*. Leiden: Brill, 174-197.

FEE, G. D. 1978a. Modern textual criticism and the revival of the Textus Receptus. *JETS* 21, 19-33.

FEE, G. D. 1978b. Modern textual criticism and the majority text: a rejoinder. *JETS* 21, 157-160.

FEE, G. D. 1978/79. A critique of W. N. Pickering's *"The identity of the New Testament text"* - a review article. *WTJ* 41, 397-423.

FEE, G. D. 1980. The majority text and the original text of the New Testament. *BT* 31, 107-118.

HILLS, E. F. 1956. *The King James Version defended.* Des Moines: Christian Research Press.

HODGES, Z. C. 1978a. Modern textual criticism and the majority text: a response. *JETS* 21, 143-155.

HODGES, Z. C. 1978b. Modern textual criticism and the majority text: a surrejoinder. *JETS* 21, 161-164.

HODGES, Z. C. 1980. The implications of statistical probability for the history of the text, in W. N. Pickering, *The identity of the New Testament text.* Nashville: Thomas Nelson, 159-169.

HODGES, Z. C. & A. L. FARSTAD (eds) 1982. *The Greek New Testament according to the majority text.* Nashville: Thomas Nelson.

HURTADO, L. W. 1981. *Text-critical methodology and the pre-Caesarean text.* Grand Rapids: Eerdmans. (Studies and Documents 43.)

KING, M. A. 1964. Notes on the Bodmer manuscript. *BS* 121, 54-57.

KLIJN, A. F. J. 1956/57. Papyrus Bodmer II (Jn 1-14) and the text of Egypt. *NT* 3, 327-334.

KLIJN, A. F. J. 1960/61. De stand van het onderzoek naar de geschiedenis van die teks van het Nieuwe Testament. *NTT* 15, 161-168.

LAKE, K., R. P. BLAKE & S. NEW 1928. The Caesarean text of the Gospel of Mark. *HThR* 21, 207-404.

LAKE, K. & S. LAKE 1941. *Family 13 (The Ferrar group). The text according to Mark, with a collation of codex 28 of the Gospels.* Philadelphia: University of Pennsylvania Press. (Studies and Documents 11.)

MARTINI, C. M. 1978. Is there a late-Alexandrian text of the Gospels? *NTS* 24, 285-296.

METZGER, B. M. 1966/67. Second thoughts XII: The textual criticism of the New Testament, pt 2. *ET* 78, 372-375.

METZGER, B. M. 1968. *The text of the New Testament.* 2. ed. New York: Oxford University Press.

METZGER, B. M. 1971. *A textual commentary to the Greek New Testament.* United Bible Societies.

NESTLE, E. 1909. *Einführung in das Griechische Neue Testament.* Göttingen: Vandenhoeck & Ruprecht.

OMANSON, R. L. 1983. A perspective on the study of the New Testament text. *BT* 34, 107-122.

PICKERING, W. N. 1978. 'Queen Anne...' and all that: a response. *JETS* 21, 165-167.

PICKERING, W. N. 1980. *The identity of the New Testament text.* 2. ed. Nashville: Thomas Nelson.

PORTER, C. L. 1962. Papyrus Bodmer XV (P75) and the text of codex Vaticanus. *JBL* 81, 363-376.

PORTER, C. L. 1967. An analysis of the textual variation between P75 and the codex Vaticanus in the text of John, in B. L. Daniels & M. J. Suggs (eds), *Studies in the history and text of the New Testament in honour of Kenneth Willis Clark.* Salt Lake City: University of Utah Press, 71-80. (Studies and Documents 29.)

STREETER, B. H. 1924. *The four Gospels; a study of origins.* London: Macmillan.

STURZ, H. A. 1980. *The Byzantine text-type and New Testament textual criticism.* 3. ed. La Mirada: Biola College.

TAYLOR, R. A. 1977. Queen Anne resurrected? a review article. *JETS* 20, 177-181.

TAYLOR, R. A. 1978. 'Queen Anne' revisited: a rejoinder. *JETS* 21, 169-171.

VAN BRUGGEN, J. 1976. *De tekst van het Nieuwe Testament.* Groningen: De Vuurbaak.

VON SODEN, H. F. 1902-1910. *Die Schriften des Neuen Testaments in ihrer ältesten erreichbaren Textgestalt, hergestellt auf Grund ihrer Textgeschichte.* Teil I. Berlin.

VOGELS, H. J. 1923. *Handbuch der neutestamentliche Textkritik.* Münster: Aschendorffschen Verlagsbuchhandlung.

Westcott, B. F. & F. J. A. Hort 1974. *The New Testament in the original Greek.* Pt. 2: *Introduction.* Graz: Akademie.

Zuntz, G. 1953. *The text of the Epistles: a disquisition upon the Corpus Paulinum.* London: Oxford University Press.

W. S. VORSTER

THE ANNUNCIATION OF THE BIRTH OF JESUS IN THE
PROTEVANGELIUM OF JAMES

The purpose of the article is to study the annunciation of the birth of Jesus in the Protevangelium of James from the perspective of production and reception of texts in the early
church. Both aspects, text production and text reception, throw light on how early Christians contextualized their beliefs, transmitted tradition and retold stories. These insights
are necessary for explaining and understanding the development of ideas in early
Christianity.

> "The literary phenomenon is not only the text, but also
> its reader and all of the reader's possible reactions to
> the text - both énoncé and énonciation"
> (Michael Riffaterre 1983:3)

1. *Introduction*

In chapter 11 of the so-called *Protevangelium Jacobi* (hence *PJ*), an 'infancy
gospel' from the second century, the following narrative is related:*

> "And she took the pitcher and went outside to fill it with water, when a
> voice said to her, Greetings, most favoured one. [The Lord is with you. He
> has greatly bless]ed you among the women. Mary looked around to the
> right and to the left where the voice came from. Trembling she went into
> her house and put down the pitcher. She took the purple, sat down on her
> seat and drew out the purple (threads). Suddenly an angel stood before (her)
> and said, Don't be afraid Mary. The Lord of all things has been gracious to
> you. You will conceive of his Word. When Mary heard this she thought by
> herself and said, You mean, I shall conceive of the Lord, the living God as
> every woman bears? And the angel went to her and said, No, Mary, not so;
> for the power of God will overshadow you. That is why the holy child will be
> called son of the High (= God). You will name him Jesus because he will
> save his people from their sins. Then Mary said, I am a servant of the Lord
> before him. May it happen to me as you have said".

In spite of obvious differences between the annunciation of the birth of
Jesus in the canonical gospels and this version, there can be little doubt
that *PJ* 11:2-3 is a retelling of the annunciation of the birth of Jesus in
Luke and Matthew. From this perspective, namely the retelling of stories
in early Christianity, this particular text is of great interest for the study

---

* Cf Aland 1967, 4 for the Greek text of Papyrus Bodmer V as edited by F. de
Strycker. Also Smid 1965:80ff and de Santos Otero 1975:154-5.

of text production and text reception in the early church. In this article I shall pay attention to aspects of retelling stories, the production of texts and also the reception of texts in the early church by studying *PJ* 11:2-3. Attention will be paid to the following aspects: Retelling as a means of text production and reception, *PJ* an infancy gospel? and 'Canonical' and 'apocryphal': the New Testament and *PJ* 11:2-3.

2. *Retelling as a means of text production and reception*

Storytelling is one of the characteristic features of early Christianity. Jesus was a storyteller and much of his life and preaching was transmitted in narrative form by his followers. The New Testament as well as great parts of other early Christian literature bear witness to this statement. It is therefore not surprising to find many traces in the canonical gospels of what happened when the Jesus story or parts of it were retold by his followers.

Historico-critical investigation of the formation and growth of the gospel tradition has afforded us with a considerable amount of information about the processes at work in the transmission of the Jesus tradition. By decomposing the written texts of the gospels and constructing possible situations of communication, growth of individual forms and so on, we have a relatively good idea of how the written texts about the life and teaching of Jesus developed through oral stages into written texts. We have, however, also learnt how difficult it is to reconstruct the original words of Jesus, let alone the original contexts of communication, persons, events and processes involved and many other important aspects which are clouded by our ignorance and lack of information. It has furthermore become clear that sayings of Jesus, events in his earthly life and persons with whom he had contact during and before his ministry were transmitted in different ways for different purposes before they were written down. In short, what lies behind the gospel texts is not necessarily reflected by what is related in these texts. To put it differently, the gospels are not verbatim reports of 'what happened'.

The gospels are products of retelling the story and stories of Jesus. His sayings and deeds were put into narrative frameworks, new sayings and stories were created after the models of earlier ones and put onto the lips of Jesus, series of sayings were collected and arranged into narrated discourses and so on. How the written texts of the canonical gospels came about, what lies behind them in the history of their growth and what happened to these texts after they were written down, has been the object of study for very long.

It is, however, not only that which lies behind these texts or the texts themselves that has been studied. Attention has also been paid to the way in which these texts were used and interpreted in and by the early church, that is their *Wirkungsgeschichte*. There nevertheless remains a lot to be done since much of what has been done was done in terms of evaluation and not in terms of explanation. Notwithstanding the results of previous and very useful investigations there is much yet to be learnt about the transmission of tradition in the early church, that is transmission of tradition before and after these texts became inscripturated.

New insights into aspects of the gospel tradition are often gained only by posing 'new' and other questions to the texts involved. Although the narrative character, for example, of many parts of the New Testament and other early Christian literature has been recognized very long ago, the serious study of these texts as *narratives* started only recently. Many of the implications of this approach still await serious investigation. This includes the implications of the phenomenon of *retelling* as a means of text production and reception. New Testament scholars have been aware of the fact that retelling played an enormous role in the transmission of tradition. But have all the problems and possibilities of retelling stories been fully explored? I have elsewhere indicated how this phenomenon of retelling affects our understanding and interpretation of the parables and in particular the reconstruction of the 'original' meaning of the parables (cf Vorster 1985). What are the implications of retelling the Jesus tradition? Let us consider the phenomenon of retelling.

The question to be addressed here is whether the *same* story, a parable for example, can be told more than once and what happens when the same story is retold. Or to put it into New Testament terms, is it possible that Mark, for example, could have retold a parable in exactly the same way that Jesus had done? Narratologists and ethnomethodologists disagree about the matter (cf Polanyi 1981). The answer to the problem obviously depends on one's definition of 'story' and 'the same'. It has on the one hand been pointed out that, when a story is retold orally the exact words are almost never used in telling the same story and that "...each telling will be tuned to the circumstances in which it is told, delicately reflecting the concerns of the participants and their relationships to each other, to the events and circumstances in the story and to the fact that the story is being told at a particular point in a particular conversation *to make a point* (my italics) relevant to the topics under discussion at that time" (Polanyi 1981:319). The same also holds true of stories not embedded into conversations, for example, texts embedded into written narratives (cf the speeches of Jesus in the Gospel of Matthew). The main point of the argument is that a story is told with a *purpose* in mind and that the 'same' story can be told for different purposes and therefore become a different story (stories)—not only a different version of the same story. The parables of Jesus are a good illustration of this.

Context determines the meaning of parables—be it literary context or the context of communication. The meaning of the parable of the good Samaritan, for example, is evidently influenced directly by the immediate context into which Luke put the narrative. As it now stands, it has become part of a narrative on neighbourly love, especially in view of the words, 'you go and do likewise' (Lk 10:37). Luke tells the story with the purpose of illustrating neighbourly love. Stripped of its Lucan context, it can, however, easily be told for many other purposes too to make different points depending on the context into which it is fitted. Each retelling of the story of the good Samaritan would thus become a 'new' story, although superficially it seems to be the 'same' story. What is observed here of the parable of the good Samaritan holds true of other stories in the gospel tradition. Each time a story of Jesus is retold, it becomes in principle another story or a new story according to this view. One of the implications of this particular approach to the problem is that any attempt to reconstruct the 'original' meaning of a particular narrative is doomed to fail unless the 'original' story and its communication context can be reconstructed. Another is that the retelling of stories is in fact a means of text production. New texts are created by retelling the 'same' story for a different purpose. We will return to this aspect below.

Polanyi (1981:315) has on the other hand correctly pointed out that on a more abstract level it can be argued that '...multiple tellings may reduce to the same underlying semantic structure in which the same events, set in a similarly constructed storyworld communicate the same global point'. Seen from this perspective it seems possible to retell the 'same' story and even 'other' stories more than once (for the same purpose). The tellings will be the same if they comply with the conditions given in the quote. In other words, if the semantic structure, the storyworld and global point of a story are the same as another telling of that story or any other story, they are the 'same'. It therefore seems possible that two different stories can be told to say the same thing. Is that perhaps illustrated by the seed parables in Mark 4:26-33 for example?

What one should, in view of the aforesaid, keep in mind is that different versions of the same story or even different stories in retold form may or may not be the 'same'. Secondly, that retelling is a kind of text production because retelling can be a way of creating new texts.

Let us pursue the matter a little further and make a few remarks about text reception. During the past decades there has been a shift in the interpretation of texts from the author, via the text to the recipient. Reception criticism (cf Holub 1984) has become the object of interest in many fields of the study of texts, including New Testament studies. The focus in reception criticism is on two aspects namely the constraints in a text which direct the reader in his reading or reception of that text and secondly on empirical research of how different readers read (receive) a particular text (cf Segers 1980:9ff). These reactions of readers of a text are not unimportant to the explanation and understanding of texts. Texts prompt readers in different ways to assign a particular meaning to a given text. That is why Riffaterre (1983:3) can say, "The explanation of an utterance should not, therefore, be a description of its forms, or a grammar, but rather a description of those of its components that prompt rationalizations. The explanation of a rationalization should not consist in confirming or disproving it in terms of the external standards or yardsticks to which critics have traditionally turned... A relevant explanation of a rationalization will consist first in accepting the rationalization as a way of perceiving the text...".

In studying the Jesus tradition in its various receptions in the early church the specific role played by reader's reception deserves special attention. Why did a specific reader in the early church read a text as he did? Did the text prompt that rationalization or were there other factors responsible for a particular reading? Obviously this approach is not the same as seeking the *Sitz im Leben* of a text although results may sometimes concur. In comparing later receptions of a text with the 'original', the focus should in the first place be on the explanation of the rationalization of a particular reading. In this way it seems possible to detect and explain trajectories which were later accepted or rejected by the early church.

Given the fact that storytelling was a common practice in the early church and that stories are told for a specific purpose (e.g. to entertain, inform, persuade, confirm, etc), retelling of stories found in the canonical gospels seems to contribute considerably to our knowledge about attempts to contextualize the story of Jesus. The early church did not simply transmit tradition. Tradition was used creatively. It is even possible to speak of transmission of tradition as imagination. Let us now turn to *PJ*.

3. *PJ an infancy gospel?*

It is well known that the childhood of Jesus is dealt with in the New Testament only by Matthew and Luke. Mark and John don't include any narratives about the birth and childhood of Jesus. They concentrate on other aspects of his life and teaching. In the period after the New Testament, however, a great variety of writings, the so-called apocryphal gospels, came into existence. These texts are modelled on and focus or elaborate on aspects of the Jesus tradition found in the canonical gospels. They even contain information not found in the canonical gospels—one of the reasons why they are often regarded as 'apocryphal'. These texts do not form a body of similar texts, not with regard to form nor with regard to contents. Schneemelcher (1968:48-51) divides them into three groups:

1. Texts which are clearly related to the canonical gospels, specifically the synoptic gospels, possibly because of common traditions;

2. So-called gnostic gospels in which revelation of the resurrected Lord plays a significant role. Their contents tie in with information found in the canonical gospels but in a 'developed' form and content;

3. Texts which are (legendary) elaborations of aspects of the life of Jesus. The infancy gospels fall into this category because they supplement or expand the infancy stories of Jesus found in Matthew and Luke. *PJ* is normally regarded as an infancy gospel.

Why were these infancy gospels written? In his treatment of the question, Cullmann (1968: 272-4) correctly observes that various reasons can explain the origin of these texts. In the first place we are all aware of how little information is given in the New Testament about the early years of Jesus on earth. Lack of information gives rise to inquisitiveness, a natural eagerness to be informed. One could therefore expect that a considerable amount of information (factive of fictive) could have originated in the early church on this score. Secondly, and I shall return to this below, the need to develop christology also explains some of this information in these texts. Christological thought originated with the resurrection and developed backwards to pre-existence christology (cf Brown 1977:311ff). The need to relate the moment of the birth of Christ to christology, forms part of this process. And in the third place early Christian apologetic (in view of Jewish polemic) also explains the origin of some of the material. How Jesus of *Nazareth* could be the promised Messiah who was to come from Bethlehem, demanded explanation. One already notices how Matthew and Luke solve the problem. According to Matthew Jesus and his parents had to leave his birthplace, Bethlehem, for Egypt because of the massacre of the children. On their return they went to Nazareth. Luke on the other hand tells us that Jesus was born in Bethlehem because of a census which caused his parents to go there from Nazareth, their home town. In view of this, obviously a variety of themes found in the Jesus tradition could have been developed for various purposes and because of various needs. Where does *PJ* fit into the picture?

The title of the book *Protevangelium Jacobi*, which goes back to G. Postel (1510-1581), has become the accepted one. It indicates that the book contains material about the infancy of Jesus which is older than the information contained in the canonical gospels. In the oldest existing manuscript of the book, Papyrus Bodmer V (3rd to early 4th century AD), the title is: *The birth of Mary. Revelation of James.* Origen in his commentary on Matthew (10:17) refers to it as *biblos Iakōbou* (cf Delius 1973:17), according to which the brothers of Jesus were born from an earlier marriage of Joseph. In 25:1-2 we read:

> "I, James, who wrote this (hi)story when a tumult arose in Jerusalem on the death of Herod, withdrew into the wilderness until it was over. I will praise the Lord, God, who gave me the gift of wisdom to write this story. Grace will be with all those who fear our Lord. Amen.
> Birth of Mary.
Revelation.
James.
> Peace to the author and the reader."

The James referred to here is presumably James, the brother of Jesus who recounts the life story (*historia*) of Mary, the mother of Jesus. Except for this pseudonymous reference, the author is completely unknown to us and so is also the place of writing. Because of ignorance of the author concerning the geography of Palestine and religious practices there, this country is normally dismissed as a possible place of origin (cf Smid 1965:20). Other places which are mentioned as places of origin are Syria and Egypt. Although there seems to be no definite reason why Egypt should be preferred to Syria or vice versa, it might be of interest to remind ourselves that most of the virgin birth material probably originated in Syria (cf Von Campenhausen 1963:13ff. and Hamman 1966:62-69). The book is furthermore normally dated on external grounds in the second century (cf Wilson 1978, Smid 1965 *et al.*) because it was already known to Clement of Alexandria and Origen. Justin has similar views on related matters (cf *Apol.* I.23,33) which makes it possible that he also knew the book. But that is disputable. It has been transmitted in various translations contributing to the popularity of the book in the East.

Despite rejection in the West by the Gelasian Decree (ca 500 AD), where it is listed as an apocryphon not received by 'the catholic and apostolic Roman Church' (cf Brown *et al.* 1978:248), its influence on the development of mariological tradition and dogma cannot be underestimated. This is confirmed by catholic piety, in art and also in dogma-historical developments within Roman Catholicism (cf Brown *et al.* 1978:248 and Cullmann 1968:279). The infancy gospels, and in particular *PJ* had a tremendous impact in the early church, the Middle Ages and the Renaissance—even greater than the Bible—on literature and art (cf Quasten 1950:106). Although Luther rejected the infancy gospels at a later stage in his life, Anne, the mother of Mary, whose name is known to us through *PJ*, was hailed by him when he entered the monastery (cf Cullmann 1968:275). Needless to say that its reception and influence on Mariology have greatly influenced interpreters of the text. This is obvious from the anti-Roman Catholic as well as Roman Catholic readings and evaluation thereof.

It has been mentioned above that the infancy stories developed certain themes of the childhood of Jesus. In *PJ* the theme is the birth of Christ from the perspective of the virgin Mary. It relates the life story of Mary, the daughter of a *rich* man Joachim and Anne (Anna); her birth based on the Old Testament story of Hannah (1 Sm 1-2, cf *PJ* 1-5); childhood in the temple (6-8); 'marriage' (cf 19) to a widower, Joseph, who already had children (9-10); annunciation of the birth of Jesus in Jerusalem (11); visit to Elizabeth (12); Joseph's doubt and comfort by an angel (13-14); vindication of Mary before the High Priest (15-16); birth of Jesus in a cave outside Bethlehem (17-18); vision of Joseph (18); Salome's unbelief about a miraculous virgin birth (19-20); and adoration of the Magi (21). The story ends with Herod's infanticide and the murder of Zechariah, the father of John the Baptist, in the temple (22-24) and the postscript (25) referred to above. In short, the book develops the birth story of Jesus by retelling the annunciation and birth of Jesus within a narrative about his mother.

PJ is a *narrative* consisting of various episodes. Except for chapter 18:2 which contains a vision of Joseph and the postscript in 25, narrated in the first person, the narrative is narrated from a third person omniscient narrative point of view (cf Chatman 1978:151ff). The *narrated time* covers the period of the parents of Mary through her birth and childhood, the birth of Jesus to the massacre of the children by Herod and the death of Zechariah. The *narrated space* is mainly Palestine and in particular Jerusalem. The temple, house of the parents, house of Joseph and Mary, the road to Bethlehem and the cave also play a role. The *characters* and the way in which they are presented are determined by the scenarios in which they act. I will mention only the more important ones: *Joachim and Anne*: two pious, godfearing, rich, but childless parents who are presented in their emotions from despair to happiness; *Mary*: the protagonist of the story—a long expected child whose childhood is based on the example of Old Testament characters. Her name is hailed by the whole nation because it will be an eternal name remembered by all generations (cf 6:2, 7:2, 12:2). She is raised for the service of the Lord; kept safely (holy) for the Lord (6:3); beloved of the whole of Israel (7:3). She is fed like a dove by an angel, a *Davidid*, undefiled, pure virgin (10:1). She is put into the care of a widower at the age of 12 (9:1); a willing servant of the Lord (11:3), working for him in his temple. She is visited by the angels (cf 11 *et al*), bearer of a child not conceived in a normal way (11); mother of the Lord (12:2), chaste and complying to the morality of Israel (12:3). She is accused of unchastity like her predecessor Eve (13:1), but vindicated (16:3). She is a virgin who abstained from intercourse with Joseph (her husband, betrothed 13:3, 15:3, 19), betrothed to Joseph (19:1), a mother who cares for her child (cf 17:2, 19:2, 22:2); *Joseph*: a widower with children, elected to take care of Mary (9:1), a builder (9:3), a man of emotion: fear (9:3, 14:1, 17:3), reproach, doubt, suspicion (9:3, 13:1-2) and joy (13:2). He is a 'father' who cares for the girl (his wife) and her child (17:3, 22:2); *Jesus*: the child conceived in an abnormal manner (9:2), whose name shall be Jesus because he will save his people from their sins (11:3, 14:2, 19:2). He is conceived of the Holy Spirit (14:2, 19:1), he is the Christ (21:2,4) and the Christ of the Lord (21:4), the king to be born for Israel (20:2, 21:2). Soon after his birth he is capable of taking his mother's breast and being a great salvation to Salome (20:3). He is a king to be worshipped (21:2,3) and is taken care of as a baby (22:2). The *Jewish religious leaders* are presented in a positive manner unlike the way they are characterized in the canonical gospels. They perform religious rites (cf 6:2, 8:2,3, 24:1 *et al.*), bless (17:3 *et al.*), pray (8:3 *et al.*), take care of the temple and determine the norms (cf 10:1, 15:3 *et al.*). They seek the will of God in prayer and reveal it (8:3ff). They are helpers and not opponents of the protagonist. This is in agreement with the very positive picture painted of Israel (people of Israel, the whole nation of Israel, sons of Israel) in *PJ* (cf 1:2, 7:2 *et al.*). Their characterization is such that one gets the impression that the story is told on their behalf. Since the child is born *from* Israel *for* Israel they are presented as co-operators in his coming. From a narrative point of view this is very interesting because there is reason to believe that the story polemises against views held by Jews who were contemporaries of the author. In order to convince his readers he presents the Jews who were 'involved' in the coming of the child positively.

Other helpers in the story are characters like Elizabeth, Zechariah, the midwives, Simeon, the Magi and angels. Euthine, Herod and the Romans act as opponents in the development of the story.

The story is built up of short episodes which relate to each other by various narrative techniques like pro- and retrospection. Previews are given, for example, in terms of lack which is then later liquidated (cf 1-8). In 8:2 it is related that Mary became twelve and that the priests held a meeting about her presence in the temple. This information is not, in the first instance, given to inform the reader about the 'Mary of history' or her biography. It serves a purpose in the development of the plot, because the age of Mary is the reason why she has to leave the temple.

This theme is worked out in 8:3 ff and leads to Joseph being chosen to take care of the virgin girl from the temple. These and other narrative techniques such as repetition of formulas (cf 6:1, 13:3, 15:3,4, 19:3) and narrative commentary are used in plotting the episodes. One can agree with Cullmann (1968:279) when he says, "Die ganze Darstellung ist eindrucksvoll und höchst anschaulich und zeugt von Diskretion, Innerlichkeit und Poesie. Wenn der Verfasser auch Quellen aus mündlicher und schriftlicher christlicher Tradition benutzt hat, besonders aber auch viel Stoff aus dem AT, vor allem die Samuelgeschichte, so hat er es doch verstanden, sie zu einem kunstvollen Ganzen zu verbinden. Nur wo die Apologetik es erfordert, scheut er sich nicht, auch größere, ja geschmacklose Züge beizubehalten".

The contents of the book are couched in Old and New Testament imagery and thought and the author was evidently influenced by conventions of the Old and New Testament. Even in language usage and narrative structures similarities between *PJ*, the Septuagint and the New Testament abound.

Scholars normally agree that *PJ* does not supply us with new information about the 'Mary of history'. On the contrary, it is mostly regarded as fiction written with an apologetic interest (cf Brown *et al.* 1978:258). The story is based upon the canonical gospels, but is also the result of the author's vivid imagination (cf the Salome-episode). This, however, does not imply that the story is completely worthless for historical construction or that it can be dismissed as invented and therefore not true or genuine (cf Koester 1980: 105ff). This atitude leads to oversimplified statements like the following, "As it can be shown in several instances that the author arranges his narrative after O.T. examples, it is certain that he is relating a fictitious historia. As he lived in the second half of the second century no authentic data were available to him. 'Amore Mariae' he writes his tale..." (Smid 1965:11). Without arguing the point, I would rather subscribe to the following statement, "The author of the *Protevangelium* betrays no use of significant, independent sources for the life of Mary; seemingly, his principal source was the canonical Gospels" (Brown *et al.* 1978:260). It is a retelling of the virgin birth story.

4. *'Canonical' and 'Apocryphal': the New Testament and PJ xi: 2-3*

New Testament scholars are in agreement that Matthew and Luke offer two *different* accounts of the infancy of Jesus. The stories are narrated from two different points of view with different purposes in mind. They agree only on a very few points. Brown (1977:34-35, cf Fitzmyer 1973: 564) notes the following aspects which they share: Mary and Joseph are the parents, legally engaged or married but not living together yet; Joseph is of Davidic descent; an angelic announcement of the birth of Jesus; conception of the child not through intercourse with her husband; conception is through the Holy Spirit; angelic directive about the name Jesus; the angel states that he is to be Saviour; birth takes place after the parents have come to live together; the birthplace is Bethlehem; the child is born during the reign of Herod the Great and the child is reared at Nazareth. Although commentators have often harmonized the two versions into one consecutive narrative the differences and contradictions (cf Brown 1977:35-36) cannot be wished away or explained in such a manner. In addition to the differences in the genealogies and the lack of parallels in Luke for Matthew 2:2-22 and in Matthew for Luke 1-2 (with the exception of Lk 1:26-35) there remains a considerable amount of detail in Matthew that can be explained only in view of each evangelist's telling of the story for his own purpose and from his own perspective.

If we compare *PJ* to the Matthean and Lucan versions with a view to the agreements between Matthew and Luke, there are remarkable agreements and differences. With regard to the agreements the following should be mentioned: an angelic announcement of the birth of Jesus; conception of the child, not through intercourse with her husband; conception through the 'Holy Spirit'; angelic directive about the name of Jesus; the angel states that he is to be Saviour; birth takes place after the parents have come to live together; the child is born during the reign of Herod. On the other hand there are also important differences in this respect: Joseph is an old widower with children to whom the virgin is allotted as wife (cf 8:3) and whom he takes into his care (παραλάβαι εἰς τήρησιν αὐτῷ cf 9:1,3); *Mary* is a Davidid (10:1); the birth takes place near Bethlehem in a *cave* (18:1, 19:1-3, 20:3, 21:3) and Nazareth does not play any role in *PJ*. The author of *PJ* made use of the New Testament but retold the story just as Matthew and Luke had done with the traditions they used in their narratives.

Let us now consider *PJ*'s retelling of the annunciation of the birth of Jesus which is narrated in Luke 1:26-38 in an angelic appearance to Mary in Nazareth and incorporated into Matthew's version of the birth of Jesus (Mt 1:18-25) in an angelic appearance to *Joseph* in Bethlehem.

From a form-critical perspective it is interesting to note that the form of biblical annunciations of birth normally has the following pattern: 1. *Appearance* of an angel of the Lord (or the Lord); 2. *Fear* or prostration of the visionary; 3. *Divine message*; 4. An *objection* by the visionary (as to how it can be, or request for a sign); 5. Giving of a *sign* of reassurance (cf Brown 1977:156). This pattern is found in the birth stories of Ishmael (Gn 16:7ff), Isaac (Gn 17:1ff), Samson (Jd 13:3ff), John the Baptist (Lk

1:11ff) and Jesus (Lk 1:26ff, cf Mt 1:20-21). "Such an annunciation was a standard biblical way of preparing the reader for the career of a person who was destined to play a significant role in salvation history, a role already known to the author" (Brown *et al.* 1978:114). Luke has followed this pattern in the annunciation stories of both John the Baptist and Jesus while Matthew, since he inserted this story into another narrative, only partly used the form. A close comparison of Luke 1:26-38 with Matthew 1:20-21 reveals that the authors used the same tradition (not necessarily the same version of the pre-gospel story) to tell *different* stories about the birth of Jesus. Brown (1979: 162) summarizes the probable history of the formation of the gospel stories as follows, "This pre-Gospel annunciation pattern developed in each evangelist's tradition in a different way. As part of an elaborate parallelism between the infant JBap and the infant Jesus, Luke rewrote it and used it to fashion a companion annunciation of the birth of JBap. Since he directed the JBap annunciation to Zechariah, he directed the Jesus annunciation to Mary... Matthew (or his tradition) combined the pre-Gospel angelic annunciation of the birth of the Davidic Messiah (with its christological message of begetting through the Holy Spirit) with a popular narrative in which a story of Joseph and the infant Jesus had been modeled upon the adventures of the patriarch Joseph and the infant Moses, a narrative structured on a series of angelic dream appearances". This explains why Luke has the annunciation made to Mary and Matthew to Joseph.

In *PJ*'s retelling of the New Testament material, the author used both Luke's (cf *PJ* 11:2-3) and Matthew's version (cf *PJ* 14:1-2) of the annunciation. This gave him the opportunity to make two separate episodes of the story to develop his plot. In fact, in his reception of the text(s) of the infancy stories of Luke and Matthew the two versions offered him material for retelling the birth story more extensively. Instead of harmonizing, he relates 'Luke's' version to narrate the annunciation of the birth to Mary, and Matthew's version to elaborate on Joseph's dilemma and fill out the 'open spaces' in the gospel stories. The differences between Matthew and Luke thus gave him the opportunity to retell the story in the way he did. Let us now consider the three versions in more detail:

James 11:1-3

18 Τοῦ δὲ Ἰησοῦ Χριστοῦ ἡ γένεσις οὕτως ἦν. μνηστευθείσης τῆς μητρὸς αὐτοῦ Μαρίας τῷ Ἰωσήφ, πρὶν ἢ συνελθεῖν αὐτοὺς εὑρέθη ἐν γαστρὶ ἔχουσα ἐκ πνεύματος ἁγίου. 19 Ἰωσὴφ δὲ ὁ ἀνὴρ αὐτῆς, δίκαιος ὢν καὶ μὴ θέλων αὐτὴν δειγματίσαι, ἐβουλήθη λάθρα ἀπολῦσαι αὐτήν. 20 ταῦτα δὲ αὐτοῦ ἐνθυμηθέντος, ἰδοὺ ἄγγελος κυρίου κατ' ὄναρ ἐφάνη αὐτῷ λέγων· Ἰωσὴφ υἱὸς Δαυίδ, μὴ φοβηθῇς παραλαβεῖν Μαρίαν τὴν γυναῖκά σου· τὸ γὰρ ἐν αὐτῇ γεννηθὲν ἐκ πνεύματός ἐστιν ἁγίου. 21 τέξεται δὲ υἱόν, καὶ καλέσεις τὸ ὄνομα αὐτοῦ Ἰησοῦν· αὐτὸς γὰρ σώσει τὸν λαὸν αὐτοῦ ἀπὸ τῶν ἁμαρτιῶν αὐτῶν. 22 Τοῦτο δὲ ὅλον γέγονεν ἵνα πληρωθῇ τὸ ῥηθὲν ὑπὸ κυρίου διὰ τοῦ προφήτου λέγοντος· 23 Ἰδοὺ ἡ παρθένος ἐν γαστρὶ ἕξει καὶ τέξεται υἱόν, καὶ καλέσουσιν τὸ ὄνομα αὐτοῦ Ἐμμανουήλ, ὅ ἐστιν μεθερμηνευόμενον μεθ' ἡμῶν ὁ Θεός. 24 ἐγερθεὶς δὲ ὁ Ἰωσὴφ ἀπὸ τοῦ ὕπνου ἐποίησεν ὡς προσέταξεν αὐτῷ ὁ ἄγγελος κυρίου, καὶ παρέλαβεν τὴν γυναῖκα αὐτοῦ· 25 καὶ οὐκ ἐγίνωσκεν αὐτὴν ἕως οὗ ἔτεκεν υἱόν· καὶ ἐκάλεσεν τὸ ὄνομα αὐτοῦ Ἰησοῦν.

26 Ἐν δὲ τῷ μηνὶ τῷ ἕκτῳ ἀπεστάλη ὁ ἄγγελος Γαβριὴλ ἀπὸ τοῦ Θεοῦ εἰς πόλιν τῆς Γαλιλαίας ᾗ ὄνομα Ναζαρὲθ, 27 πρὸς παρθένον ἐμνηστευμένην ἀνδρὶ ᾧ ὄνομα Ἰωσὴφ ἐξ οἴκου Δαυίδ, καὶ τὸ ὄνομα τῆς παρθένου Μαριάμ. 28 καὶ εἰσελθὼν πρὸς αὐτὴν εἶπεν· χαῖρε, κεχαριτωμένη, ὁ κύριος μετὰ σοῦ. 29 ἡ δὲ ἐπὶ τῷ λόγῳ διεταράχθη, καὶ διελογίζετο ποταπὸς εἴη ὁ ἀσπασμὸς οὗτος. 30 καὶ εἶπεν ὁ ἄγγελος αὐτῇ· μὴ φοβοῦ, Μαριάμ· εὗρες γὰρ χάριν παρὰ τῷ Θεῷ· 31 καὶ ἰδοὺ συλλήμψῃ ἐν γαστρὶ καὶ τέξῃ υἱόν, καὶ καλέσεις τὸ ὄνομα αὐτοῦ Ἰησοῦν. 32 οὗτος ἔσται μέγας καὶ υἱὸς ὑψίστου κληθήσεται, καὶ δώσει αὐτῷ κύριος ὁ Θεὸς τὸν θρόνον Δαυὶδ τοῦ πατρὸς αὐτοῦ, 33 καὶ βασιλεύσει ἐπὶ τὸν οἶκον Ἰακὼβ εἰς τοὺς αἰῶνας, καὶ τῆς βασιλείας αὐτοῦ οὐκ ἔσται τέλος. 34 εἶπεν δὲ Μαριὰμ πρὸς τὸν ἄγγελον· πῶς ἔσται τοῦτο, ἐπεὶ ἄνδρα οὐ γινώσκω; 35 καὶ ἀποκριθεὶς ὁ ἄγγελος εἶπεν αὐτῇ· πνεῦμα ἅγιον ἐπελεύσεται ἐπὶ σέ, καὶ δύναμις ὑψίστου ἐπισκιάσει σοι· διὸ καὶ τὸ γεννώμενον ἅγιον κληθήσεται υἱὸς Θεοῦ. 36 καὶ ἰδοὺ Ἐλισάβετ ἡ συγγενής σου καὶ αὐτὴ συνείληφεν υἱὸν ἐν γήρει αὐτῆς, καὶ οὗτος μὴν ἕκτος ἐστὶν αὐτῇ τῇ καλουμένῃ στείρᾳ· 37 ὅτι οὐκ ἀδυνατήσει παρὰ τοῦ Θεοῦ πᾶν ῥῆμα. 38 εἶπεν δὲ Μαριάμ· ἰδοὺ ἡ δούλη κυρίου· γένοιτό μοι κατὰ τὸ ῥῆμά σου. καὶ ἀπῆλθεν ἀπ' αὐτῆς ὁ ἄγγελος.

Protev. Jacobi 11,1-3 (sec. Pap. Bodmer V et ed. de Strycker): ¹Καὶ ἔλαβεν τὴν κάλπιν καὶ ἐξῆλθεν γεμίσαι ὕδωρ. Καὶ ἰδοὺ [αὐτῇ] φωνὴ λέγουσα <αὐτῇ>· Χαῖρε, κεχαριτω<μένη>· ὁ Κύριος μετὰ σοῦ· εὐλογη<>μένη σὺ ἐν γυναιξίν. Καὶ περιέβλεπεν τὰ δεξιὰ καὶ τὰ ἀριστερὰ Μαρία πόθεν αὕτη εἴη ἡ φωνή. Καὶ ἔντρομος γενομένη εἰσῄει εἰς τὸν οἶκον αὐτῆς καὶ ἀναπαύσασα τὴν κάλπιν ἔλαβεν τὴν πορφύραν καὶ ἐκάθισεν ἐπὶ τοῦ θρόνου καὶ ἦλκεν τὴν πορφύραν. ²Καὶ ἰδοὺ ἔστη ἄγγελος ἐνώπιον <αὐτῆς> λέγων· Μὴ φοβοῦ, Μαρία· εὗρες γὰρ χάριν ἐνώπιον τοῦ πάντων Δεσπότου. Συλλήμψῃ ἐκ Λόγου αὐτοῦ. Ἡ δὲ ἀκούσασα Μαρία διεκρίθη ἐν ἑαυτῇ λέγουσα· Ἐγὼ συλλήμψομαι ἀπὸ Κυρίου Θεοῦ ζῶντος ὡς πᾶσα γυνὴ γεννᾷ; ³Καὶ ἰδοὺ ἄγγελος ἔστη [αὐτῇ] λέγων αὐτῇ· Οὐχ οὕτως, Μαρία. Δύναμις γὰρ Θεοῦ ἐπισκιάσει σοι· διὸ καὶ τὸ γεννώμενον ἅγιον κληθήσεται υἱὸς Ὑψίστου. Καὶ καλέσεις τὸ ὄνομα αὐτοῦ Ἰησοῦν· αὐτός γὰρ σώσει <τὸν> λαὸν αὐτοῦ ἐκ τῶν ἁμαρτιῶν αὐτῶν. Καὶ εἶπεν Μαρία· Ἰδοὺ ἡ δούλη Κυρίου κατενώπιον αὐτοῦ. Γένοιτό μοι κατὰ τὸ ῥῆμά σου.

* (Double underlining refers to agreements between Matthew and PJ only).

I shall not discuss minor differences and agreements like the narrative framework of each version as well as the locality of the appearances in Bethlehem (Mt), Nazareth (Lk) and Jerusalem (*PJ*) which can be explained in view of each author's own presentation of his story.

The form in which the author of *PJ* presented his announcement story closely relates to the 'biblical' form of annunciation stories. It has the following motifs in common with Luke's version: 1. Appearance of an angel; 2. Fear of the visionary; 3. The divine message including a. a qualifying description of the visionary, b. the visionary is addressed by name and urged not to fear because God has interfered in her life, c. a woman is to conceive and bear a child, d. the name by which the child should be called, e. future accomplishments of the child; 4. Objection of the visionary as to how this can be done; 5. Answer to objection. Although the order and contents of these motifs are not exactly the same there is a number of obvious agreements between the stories. These agreements are also not superficial and one might even ask whether the semantic structure and 'global point' of the stories are the same in view of this. Even on the surface it is clear from the underlined words that the author of *PJ* was influenced by Luke in his choice of wording, but also by Matthew. The doubly underlined words indicate agreements between Matthew and *PJ*.

Are the three 'versions' of the annunciation in view of the apparent agreements perhaps then after all not different but the same? To answer the question we will first have to discover the 'global point' of each. It will take us too far to discuss all the detail problems involved that have been addressed from various perspectives during the history of research (cf Von Campenhausen 1962, Dibelius 1932, and Brown 1977).

Matthew and Luke told the infancy stories and parts of it with specific purposes in mind. These relate to curiosity, apologetics and christology (cf Brown 1977:28ff). In view of all the differences and contradictions between the versions of Matthew and Luke in their presentations of the infancy stories, it has become evident that both took a greater interest in the theological (= christological) aspects of their stories rather than in the historical or biographical ones. Jesus' origins were made intelligible to their readers against the background of the fulfilment of Old Testament expectations as they understood it (cf fulfilment quotations in Matthew) or with a view to the history of salvation, that is as *theologoumena*.

There is general agreement that the infancy stories represent the latest phase in the development of the gospel tradition and that Matthew and Luke differ from the rest of the New Testament in this respect. In contrast to Mark they relate christology not only to the resurrection and ministry of Jesus (two-stage christology), but also to his birth and infancy (three-stage christology). It is a very particular kind of three-stage christology which is also different from that of Paul and John who both have a pre-existence christology. "Their major affirmations in these Gospel introductions bear then on His Christological identification: He is born of God, son of Abraham, son of David, Messiah, Savior, Lord, and Son of God. To fail to perceive this is to miss the thrust of the infancy narratives" (Fitzmyer 1973:564). It is furthermore argued that christology developed from the resurrection backwards through Jesus' ministry and baptism to his birth and pre-existence. In the pre-gospel traditions found in Paul (compare the sermons in Acts) the identity of Jesus is associated with his being raised from the dead by God (cf Rm 1:3-4, Ac 2:32 *et al.*). In Mark (1:11) he is proclaimed Son of God at his baptism and transfiguration (9:7) while in Luke he is born Son of God (cf also Matthew). "The same combined ideas that early Christian preaching had once applied to the resurrection (i.e., a divine proclamation, the begetting of God's Son, the agency of the Holy Spirit), and which Mark had applied to the baptism, are now applied to the conception of Jesus in the words of an angel's message to Joseph and to Mary..." (Brown 1977:31). In view of this the infancy of Jesus is narrated in Matthew and Luke from the perspective of the identity of Jesus—*who* he is and *how* it happened that he is who he is. His being Son of God and being Son of David are related to each other by associating his sonship with the moment of his conception. Matthew and Luke made their own stories of it by presenting the material each in his own way. With this in mind, let us now consider the 'virginal conception' which is the focal point in *PJ*.

One of the differences between Matthew and Luke with regard to the conception of Jesus is the fact that Matthew leaves no doubt that the conception of Jesus has already taken place when the angel appears to Joseph. Joseph was not involved in it in any way. (In Luke's version it is a future conception.) Exactly how the conception happens is not told by Matthew. His story, which is unmistakably a story about virginal conception, has definite apologetic nuances. In 1:18 he tells the reader that Mary conceived *before* she and Joseph started living together (got married) but also that he did not have intercourse with her until she bore Jesus (1:25). Added to the angel's announcement, is a *formula citation* (1:22-23) to prove that the conception is a fulfilment of Isaiah's prophecy of a young girl conceiving and bearing a son. In this way Matthew undoubtedly stresses the virginal conception through the Holy Spirit. The child is a Davidid through naming. His father is an ancestor of David (1:19). Through conception, however, he is Emmanuel. Unlike in Luke where Mary plays a more important role in the infancy story, Mary is an

instrument of God's action in Matthew. "Once she has given birth to
Jesus, she and the child become the object of Joseph's care (2:13-14,
20-21); and it is Joseph who is given the center stage of drama" (Brown *et
al.* 1978:86). The primary emphasis of the story is the virginal conception
by the Holy Spirit.

In Luke it is different. His is not in the first instance a story about
virginal conception. In his version the focus is on the future greatness of
Jesus, on christology and exceptional conception. "We should not forget
this christology even though there has been more Marian reflection (and
literature) based on this scene than on any other in the NT" (Brown *et al.*
1978:112). Having given a rather extensive divine message, Luke tells
the reader that Mary is confused about the fact that she will become the
mother of the Davidic Messiah, eternal king of the house of Jacob, about
this future conception. Mary objects by saying that she does not have intercourse with a man (1:34). This objection and the reference to her being a
betrothed virgin are the only indications of her virginity. Fitzmyer
(1973:567) therefore correctly maintains that, "When this account is
read in and of itself... every detail in it could be understood of a child to
be born of Mary in the usual human way, a child endowed with God's
special favor, born at the intervention of the Spirit of God, and destined
to be acknowledged as the heir of David's throne as God's Messiah and
Son. Chap. 2 in the Lucan Gospel supports this understanding even further with its references to Mary and Joseph as Jesus' 'parents' (2:41) or
as 'your father and I' (2:48)".

The global point of the annunciation story in Luke reminds one of
Paul's statement in Romans 1:3-4: "It is about his Son, our Lord Jesus
Christ: as to his humanity, he was born a descendant of David; as to his
divine holiness, he was shown with great power to be the Son of God by
being raised from death" (GNB). Luke's story is a story about an extraordinary child and its conception. That Luke's annunciation story has
been read as a story about virginal conception since the early days of
church history cannot be denied. It is well known that Mary's objection,
and in particular her question, 'how can this be?', gave rise to much
speculation about Mary's ignorance of how children are conceived,
perpetual virginity and a hypothetical vow to remain a virgin for the rest
of her life (cf Brown *et al.* 1978:114). Luke 1:34 has ever since been a bone
of contention and debate. If one realizes, however, that an objection or
request for a sign very often occurs in annunciation stories, in other
words, that it need not be a biographical statement, and notice how it
contributes towards the development of the plot, it becomes another matter. In the case of Luke it offers the opportunity to inform the reader that
the conception will be through the Holy Spirit, and to refer to the fact

that Elizabeth, who used to be barren, is pregnant *because there is nothing God cannot do* (1:37). After this Mary is satisfied and the angel leaves. It is the Matthean version with its nuances which influenced readers of Luke to interpret Luke's story in view of Matthew's. On the other hand, it is also clear that the lack of clarity in Luke's version (cf also Matthew) of how the Holy Spirit will be involved in the conception of Jesus; the accusations of Jesus being an illegitimate child (cf e.g. Celcus, *Logos, Alēthēs* 1:32); attempts to explain how Jesus could have been Son of God from his childhood, and many more aspects of which we find vestiges in the New Testament, could have given rise to readings of Luke with the focus on virginal conception.

The author of *PJ* used the material of the annunciation stories of the New Testament to propagate the virginal conception, most probably in an attempt to convince his readers of the extraordinary birth of Jesus. The global point of his version ties in with the rest of his narrative. It is an annunciation narrative about a virginal conception which is elaborated upon in various episodes which follow. It serves the purpose of a preview of what is to follow in the rest of the narrative. In telling the story of the virginal conception, *PJ* is closer to Matthew than to Luke even though he uses Luke's version as his main 'Vorlage', and despite the christological information Luke's version contains. This is mainly due to the fact that the author of *PJ* embedded this narrative into a virginal conception-context. What *PJ* 11 amounts to, or why it was told, is determined by its literary environment. In spite of its christological content (Son of the Highest, Saviour of his people from their sins), its meaning and reference is determined by the fact that it forms part of the story of *Mary's* virginal conception. This is made clear by the narrative framework of the annunciation story in *PJ*, the contents thereof and the integration of the material into the complete story.

One of the remarkable differences between *PJ* and Luke is in the wording of the promise of future conception. According to Luke the angel says χαὶ ἰδοὺ συλλήμψῃ ἐν γαστρὶ while *PJ* has χαὶ συνλήμψῃ ἐκ λόγου αὐτοῦ. What does the expression in *PJ* mean? Unfortunately the question is not completely answered by the text. Mary finds the remark puzzling and deliberates whether she will conceive of the Lord, the living God and give birth like every other woman does. That will not be the case. The power of God will overshadow her. Is συνλήμψῃ ἐκ λόγου αὐτοῦ the same as, or paraphrased by δύναμις γὰρ θεοῦ ἐπισκιάσει σοι? This is of course a possibility because αὐτοῦ refers to δεσπότου in the preceding phrase and δεσπότης is a substitute for θεός in *PJ* (cf 2:4, 7:1 *et al.*). λόγος would thus refer to or be the same as δύναμις θεοῦ a term used for the Holy Spirit (cf Luke 1:35). In 19:1 it is overtly stated that, '... ἀλλά συλλήμψιν ἔχει ἐκ

πνεύματος ἁγίου (cf The Gospel of the Hebrews in Delius 1973:8). Nevertheless, it is clear that the author did not fill out the 'open space' in the
New Testament versions by telling the reader in detail how the conception through the Holy Spirit took place or through which medium the
conception happened. Later readings of the phrase gave rise to speculation and even explanation of how conception took place ἐx λόγου for example, the idea of conception through the ear (cf Smid 1965:84). In addition it may rightfully be asked whether this formulation shows traces of
the *logos* christology of the second century (cf Justin, *Apol.* 1:33 and Bauer
1967:48ff).

The omission of the extensive identification of the child by Luke in *PJ*
and the reformulation of Mary's question, πῶς ἔσται τοῦτο, ἐπεὶ ἄνδρα οὐ
γινώσκω; into ἐγὼ συνλήμφομαι ἀπὸ κυρίου τοῦ θεοῦ ζῶντος ὡς πᾶσα γυνὴ
γεννᾷ; the answer of the angel, οὐχ οὕτως Μαριάμ and what follows, is a
deliberate attempt by the author to prompt his reader to understand that
the birth is an exceptional one. It is also a preview of an episode which is
later taken up and developed in the gynaecological test case story in
chapter 19ff. In chapters 17-19 a new episode in the story of Jesus' birth
is invented in which the occasion is taken to elaborate upon Mary's
remark ἐπει ἄνδρα οὐ γινώσκω (cf 17:1 and 19:1). Most probably it also
already points to what is being stated in 20:1 as οὐ γὰρ μικρὸς ἀγὼν
περίκειταί μοι. Interestingly enough, the author of *PJ* did not elaborate on
the *how* of the conception through the Holy Spirit. Similar to Luke, the
answer to Mary's question concerns the *who* that will be conceived rather
than the *how*.

Did Matthew, Luke and the author of *PJ* tell the same story? Superficially one would have to say yes. It seems like yet another story of the
annunciation of the birth of Jesus. However, does this reply in the affirmative comply with the conditions discussed above, according to which
various versions of the 'same' story can be the 'same'? Matthew and
Luke did not in fact tell the same story. Their purposes were different
and so were the 'points' of their stories. The author of *PJ* retold Matthew's and Luke's versions and in his retelling he came closer to telling
the same story that Matthew did, where the emphasis is on the virginal
conception, even though he relied more on Luke's version of the
material. But again he did not tell the same story as Matthew because
Matthew used the virginal conception in telling the story of Emmanuel
and how he is 'God with us' through conception to resurrection. In *PJ* the
virginal conception is not told—not even in the annunciation story—to
explain christology, but to explain the extraordinary birth of the
Messiah.

There should be no doubt that the author of *PJ* was prompted by the New Testament texts to retell the annunciation story, and for that matter his whole story in the way he did. By emphasizing certain motifs found in the New Testament, he retold the virginal conception story for a purpose which most probably can be linked to the difficulties which arose when christology was associated with the moment of conception. When theologoumena became part of the life story of Jesus (cf Dibelius 1932: 38ff) a whole set of problems was generated (cf Von Campenhausen 1962). The following remark of Brown about Luke's version (1977: 312) is helpful in this connection, "The action of the Holy Spirit and the power of the Most High came not upon the Davidic king but upon his mother. We are not dealing with the adoption of a Davidid by coronation as God's son or representative; we are dealing with begetting of God's son in the womb of Mary through God's creative Spirit". *PJ* lays stress on this mariological directive of the Lucan text and follows Matthew in his identification of Jesus. *PJ* is a retelling of a theologoumenon which had already been told for various purposes (cf Matthew and Luke). It originates from a period when speculation about the origins of Jesus was in the air (cf Bauer 1967:29ff), and unity and diversity in teaching became a problem of orthodoxy and heterodoxy (cf Bauer 1964). With *PJ* we have, however, not reached a stage where full-fledged doctrines about the humanity and divinity of Christ have been worked out. *PJ* reveals a stage of imitative and imaginative retelling of New Testament material, in many respects similar to retellings found in the New Testament.

The author of *PJ* knew the New Testament versions of the conception of Jesus. These versions prompted him in his own situation to retell the story of Jesus' conception with his own purpose in mind. In order to smooth out some of the difficulties of the New Testament versions, he produced a new text, but a text which can be explained as a rationalization of what is given in the New Testament. He undoubtedly invented some of the material he offered his reader and most probably does not supply the person in search for 'how things really happened' with any 'new' information. The points in which it deviates from the 'canonical' versions of the infancy story of Jesus, with which I have dealt above, can be accounted for either in terms of the 'integrity' of his story or perhaps as rival traditions.

The purpose of *PJ* is often said to be the *glorification of Mary* (cf Smid 1965:14). It is stated as follows by Cullmann (1968:279), "Das Ganze ist zur Verherrlichung der Maria geschrieben. Nicht nur werden implizit die jüdischen Verleumdungen ... besonders kräftig abgelehnt, sondern alle künftigen mariologischen Themen kündigen sich schon an...". I am afraid that Cullmann and others who share this view are led by the fact

that *PJ* was used and received by many of its readers as a glorification of
Mary and a clear plea for asceticism. But is that the purpose of the story?
Is that why it was written or what the text tells? Granted the fact that the
virginal conception, virgin birth and enduring virginity (cf 20:1), is narrated by *PJ*, one should nevertheless be careful to conclude that its purpose is to glorify Mary. The purpose of the story should rather be looked
for in *PJ* as a retelling of the birth story of Jesus from the perspective of
his mother. The author's object was probably *not* ''...to write a (pretty
elaborate) mariology in the form of a novel'', as Smid (1965:19) contends. Intertextual relationships with texts of the same period (cf Delius
1973:5ff) prove that discussions about the origin of Jesus, his birth, and
for that matter the virgin birth and Mary's role in the birth of Jesus, was
in vogue, so to speak, when our author retold the story of the birth of
Jesus. *PJ* was told primarily with a view to the birth of Jesus, and from
the perspective of his mother. That is why it is rightfully called an infancy
gospel.

Because retellings of stories are in principle more often not the same as
the 'original' it is a pity that extracanonical narratives have been called
'apocryphal'. 'Canonical' and 'apocryphal' reflect, as Koester (1980:
105ff) correctly observes, deep-seated prejudices that have far-reaching
consequences. Especially in (fundamentalist) Protestant-dominated areas
or countries where the 'sola scriptura' doctrine has unintentionally given
rise to ignorance about developments in the early church and neglect of
the study of early Christian documents, these terms are naively equated
to 'authentic' versus 'inauthentic', 'factive' versus 'fictive', 'historical'
versus 'unhistorical', 'true' versus 'false' and so on. The following
remark by Brown (1977:33 n.21) is useful in this connection, ''The
relative sobriety of the canonical infancy narratives when compared to
the non-canonical ones has been used as an argument for their historicity. But is this a difference of kind (history vs. fiction) or a difference of
degree? One might argue that both canonical and non-canonical narratives result from the attempts of Christian imagination to fill in the
Messiah's origins, and that in the case of the apocryphal narratives the
imagination had a freer and further exercise'' (cf Vorster 1984).

BIBLIOGRAPHY

ALAND, K. 1967. *Synopsis Quattuor Evangeliorum.* Stuttgart: Württembergische Bibelanstalt.
ALTANER, B. & A. STUIBER 1966. *Patrologie. Leben, Schriften und Lehre der Kirchenväter.* 7.
   Aufl. Freiburg: Herder.
BAUER, W. 1964. *Rechtgläubigkeit und Ketzerei im ältesten Christentum.* Hrsg. von G. Strecker.
   2. Aufl. Tübingen: Mohr. (BHTh 10.)
BAUER, W. 1967. *Das Leben Jesu im Zeitalter der neutestamentlichen Apokryphen.* Darmstadt:
   Wissenschaftliche Buchgesellschaft.

BROWN, R. E. 1977. *The birth of the Messiah. A Commentary on the infancy narratives in Matthew and Luke.* London: Chapman.

BROWN, R. E. *et al* (eds) 1978. *Mary in the New Testament. A collaborative assessment by Protestant and Roman Catholic scholars.* Philadelphia: Fortress.

CHATMAN, S. 1978. *Story and discourse. Narrative structure in fiction and film.* Ithaca: Cornell University Press.

CULLMANN, O. 1968. Kindheitsevangelien, in E. Hennecke, *Neutestamentliche Apokryphen in deutscher Übersetzung.* 4. Aufl. Hrsg. von W. Schneemelcher. Tübingen: Mohr.

DELIUS, W. 1973. *Texte zur Geschichte der Marienverehrung und Marienverkündigung in der Alten Kirche.* 2. Aufl. von H.-U. Rosenbaum. Berlin: De Gruyter.

DE SANTOS OTERO, A. 1975. *Los evangelios apocrifos.* 3. ed. Madrid: Biblioteca de Autores Christianos.

DIBELIUS, M. 1932. *Jungfrauensohn und Krippenkind. Untersuchungen zur Geburtsgeschichte Jesu im Lukas-Evangelium.* Heidelberg: Carl Winter.

DIHLE, A. 1970. *Studien zur griechischen Biographie.* 2. Aufl. Göttingen: Vandenhoeck. (AAWG 37.)

FITZMYER, J. A. 1973. The Virginal conception of Jesus in the New Testament. *TS* 34, 541-75.

GERHART, M. 1979. Imagination and history in Ricoeur's interpretation theory. *Philosophy Today* 23, 51-68.

HAMMAN, A. 1966. Sitz im Leben des Actes Apocryphes du Nouveau Testament, in F. L. Cross (ed), *Studia Patristica 8, Part 2: Patres Apostolici, Historica, Liturgica, Ascetica et Monastica.* (TU 93). Berlin: Akademie.

HELM, R. 1956. *Der antike Roman.* 2. Aufl. Göttingen: Vandenhoeck.

HOLUB, R. C. 1984. *Reception theory. A critical introduction.* London: Methuen. (New Accents.)

HORBURY, W. 1982. The benediction of the *minim* and early Jewish-Christian controversy. *JThS* 33, 19-61.

KOESTER, H. 1980. Apocryphal and Canonical Gospels. *HThR* 73, 105-30.

OSBORN, E. 1981. *The beginning of Christian philosophy.* Cambridge: The University Press.

POLANYI, L. 1981. Telling the same story twice. *Text* 1, 315-36.

QUASTEN, J. 1950. *Patrology* I. Utrecht: Spectrum.

RIFFATERRE, M. 1983. *Text production.* New York: Columbia University Press.

SCHNEEMELCHER, W. 1968. Typen apokrypher Evangelien, in E. Hennecke, *Neutestamentliche Apokryphen in deutscher Übersetzung.* 4. Aufl. Hrsg. von W. Schneemelcher. Tübingen: Mohr.

SCHÜRMANN, H. 1969. *Das Lukasevangelium.* 1 Teil. HThK 3. Freiburg/Basel/Wien.

SEGERS, R. T. 1980. *Het lezen van literatuur. Een inleiding tot een nieuwe literatuurbenadering.* Baarn: Ambo.

SMID, H. R. 1965. *Protevangelium Jacobi. A commentary.* Assen: Van Gorcum.

VIELHAUER, P. 1978. *Geschichte der urchristlichen Literatur. Einleitung in das Neue Testament, die Apokryphen und die Apostolischen Väter.* Berlin: De Gruyter.

VON CAMPENHAUSEN, H. 1962. *Die Jungfrauengeburt in der Theologie der alten Kirche.* Heidelberg: Carl Winter (SHAW).

VON TISCHENDORF, K. 1966. *Evangelia Apocrypha.* Hildesheim: Georg Olms.

VORSTER, W. S. 1984. The historical paradigm. Its possibilities and limitations. *Neotestamentica* 18, 104-123.

VORSTER, W. S. 1985. Meaning and reference. The parables of Jesus in Mark 4, in B. C. Lategan & W. S. Vorster, *Text and reality. Aspects of reference in biblical texts.* Philadelphia: Fortress. (Semeia Supplements.)

WILSON, R. M. 1978. Apokryphen des Neuen Testaments. *TRE* 3, 316-62.

J. N. SUGGIT

THE PERILS OF BIBLE TRANSLATION: AN EXAMINATION OF THE LATIN VERSIONS OF THE WORDS OF INSTITUTION OF THE EUCHARIST

Among the many contributions which Professor Bruce Metzger has made to the study of the New Testament, the fields of textual criticism and Bible translation have been specially prominent. It is therefore appropriate that this study should deal with ways in which the translation of a New Testament text may well have affected the development of eucharistic theology and indeed perhaps even the whole history of the western Church. At the same time we shall note some of the problems posed by the relation between the text of the New Testament and the wording of the Church's liturgies. Of all the influences on the history of the text that of liturgical use has been one of the most significant. Most Christians, at any rate in pre-Reformation times, would be more familiar with the words of the liturgy than with the words of Scripture.

We are not concerned here with attempts to recover the words used by Jesus at the Last Supper, but simply with the way in which the words recorded in the Synoptic Gospels and Paul have been translated into Latin, both in Scripture and in liturgical texts. In the following table of relevant texts some of the *variae lectiones* in the Greek have been appended. For reasons mentioned below the Latin text of the Vulgate is that of the Clementine edition of 1592.

Mk 14:22   λάβετε, τοῦτό ἐστιν τὸ σῶμά μου. (post λαβετε f 13 plur add φαγετε// εστιν om W)
               Sumite, hoc est corpus meum.

Mk 14:24   τοῦτό ἐστιν τὸ αἷμά μου τῆς διαθήκης τὸ ἐκχυννόμενον ὑπὲρ πολλῶν. (post μου add το A D* W f 1 f 13 plur// post της add καινης A f1 f 13 plur)
               Hic est sanguis meus novi testamenti qui pro multis effundetur.

Mt 26:26   λάβετε φάγετε, τοῦτό ἐστιν τὸ σῶμά μου.
               Accipite et comedite, hoc est corpus meum.

Mt 26:28   τοῦτο γάρ ἐστιν τὸ αἷμά μου τῆς διαθήκης τὸ περὶ πολλῶν ἐκχυννόμενον εἰς ἄφεσιν ἁμαρτιῶν. (post μου add το A C W 074 f 1 f 13 plur// post της add καινης A C D W f 1 f 13 plur)

Hic enim est sanguis meus novi testamenti qui pro multis
effundetur in remissionem peccatorum

Lk 22:19 τοῦτό ἐστιν τὸ σῶμά μου τὸ ὑπὲρ ὑμῶν διδόμενον· τοῦτο ποιεῖτε
εἰς τὴν ἐμὴν ἀνάμνησιν. (το υπερ - αναμνησιν om D it)
Hoc est corpus meum, quod pro vobis datur: hoc facite in
meam commemorationem.

Lk 22:20 τοῦτο τὸ ποτήριον ἡ καινὴ διαθήκη ἐν τῷ αἵματί μου τὸ ὑπὲρ
ὑμῶν ἐκχυννόμενον. (versum om D it)
Hic est calix novum testamentum in sanguine meo, qui pro
vobis fundetur.

1 Cor 11:24 τοῦτό μού ἐστιν τὸ σῶμα τὸ ὑπὲρ ὑμῶν· τοῦτο ποιεῖτε εἰς τὴν
ἐμὴν ἀνάμνησιν. (post υμων add κλωμενον ℵ² C³ D² F G,
θρυπτομενον D*, διδομενον co // C³ Ψ plur add ad initium
λαβετε φαγετε)
Hoc est corpus meum quod pro vobis tradetur: hoc facite
in meam commemorationem.

1 Cor 11:25 τοῦτο τὸ ποτήριον ἡ καινὴ διαθήκη ἐστὶν ἐν τῷ ἐμῷ αἵματι·
τοῦτο ποιεῖτε, ὁσάκις ἐὰν πίνητε, εἰς τὴν ἐμὴν ἀνάμνησιν.
(αιματι μου p⁴⁶ A C P 33 365 pc)
Hic calix novum testamentum est in meo sanguine. Hoc
facite quotiescunque bibetis, in meam commemorationem.

The Clementine edition of the Vulgate has been followed since this was
based on the texts used in the later Middle Ages. It should however be
noted that the Stuttgart edition (Weber *et al* 1975) follows variant
readings and prints the present tense in each case (*effunditur, funditur*).
The mss of the Vulgate are divided between the future and the present
tense, with numerically stronger support for the future. The same is true
of the mss of the Old Latin versions, on which the Vulgate was largely
based. The Stuttgart edition tends to follow the Greek, as witnessed particularly at 1 Cor 11:24 where *hoc est corpus meum pro vobis* is the reading
adopted, although only one 9th century ms is cited in its support. It may
be that the future was sometimes mistakenly written for the present, since
there is a difference of only a single letter between them, except in the
case of Lk 22:19 where *dabitur* would be too different from *datur* to be
merely a copyist's error. It is therefore perhaps significant that this is the
one occasion when the present is found in all mss of the Vulgate.

The influence of the liturgy on the text is clearly to be seen in the *variae
lectiones* of the Greek given above, all of which are to be found in the
Greek liturgies. The addition of φάγετε, for example, in mss of Mk 14:24
is due more probably to assimilation to the liturgical texts than to Mt
26:26. The same is true of the additions to 1 Cor 11:24, and may help to

explain the complex problem of Lk 22:19f. The same process was doubtless at work in the Latin texts, as will be indicated below.

From the foregoing quotations from the text of the New Testament it can be clearly seen that in Greek the verb is always in the present participle passive (διδόμενον, κλώμενον, ἐκχυννόμενον), and even the additions to 1 Cor 11:24 are found only in the present. When these present participles are rendered into Latin they are (with the exception of Lk 22:19) rendered by a relative clause with the future indicative.

The Greek present participle should normally be translated by an English present continuous (*is being given, is being shed*), though it can regularly describe a repeated or habitual action. It is linguistically possible for a present indicative or participle in Greek to represent the future. This occurs especially in confident assertions, when the future event is seen as so certain as to be considered as present (cf Burton 1976:9f). A good example is Mk 9:31 (ὁ υἱὸς τοῦ ἀνθρώπου παραδίδοται εἰς χεῖρας ἀνθρώπων). This literally means "The Son of Man is being handed over into the hands of men", where *RSV* translates "will be delivered". While this rendering is quite possible, it disguises the tense of the Greek and obscures the difference between this text and the parallels in Mt and Lk, and in Mk 10:33 and parallels, where in every case the future in one form or another is employed. Another example is Mt 27:63, where ἐγείρομαι literally means "I am rising" and where *RSV* translates "I will rise again". Jn 17:20 (οὐ περὶ τούτων δὲ ἐρωτῶ μόνον, ἀλλὰ καὶ περὶ τῶν πιστευόντων διὰ τοῦ λόγου αὐτῶν εἰς ἐμέ) furnishes an example of the use of the present participle with a future reference: whereas the literal meaning is "those who believe in me" *RSV* renders "those who are to believe in me", a translation, interestingly enough, found in most Latin versions, including the Vulgate. In this particular instance the words are probably to be understood as words of the risen Christ formed by John and addressed to Christians of John's generation some sixty years after the crucifixion as words of constant encouragement to the Church, rather than as being simply a historical record of what Jesus is supposed to have said.

In spite of this use of the present to refer to the future, there is a difference between the two tenses. The use of the present participle in communities already celebrating the Lord's Supper is a vivid declaration that the Lord is giving himself to the communicants in the sacrament as surely as he gave himself once for all on the cross. The present tense therefore helps the participants to realise that they are not simply commemorating a past event, but are rather entering into a present experience as the Lord gives himself to them and they share in his passion and risen life.

The history of the development of the words of institution in east and west makes interesting reading. The earliest evidence is furnished in the Latin text of Hippolytus at the beginning of the third century. The best mss read *hoc est corpus meum quod pro vobis confringitur* and *hic est sanguis meus qui pro vobis effunditur* (Dix 1968:8), though there is a variant reading in the former case in the future. Doubtless the Greek original (which is lacking) was in the present as in the New Testament, and the Apostolic Constitutions furnish evidence for the present θρυπτόμενον (Dix 1968:8). Ambrose *de Sacr* 4:5:21f has the future in the words over the bread—*hoc est enim corpus meum quod pro multis confringetur*, while over the cup he has simply *hic est sanguis meus*. In all later Latin rites the words over the bread are *hoc est enim corpus meum* and over the cup *hic est enim calix sanguinis mei, novi et aeterni testamenti, mysterium fidei, qui pro vobis et pro multis effundetur in remissionem peccatorum*. Though the difference from Ambrose can be readily seen, both Ambrose and the Latin mss have the verbs in the future. The only exception to the use of the future appears to be in the Bobbio missal (Lowe 1920:12) where the present *effunditur* occurs, possibly simply a copyist's error since *e* and *i* are frequently confused in this ms, as is shown even in the words of institution—*sanguenis, faciates* (corrected by a later hand to *facietes*), *mistirium* (corrected to *mystirium*). In the *Ordo Missae Romanae* 1969 the words over the cup are the same as previously, without *mysterium fidei* which occur in another position: over the bread the words become *Hoc est Corpus meum, quod pro vobis tradetur*.

In the Latin rite therefore from the time of Ambrose there is a consistent emphasis on the future tense, and it is presumably this liturgical use which was responsible for the occurrence of the future in most manuscripts of the Vulgate. Now the use of the future gives an altogether different meaning to the words, for the future looks back to the words supposedly said at the Last Supper, and so views them as the historical record of a saying which was fulfilled on the cross. The future tense historicises the rite instead of stressing the present self-giving of the Lord to the communicants and their participation in his death and resurrection. It is therefore not surprising that at the Reformation the debate centred very largely on the meaning of this historical element: was the eucharist to be seen especially as a commemoration of a past event or was it some kind of repetition of the sacrifice of the cross? Viewed from such a historical perspective it is not surprising that the language of sacrifice proved ambiguous or misleading.

Not only was the text of the New Testament in later times affected by the liturgy, but it would also seem that the formulation of the words of the eucharist as we have them in the Gospels and 1 Corinthians was largely influenced by the liturgical practice of the time when the authors wrote.

They wrote in terms which could speak loud and clear to those who read or heard them. In this way, as has been frequently pointed out (e.g. Thurian 1960, 1961 and von Allmen 1969:ch 1), the significance of the eucharist is similar to that of the Passover. In each case the worshippers are participating in a present act of redemption rather than simply commemorating a past event, even though in each case there is no attempt to deny the historical reality of the event on which the celebration is based.

The Greek liturgies without exception retain this understanding. Present participles are consistently used in the words both over the bread and over the cup. So the Liturgy of St James, with which Chrysostom, Basil and Mark substantially agree, has λάβετε, φάγετε· τοῦτό μου ἐστὶ τὸ σῶμα, τὸ ὑπὲρ ὑμῶν κλώμενον καὶ διαδιδόμενον εἰς ἄφεσιν ἁμαρτιῶν and ... τὸ αἷμα, τὸ τῆς καινῆς διαθήκης, τὸ ὑπὲρ ὑμῶν καὶ πολλῶν ἐκχεόμενον καὶ διαδιδόμενον... (Neale 1868:60). The so-called Clementine liturgy has ...τὸ περὶ πολλῶν θρυπτόμενον... and τὸ αἷμά μου, τὸ περὶ πολλῶν ἐκχυνόμενον... (Neale 1868:101). As the eastern liturgies were attributed to the apostles it was possible to make this sense of present involvement even more vivid, as happens, for example, in the Liturgy of St James, where the words over the cup are prefaced by the sentence ἔδωκεν ἡμῖν τοῖς αὐτοῦ μαθηταῖς... ("He gave to us his disciples, saying..."). In the same way the Liturgy of St Basil expands the words of 1 Cor 11:26—ὁσάκις γὰρ ἂν ἐσθίητε τὸν ἄρτον τοῦτον καὶ τὸ ποτήριον τοῦτο πίνητε, τὸν θάνατον καταγγέλλετε καὶ τὴν ἐμὴν ἀνάστασιν ὁμολογεῖτε ("For as often as you eat this bread and drink this cup you proclaim my death and confess my resurrection") (Neale 1868:60, 160).

That the tense of the verbs in the words of institution should be taken with all seriousness is shown by the use of the imperfect tense to describe the occasion of the Supper in 1 Cor 11:23—ἐν τῇ νυκτὶ ᾗ παρεδίδετο ("On the night in which he was being handed over"). Here the use of the imperfect is emphasised by its contrast with the series of aorists which immediately follow it—ἔλαβεν, ἔκλασεν, εἶπεν. This imperfect is retained in all the Greek liturgies, though in different forms. The meaning of them all, as in 1 Cor 11:23, is that the eucharist is the moment when the Lord was handed over "for the life and salvation of the world" (Liturgy of St James) by one of his own disciples present with him at the Last Supper. All the Gospels stress the treachery of Judas, because Judas is the type of those who may be present at any or every eucharist when the Lord nevertheless gives himself to them in love. Some of the liturgies (e.g. St James) stress this by adding an additional clause—...ἐν τῇ νυκτὶ ᾗ παρεδίδοτο, μᾶλλον δὲ ἑαυτὸν παρεδίδου, ὑπὲρ τῆς τοῦ κόσμου ζωῆς καὶ σωτηρίας ("...on the night in which he was being handed over, or rather was handing himself over, for the life and salvation of the world") (Neale 1868:59).

The Vulgate translates the Greek imperfect correctly at 1 Cor 11:23—
...*in qua nocte tradebatur*, but in the prediction of Judas' betrayal the
present παραδίδοται (Mk 14:21 par) is rendered by the future *tradetur*. In
the Latin liturgy from the time of Ambrose the phrase becomes *qui pridie
quam pateretur* ("Who on the day before he suffered"), and this has been
retained in the Roman Canon, though the three new *Preces Eucharisticae* of
1969 have other wording, two of which recapture something of the drama
of 1 Cor 11:23 and the Greek liturgies. Thus *Prex* II has *Qui cum Passioni
voluntarie traderetur...*, following Hippolytus; and *Prex* III reproduces the
Vulgate, *Ipse enim in qua nocte tradebatur...* The Latin liturgies of earlier
times however are content with the simple historical statement to indicate
the occasion of the Supper.

The upshot of all this is that the Latin rites, of which we have the
earliest evidence in Ambrose in the late 4th century, reflect what Dix
(1945:265) calls the historicising of the liturgy, as opposed to the
eschatological idea found in Passover as well as in the earliest understanding of the eucharist as is preserved in the Greek liturgies. The Latin
rite achieves this historicisation by putting the words of institution into
the future, so that they become a historical record of what Jesus said at
the Last Supper, and by changing the dramatic ἐν τῇ νυκτὶ ᾗ παρεδίδετο into the purely historical statement of a past event.

As a result of this change of emphasis, the west looked for a change in
the elements resulting from the words of Jesus which were now seen not
simply as authority for the performance of the eucharistic action but as
having consecratory value. This is clearly shown in Ambrose *de Sacr*
4:23—*Antequam consecretur panis est; ubi autem verba Christi accesserint, corpus
est Christi ...Et ante verba Christi calix est vini et aquae plenus; ubi verba Christi
operata fuerint, ibi sanguis efficitur qui plebem redemit. Ergo videte quantis
generibus potens est sermo Christi universa convertere.* Instead of a rite in which
the Lord Jesus through the power of the Spirit gives himself in the sacrament so that the communicants are involved in his passion and resurrection there developed the tendency to look back to the Last Supper in a
historical way. But because the eucharist was clearly recognized as the
central act of Christian worship, its importance was stressed by ascribing
to the Lord's words a quasi-magical power. Here was one of the important factors leading to the Reformation and the dissolution of the unity of
the western Church. It is to be noted that Cyril of Jerusalem, writing a
little later than Ambrose, refers to the part of the Spirit in making the
elements the body and blood of Christ (*Cat Myst* 5:7).

The English revision of 1549 and later revisions were on the right track
when they referred to "the night in which he was betrayed" and "this is
my body which is given for you", "this is my blood which is shed for

you''. This wording has been substantially retained in the first and second eucharistic prayers in *Liturgy 75* of the Church of the Province of Southern Africa. The English however is ambiguous: *was betrayed* can be simply a past tense, and *is given, is shed* is normally regarded as a past, *has been given, has been shed*. A growing awareness in the present generation of the meaning of the eucharist has meant that modern liturgies try to recapture more of the drama of the original. This is one of the most encouraging aspects of the ecumenical movement, as is shown especially in the Lima statement of the World Council of Churches (1982:10-17). In English it would not be difficult to refer to ''the night in which he was being betrayed'' (or, perhaps, ''handed over''), though it would seem rather clumsy to talk of ''This is my body which is being given for you''. Perhaps one should follow the wording of the revised rite of the Holy Communion of the Methodist Church—*This is my body given for you..., my blood shed for you*. English is perhaps incapable of really recapturing the dramatic meaning of the Greek present participle, just as Latin has no exact equivalent to it.

Other changes are needed in the English rites if they are to avoid the historical emphasis and stress the present reality, especially in the words of administration since 1549. *Liturgy 75* of the Church of the Province of Southern Africa reverts to the early custom of saying simply *The Body of Christ* and *The Blood of Christ* which are phrases capable of different interpretations, as they draw attention not only to the elements but to the communicants' involvement in the Body of Christ, the Church, and in the passion of Christ. In this respect too the eastern rites avoid the historicisation of the west which is here more prominent in the English than in the Roman rite.

In drawing attention to the dangers of translating the text of the Bible this paper has incidentally indicated the close connection which must always exist between the Bible and the Church's liturgy. Not only is the liturgy dependent on the Scripture: Scripture is itself to be interpreted and understood in the light of the liturgy, which celebrates the act of redemption to which the Scripture bears witness. The present growth in understanding of the eucharist may well be encouraged by reconsidering our earliest liturgical texts not only as words spoken by the Lord at the Last Supper, but rather as words addressed to participants in every eucharist. Was the lack of a present participle passive in Latin a contributory factor to the Reformation?

BIBLIOGRAPHY

BURTON, E. DE W. 1976. *Syntax of the moods and tenses in New Testament Greek*. 3. ed. Edinburgh: Clark.

CHADWICK, H. (ed) 1960. *St Ambrose: on the sacraments*. London: Mowbray. (Studies in eucharistic faith and practice.)

CROSS, F. L. (ed) 1960. *St Cyril of Jerusalem's lectures on the Christian sacraments*. London: SPCK. (Texts for students 51.)

DIX, G. 1945. *The shape of the liturgy*. 2. ed. Westminster: Dacre.

DIX, G. (ed) 1968. *The apostolic tradition of Hippolytus*. London: SPCK.

LOWE, E. A. (ed) 1920. *The Bobbio missal*. London: Henry Bradshaw Soc. (vol 58.)

NEALE, J. M. (ed) 1868. *The liturgies of S. Mark, S. James, S. Clement, S. Chrysostom, S. Basil*. 2. ed. London: Hayes.

THURIAN, M. 1960. *The eucharistic memorial, Pt 1. The Old Testament*. Richmond: John Knox. (Ecumenical Studies in worship 8.)

THURIAN, M. 1961. *The eucharistic memorial, Pt 2. The New Testament*. Richmond: John Knox. (Ecumenical Studies in worship 19.)

VON ALLMEN, J.-J. 1969. *The Lord's Supper*. London: Lutterworth. (Ecumenical Studies in worship 19.)

WEBER, R. *et al* (eds) 1975. *Biblia Sacra Vulgata*. Tom II. 2. ed. Stuttgart: Württembergische Bibelanstalt.

WORLD COUNCIL OF CHURCHES 1982. *Baptism, eucharist and ministry.* Geneva: WCC. (Faith & Order paper 111.)

A. G. VAN AARDE

PLOT AS MEDIATED THROUGH POINT OF VIEW.
MT 22:1-14 – A CASE STUDY

The notion 'plotted time', or plot as 'sujet', corresponds with the concept 'plot as mediated through point of view'. This concept is employed in the Gospel of Matthew as a whole *inter alia* by way of two equivalent narrative-lines, namely the pre-Easter Jesus-commission and the post-Easter disciples-commission. The article's aim is to indicate on the one hand that the so-called 'allegory' of the wedding-banquet in Mt 22:1-14 is in this regard an illustration of Matthew's 'plotted time' in a nutshell, and on the other hand, built on the preceding results, that Adolf Jülicher's distinction between an 'allegory' and a 'parable-proper' does not hold good in narrative criticism.

The following comments of R. C. Tannehill about the way Mark employed the Jesus-commission and the disciples-commission as two narrative-lines in the arrangement of his gospel also apply to a certain extent to Matthew's narrative. Tannehill transmutes the structuralist's term 'mandate', replaces it with the term 'commission', and uses this concept in narrative criticism: ''In my usage, the term 'commission' will have a meaning similar to the term 'mandate' in recent structural analysis of narrative... For my purposes, the most important observation is that a unified narrative sequence results from the communication of a commission to a person and the acceptance of this commission. The narrative sequence will then relate the fulfilment or nonfulfilment of the commission... The sequence is over when the commission is fulfilled or is finally abandoned... The Gospel of Mark is the story of the commission which Jesus received from God and of what Jesus has done (and will do) to fulfill his commission... Although Jesus' commission is central in Mark, many other commissions and tasks are suggested... In 1:16-20 Jesus calls four fishermen to follow him. This establishes the disciples' commission and begins a sequence of events...'' (Tannehill 1980:60ff).

Tannehill's notification of the two major commissions in Mark's gospel is part of a notion to which N. R. Petersen refers as 'plotted time'. Petersen (1978:47f) elaborated in this regard on the Russian Formalist's category *sujet* in distinction to *fabula*. The term 'fabula' alludes to the story-stuff of a narrative. Viktor Šklovskij (in Silberman 1983:24) elucidated it in this way: ''Too often one confuses the concept of the plot with the description of events, that is, with what I provisionally call

Fable. In reality this Fable is only the material out of which the plot is fashioned.'' On the other side, the term 'sujet' refers to the arrangement (selection and combination) of the story-stuff in such a way that the different episodes and commissions in a narrative are related causally. Therefore, it is significant to bear in mind that *causality* is the underlying principle that constitutes plot (cf Foster 1962:460).

The notion 'plotted time', or plot as 'sujet', corresponds also with Wellek and Warren's (1956:218) concept of *plot as mediated through point of view* (cf also Petersen 1978:48). Petersen (1978:46) particularizes this concept by employing Roman Jakobson's communication's model, especially the fundamental principle of the so-called 'poetic function', namely *equivalence* and its recessive notions *parallelism* and *repetition*. Petersen (1978:37) suggests that if the above-mentioned linkage of literary theoretical categories includes the current 'speech-act theory', biblical critics can probably find criteria for determining the narrator's/implied author's *point of view* on what he is speaking about. He refers to a narration as ''a time art in which writers orchestrate their reader's experience by relating story time, plotted time and reading time'' (Petersen 1978:50). Seen from this perspective, 'plotted time' accords with the notion *plot as mediated through point of view*, particularly against the purport of Boris Uspenky's (1973) treatise on 'narrative point of view'.

Regarding Uspensky's comprehensive way of handling 'point of view', Janice Anderson (1981) in a paper on the Gospel of Matthew disapprovingly described it as an ''ubiquitous nature of 'point of view''''. She requested: ''Where does point of view end and character or plot begin? I would prefer a narrower definition of point of view. Much of what Uspensky discusses under point of view could then be treated under the category of rhetoric or communication'' (Anderson 1981:1). Her choice is a preference for an approach to 'point of view' as it functioned in '''old' New Criticism'' (cf Polzin 1980:100).

However, from a perspective of present-day 'speech-act theory', Susan Lanser (1981:77) expounds the insufficiencies of the earlier notion of point of view. Like for example Fowler (1982), she welcomes the synthesis Uspensky made between the narrating *technique* and the narrator's underlying *idea*. According to the earlier definition of 'point of view', the notion designated the technical angle of vision from which the narrator/implied author presents the narrative world, for example an heterodiegetic or autodiegetic (or mingled) perspective. Strictly spoken, the term 'point of view' is ambivalent and comprises two components of referential meaning: the indicated *technical perspective* which corresponds with the 'emotive function' in Jakobson's model (cf Petersen 1978:35) and the *ideological perspective* from which the narrator/implied author observes the story-stuff of the narrative world and evaluates (selects and combines) it with the result that the narrated world is arranged in a plot as an orchestration to the ideal/implied reader. The narrative point of view on the ideological plane corresponds on the one hand with Jakobson's 'poetic function' and on the other with his 'conative function'.

Thus, there is in this regard a contingency among the literary theoretical notions speech-act theory (cf Chatman), equivalence (cf Jakobson) and parallelism/repetition (cf Petersen) and plot as mediated through point of view (cf Wellek and Warren). Concerning the Gospel of Matthew, Petersen (1978:46) noteworthily refers to the equivalence of the five repetitious Jesus' discourses (cf also D. L. Barr 1976) and Combrink (1983) analyses the linear sequences of episodes. Yet, there is an aspect of another, in my opinion very important, feature of Matthew's plot, and that is the equivalence of the two notable commissions: the pre-Easter Jesus-commission and the post-Easter disciples-commission.

'Plotted time' presumes at least one sequence of episodes which causally extends from a *beginning* across a *middle* to the *end*, according to the Aristotelian paradigm regarding the linear and chronological arrangement of a plot (cf Butcher 1951:82). In the *beginning* of the plot an intrigue of chronological and causal related events and episodes commences and suspense is created; in the *middle* the sequence of events which have been initiated, is developed and finally at the *end* terminated when the denouement is reached. Eberhard Lämmert (1972:43ff) refers to this sort of consummated sequence as a 'Handlungsstrang'.

As a clarification on Tannehill's above-mentioned notion of 'commission', one may define a 'Handlungsstrang' as a 'commission' of a protagonist who succeeded or failed in the act of bearing ideological values. When these values are received and even concretized by another narrated character, he/she is functioning in the narrative as 'an object of desire' (cf Vandermoere 1976:30). If the commission ends abortatively, the object of the commission is 'an object of aversion'.

Be that as it may, there are many narratives with more than one narrative-line ('Handlungsstrang'). Indeed, there may be an indefinite number of narrative-lines in a narrative (cf Prince 1982:75). In a 'Rahmenhandlung' (Lämmert 1972:44) one of the narrative-lines is dominant ('übergeordnete Handlung') and the other are subordinated ('eingelagerten Handlungssträngen'). If the narrative is a cohesive unit, the various subordinated narrative-lines should be in a structured way conjoined with or embedded into the main narrative-line. However, in spite of the contingency among the various narrative-lines, each of the subordinated sequences has to be self-reliant at least in respect of setting, time or characters. The principle underlying the conjunction or embeddedness ('Verknüpfungsprinzip') can be addition, parallelism, repetition, flashback, anticipation, symbolization, contrast, transparency, *et cetera* (cf Lämmert 1972:45-62). Nevertheless, the critic's pinpointing of the 'Verknüpfungsprinzip' is in my view one of the most important criteria to determine the narrator's/implied author's ideological point of view which causes the nature of his orchestration of events in the plot. "Once we have determined that a particular narrative is characterized by certain kinds of events or a certain way of linking them, we can begin to wonder why" (Prince 1982:77).

We have already mentioned Matthew's employment of two correlative narrative-lines in the plotting of his gospel, namely the pre-Easter Jesus-commission and the post-Easter disciples-commission. This feature makes Matthew's gospel, seen holisticly, a piece of 'time art'. In earlier days, working in a historical-critical framework, Willi Marxsen perceived something of this important Matthaean phenomenon which makes the end of the Gospel, just as in the case of the Gospel of Mark (cf Petersen 1980a) eventually open-ended: "If Mark lived during the immanent expectation of the Parousia, for Matthew time is beginning to draw out. He then offers a kind of 'interim solution' by inserting the period of missionizing... this motif is definitely present also in Mark (cf Mk 13:10— A.G.v.A.). But it is not yet an epoch with independent significance. In Matthew, on the other hand, this interval takes on significance with the task of making *pánta tà ethnē* (cf Mt 28:16-20—A.G.v.A.) disciples... The period of missionizing follows the time of Jesus. It extends from Easter until at least the time of Matthew. It can extend still further, in fact, to our own time. The Matthaean ending is thus all but timeless, since after concluding one epoch he allows another to begin which continues till the end of the world" (Marxsen 1969:98).

Although the disciples-commission commenced when the Jesus-commission had ended, it alternates the Jesus-commission by way of analogical and often symbolical anticipation. Sometimes the disciples-commission is even embedded into the Jesus-commission. To create sympathy for Jesus and what his commission involved, Matthew associates the implied reader of his gospel with the twelve disciples and their commission. The disciples-commission, which is supposed to be correlated with the Jesus-commission, ought to concretize a radical obedience to the will of God (the 'law and the prophets'). However, the disciples as well as those who are being associated with them, are inclined to disobedience, just like the Jewish leaders who are the antagonists in both narrative-lines (cf Van Aarde 1982:84-114). The so-called 'allegory' of the wedding-banquet in Mt 22:1-14 is in this regard an illustration of Matthew's 'plotted time' in a nutshell.

To my mind it is really inappropriate to use in narrative criticism the 'formgeschichtliche' categories of Adolf Jülicher and others in distinguishing between an *allegory* on the one side and a *parable* or *example-story* on the other side. We enter later into the matter of the irrelevancy of this distinction on account of our treatment below of the story of the wedding-banquet as a *narrative*. As a matter of interest, Rhoads and Michie's (1982:55-8) designation of Jesus' parables in Mark's narrative as *riddles*, irrespective of the question whether it is an 'allegory' or a 'parable-proper', is at least very provocative. It is my aim to indicate that the Matthaean 'riddle' of the wedding feast can dissolve itself within text-immanent boundaries when one recognizes the 'Verknüpfungsprinzip' among the (four) narrative-lines in the plot of this story.

Although D. O. Via (1971) treated the story of the wedding-banquet in Mt 22:1-14 as a 'narrative parable', he did not estimate the narrativity of this story very high. However, his approach as well as his results are unconvincing. The reason, in my opinion, is his failure to determine the narrator's point of view on what he is speaking about, because he did not reckon with the combinational pattern of the various narrative-lines in the plot of the story. According to Via there is less cohesion in the parts. He commented: "The Wedding Feast is a parable, and the story element —the narration of events in time—is there. There is some movement and there is structure, but it is content or theme which generates the structure. Theme and plot are two sides of the same formal principle with plot being theme in movement and theme being plot in stasis. Of theme we ask, 'What is the point?' and of plot we ask, 'How will it turn out?' Usually one or the other is dominant in any given story, and in the Wedding Feast it is theme".

These remarks of Via about the story of the wedding-banquet have to be seen against the purport of one of his earlier comments: "The parable does not present the organic inclusion of one of the motifs within the other, but rather the narrative structure is a juxtaposition of two fragmented forms with the continuity being provided by theme..." Contrarily, there is in my opinion a coherence in the narrative structure of the story and the evangelist's redactional activity did not cause accidental linear juxtaposition between the two alleged fragmented sequences of events, but the one is correlatively modelled on the previous one. And that is exactly what is meant by the notion *plot as mediated through point of view*.

Two of the above-mentioned four narrative-lines in the story of the wedding-banquet are consummated 'Handlungssträngen'. Each of the two sequences consists of either a successful or unsuccessful commission of protagonists, sent by a king, to respectively an 'object of aversion' (the 'city people') and an 'object of desire' (the 'street people'). The first complete narrative-line comprises a commission of slaves (the protagonists) to the initially invited guests in the city (the object). These people refused the invitation to take part in the wedding feast for the sake of the king's son and they were punished (vv 4-7). The second narrative-line consists of another commission of slaves to the (initially uninvited) people outside the city, good and bad people alike from the streets. They accepted the call and nevertheless, one among them has to be punished and excluded from the wedding hall (vv 8-14).

Seen from a linear, chronological perspective according to the mentioned Aristotelian paradigm, the sequence of episodes in the two narrative-lines is respectively as follows: 1. A king sends his slaves to request the invited persons in the city (a 'particularistic mission') to be present at his son's wedding feast, because it is ready (the *beginning*); they turn down the invitation and some grab the slaves, insult them and kill them (the *middle*); the commission ends in a futile way, but the king punishes the murderers by ordering his soldiers to kill them and burn down their city, for they are not suitable to take part in the wedding-banquet (the *end*). 2. The king sends his slaves with the wedding feast invitation to the 'street people' outside the city (a 'universalistic mission'), because it is ready (the *beginning*); they accept the invitation and the wedding feast becomes realized (the *middle*); the king inspects the participants, finds one among the 'street people' who does not really belong to the wedding feast (he does not wear a wedding garment) and commands his servants to shut him out irrevocably from the banquet (the *end*).

It is clear that there is a remarkable equivalence between these two narrative-lines. The narrator's ideological point of view can be recognized when the principle which underlies the conjunction ('Verknüpfungsprinzip') is pinpointed.

In view of the law-of-end stress in folk literature to which Via as a matter of fact did pay attention in the above-mentioned article, it seems that the story's main interest is not in the invited guests in the city, but in the initially uninvited people from the street outside the city, since they are dealt with in the climax at the end. However, the end stress is laid upon the one among the 'street people' whose hands and feet were tied up and who was thrown out in the dark, because he wasn't dressed in wedding clothes. Actually, the Jesus-logion at the end of the story, "Many are invited, but few are chosen", indicated that the point about which the narrator is speaking, is not his interest as such in the person without the wedding garment (Via), but in the nature of the correlative analogy which is created between the reason for the burning down of the city in the first narrative-line and the brutal exclusion from the wedding feast in the second. It is also clear that these two narrative-lines should not be treated merely as fragments in juxtaposition which had been taken from the tradition.

From the perspective of 'plotted time', it is striking that one in the midst of the 'street people', though he accepted the wedding feast invitation along with the other in contrast with the 'city people', is rebuked in the same fashion as the 'city people' in a sort of correlative action. One conclusion to this equivalence of events is that the absence of wedding clothes which made the apparent unlucky person unsuitable for the banquet (v 11f) does have a textimmanent reference: his ideological point of view, in spite of his acceptance of the invitation, concurs with that of the antagonists in the first narrative-line. Therefore, one may say that the events in the first narrative-line are presented by the narrator/implied author as a *transparency* with regard to the second narrative-line. In other words, the continuing principle between the two sequences does not exist in terms of theme/ideology alone, as Via would have it, but also in terms of plot; in short, in terms of plot as mediated through point of view.

How does this conclusion fit in with the equivalent pre-Easter Jesus-commission and the post-Easter disciples-commission which constitutes the 'plotted time' of Matthew's narrative as a whole? A particularization of this question leads us to the following two issues: firstly, the problem concerning the extrinsic reference of narrative texts, and secondly, the 'formgeschichtliche' distinction between an 'allegory' on the one side and a 'parable' on the other side. We already mentioned that this distinction does not hold good in narrative criticism. Nevertheless, this differentiation usually intrudes itself upon the exegesis of the story about the wedding-banquet. The reason is that the pericope in Mt 22:1-14 is the one passage in the New Testament which has been reckoned in the past to be the only undisputable 'allegory' among Jesus' parables (cf Linnemann 1977:8). Contrary to the Matthaean presentation, the wedding feast's parallels in the Gospel of Luke and in the Gospel of Thomas are moulded into the form of the so-called 'parable-proper'.

The motive for my opinion why it is inappropriate to draw in narrative criticism the distinction between an 'allegory' and a 'parable' is rooted in the recently debated question regarding the way a narration 'mirrors' or 'windows' the real world (cf Murray Krieger's distinction between 'window' and 'mirror'—see Petersen 1978:34,38ff). On quite different grounds Via (1967) (in his more elaborate work on the parables), among other scholars like for example G. Sellin (1978) and H.-J. Klauck (1978), also disputed Jülicher's distinction. It is in this regard also important to notice that Klauck furthermore rejected Jülicher's differentiation between a similitude/parable and a metaphor. Traditionally seen, a similitude/parable arises from an *Ähnlichkeitsrelation* while a metaphor alludes to the literary phenomenon that two comparable objects (a 'subject' is like a 'predicate') are articulated in an *uneigentliche* discourse (cf Klauck 1978:6f). Today, metaphoricity is not viewed as mere 'ornamental diction' in the sense of a 'Mimesis des Seienden' where the 'subject' does not create new information about the 'predicate' (Weder 1978: 76f). Like the ability of language in general ('Sprachkraft der Existenz'— Fuchs 1958:211ff,214; cf also Kingsbury 1972:102), a metaphor is co-productive in the constituting of an experience of reality. According to Weder (1978:75) the metaphor 'spricht dem Wirklichen mehr zu, als dieses in Wirklichkeit ist'.

The two aspects, 'Ähnlichkeitsrelation' and 'uneigentliche Rede' ought therefore not to be seen as the two distinguishing features between respectively a similitude/parable and a metaphor. This distinction originated, according to Klauck, in Jülicher's campaign against first century allegorical exegesis. Jülicher had mistakenly muddled up the so-called literary form 'allegory' with the fundamental features of allegorical exegesis, the latter which was not merely a hellenistic theoretical phenomenon, as Jülicher would have it, but was also known by the Old Testament, early Judaism and Qumran. These features are (cf Klauck 1978:354-61): (a) an aesthetical and historical uninterest, (b) anachronistic eisegesis from a presupposed perspective, (c) an esoteric code of communication on the assumption that the intention of a text is hidden and addressed to a certain elected hearer, an interpretation model to which Kümmel (1982:357) refers to as 'dechiffrierenden Interpretation', and (d) a process by which units or items are isolated and pushed into a new context.

Concerning the so-called literary form 'allegory', Klauck (1978:136) opposed the view that an 'allegory' is not a realistic sketch ("...die Allegorie vertrage sich nicht mit realistischer Schilderung") as in the same manner a 'metaphor' symbolises the reality. Klauck (1978:143) indicated that a "Metapher, die einem klar strukturierten Bildfeld angehört, ...von einem Netz oder Bündel möglicher Assoziationen (umgeben ist)". Unfortunately, Klauck did not elaborate on this important insight. At most, it seems that he wanted to underline particularly that the so-called literary form 'allegory' must not be confused with allegorizing exegesis. He defines the latter as "ein Kommentar, der von der intentionalen Textur (of a text—A.G.v.A.) absieht und eigene Einsichten und Überzeugungen im Text bestätigt findet, ...allegorisch (ist)"

(Klauck 1978:147). Thus, Kümmel (1982:357f) rightly criticised Klauck for his negligence to carry over principles into practice.

Dan Via's approach, on the other hand, is partially rooted in Ernst Fuchs' 'new-hermeneutics'. Still distinguishing between a 'parable' and a 'metaphor', Fuchs holds that *analogy* is most readily apparent in a metaphor which is a type of parabolic speech. 'Analogy' refers in such types of 'ornamental diction' to the feature that there is talk about one thing even though something else is intended. 'Analogy' does not intend to increase the hearer's knowledge concerning the subject matter (the 'predicate') which the words bring to expression (Fuchs 1958:214). Instead, 'analogy' functions, according to Fuchs (1958:213f,217ff), to shape the point of view ('Einstellung') of the hearer and thereby to change it. This specific point of view is the identical one the narrator would wish the hearer to adopt. The upshot, then, is that through 'analogy' the narrator aims at achieving a transference of point of view on the part of the hearer; thus bringing him into agreement ('Einverständnis') with the narrator concerning the 'reality' the pictorial speech is bringing to expression (cf also Kissinger 1979:183).

An elaboration on Fuchs' (and Eberhard Jüngel, a pupil of Fuchs) treatment of the parabolic speech is found in the book of Robert Funk (1966). Funk preferred to speak of 'the parable as metaphor' instead of 'the parable as analogy'. Nevertheless, in spite of the valuable contribution of the 'new-hermeneutics' regarding the emphasis which is laid on the language-power of existence, expressed by metaphoricity, the parables of Jesus were not studied as forms of narrative art. Although this kind of research was initiated in a certain sense by G. V. Jones (1964), Via (1967) in particular called attention to the need to interpret the synoptical parables existentially as 'genuine works of art', or in other words, as 'real aesthetic objects', unyoked from their historical setting in the life of Jesus (Via 1967:ixf). Unfortunately, this meritorious assertion lets a parable of Jesus become a mere 'free-floating' object (cf Kingsbury 1972:107). The consequence is that the parables, because they are aesthetic objects, resist according to Via (1967:178f) the effort to interpret them as part of the holistic context of a Gospel as narrative. Contrarily, Güttgemanns (1979:290), rightly, is of opinion that "the evangelist, in his selection, insertion, and expansion of the materials, would be guided by the viewpoint of the 'Gestalt'—*affiliation*, i.e., the 'material' being so shaped in the production of the form of the gospels that it accords with the linguistic 'Gestalt' he intends. The gospel form would then in gestaltist terms be seen as intentional, individual compositional act, which dissolves the collective tradition of the 'material' by the creation of a new form, in which he freely and at the same time dialectically 'takes up' the 'material' into the 'framework' in the truest sense of the word: By means of the gestaltist and intentional circumscription of the 'material' in selection, insertion, and redactional framing following the principle of affiliation with the intended gospel form, the 'material' is raised onto another linguistic level; *it now serves a linguistic effect which is not produced solely by means of its sum, but also, by means of the intentional composition of the form of the gospels, bestows the contextual sense-horizon upon the 'material'* ".

Thus, with reference to Güttgemanns in this regard, my reasons and those of Via for rejecting Jülicher's distinction between an 'allegory' and a 'parable', do not have the same grounds. Via builds his arguments especially on his campaign against the unconvincing theory that a 'parable' would have only one point of reference (*tertium comparationis*) to the reality outside the text, and an 'allegory' more than one. He argues that if that would be correct, it has the effect that a 'parable' is read from the perspective of one subjectively delineated point of view, 'windowing' out on the real world. And that is exactly the same as falsely allegorizing the parables of Jesus.

If one considers on this point Klauck's above-mentioned contribution concerning the necessary distinction between allegorizing exegesis and the theoretical from 'allegory', as well as Weder's thesis that *metaphoricity* is a constituting element in both theoretical forms, 'parable' and 'allegory', Via's objection against traditional classification can be amended. An important condition is that the *narrativity* of Jesus' parables, irrespective of the question whether it is an 'allegory' or a 'parable', has to be taken seriously. If this is done, it would have the effect that, on the one side, metaphoricity (or with reference to Fuchs, 'analogy') becomes an element of the poetics of a parabolic speech, and, on the other side, it allows us to assume Jesus' parables as fully part of the selected, arranged and integrated story-stuff of a Gospel as a whole. A parabolic speech in a Gospel as narrative, therefore, can be understood as a 'riddle' within the 'plotted time' regarding the holistic context. Seen in this way, scholars cannot deny any more that a 'parable-proper', so to speak, contains within it 'allegorical' traits.

Therefore, Via (1967:24f) is correct in denouncing that different text types of metaphorical discourses can be distinguished barely on account of the question whether there exists one point of reference or more. However, he misses the mark when he maintains the distinction as such between an 'allegory' and a 'parable' on the grounds that the two text types have different ways in which the reference items are related to the reality or world of thought outside the ext itself. If the narrativity of metaphorical narration is taken seriously, there is no need in principle for such a contrariety regarding both types of texts. This judgment can be substructured by Roman Jakobson's communication model, simply diagrammed as follows:

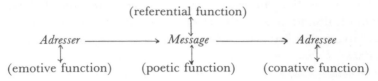

(referential function)

Adresser ──────────→ Message ──────────→ Adressee

(emotive function)   (poetic function)   (conative function)

In narration, from the viewpoint of Jakobson's model, the 'poetic function' corresponds to the notion of plot, but the notion of plot also interacts with the 'emotive function' and this includes the 'conative function' (cf Petersen 1978:36f). Although the 'poetic function' calls attention to the signifier, not to the propositional content it signifies (the 'referential function'), it provides evident 'windows' opening out on extrinsic horizons. Applied to the Matthaean story of the wedding feast (the so-called 'allegory') in comparison with its Lucan parallel (the so-called 'parable-proper'), one cannot differentiate in principle between the nature of reference (extrinsic or intrinsic) of these two stories, simply because they are in my opinion not of different text types, although the interpretation of the parallel reference items would not be the same.

From the intrinsic evidence of Luke's holistic context one can assume that the story of Jesus becomes a story of Jesus' journey to Jerusalem. Since the work of Hans Conzelmann on the Gospel of Luke, it is widely assumed that the reason why the Gospel of Luke is shaped in a form of a story of a journey has to do with the evangelist's peculiar notion of the history of salvation. However, this notion is not primarily a historical one, but a feature Vorster (1984) refers to as 'endophoric' in contrast with the 'exophoric' use of reference items in language (Halliday and Hasan's terminology). The latter has to do with the reference to the world outside the text (situational context). The 'endophoric' use of items should be interpreted in reference to the 'co-text', that is the information of the holistic context within which it occurs. Part of this information, regarding Luke's gospel, is his portrayal of the disciples which is totally different from that of Mark or Matthew. Luke regularly refers to Jesus' adherents as his 'disciples', but they do not stand apart from Israel (cf Kingsbury 1981:122f).

Seen from this perspective, Luke, by casting the story of Jesus in the form of a journey through Galilee and toward Jerusalem with its temple as the centre of Israel, deftly directs attention on the theme of Jesus' proffering salvation to Israel (Kingsbury 1981:97). The disciples of Jesus are those out of the midst of Israel who hear his authoritative summons and follow after him.

In terms of the Lucan 'co-text' the story of the wedding-banquet (Lk 14:15-24) is part of a scenario in the episode of the journey itself which commences in Lk 9:51 and ends in Lk 19:44. According to Matthew, Jesus had told the story after his arrival in Jerusalem. This positional change in 'co-text' does in fact alter the 'endophoric' use of reference items within respectively the two stories, but it does not make them two different text types.

An important consequence of the particular position of the story of the wedding-banquet in the Lucan 'co-text' is *inter alia* that the declination of the invitation by the initially invited guests should not be understood as refusals, but as excuses for coming late (cf Linnemann 1977:89). Against the purport that God offers in Jesus Messiah salvation to Israel, these excuses serve to stress the point that each one who does not unreservedly and immediately accept the invitation, is actually asking for delay to engage in Jesus' journey to Jerusalem. Thereby, such a person excludes himself/herself from the community of true Israel (cf Lk 22:30) and is indeed not fit (cf Lk 9:60,62—from a post-perspective) to continue the journey from Jerusalem onwards (cf Lk 24:52f - from a pre-perspective)—in fact, according to Acts, towards Rome.

Thus, it is clear that there is more than one point of reference in Luke's story of the wedding-banquet which point outside the story as micro-text. Just as in the case of the Matthaean parallel, the 'street-people' as well as the initially invited people are such reference items.

From the evidence of the Matthaean 'co-text', one can assume that the characters and the events in the story of the wedding feast refer 'endophoric' in a symbolical manner to the attitude/point of view of the Jewish leaders against Jesus (the first narrative-line) and on the other side 'exophoric' to the members of the Matthaean community who are actually the implied readers of the Gospel. The narrator's guiding voice (cf Petersen 1980b:36ff) lures the addressee into the narrated world, associates him with the 'street-people', and tries to change his point of view existentially so that it would not concur with the antagonist's point of view, just as the person in the story without the wedding garment, but rather concurs with the ideological point of view of the narrator/implied author whose 'limited point of view', seen from a technical angle, makes Jesus the vehicle of his ideas.

BIBLIOGRAPHY

ANDERSON, J. C. 1981. Point of view in Matthew: evidence. Unpublished paper presented at the AAR-SBL Meeting. Symposium on literary analysis of the Gospels and Acts.
BARR, D. L. 1976. The drama of Matthew's Gospel: a reconsideration of its structure and purpose. *ThD* 24, 349-59.

74 A. G. VAN AARDE

BUTCHER, S. H. 1951. *Aristotle's theory of poetry and fine art. With a critical text and translation of the Poetics.* 4. ed. New York: Dover.
CHATMAN, S. 1978. *Story and discourse. Narrative structure in fiction and film.* Ithaca: Cornell University Press.
COMBRINK, H. J. B. 1983. The structure of the Gospel of Matthew as narrative. *TynB* 34, 61-90.
FORSTER, E. M. 1962. *Aspects of the novel.* New York: Penguin Books.
FOWLER, R. 1982. How to see through language: perspective in fiction. *Poetics* 11, 213-35.
FUCHS, E. 1958. *Hermeneutik.* 2. Aufl. Bad Cannstatt: Müllerschön Verlag.
FUNK, R. 1966. *Language, hermeneutic, and Word of God.* New York: Harper & Row.
GÜTTGEMANNS, E. 1979. *Candid questions concerning gospel form criticism. A methodological sketch of the fundamental problematics of form and redaction criticism,* tr by W. G. Doty. Pittsburgh: Pickwick.
JONES, G. V. 1964. *The art and truth of the parables.* London: SPCK.
KINGSBURY, J. D. 1972. The parables of Jesus in current research. *Dialog* 11, 101-107.
KINGSBURY, J. D. 1981. *Jesus Christ in Matthew, Mark and Luke.* Philadelphia: Fortress.
KISSINGER, W. S. (1979). *The parables of Jesus. A history of interpretation and bibliography.* Metuchen: Scarecrow.
KLAUCK, H.-J. 1978. *Allegorie und Allegorese in synoptischen Gleichnistexten.* Münster: Aschendorff.
KÜMMEL, W. G. 1982. Jesusforschung seit 1965: Nachträge 1975-1980. *ThR* 47, 348-83.
LÄMMERT, E. 1972. *Bauformen des Erzählens.* 5. Aufl. Stuttgart: Metzlersche Verlagsbuchhandlung.
LANSER, S. S. 1981. *The narrative act. Point of view in prose fiction.* Princeton: Princeton University Press.
LINNEMANN, E. 1977. *Parables of Jesus. Introduction and exposition,* tr by J. Sturdy. 4. impression. London: SPCK.
MARXSEN, W. 1969. *Mark the evangelist. Studies on the redaction of the Gospel,* tr by J. Boyce, D. Juel *et al.* Nashville: Abingdon.
PETERSEN, N. R. 1978. *Literary criticism for New Testament critics.* Philadelphia: Fortress.
PETERSEN, N. R. 1980a. When is the end not the end? Literary reflections on the ending of Mark's narrative. *Interp* 34, 151-66.
PETERSEN, N. R. 1980b. Literary criticism in biblical studies, in R. A. Spencer (ed), *Orientation by disorientation. Studies in literary criticism and biblical literary criticism* (presented in honor of William A. Beardslee). Pittsburgh: Pickwick, 25-50.
POLZIN, R. M. 1980. Literary and historical criticism of the Bible: A crisis in scholarship, in R. A. Spencer (ed), *Orientation by disorientation. Studies in literary criticism and biblical literary criticism* (presented in honor of William A. Beardslee). Pittsburgh: Pickwick, 99-114.
PRINCE, G. 1982. *Narratology. The form and function of narrative.* Berlin: Mouton.
RHOADS, D. & D. MICHIE 1982. *Mark as story. An introduction to the narrative of a gospel.* Philadelphia: Fortress.
SELLIN, G. 1978. Allegorie und 'Gleichnis'. Zur Formenlehre der synoptischen Gleichnisse. *ZThK* 75, 281-335.
SILBERMAN, L. H. 1983. Listening to the text. *JBL* 102, 3-26.
TANNEHILL, R. C. 1980. The Gospel of Mark as narrative christology. *Semeia* 16, 57-95.
USPENSKY, B. 1973. *A poetics of composition. The structure of the artistic text and typology of a compositional form,* tr by S. Wittig. Berkely: University of California Press.
VAN AARDE, A. G. 1982. *God met ons. Dié teologiese perspektief van die Matteusevangelie.* Pretoria: Unpublished diss, University of Pretoria.
VANDERMOERE, H. 1976. *The study of the novel. A structural approach.* Leuven: Acco.
VIA, D. O. 1967. *The parables. Their literary and existential dimension.* Philadelphia: Fortress.
VIA, D. O. 1971. The relationship of form to content in the parables: The wedding feast. *Interp* 25, 171-84.
VORSTER, W. S. 1985. Reader-response, redescription and reference. 'You are that man'

(2 Sm 12:7), in B. C. Lategan & W. S. Vorster, *Text and reality. Aspects of reference in biblical texts*. Philadelphia: Fortress.

WEDER, H. 1978. *Die Gleichnisse Jesu als Metaphern. Traditions- und redaktionsgeschichtliche Analysen und Interpretationen*. Göttingen: Vandenhoeck & Ruprecht.

WELLEK, R. & A. WARREN 1956. *Theory of literature*. Rev. ed. New York: Harcourt.

P. J. MAARTENS

THE SON OF MAN AS A COMPOSITE METAPHOR
IN MARK 14:62

1. *The Son of Man as a Messianic Metaphor*

In the history of New Testament research the suffering Son of man sayings enjoy a special claim to originality. Those passion predictions give
expression to Jesus' messianic consciousness of His calling. The predictions, such as Mk 8:31; 9:12,31; 10:33 are fulfilled in the report of the
passion events. In Mk 14:62 the development of the passion theme is
'unexpectedly' broken by the theme of the coming of the eschatological
Son of man. Jesus, in Mk 14:62, is the Son of man who is exalted as the
eschatological judge. The exaltation of the Son of man in Mk 14:62
replaces the passion motif. The purpose of this enquiry is to investigate
the correlation of both these motifs in the Gospel of Mark.

A theoretically-founded explanation of the term Son of man is indispensable for the purposes of interpretation. Both the passion-motif (cf
Mk 8:31; 9:31 and 10:33) as well as the authority of the Son of man as
eschatological judge (cf Mk 8:38; 13:26 and 14:62) are particularised
through the use of parallelisms in the Gospel. The use of parallelisms
gives a decisive indication of the fact that poetical linguistics is a relevant
aspect for the meaning and interpretation of the Son of man. In order to
determine the meaning of the expression it is necessary first of all to investigate the development of the term, Son of man, in the Jewish
literature of the intertestamental period. Thereafter, the use of the title
must be investigated in the Gospel of Mark. Two stages of investigation
are necessary for the interpretation of the meaning of the title. Consequently, attention will be given first of all to the Jewish sources.

In Daniel 7:13ff the title Son of man appears in connection with the
term 'saints of the Most High' (Dn 7:18ff) which refers to the nation.
Casey (1979:48 and 112) is convinced that the Son of man in Dn 7:13 is
consequently not yet a title. The meaning of the term is indeed specified
in the parables of Enoch 37-71, but it is even here not yet a title. Perrin
(1968:19) shows that the meaning of the Son of man in the 17th psalm of
Solomon has been reduced to the features of a Davidic prince. In his further elaboration Perrin considers 4 Ezra 13 as an apocalyptic midrash on
the 17th psalm. In 4 Ezra 13 the qualities of the Son of man are restricted
to the qualities of an eschatological redeemer who has a kingly origin. In

late Judaism, the Son of man developed into a title for the end of time, kingly saviour. The influence of 4 Ezra 13 cannot be accepted as self-evident. Higgins (1980:9) denies that 4 Ezra exercised any meaningful influence on the background of the Gospels. Even if this were the case, 4 Ezra 13 nevertheless illustrates the development of the Son of man towards a royal title in the writings of late Judaism.

In the writings of late Judaism the title, Son of man, appears in connection with the semantic features which have a reference to a Davidic king. Semantic features are by notational convention indicated between parentheses. The semantic features of the Davidic king, which have been transferred in the sources of late Judaism to the Son of man, can be expressed as follows: (sovereignty) (majesty) (nationality) (justice) (righteousness) (glory) (kingly power) (immortality). The eschatological expectation, which is expressed by means of this list of features, is irreconcilable with the suffering of the Son of man which occupies a central role in the Gospel of Mark. A suffering Messiah becomes hard pressed when viewed together with the semantic features such as (majesty) (sovereignty) and (glory) taken from the Jewish eschatological expectations.

The Son of man is, secondly, used in the New Testament as a title. Different authors such as Marshall (1964:64) and Moule (1977:11ff) make reference to the use of the definite article before the expression υἱὸς τοῦ ἀνθρώπου in support of this consequence. In so far as the Son of man is used as a Messianic title, the metaphorical theory offers the most comprehensive framework by which one can describe the title. Consequently, the Son of man must be classified as a metaphor and the 'proper term' of the vehicle must be identified.

The Son of man belongs to the same category of 'genitive link' metaphors which Brooke-Rose (1958:40) identifies with the titles of Son of God and Son of David. The Son of man belongs to this class of genitive link metaphors which Brooke-Rose calls 'attributive'. The vehicle Son of man belongs, consequently, to the class of genitive link metaphors, which Brooke-Rose proposes with the 'three term formula': A = B is C. The third term indicates the genitive-link, term C, and it attributes the semantical feature [+ human] to the metaphor 'Son of man'. It is exactly the violation of selection restrictions, which refers to the feature [+ human] which identifies the use of the Son of man as a metaphor and as a Messianic title in the Gospel of Mark. The violation of selection restrictions become obvious when the tenor/vehicle relationship is investigated in the context.

In the Gospel of Mark the Son of man sayings are reserved exclusively for Jesus. Jesus, with special reference to His Messiahship, is thus as

tenor distinguished from the vehicle 'Son of man'. As the majority of
New Testament scholars indicate (cf e.g. Hahn 1974:32-53) the tenor of
the Son of man can be divided into three categories:
(a) present authority (for example Mk 2:10 and 28);
(b) suffering and vindication (for example Mk 8:31; 9:31 and 10:33);
and
(c) eschatological authority (for example Mk 14:62) of the Son of man.
From the violation of selection restrictions it appears that the Son of man
is both a metaphor and as a consequence a title. Mk 2:10 offers a
convincing example: "the Son of man has authority on earth to forgive
sins". It is the prerogative of God to forgive sins. The divine authority to
forgive sins violates the semantic features [+ human] which apply to the
Son of man. The same observation is valid for Mk 2:28 which says that
the "Son of man is Lord even of the Sabbath". This feature of a
metaphor is also valid for the vindication of the suffering Son of man (e.g.
Mk 8:31) and the eschatological authority of the Son of man (Mk 14:62)
as the ultimate judge of humanity.

The Son of man has as a consequence the status of a title in the Gospel
of Mark. As a vehicle the Son of man points to the Messiahship of Jesus
as an actual point of reference of the metaphor. Because the suffering Son
of man sayings are important for the present investigation, the interplay
of meaning between the passion motif and the Son of man will be investigated further.

From the previous introduction it is clear that the central viewpoint of
the Gospel of Mark is of decisive importance for the meaning of the title
Son of man. In the macro-context of the Gospel a correlation is made between the Son of man as coming judge in Mk 8:38; 9:1; 13:26 and 14:62
and the passion motif. The correlation of the passion motif and the function of the Son of man as eschatological judge demands a further investigation of the context of the Son of man sayings.

2. The Passion motif as counter-determining context of the Son of Man sayings

2.1 Context and tradition

It is generally accepted today that Judaism, with a few exceptions was not
well-acquainted with a suffering Messiah. Goppelt (1975:190) traces this
observation back to Dalman (1887). Cullmann (1971:55/56) maintains
that to a certain extent there could have been traces of a suffering
Messiah in Judaism (cf the Teacher of Righteousness in Qumran). The
case of the Teacher of Righteousness belongs rather to the rank of mar-
tyrs and prophets. Even so it is not clear whether he finally did die. Also

Mowinckel (1956:410), Hahn (1974:19-23), Fuller (1965:43-46) and Casey (1979:206) are in agreement that late Judaism did not identify the Messiah with the suffering servant. The passion motif of the Gospel of Mark is directly opposed to the triumphalistic eschatological expectations of Judaism. It is consequently of utmost importance to determine the semantic features which Judaism attributed to the Son of man.

The features of the Son of man in Jewish literature must be derived from the following: Dn 7:13 (cf Casey 1979:7), the Jewish Midrash on Dn 7 (cf Perrin 1966:18), and the apocryphal and pseudepigraphical writings (cf Hooker 1967:57-74 and Casey 1979:99-141). Casey (1979:48), just as other authors before him dates Dn 7 between 166 to 165 B.C. The Son of man in Dn 7:13 is a submerged metaphor with a proleptic function which is descriptive of the future rule of God over an independent Judaism. The chosen one of God is, according to Casey (1979:37) coming on the clouds. He is coming so that he, as Tödt (1965:24) shows, may take possession of everlasting glory, rule and the kingdom. He will reveal the rule of God. As Casey (1979:29) rightly shows, he does not possess a throne and he is not crowned. In Dn 7:25 and 27 he is replaced by Brooke-Rose's (1958:68) "simple replacement" by the "saints of the Most High". The latter will be subject to a king (Dn 7:24) who blasphemes against the Most High. The king will persecute them (Dn 7:25). Moule (1967:89) and Hooker (1967:30) try by means of the theme of oppression and persecution (Dn 7:23-25) of the saints to make provision for Mark's theme of a suffering Son of man. However, Moule and Hooker's arguments are not convincing. It is a forced interpretation. The Son of man of Dn 7:13 does not suffer, He is called to glory. He is the conqueror. Although it is not identical, the Son of man is identified with the vehicle: 'saints of the Most High' which places him within the micro-context of Daniel 7. They are the object of his rule. The features of the Son of man are taken over by the 'saints of the Most High' as the vehicle. Higgins rightly remarks (1980:8): "Thus the one like a Son of man becomes representative of the true Israel. In both cases he is a collective figure, without becoming directly a messiah or redeemer". Within the micro-context of Daniel 7 the Son of man is the tenor of the vehicle: 'saints of the Most High'. The latter is the 'true Israel' who perseveres in the faith and triumph during the Maccabean rule.

The Son of man of Dn 7:13 is a metaphor which refers to the rule of God as the proper point of reference. The 'saints of the Most High', who are the object of his rule, are subjected to persecution and as a consequence to suffering (Dn 7:25). With the particularisation of the methaporical title of the 'Son of man' as an eschatological saviour, the passion motif recedes into the background in late Jewish writings. Not-

withstanding Hooker's associations (1967:30) with Moule's interpretation of a suffering Son of man in Daniel 7, he proposes this development
as follows:

> "It is easy to understand, however, why, when the 'one like the Son of man'
> ceased to be understood of Israel and became a distinct and separate figure,
> he was thought of in connection with the glory of the future, and not the suf-
> ferings of the present. Both because it was a little fitting for one given
> authority by God, and because the emphasis was thrown more and more
> upon the future glory, in contrast to the all too familiar reality of the pre-
> sent, the Son of man grew apart from the concepts of suffering and humilia-
> tion''.

It is obvious from the above quotation that Moule and Hooker consider
the 'Son of man' and 'the saints of the Most High' as one and the same
reality. It has already been shown that the proper point of reference for
the 'Son of man' is the *rule of God* and the tenor of the 'saints of the Most
High' is the *true Israel*. Consequently, both vehicles refer to two different
tenors: the 'Son of man' refers to the *rule of God* and the saints of the Most
High' to the *true Israel*. As substitution metaphors both metaphors, namely the 'Son of man' and 'saints of the Most High' respectively as tenor
and vehicle, are in a relationship of identification. The *true Israel*, as object of obedience, is here in a relationship of identification with the *rule of
God*. This does not mean that the Son of man suffers whenever the saints
of the Most High suffer.

Among the writings of late Judaism 1 Enoch 37-71 and 4 Ezra 13
deserve special attention. Both sources are dependent upon Dn 7. The
parables of 1 Enoch 37-71 give the most encompassing description of the
Son of man. Casey (1979:99) dates 1 Enoch to the period between 100
B.C. and A.D. 70. 4 Ezra originates from the Roman period of the corresponding dates.

In 1 Enoch the Son of man is pre-existent. He was chosen before the
foundation of the world (48:3-6 and 46:3). Under the protection of the
wings of God He is present in a mysterious way in the ranks of believers.
He reveals the mystery of the kingdom (46:3). He is not a king, according
to Casey (1979:111). He is rather the anointed one (48:10 and 52:4). The
latter title is a conscious evasion of the eschatological hope in a kingly
monarchy of Davidic origin. Casey (1979:111) qualifies this expectation
in this way: "But Enoch could be said to have been given the reality of
kingship—he is enthroned and clearly is the leader of the community of
the righteous and elect, and on his act in vindicating the elect and
righteous by condemning the kings and mighty depends their salvation''.
Because he is righteous (1 Enoch 1:2; 12:4; 14:1; 15:1 and especially
71:14), he is the post-existant judge of mankind.

4 Ezra reduces the symbolism of the Son of man to a title for the eschatological redeemer of Judaism. He exercises the eschatological rule which will determine the final succession of events. Here, just as in other apocryphal and pseudepigraphical writings, there is no indication for a suffering Son of man.

Around the beginning of the Christian era, Judaism united the different features of the Son of man into an eschatological expectation. An analysis of components of the most important semantic features which are relevant for the Son of man in late Judaism, can *inter alia* be specified as follows: (judge[1]) (ruler[2]) (redeemer[3]) (revelation[4]) (sovereignty[5]) (majesty[6]) (pre-existence[7]) (authority[8]) (transcendence[9]) (immortality[10]) (praiseworthiness[11]) (glory[12]) (election[13]) (righteousness[14]) (justice[15]) (humanity[16]) (victory[17]).

---

[1] Tödt (1965:27), Perrin (1966:23 and 1974:30), Jeremias (1971:268), Cullmann (1971:157-58) and Higgins (1980:8) with reference to Dn 7:13; 1 Enoch 45:3; 47:3; 55:4; 61:8ff; 62:3 and 69:27; 4 Ezra 13 and Ps Sol 17. Also features such as (finality) (sovereignty) are relevant for the Son of man as eschatological judge.

[2] Cullmann (1971:140), Perrin (1974:31) and Casey (1979:102/3) with reference to Dn 7:13; 1 Enoch 46:4ff and 52:4.

[3] Tödt (1965:29) and Casey (1979:106) with reference to 1 Enoch 46-48; 48:4 and 62:14.

[4] Hooker (1967:39ff) and Casey (1979:103) with reference to 1 Enoch 46:6; 62:1-7.

[5] Jeremias (1971:274) with reference to Dn 7:13; Mowinckel (1956:394) with reference to his universal rule in 2 Baruch 29:1 and 1 Enoch 48:5; Hahn (1974:31) with reference to his universal appearance. Casey (1979:111) makes the following remark: "Terms such as 'king', 'kingship', 'kingdom', 'reign', seem to have been alien to the author of the Similitudes as a means of expressing the position of the exalted Enoch". Casey shows further that the Son of man is the "anointed one" (cf 1 Enoch 48:10 and 52:4) and the "reality" of the kingship is entrusted to him (cf also Perrin 1974:31).

[6] Mowinckel (1956:360) and Perrin (1974:31) with reference to 1 Enoch 68:2; 4 Ezra 7:28; 12:32 and 13:3.

[7] Tödt (1965:28) and Casey (1979:106) with reference to 1 Enoch 39:6ff; 48:6; 62:7 and 70:4. Hooker (1967:42-43) expresses rather well her doubts about this feature.

[8] Mowinckel (1956:361), Perrin (1974:31) and Casey (1979:28) with reference to Dn 7:13; 1 Enoch 50; 56:5-8; 57:1-3; 62:5 and 66:22.

[9] Mowinckel (1956:366), Tödt (1965:28-30), Hooker (1967:45) and Casey (1979:102) with reference to Dn 7:13; 1 Enoch 46:1-3 and 71:14.

[10] Tödt (1965:28) and Casey (1979:106) with reference to Dn 7:14; 1 Enoch 46:3-5; 48:5 and 71:6-17.

[11] Mowinckel (1956:361), Perrin (1966:24; 1974:31), Hooker (1967:39), Jeremias (1971:270), Cullmann (1971:155), Casey (1979:25) and Dunn (1980:75) with reference to 1 Enoch 45:3; 48:5; 55:4; 61:8; 62:2 and 69:27. Semantic features can be included here, such as (exaltation) (worthy of adoration).

[12] Jeremias (1971:276), Cullmann (1971:155) and Perrin (1974:31) with reference to 4 Ezra 13:3.

[13] Mowinckel (1956:366) with reference to the Targum on Isaiah 53. Thus, also Hooker (1967:35 and 38), Perrin (1974:31) and Casey (1979:103) with reference to 1 Enoch 39:6; 40:5; 45:3-4; 49:2-4; 51:3 and 4; 56:9; 55:4; 61:5,8, and 10; 62:1; 4 Ezra 7:28 and 13:32.

[14] Perrin (1966:22), Hooker (1967:38), Jeremias (1971:270), Cullmann (1971:143),

Perrin (1966:26), Donahue (1979:183) and Casey (1979:236) hold the
opinion that psalm 110:11 and Dn 7:13 in the light of Jewish expectations
created a tradition which is possibly older than the Gospel of Mark. This
old tradition finds its precipitation in Mk 8:38; 9:1 and par.; 13:26 and
14:62[18]. The passion motif of the Gospel of Mark contrasts (Lämmert)
the eschatological Son of man sayings. The suffering Son of man sayings
can consequently be considered with great probability as an original
motif of the Gospel of Mark.

There is a noteworthy tension between the passion motif of the Gospel
of Mark (cf Mk 8:31; 9:31; 10:33 and 45) and the eschatological struggle
for freedom of late-Judaism such as is reflected in the above mentioned
semantic features. The passion motif consequently surpasses the
eschatological expectations of late Judaism. There is absolutely no indication in late Judaism that the Son of man would die. On account of
the violation of the eschatological conventions the passion motif, of either
a suffering righteous one or a suffering servant, is that of the counter-
determining context (cf Weinrich 1967:6) of the suffering Son of man.

2.2 The suffering Righteous one (Servant) as counter-determining context of the Son of Man

The passion sayings of the Son of man in the Gospel of Mark (cf Mk
8:31; 9:31; 10:33 and 45) counter-determine the eschatological expectations which are connected to the title. Perrin (1968:357) attributes the
passion sayings redactionally to Mark. He expresses himself about their
meaning in this way:

> "To him (Mark) we owe the general picture we have from the Gospels that
> 'Son of man' is Jesus' favourite self-designation and that Jesus used it to
> teach His disciples to understand both the true nature of His Messiahship as
> including suffering and glory, and the true nature of Christian discipleship
> as the way to glory through suffering".

The correlation of the Son of man and the suffering righteous one is
characteristic of the Gospel of Mark. The vindication motif of the suffer-

and Casey (1979:103, 108) with reference to 1 Enoch 46:3; 48:4; 4 Ezra 7:28 and 13:32.
The semantic features (holiness) (righteousness) can be included here.

[15] Perrin (1966:23) and Casey (1979:103) with reference to 1 Enoch 1:2; 12:4; 14:1;
15:4; 47:3; Wisdom 4; and Jub 10:17.

[16] Mowinckel (1956:366), Cullmann (1971:137), Perrin (1974:31), Casey (1979:104)
with reference to 1 Enoch 60:10.

[17] Mowinckel (1956:361), Casey (1979:25 and 106) and Dunn (1980:75) with reference
to Dn 7:14 and 27; 1 Enoch 50; 52:6-9; 55:4; 56:5-8; 57:1-3 and 61:8.

[18] Tödt (1965:33), Hahn (1974:32ff), Jüngel (1979:243), Nineham (1963:46), and
Fuller (1965:34-43) maintain that the apocalyptic Son of man is derived from the pre-
Christian Jewish apocalyptic.

ing righteous one is of essential importance for the central direction of the Gospel. Finally, Mark wishes to strengthen the faith of his reader with the knowledge that Jesus is the exalted and returning Son of man. The distribution of christological titles takes place in correlation with the central direction of the Gospel: a high frequency of titles appears at the beginning of the Gospel in the prologue (cf also Mk 2:10 and 28), the Caesarea-Philippi confession (Mk 8:27ff) the passion sayings (Mk 8:31 and par., also 10:45), the prophetic discourse (Mk 13) and the trial of Jesus. Perrin (1968:357) had earlier already indicated that Mark has preserved his 'true christology' for the passion announcements of the Son of man. The christology develops through a reciprocial exchange of meaning among the Messianic metaphors which Mark uses. The titles interpret one another. Peter's confession at Caesarea-Philippi in Mk 8:29ff causes a turn in the correlation and exchange of meaning among the christological titles. The progression which takes place within the exchange of meaning is expressed by Donahue (1973:162) in this way:

> "The 'Galilean springtime' is over and Jesus turns His face to Jerusalem where He will suffer and die. In a very real sense Mark begins his christology here. The title *christos* forgotten since the superscription (1:1) reappears. All the uses of Son of man, except 2:10 and 2:28, are found after 8:27 and the whole subsequent section is built around the three Passion predictions."

Against the background of the passion motif as counter-determining context there is, in so far as it concerns the passion predictions, also a question of a re-interpretation which the suffering Son of man gives to christology. The 'true christology' re-interprets the 'false christology' of the disciples, and others (cf Mk 8:27ff; 9:33ff; 10:35ff and the commands to silence 1:25,44; 3:12; 5:43; 7:36; 8:30 which reaches a climax with 9:9). From the prologue of the Gospel there is continuously present the contrasting of the expectations with their fulfilment. According to Tödt (1965:146) the passion sayings also appear in interaction with the apocalyptic Son of man sayings (cf Mk 8:38; 9:1; 13:26 and 14:62). The apocalyptic Son of man as returning redeemer and judge of humanity re-interprets the passion sayings (cf Mk 2:20; 8:31; 9:12,13; 10:33,45; 12:7ff; 14:7ff and 21). The vindication motif contrasts the passion motif which counter-determines the eschatological expectations. This counter-determination takes place through the central direction of the christology with regard to Jesus as the suffering righteous one.

An inclusive description of the counter-determining context of the suffering righteous one is offered in Kleinknecht (1981). Kleinknecht (1981:25) reinforces a summary of the conventions of the suffering righteous one as follows:

"Mit grosser Wahrscheinlichkeit sind die ältesten greifbaren Texte vom 'Leiden des Gerechten' kultische Gebrauchstexte gewesen, deren Funktion es war, die durch (Feind-) Bedrängnis gestörte צדקה-Beziehung des Beters zu Jahwe durch einen צדקה-Erweis Jahwes wiederherzustellen. Dieser Erweis wurde in der kultischen Situation unmittelbar erwartet. Der jeweilige Beter trat dabei in das kultischen Urbild des צדיק ein, das in den verschiedenen Psalmen durch Parallelbegriffe verschiedener Nuancierung konkretisiert und akzentuiert wird".

Pesch (1977b:13ff) and Kleinknecht (1981:18) consider, among others, the following psalms as relevant for the conventions of the suffering' righteous one: 3, 5, 6, 7, 13, 18, 22, 26, 27, 28, 30, 31, 34, 35, 41, 43, 44, 49, 54, 56, 57, 59, 64, 69, 80, 89, 109, 110, 118 and 142. Pesch and Kleinknecht show convincingly that these conventions were decisive for the life and conduct of Jesus. Goppelt (1975: 239) distinguishes above all the themes, e.g. humiliation and exaltation which are correlated throughout in the Gospel of Mark. "In seiner jüdischen Umwelt lebte das Bild des Gerechten, der um seiner Treue gegenüber dem Gesetz willen verfolgt, von Gott aber schliesslich, gerade wenn er Märtyrer geworden ist, erhöht wird". Goppelt illustrates in a very decisive way the dependence of the Gospel of Mark on these conventions by means of references, among others to Ps 22. The linguistic dependence appears clearly from the mocking of Jesus (Mk 14:65; 15:20 and 29; Ps 22:7), the rending of His clothes (Mk 15:24; Ps 22:7) and Jesus' cry: "My God, my God, why hast thou forsaken me?" (Mk 15:34; Ps 22:2). On account of the impulse which this latter gives, it is, with the exception of Mt 27:46, suppressed by the other evangelists. The suppression of this cry in the other evangelists confirms for Goppelt its historical originality. Goppelt (1975:240) makes the following deduction from it: "So war es wohl von Jesus selbst angeregt, wenn die Passionsgeschichte in laufender Anlehnung an die Psalmen vom leidenden Gerechten dargestellt und ausgestaltet wurde".

Kleinknecht (1981:40) illustrates a chiastic correlation of the themes vicariousness and exaltation in the text of Is 52:13-53:12. The suffering servant therefore belongs inseparably to the conventions of the suffering righteous one. Besides, in the Gospel of Mark, the motif of the suffering servant is used to specify the central direction of the Gospel on Jesus as the suffering righteous one. The Gospel of Mark does not have quotations from Isaiah, only some references. The suffering servant is as a consequence a suspended tenor which is recoverable only through some references from the context. Possible references to the suffering servant are spread throughout the macro-context of Mark in the following texts: 1:11; 8:31; 9:7,12,32; 10:33,34,45; 12:32; 14:7,8,21,24,49,65; 15:27 and 32.

Bultmann (1968:152f) and Conzelmann (1969:133ff) have considered the passion predictions of the Son of man as *vaticinia ex eventu* which owe their existence to the Hellenistic church. As a consequence, texts such as 8:31; 9:12,31; 10:33,34,45 and 14:24 are rejected as secondary editions. Tödt (1965), Hahn (1974), Fuller (1965) and Hooker (1967) differ from the absolute scepticism with which Bultmann treats the passion predictions. They attribute the passion predictions to the early Aramean speaking Christian church of Palestine. Fuller (1965:119 and 161) places the existence of this tradition on the basis of agreement between the passion predictions of Mark 8:31; 9:12b and 10:45 and 1 Cor 15:3b. This would date it between the Easter of A.D. 31 and Paul's conversion in A.D. 33. Tödt, Hooker and Barrett and, to a lesser degree also Fuller and Hahn, reject the viewpoint of Cullmann (1971:63ff) and Jeremias (1968: 709-717) that the passion predictions of the Son of man in, *inter alia*, Mk 8:31; 9:12,31; 10:33 and 34, are linguistically dependent upon Is 53. Hahn (1974:56) accepts that there are some expressions which are dependent on Is 53. He proposes rather the following conditions: "Nur die Aussagen, die von einem Stellvertretenden sterben 'für viele' sprechen oder sonst noch deutliche Bezugnahmen auf die Sühnevorstellung von Jes 53 enthalten, dürfen mit dem prophetischen Kapitel in Verbindung gebracht werden".

Subject to the conditions that references must have a connection with the vicarious death and reconciliation, Hahn finds two references which are dependent on Is 53. The first reference is the expression δοῦναι τὴν ψυχὴν αὐτοῦ λύτρον ἀντὶ πολλῶν in Mk 10:45b which Hahn content wise traces back to Is 53. The second reference is the expression (τὸ αἷμά μου) ...τὸ ἐκχυννόμενον ὑπὲρ πολλων which Hahn (1974:60) derives from Is 53:12 on the basis of reconciliation as a criterion. The criteria which Hahn applies are rather inadequate. The central theme of Is 53 is not only the correlation of the themes of the 'vicarious death' and 'reconciliation' of the suffering servant. As Kleinknecht (1981:18) shows, the central theme of Is 53 is to be found in the poetical antitheses of the themes 'vicarious death' and the 'exaltation' of the suffering servant. Hahn (1974:56) insists on the fact that references not be brought 'atomistically' into connection with Is 53, but that there must be a clear agreement between the reference and the central theme of Is 53. If the antithetical opposition between vicarious death and exaltation is the criterion, the claims which Mk 9:21,31; 10:33 & 34 make on Is 53, must be acknowledged. Hahn rightly indicates that the references to Is 53 specify more clearly the atonement-theme of the suffering righteous one.

The atonement theme (cf Mk 10:45) is decisive for the meaning of the Gospel. Right from scratch the Gospel of Mark draws a connection between Jesus' messianic calling and the suffering servant. Ernst (1972:50), Lane (1974:57) and Anderson (1976:79) acknowledge a quotation of the Hebrew text of Is 42:1 in the expression ἐν σοὶ εὐδόκησα in Mk 1:11 and 9:7. The suffering servant particularises the atonement theme which Mark sees to be of decisive meaning for Jesus' messianic calling. The goal of His messianic call consists in the fact that according to Mk 10:45 He gives His life as a ransom for the atonement of many people. In Mk 14:3-9 Jesus is anointed in Bethany by a woman. In Mk 14:4 & 5 some bystanders protest against the unnecessary waste of money which the gesture involved. Jesus considers the action (cf Mk 14:8) as a foretaste of the anointing of His body for burial. According to Cullmann (1957:62) the passion prediction in Mk 14:7 is derived from Jesus: "For you always have the poor with you... but you will not always have me". According to Lane (1974:491) Jesus distinguishes Himself also with the words "For you always have the poor (τοὺς πτωχούς) with you" from the suffering righteous one. Jesus is more than the suffering righteous one. Jesus is the suffering servant. He is the Messiah because His death brings atonement with it. Hengel (1981:41) expresses himself as follows concerning the suffering righteous one:

> "A one-sided introduction of this theme, however, misinterprets the intention of the passion in Mark. The pattern of the humiliation and exaltation of the righteous is far too general and imprecise to interpret the event which Mark narrates so skilfully and with such deep theological reflection. He is concerned with the utterly unique event of the passion and crucifixion of the Messiah of Israel which is without any parallel in the history of religion. For Mark, the few psalms of suffering which illuminate individual features of the suffering and death of Jesus, like Ps 29 and 69, are exclusively Messianic psalms, such as psalm 110 and 118 ...Where features from the suffering of the righteous man appear, for example in the mocking of Jesus, they are also in a messianic key. The suffering of the righteous is to be integrated completely and utterly into the suffering of the Messiah. *The Messiah alone is the righteous and sinless one par excellence.* His suffering therefore has irreplaceable and unique significance".

The features of the suffering righteous one and the suffering servant are applicable collectively to the christology of Mark in reciprocal interchange. The re-topicalised semantic features of the suffering of the righteous (servant) which can be transferred to Jesus as tenor, can be specified as follows: (mockery[19]) (service) (obedience) (voluntariness)

---

[19] Tödt (1969:161) refers only to Ps 21:8 LXX; Pesch (1977b:52,149); Lane (1974:375) and Hengel (1981:42) with reference to Mk 10:34 (Is 50:6); 14:56; 15:23, 36 (Ps 69:22) and 15:29 (Ps 21:8 LXX; 22:8 and 109:25).

(humility) (invincibility[20]) (trustworthiness[21]) (power[22]) (praise-worthiness[23]) (blamelessness[24]) (defencelessness[25]) (vicariousness[26]) (righteousness[27]) (mortality[28]) (universality[29]) (suffering) (atonement[30]) (truth[31]).

---

[20] Tödt (1965:186) views Jesus' acceptance of the cup of suffering as a free act (cf Mk 14:41). As regards the δεῖ-formula in Mk 8:31, Tödt (1965:191) says: "The must in Mk 8:31 thus has the same meaning as the phrase in Mark 9:12b 'it is written'... The reason for the 'must' of the Son of man's suffering is rather God's will as revealed in Scripture". Tödt (1965:210-211) further accepts also the reference to Is 53:10ff below. Pesch (1977b:49) is in agreement with Tödt: "Mit δεῖ ist das 'Muss' der den Willen Gottes bekundenden Schriftnotwendigkeit ausgedruckt (cf 9:12; 14,21,49)". The obedience which Jesus shows, must rather be qualified with (sovereignty). Cf also Fuller's (1965:150,153) emphasis on the vindication-motif (conquest), Lohmeyer (1967:160), Taylor (1969:378), Jeremias (1965:710,717) who also wishes to derive the ὑπέρ-formula from Is 53, and Colpe (1972:448) with reference to Mk 8:31; 9:12b (Ps 118:22); 10:45 (Is 53:10); 13:32; 14:35ff and 14:41. The features (service) (obedience) (sovereignty) (faithfulness) (invincibility) interpret one another interchangeably.

[21] Cf Pesch's (1975:22,189) emphasis on (divine fidelity) with reference to Mk 14:38 (Ps 51:14); 14:65 (Ps 110:1 and Psalms 5:11; 24:31,32; 35:24).

[22] Also (authoritativeness). Tödt (1965:178,180 and especially 186). Tödt refers to the contrasting of the verbs 'will be handed over' (passive) with 'will rise' (active). In Mk 9:31 a dynamic degree of sovereignty for Jesus is preserved. On page 188 Tödt says, in reference to Mk 14:21,41: "The Son of man is he who goes his way... he himself announces that the hour has come, he himself summons the disciples to set out on the road. Thus the two expressions *hour* and *he goes* suggests Jesus' 'exousia'". Cf also Pesch (1975:194) with reference to Mk 14:38 (Ps 51:14); 14:62 (Ps 110:1) and (Psalms 5:11; 7:9; 18:21, 25; 24:31,32; 35:24).

[23] According to Tödt (1965:181) Mark correlates a christology of the resurrection with a christology of glorification. Pesch (1975:175) and especially his utterance on 185: "Die sessio ad dexteram ist der Lohn für besonders Gerechte, für Martyrer unmittelbar nach ihrem Tod, als Platz des Menschensohn entspricht sie seiner Richterfunktion". Cf also Pesch (1977b:49) and Higgins (1980:30 and 77ff) with reference to Mk 8:31; 9:12; Phlp 2.7 (Ps 22.2, 94.20 and Is 53.3,6-11) and also Mk 14:62 (Ps 110:1; Is 52:15; Dn 7:13 and 1 Enoch 62:3 and 5).

[24] Jeremias (1968:717) and Lane (1974:384) with reference to Mk 14:49,61 (Is 53:7); 10:45 (Is 53:11).

[25] Also (powerlessness). Pesch (1975:181) with reference to Mk 14:18; (Ps 41:10; 55:14); 14:41 and 14:49 (Is 53:7); 15:24 (Ps 22:19; 109:25).

[26] Cullmann (1971:64,163) and Fuller (1965:118,150). Taylor (1967:444) says amongst all things: "λύτρον (is) used metaphorically but forcibly to describe an act of redemption" (cf also p. 546). Thus also France (1968:33) and Jeremias (1968:713ff). Barrett (1972:21 and 26) rejects Jeremias' position that Mk 10:45b can be linguistically derived from Is 53. Hahn (1974:20,55) derives the ὑπέρ-formula from Is 53. Above all Mk 10:45b δοῦναι τὴν ψυχήν is linguistically dependent on תשים אשם נפשו of Is 53:10. Thus also Lane (1974:383,4), Kertel (1975:231,237), Pesch (1977b:164 and 359-60) and Hengel (1981:35,53). Kleinknecht (1981:148) views Is 43 as relevant: "die Stellvertretung des Gottesknechts wird von Jes 43 her als כפר, das Gott aus freier Liebe gibt, verstanden". Cf Mk 8:37 (Ps 49:8,16); 10:45 (Is 43 and 53:10ff); 14:12 (Is 53:12 LXX); 14:24 (Is 53:11) and Rm 4:25 and 1 Cor 15:3.

[27] Pesch (1975:172 and 191). It is as eschatological judge that Jesus is the righteous one. Herein lies His proper authority. Mk 8:33; 14:38 (Ps 51:14); 14:61; 15:4,14 (Is 53:7,9 and 11).

[28] Tödt (1965:153,164) rejects the passion sayings' dependence on Jesus in favour of a

2.3 *An historically-based analysis of the Passion sayings*

In section 2.1-2 above it has been shown that authors such as, *inter alia*, Tödt, Hahn and Fuller, derive the passion predictions of the Gospel of Mark from Aramaic speaking Palestinian Christianity. This observation has above all reference to the sayings in Mark 10:45 and 14:24, the ὑπέρ-formula (Jeremias) and the παραδιδόναι-formula (Jeremias and Tödt) in Mk 9:31 and 10:31 (cf also Rm 4:25 or 8:32). It is important for the present investigation to examine the possibility that the passion-predictions could be derived from the historical Jesus. The possibility that Jesus Himself could have been the source of the passion predictions, can be judged favourably in the light of the following arguments.

There are independent passion sayings in the Gospels of Luke and John which probably could be derived from the historical Jesus. This argument rests on Burkitt's criterion of multiple attestation of independent sources. Black (1969:2-3) refers to the following 'non-Marcan' features of Lk 24:7. The sentence begins with a *huperbaton* construction: λέγων τὸν υἱὸν τοῦ ἀνθρώπου ὅτι ...This is an Aramaic (as well as Hebraic) rather than a Greek construction. Lk 24:7 is not derived from Mk 9:31 because the latter does not have the 'apocalyptic δεῖ' nor the addition of ἁμαρτωλῶν as it appears in Luke in the expression: δεῖ παραδοθῆναι εἰς χεῖρας ἀνθρώπων ἁμαρτωλῶν. Jeremias (1968:715) had already noted the Aramaic play on words between בר נשא and בני נשא in Mk 9:31 and Lk 24:7. Black (1969:3) shows that Lk 24:7 developed the vocabulary to בני נשא רשעין (ἄνθρωποι ἁμαρτωλοί).

Following Schnackenburg Black finds a second independent passion tradition in Jn 3:14 and 12:32. The expression ὑψωθῆναι in Jn 3:14 is a verbal metaphor which refers to the crucifixion as its proper point of reference. The figurative language which is taken up here, refers amongst other things to the expression: "My servant shall prosper; he shall be exalted and lifted up and shall be very high" (Is 53:13). The same 'elevation christology' (according to Black) one comes across as well in Phlp 2:9 and Acts 2:33 and 5:31. Black also finds independent cor-

---

reference to Ps 118:22. Cf rather Pesch (1977b:358) and Lane (1974:375) with special reference to ἐκχυννόμενον ὑπὲρ πολλῶν in Mk 14:24. Cf Mk 8:3 (Ps 22; 118:22); 9:31; 10:33; 14:21 and 24; 15:20-39,44 (Is 53:10,12).

[29] Lane (1974:376), Hahn (1974:55), Pesch (1977b:360) and Hengel (1981:73) with reference to ἀντὶ πολλῶν. Mk 10:45 and 14:24 (Is 53:10-12); 11:17 (Is 56:7); Enoch 46:4ff; 48:8 and 55:4.

[30] Also (humility) (redemption). Tödt (1956:202) says with reference to Mk 10:45: "It relies on Is 53 as Mk 14:24 also does for the interpretation of the cup-word". So also Colpe (1972:455), Hahn (1974:55), Pesch (1975:183 and 1977b:358 and 360). Hengel (1981:45) and Kleinknecht (1981:148) with reference to Mk 10:45; 14:24 (Ps 22 and Is 53:10-12).

[31] Ernst (1972:50) and Lane (1974:432) with reference to Mk 13:31-32 (Is 51:6).

roborating witness to the passion sayings in Rm 8:25 and in 1 Cor 15:4. Briefly, Black's arguments rest firstly on the multiple attestation of the passion sayings in independent sources of the New Testament. Secondly, his conviction rests on linguistic criteria which are connected with Aramaic poetical linguistic usage, as it appears from Aramaisms, the use of word play and a co-ordination of a resurrection and exaltation kerygma. Black (1969:8) draws the following conclusion:

> "No doubt the identification of a non-Markan tradition of passion sayings simply emphasizes the heterogeneous nature of the expression given, through the use of Old Testament testimonia, to the original kerygma, but the possible Aramaic root of this tradition is as powerful an argument in favour of its dominical origin as any similar considerations regarding the Q tradition. The post-easter 'resurrection-ascension' kerygma may well be grounded in a pre-easter 'exaltation-resurrection' didache traceable to the mind of the Lord Himself".

A further important observation to which attention must be given is the fact that the suffering righteous (servant) of the Old Testament is the counter-determining context for the passion predictions. The suffering servant counter-determines the exalted Jewish eschatological expectations. Judaism is, as Cullmann (1971:56) and Jeremias (1968:666) show, conversant with a martyr-prophet, even the teacher of righteousness suffers. It is however not certain whether the teacher of righteousness died a martyr's death. The passion sayings connect with the theme of prophetic suffering. But the Son of man does not suffer in Judaism. Casey (1979:14) adopts a strong position in this regard: "The manlike figure cannot suffer, and it is only when he has been identified as the saints of the Most High that Daniel can see them humiliated". Mark's suffering Son of man is an incomparable figure. The suffering Son of man sayings can consequently be traced back to the historical Jesus on the basis of the criterion of dissimilarity with Judaism.

The probability that the suffering Son of man can be derived from the historical Jesus, is strengthened by the fact that the Son of man sayings are reserved exclusively for the use of Jesus. The 'true christology' of Mark is resumed in the Son of man sayings. If the genuineness of the suffering Son of man is historically based, the 'true christology' can be derived from the historical Jesus. Jesus probably rejected the popular messianic eschatological expectations. The 'true christology' theocratised the contemporary eschatological expectations. Consequently, he dedicated the monarchy of Israel to God. This was decisive for the 'true christology' of the Gospels that Jesus identified the exalted eschatological expectations, such as among others, expressed by Dn 7:13, with the suffering righteous one (Is 53 and different Psalms). The exalted Son of man is the invincible Son of man (cf Mk 8:31; 9:12,31; 10:33 and 45).

3. The Son of Man as Compound Metaphor

3.1 The identification of the Son of Man as a compound metaphor

The Messiahship of Jesus is the 'proper point of reference' for the christological titles. As it appears from among other texts, in Mk 9:9 the messianic authority of Jesus is temporarily submerged in His crucifixion and His resurrection in the macro-context of the Gospel. In literary theory the tenor of a suspended metaphor is always recoverable from the context, as Ingendahl (1971:44) showed. A tenor which is temporarily submerged, can enter into the macro-context in reciprocal interaction by means of a chain of vehicles. Miller (1971:31) calls a metaphor which constructs a relationship with a chain of vehicles—a 'compound' metaphor. The chain of vehicles which is distributed through the macro-context, anticipates and particularises the meaning of the submerged tenor.

Jesus is identified in the Gospel of Mark with a chain of messianic titles. The titles, Christ, Son of God and Son of man, are vehicles which refer to the *messiahship of Jesus* as temporarily suspended tenor. Brooke-Rose (1958:19) calls the vehicles which can replace one another under certain circumstances 'replacement metaphors'. The following texts can serve as examples. The Son of man in Mk 8:31 replaces the title of Christ used by Peter in Mk 8:29 in his capacity as the suffering righteous one. The popular messianic confession of Peter (Mk 8:29) is re-interpreted with a 'true christology' (Perrin) of the Son of man. Formulae such as "handed over" (Mk 8:31 etc.) "must suffer much and be treated with contempt" (9:12) and "a ransom for many" (Mk 10:45) refer to the counter-determining context of the suffering righteous one.

In Mk 14:62 the High Priest asks Jesus: "Are you the Christ, the Son of the Blessed?" The expression 'the Son of the Blessed' defines the messianic title 'Son of God'. The two titles *Christ* and *Son of God* are identified in Mk 14:61. Both titles are replacement metaphors. Jesus answers the High Priest's question of Mk 14:61 in Mk 14:62. The answer which Jesus gives in Mk 14:62, replaces both the Christ-title and the Son of God title with the Son of man title in his capacity as eschatological judge (Dn 7:13).

Ingendahl's (1971:44) observation that a vehicle sometimes appears independently in a text is applicable to the title Son of man in the above cases. An independent vehicle can, as is the case above with the Son of man in Mk 8:31 and 14:62, appear as tenor for other vehicles. Mk 8:31 proposes the Christ title in reciprocal exchange with the suffering of the righteous one as a counter-determining context of the metaphor. In Mk

14:62 the messianic expectations (expressed by the titles Christ and the
Son of God) are counter-determined by the meaning of the eschatological
Son of man.

Compound metaphors are not only characterised by a vehicle which is
independent, they also replace the suspended tenor in the macro-context.
A compound metaphor is also characterised by literary strategies which
Brooke-Rose (1958:68) calls "pointing formulae". Under "pointing formulae" Brooke-Rose includes demonstrative expressions, articles,
parallelisms, and apposition. Above all the article and parallelisms are
relevant for the Son of man.

Moule (1978:16) who worked independently of Brooke-Rose's
metaphorical theories, arrived at conclusions which agree with deductions which Brooke-Rose, *inter alia*, makes. Moule (1978:16) refers to the
fact that the article is not used in Dn 7:13 before the vehicle *Son of man* in
the expression "someone like a human being". In the apocalyptic Son of
man sayings the article is used before the vehicle.[32] In similar cases like
Mk 14:62 the article refers back to the context of Dn 7:13. As a
'demonstrative formula' the article establishes that the Son of man is a
composite metaphor. Parallelisms are also a feature of pointing formulae.
The parallelism of the suffering Son of man (Mk 8:31; 9:12,31; 10:33 and
45) characterise the vehicle *Son of man* as a composite metaphor. The
function of demonstrative formulae is to specify the submerged or hidden
tenor, namely the *Messiahship of Jesus*, within the macro-context. The
parallelisms of *inter alia* the 'handing over formulae' (cf Mk 9:31; 10:33),
the antithesis of suffering and exaltation (cf Mk 8:31; 9:31, 10:34), the
condemnation, rejection, mockery, and derision of the Son of man (cf
Mk 8:31; 10:33 and 34) particularise the meaning of the suffering
righteous one. The Son of man as composite metaphor strengthens the
central point of view on the re-enactment of Jesus as the suffering
righteous one. As composite metaphor which appears independently in
the context, the Son of man sayings interpret other Messianic titles. The
Son of man re-interprets, as tenor, the meaning of the titles, Christ and
Son of God.

3.2 *The particularising of Jesus' Messiahship with the Son of man sayings*

An investigation of the distribution of christological titles shows that the
titles Son of God and Christ were used at the climax of Jesus' ministry. In

---

[32] Moule (1978:16) expresses himself as follows about the article for the vehicle *Son of man*: "I am postulating for Jesus himself—the use of the equivalent of the definite article or a demonstrative pronoun by way of allusion back to an initial mention (or an assumed knowledge among the hearers) of Daniel's human figure".

the Gospel of Mark it appears that the Son of man interprets the christological confessions which are expressed by the titles, Son of God and Christ. Consequently, attention is firstly focused on the correlation of the titles of Son of man and Son of God.

Perrin (1968:358) views the meaning of the Son of man as "crucial for an understanding of the nature of that divine sonship". He describes the correlation of both titles as follows: "in effect, he uses Son of man to interpret and to give content to the conception of Jesus as the Son of God".

Donahue (1973:178-180) supports the viewpoint of Perrin. Donahue further distinguishes also a certain pattern in the development of the Son of God title. Just as Hahn (1974:297-308) and Fuller (1965:144 and 194ff) Donahue's investigation yields two categories. He classifies Mk 3:11; 5:7 and 15:39 as belonging to a Hellenistic category. Mk 1:11; 8:38; 9:7 and 14:61 he classifies according to the Jewish-Christian categories of proverbs.

In the Hellenistic category Mk 3:11 and 5:7 are considered as public confessions of Jesus which put Jesus' commands for silence under restraint. Both statements are made by demons or by people who are possessed by demons. These 'confessions' come at the wrong time and are from the wrong source. Betz (1968:122) and Weeden (1971:57) associate the utterances with a *theios-aner* christology. Dunn (1969:9) shows that Jesus rejects these statements just as He rejected the popular Messianic confessions. As Robinson (1973:27) shows the goal of Mk 3:12 is to put the 'false christology' under restraint, just as is the case with other commands for silence (Mk 1:25,44; 5:43; 7:36; 8:30 and 9:9).

The second Jewish-Christian class of utterances (cf Mk 1:11; 8:38; 9:7 and 14:61) is correlated with the Son of man sayings. In 1:21-28 the theme of the authority of Jesus as "Holy One of God", is chiastically foregrounded. This theme of authority correlates with the power of the Son of man to exercise the divine prerogative of the forgiveness of sins (Mk 2:10) and sovereignty (Mk 2:28).

The structuring principles of composition contrast the authority of the Son of man retrospectively and prospectively. In Mk 8:37 the eschatological authority of the Son of man is considered. Seven verses later, after the transfiguration of Jesus on the mountain, Jesus is addressed in Mk 9:7 as the "beloved Son". In Mk 14:61 the title of Christ is identified with the expression "the Son of the Blessed". Jesus answers the High Priest in Mk 14:62. In His answer Jesus replaces both titles which the High Priest uses with the saying of the Son of man who, as final judge will sit on the right hand of God when He comes on the clouds of heaven. On the basis of the reciprocal interchange of meaning among the titles, Perrin (1968:358) comes to the following conclusion: "For Mark the meaning of the Son of God is to be expressed in terms of a use of Son of man''. The Messiahship of Jesus comes to expression in the reciprocal interchange of meaning among the replacement metaphors. The interchange of meanings among the Messianic metaphors specifies within the context the Messianity of Jesus as submerged tenor. The 'true christology' is preserved for the Son of man sayings. This christology specifies the theme of the suffering righteous one, especially during Jesus' trial and crucifixion. Donahue (1973:180) rightly remarks: ''Therefore Mark holds the real meaning of the title in suspension until the trial scene''. This observation is also valid for the title of Christ in the Gospel of Mark. The co-ordination of both above-mentioned titles and the Son of man must be attributed to the correlative structuring devices of prose composition which are applied consciously in the Gospel of Mark.

After the use of the title of Christ in the prologue (Mk 1:1) the title again makes its appearance in Mk 8:29. The use of the title of Christ in Mk 8:29 fulfils an important function in the section of Mk 3:22-10:52 considered as a unity. Tödt's analysis (1965:145-149) of this section shows that the unity has a solid structure. The title of Christ, as it is used in Mk 8:27-33, represents a christology which is corrected in Mk 8:27-10:45. Tödt (1965:145ff) and Perrin (1968:363) indicate that the unity can be subdivided into three parallel sections which as a result of geographical references can be distinguished from one another. The first passion announcement which follows on Peter's confession of Christ took place in Caesarea-Philippi. The second announcement of the suffering Son of man was made while, according to Mk 8:31, they were travelling through the territory of Galilee. The third announcement of the suffering Son of man came shortly after they had entered the territory of Judea in Mk 10:1. The passion saying in Mk 10:33 was uttered on the road back to Jerusalem. Each separate section of this unity has its own passion saying (Mk 8:31; 9:31; 10:33). The unity reaches a dramatic climax with the announcement that it is in Jerusalem (Mk 10:32) where Jesus must suffer. Perrin (1965:363) describes the structure as follows: ''Further, each passion prediction occurs in a contextual pattern which is constant throughout: there is always a prediction, a misunderstanding, and then teaching about discipleship''.

The first passion prediction is followed by the rebuke of Peter in Mk 8:33. The second passion prediction gives rise to the observation in Mk 8:32 that the disciples did not understand it. This observation is also found elsewhere in the redaction of Mark (cf Mk 6:52 and 8:17). After the second passion prediction the disciples disputed about whom amongst them was the most important (cf Mk 10:34). The third passion prediction is followed by the ironical request of James and John to sit one on His right hand, the other on His left hand (cf Mk 10:37) when Jesus comes into His glory. This misunderstanding among the disciples shows that the popular Messianic expectations had also made inroads among Jesus' disciples. The passion predictions which reached a climax in Mk 10:45 correct the dominating misunderstandings. The misunderstanding of the disciples is followed by three discourses of Jesus on 'true discipleship'. Perrin (1968:363) describes these parallels as follows:

> "The three units of teaching on discipleship are to be found in 8:34ff, 9:35ff, and 10:38ff. Each of these sections of teaching makes its own particular point. Put together, they represent the basic Marcan understanding of the nature of Christian discipleship, and, moreover, they progress to a climax in 10:45. In the first section, discipleship is defined in terms of preparedness to take up the cross, in the second as preparedness to be last and servant of all, and in the third servanthood is defined in terms of the Son of man who 'also came not to be served but to serve, and to give His life as a ransom for many'''.

The passion sayings reach a climax with the prediction that Jesus will lay down His life as a ransom for many. In this unity the parallelisms serve as demonstrative formulae (Brooke-Rose) which specify the Messiahship of Jesus as submerged tenor. The expression "ransom" and the "for many" formulae refer to the suffering servant in Is 53:10-12 which counter-determines the Messiahship of Jesus. The reference to Is 53:10 also counter-determines the Messiahship of Jesus. The reference to Is 53:10 also counter-determines the cause of Jesus' suffering: "Yet it was the will of the Lord to bruise Him; He has put Him to grief". Mark's redactional contribution to the passion story is that it was not exclusively the fault of the Jews or the Romans which had as its consequence Jesus' death. The vicarious suffering and death was the will of God. The counter-determining context and the pointing formulae specify the initiative which God takes in the suffering and death of Jesus. The δει-formula in the passion sayings (cf δεῖ...ἀποδοκιμασθῆναι...ἀποκτανθῆναι and ἀναστῆναι in Mk 8:31) established the fact that the suffering-events are the will of God. The παραδίδοναι-formula (cf Mk 9:31 and 10:33) and the καθὼς γέγραπται-formula (cf Mk 14:21 and 41) give expression to the scriptual necessity (in Perrin's terms 1968:360) of the passion events. The Messiahship of Jesus is also counter-determined by the vindication motif of the suffering righteous one. The vindication motif reaches its climax in Mk 14:61-62.

In Mk 14:61 the High Priest asks Jesus: "Are you the Christ, the Son of the Blessed?" Jesus at this stage had already united the context with the suffering righteous one. There is no longer any room for misunderstanding. With the question which the High Priest poses, he identifies the titles Χριστός and υἱὸς τοῦ εὐλογητοῦ. For the first time Jesus accepts both titles plainly and openly: "I am".

In Mk 14:62 the titles *Christ* and the *Son of God* (the latter is expressed as υἱὸς τοῦ εὐλογητοῦ) are replaced by the eschatological *Son of man*. The eschatological Son of man sayings are the climax of the vindication motif which is connected to the theme of the suffering righteous one. Mk 14:62 contrasts the suffering Son of man sayings. The specification of Jesus' Messiahship is rounded off by the vindication of the eschatological Son of man in Mk 14:62. As compound metaphor the Son of man in Mk 14:62 is in a relationship of identification with the titles of Christ and Son of God in Mk 14:61. Jesus accepts the royal honorary titles of Mk 14:61, but interprets the meaning of them through 'simple replacement' (Brooke-Rose) with the eschatological Son of man. The epexegetical καί of Mk 14:62b explains both the honorary titles Christ and Son of God. Jesus accepts royal homage only in so far as He is the eschatological king. The kingship of Jesus is theocratised. The Son of man sits on the right hand of the one who is powerful (Mk 14:62b). The kingdom of God is also theocratised. Just as in Dn 7:13 His kingdom does not appear from the world. Although His rule breaks into the world, He comes on "the clouds of heaven" (Mk 14:62c). The kingship of Jesus is qualified by the eschatological judgment of the Son of man. As compound metaphor the *Son of man* is at the same time the tenor of the kingly titles, Christ and Son of God, in Mk 14:61.

In the relationship of identification between on the one hand the titles *Christ* and *Son of God* and on the other hand the *Son of man* as tenor, the features of the Son of man as eschatological judge (Dn 7:13) are taken over by the kingly honorary titles in Mk 14:62. As compound metaphor the vehicle *Son of man* specifies the Messiahship of Jesus through the mechanisms of 'simple replacement' and the pointing formulae. As tenor the compound metaphor *Son of man* specifies the royal titles with features of the suffering righteous one as well as the features of the returning judge. The following thesis of Hahn (1974:175) can be justified within the framework of the metaphor theory:

> "Der jüdische Messiastitel war für Jesus und die Urgemeinde als solcher nicht tragbar, aber in Verbindung mit der Menschensohnvorstellung und dem Leidensgedanken wurde er später aufgenommen und dementsprechend umgeformt".

The features of the eschatological judge (Dn 7:13) established Jesus, the suffering righteous one, in the capacity of conqueror as the returning Son of man.

4. *The function of the apocalyptic Son of man in Mk 14:62*

The apocalyptic Son of man saying in Mk 14:62 radicalises the Jewish national future hopes. It is the climax of Mark's christology. The specification of Jesus' Messiahship in this way reaches completion. The Jewish eschatological expectations are not fulfilled in an independent Jewish kingdom. The return of the Son of man is the universal destiny of the world. The apocalyptic theocracy which breaks in with the coming Son of man, also completes the theme of discipleship. With the coming of the Son of man the ναός reaches its destiny. Donahue (1973:184) describes the meaning of Mk 14:62 thus:

> "The earthly ministry is an epiphany of the Son of man. It is also a call to follow Jesus in suffering and death. The future sayings indicate that the real meaning of the earthly ministry and suffering will be known only in the return of the Son of Man. Mark thus forms a consistent schema for the past of Jesus, the present tribulation of the community and their future hope. This explains the pattern of suffering, *parousia* and new community which we have noted. Mark is enabled to find one title which applies to Jesus at all phases of His existence, earthly ministry, present status and future activity. No other title of his Gospel allowed him to do this, since all these titles receive their proper interpretation only in terms of the corrective Son of man saying of 14:62".

The eschatological tension of the Gospel of Mark begins to lift with Jesus' entry into Jerusalem. The 'cleansing of the Temple' (Mk 11:12-21) announces the beginning of eschatological judgment over Jerusalem. The purpose of Jesus' judgment on the Temple is expressed with the saying in Mk 11:17: "My house shall be called a house of prayer for all the nations". The judgment on the Temple forms an *inclusio* with the prediction of the destruction of the Temple in Mk 13:1-2. The condemnation of Judaism means that the salvation prerogative of the Jews now passes to the new community (ναός) of Mk 14:58. The end has arrived for Judaism. In Mk 14:58ff, however, it does not say who Jesus is, nor when He will establish this new community. The christology of Mk 14:62 answers these questions. The Jesus who stands trial in Mk 14:62 is the eschatological Son of man. He establishes the ναός (Mk 14:58). This is the Jesus who must suffer and die. Since the entry into Jerusalem the eschatological judgment of God has begun to work. The trial of Jesus contrasts the end of time judgment. The accused is the eschatological judge. His work is not yet complete. Until the *parousia* the circle of disciples will remain an incomplete community. They exist, remaining subject to the danger of unrest, persecution and suffering. False Christs and prophets will always make their appearance. Disputes, discord, rumours of war and famine will always be present. Just as with Jesus so must the disciples be handed over to persecution. Many will be deceived and some may even deny Him.

Mk 14:62 casts the glance onto the future. Here the suffering, resurrection and destruction of the Temple are seen passing by. The persecution of Jesus obtains a destiny-judgment. Notwithstanding defects, the disciples share in the new community. Although the future includes persecution, oppression and suffering, the new community waits in expectation. The return will unite them. The future towards which they are travelling, is not dark. This goal is not simply 'a novum' or a 'Utopia'. The goal of the believer is the *eschaton*. It is the coming of the Son of man. The goal is the Kingdom of God, His glory and justice.

BIBLIOGRAPHY

ANDERSON, H. 1976. *The Gospel of Mark.* London: Oliphants.

BARRETT, C. K. 1959. The background of Mark 10:45, in A. J. B. Higgins (ed), *New Testament essays. Studies in memory of T. W. Manson.* London: MUP, 1-18.

BARRETT, C. K. 1978. *New Testament essays.* London: SPCK.

BETZ, H. D. 1968. Jesus as divine man, in T. Trotter (ed), *Jesus and the historian.* Philadelphia: Westminster Press, 114-133.

BLACK, M. 1962. *Models and metaphors: studies in language and philosophy.* Ithaca: Cornell University Press.

BLACK, M. 1969. The 'Son of man' passion sayings in the Gospel tradition. *ZNW* 40, 1-8.

BOLKESTEIN, M. H. 1973. *Het Evangelie naar Markus.* Nijkerk: Callenbach.

BULTMANN, R. 1968. *The history of the synoptic tradition,* tr. by John Marsh from the second German edition. Oxford: Basil Blackwell.

BROOKE-ROSE, C. 1958. *A grammar of metaphor.* London: Secker and Warburg.

CASEY, M. 1979. *Son of man: the interpretation and influence of Daniel 7.* London: SPCK.

CONZELMANN, H. 1969. *An outline of the theology of the New Testament,* tr. by John Bowden. London: SCM.

CULLMANN, O. 1971. *The christology of the New Testament.* 3. imp. London: SCM.

DONAHUE, J. R. 1973. *Are you the Christ? The trial narrative in the Gospel of Mark.* Missoula, Montana: Scholars Press. (Dissertation Series 10.)

DUNN, J. D. G. 1980. *Christology in the making.* London: SCM.

ERNST, J. 1972. *Anfänge der Christologie.* Stuttgart: KBW.

FULLER, R. H. 1965. *The foundations of New Testament christology.* London: Collins.

GLÄSER, R. 1971. The application of Transformational Generative Grammar to the analysis of similes and metaphors in modern English. *Style* 5, 265-283.

GRÄBE, I. 1979. *Teorieë oor hoofaspekte van poëtiese taalgebruik: Verkenning en toepassing.* Potchefstroom: Unpublished diss, PU for CHE.

HAHN, F. 1969. *The titles of Jesus in christology: their history in early Christianity.* London: Butterworth.

HENGEL, M. 1981. *The atonement: a study of the origins of the doctrine in the New Testament.* London: SCM.

HIGGINS, A. J. B. 1959. *New Testament essays: studies in memory of T. W. Manson.* London: MUP.

HIGGINS, A. J. B. 1980. *The Son of man in the teaching of Jesus.* London: Cambridge University Press.

HOOKER, M. D. 1967. *The Son of man in Mark: a study of the background of the term 'Son of man' and its use in St Mark's Gospel.* London: SPCK.

JEREMIAS, J. 1968. παῖς θεοῦ. *TDNT V,* 21-25.

JUEL, D. 1977. *Messiah and temple: the trial of Jesus in the Gospel of Mark.* Missoula, Montana: Scholars Press.

JUNGEL, E. 1979. *Paulus und Jesus: Eine Untersuchung zur Präzisierung der Frage nach dem Ursprung der Christologie.* Tübingen: Mohr.

KATZ, J. J. 1972. *Semantic Theory*. New York: Harper & Row.

KERTELGE, K. 1975. Der dienende Menschensohn (Mk 10:45), in R. Pesch, R. Schnackenburg & O. A. Kaiser (eds), *Jesus und der Menschensohn*. Freiburg: Herder, 225-239.

KLEINKNECHT, K. T. 1981. *Der leidende Gerechtfertigte: Untersuchungen zur Altestamentlich-Jüdischen Tradition von 'leidende Gerechten' und ihrer Rezeption bei Paulus*. Tübingen: Unpublished diss, Eberhard-Karls-Universität.

KÜMMEL, W. G. 1969. *Promise and fulfilment: the eschatological message of Jesus*. London: SCM.

LÄMMERT, E. 1970. *Bauformen des Erzählens*. Stuttgart: J. B. Metzlerlersche Verlags-buchhandlung.

LOHMEYER, E. 1967. *Das Evangelium des Matthäus*. Göttingen.

LONGENECKER, R. N. 1970. *The christology of early Jewish Christianity*. London: SCM.

MAARTENS, P. J. 1977. The cola structure of Matthew 6: the relevance of the structure in the interpretation of the text. *Neotestamentica* 11, 48-76.

MAARTENS, P. J. 1978. Was die tempelreiniging 'n *coup d'état*? (Linguisties-eksegetiese teenbewyse vir 'n revolusionistiese Jesus), in V. N. Webb (ed), *Taal, Letterkunde en Maatskappy*. Port Elizabeth: UPE.

MARSHALL, I. H. 1966. The synoptic Son of man sayings in recent discussion. *NTS* 12, 327-351.

MILLER, D. M. 1971. *The net of Hephaestus: a study of modern criticism and metaphysical metaphor*. The Hague: Mouton.

MOULE, C. F. D. 1967. *The phenomenon of the New Testament*. London: SCM.

MOULE, C. F. D. 1977. *The origin of christology*. London: Cambridge University Press.

MOWINCKEL, S. 1956. *He that cometh*, tr. by G. W. Anderson. Oxford.

PERRIN, N. 1966. The Son of man in ancient Judaism and primitive Christianity: a suggestion. *Biblical Research* 11, 17-28.

PERRIN, N. 1968. The creative use of the Son of man traditions by Mark. *Union Seminary Quarterly Review* 23, 357-365.

PESCH, R. 1975. Die Passion des Menschensohnes. Eine Studie zu den Menschensohn-worten der vormarkinischen Passionsgeschichte, in R. Pesch, R. Schnackenburg & O. A. Kaiser, *Jesus und der Menschensohn*. Freiburg: Herder, 166-195.

PESCH, R., R. SCHNACKENBURG & O. A. KAISER (ed) 1975. *Jesus und der Menschensohn*. Freiburg: Herder.

PESCH, R. 1977a. *Das Markusevangelium, 1. Teil. Einleitung und Kommentar zu Kap, 1:1-8: 26*. Freiburg: Herder. (Herders Theologischer Kommentar zum Neuen Testament.)

PESCH, R. 1977b. *Das Markusevangelium, 2. Teil. Kommentar zu Kap, 8:27-16:20*. Freiburg: Herder. (Herders Theologischer Kommentar zum Neuen Testament.)

TÖDT, H. E. 1965. *The Son of man in the synoptic tradition*. London: SCM.

TROTTER, T. 1968. *Jesus and the historian*. Philadelphia: Westminster Press.

WEINRICH, H. 1967. Semantik der Metapher. *Folio Linguistica* 1, 3-17.

G. J. C. JORDAAN

THE WORD-ORDER DIFFERENCES BETWEEN THE GREEK AND THE LATIN TEXT IN CODEX BEZAE

Codex Bezae Cantabrigiensis is certainly a remarkable document. It is the only known manuscript which contains both the Greek text (D) and the Latin text (d) of the Gospels. Even more remarkable is the fact that D is the only early *Greek* witness to the Western text-type of the Gospels (Ropes 1926:ccxxxi; Epp 1966:8). If it had not been for the existence of Codex Bezae, the Western type of text would have been restricted to early versions, mainly Latin versions. Consequently the Greek text of Bezae (D) is regarded as the main authority of the Western group of texts (Epp 1966:9).

The peculiarity of D has led to much discussion among textual critics. Generally D is suspected of not being an independent Greek text. Several views have been expressed regarding the origin and nature of the text of D.

Some critics try to explain the peculiarity of D by suggesting that the text of D was submitted to strong influence by Semitic texts (Yoder 1959:317-318) or was even the result of a translation from a Semitic text (Chase 1895, *The Old Syriac element in Codex Bezae*, as quoted by Epp 1966:3; Black 1946). Scrivener (1978:xxxi), on the other hand, found certain evidence in the Greek and the Latin text of Bezae which led him to believe that the document as a whole had been exposed to Gallic influence.

Nineteenth century scholars believed D to have been dependent on a Latin text, e.g. Von Soden (1902:1340), who regarded D as a translation from Latin, and Harris (1891), who concluded: "So extensively has the Greek text of Codex Bezae been modified by the process of Latinization that we can no longer regard D as a distinct authority apart from d" (1891:114).

Less extreme is the viewpoint of Findlay (1931, On Variations in the Text of d and D, *Bulletin of Bezan Club* 9:11, as quoted by Epp 1966:9), viz. that D certainly is a distinct authority, though strongly influenced by the Latin text of d. Ropes (1926) agrees with the viewpoint of Findlay. He says: "That d has affected D seems beyond doubt...; but the proof is in most cases demonstrative only for details, many cases must remain doubtful" (1926:29).

Some critics, on the other hand, regard D as a Greek witness totally independent of the Latin. Epp (1966:9-10) and Mizzi (1968:60-66) are convinced that D has not been influenced by d at all, but that, on the contrary, d has been strongly influenced by D. Clark (1899:205,219f) even regards d as a translation from D.

It is obvious that there is marked disagreement among scholars as to whether D is an independent witness of d. The dependence or independence of D is not merely a matter of scholarly interest. If D should prove to be dependent on a Latin or any other version, the Western text-type would no longer have the support of an independent early Greek witness. Consequently the Western text-type as a whole would be restricted to the same limitations as all versions in its usefulness for the textual criticism of the Gospels.

Unquestionably there has been a mutual influence between D and d. The study of Harris (1893) removes all reasonable doubt regarding this matter. Harris made the following observations (1893:53-61):

The Greek and Latin columns in Bezae are arranged in χῶλα. A comparison between every Greek χῶλον and the corresponding Latin χῶλον displays an obvious verbal resemblance between D and d, which Harris calls a "numerical verbal equality" (1891:54). The text of Bezae in Luke 23:38-40 is a perfect example of such verbal equality:

ἦν δε και η ἐπιγραφη	*erat autem et inscriptio*
επιγεγραμμενη επ αυτω γραμμασιν	*superscripta super eum litteris*
ελληνικοις ρωμαϊκοις εβραϊκοις	*graecis latinis hebraicis*
ο βασιλευς των ϊουδαιων ουτος εστιν	*rex iudaeorum hic est*
εις δε των κακουργων εβλασφημει	*unus autem de malignis blasphemabat*
αυτον :ἀποκριθεις δε ο ετερος	*eum respondens autem alius*
επετειμα αυτω λεγων οτι ου φοβη συ	*increpabat eum dicens quoniam no times tu*
τον θ̄ν̄ οτι εν τω αυτω κριματι	*dnm. quoniam in ipso iudicio*
και ημεις εσμεν	*et nos sumus*

According to Harris the scribe of Bezae deliberately effected such "numerical verbal equality" for aesthetic reasons: He wanted the left hand (Greek) column and the right hand (Latin) column of the manuscript to look alike.

Harris (1893:61) subsequently indicates that the scribe, for the sake of "numerical verbal equality", *assimilated the word-order* of the text in the two columns. On the question whether the Latin word-order was assimilated by the Greek or the Greek word-order by the Latin, Harris answers that it was the Greek that was consistently brought in concordance with the Latin word-order. He is of such an opinion because he perceived certain word-order patterns in both D and d which do not appear in any other Greek manuscript, but which are found in some Latin versions. As an example Harris quotes John 4:9 from Bezae:

συ ιουδαιος ων πως παρ εμου   *tu cum sis ioudaios quomodo a me*
πειν αιτεις γυναικος σαμαριτιδος   *bibere petis muliere samaritanae*

In this passage the word-order of D and d agrees with that of the Latin Vulgate and the Itala, whilst all Greek witnesses have the interrogative πῶς before the pronoun σύ, viz. πῶς σύ 'Ιουδαιος ὤν... According to the theory of Harris the word-order of D could have originated only from an adaptation to or translation from a Latin text.

An objection to the theory of Harris is that it is based on only one word-order phenomenon in Bezae, viz. agreement of D and d with the Latin version(s) against the Greek witnesses. In addition to this phenomenon the following are found in Bezae:

(1) In a number of cases D and d present a word-order which is not found in any Latin manuscript, but is indeed found in the Greek manuscripts, e.g. Matthew 18:21:

τοτε προσελθων πετρος ειπεν αυτω   *tunc accedens Petrus dixit ad eum*

The Latin Vulgate and the Itala in this passage have the word-order *tunc accedens ad eum Petrus (ad eum) dixit*.

(2) There are many cases in Bezae where D and d have a singular word-order which is not found in any Latin or Greek witness, e.g. Luke 17:33:

ος αν θεληση ζωογονησαι την ψυχην   *qui uoluerit biuicare animam suam*
αυτου

In this passage the other Greek witnesses have (ἐ)ὰν θελήσῃ (ζητήσῃ) τὴν ψυχὴν αὐτοῦ περιποιήσασθαι (σῶσαι), and the Latin versions have more or less *quicumque quaesierit animam suam saluam facere* (with the infinitive in final position).

(3) There are quite a number of cases where the word-order of D in fact is different from that of d, e.g. Luke 18:27:

τα αδυνατα παρα ανθρωποις   *quae impossibilia sunt in hominibus*
δυνατα παρα θω εστιν   *apud dm possibilia sunt*

and Luke 4:6

την εξουσιαν ταυτην απασαν   *hanc potestam omnem*

Since Harris overlooked these word-order phenomena in Bezae, his theory needs amendment. The only other critic who has also made a par-

ticular study of the word-order in Bezae is Yoder (1958). Yoder indeed
observed that the theory of Harris rests upon incomplete evidence and is
therefore unsatisfactory (1958:90). Consequently Yoder made a study of
the word-order variants of codex Bezae, i.e. the cases in which the word-
order of D agrees with that of d, but differs from all Latin witnesses or all
Latin and Greek witnesses. By this means Yoder tried to explain the first
and the second of the above-mentioned phenomena which Harris had
failed to explain. At the end of his study Yoder comes to the conclusion
that a study of word-order variants leads the textual critic nowhere. He
says (1958:351): "In sum, the multiplicity and variety of transpositions
of words in a sentence testifies to an atmosphere of freedom: whether *licet*
or *illicet*, one is unable to determine".

Thus Harris and Yoder took care of the study of word-order *agreement*
between D and d. One important aspect of Bezae which remains to be
studied, is the word-order *differences* between D and d.

The study of word-order differences in Bezae is important because it
brings into view the linguistic background of the scribe of Bezae.
Schwyzer (1950:690) and Rosén (1975:24) point out the fact that the
linguistic background of non-Greek authors or translators who wrote in
Greek or translated into Greek can often be seen in the word-order of
their work. Such a non-Greek writer would in moments of inatten-
tiveness employ the word-order usual to his native language and thus
betray his linguistic background.

The same argument is true of non-Greek or non-Latin scribes who
copied the Greek or Latin texts of the New Testament. Inattentively they
would apply a non-Greek or non-Latin word-order and thus reveal their
linguistic background. Normally, however, it would be impossible to
determine whether a given word-order in a manuscript is due to the
linguistic background of the scribe or to the word-order of the archetype
from which the scribe copied. But in a bilingual document like Bezae
where the scribe *deliberately* assimilated the word-order of the Greek and
the Latin (Harris 1893:53-61), word-order difference can rightfully be
ascribed to an oversight on the part of the scribe in a moment of inatten-
tiveness. A study of such word-order differences therefore should reveal
the linguistic background of the scribe.

Information about the linguistic background of the Bezan scribe is of
great importance for the intrinsic evidence of codex Bezae. If it could be
established that the Bezan scribe was Greek-speaking, or Latin-speaking,
or spoke some other language, the peculiarity of D and d would be much
less of a problem. Such information would be enlightening for questions
like: Were D and d each copied from its own archetype, or is the one a
translation from the other? If assimilated, in which direction had the

assimilation in Bezae been done: from D to d, or from d to D? Where did codex Bezae originate: in the East or in the West, or somewhere else? It is obvious that there is a need for a thorough study of the word-order differences in Bezae. This study is presented as a startingpoint for such a study and as an indication of the possible lines along which such an investigation could be carried out. Therefore a preliminary study of the word-order differences of Bezae in the Gospel according to Luke has been made.

A survey of the word-order differences in the Bezan text of Luke shows that the following aspects are concerned:
— the order of the verb and adverbial phrases;
— the order of the noun and its adjective or adjectival phrase; and
— the position of the verb in the sentence.
From each of these categories one or more cases have been chosen to discuss.

1. Difference in the order of verb and adverbial phrase

In Luke there are 6 places where D and d differ in the order of the verb and the adverbial phrase:

Luke		
5:14	ινα εις μαρτυριον ην	ut sit in testimonium
7:12	συνεληλυθι αυτη	cum ea erat
8:39	εποιησεν αυτω	illi fecit
10:40	ου μελι σοι	non tibi cura est
11:9	υμιν λεγω	dico uobis
18:27	τα αδυνατα παρα ανθρωποις	quae impossibilia sunt in hominibus
	δυνατα παρα θω εστιν	apud dm possibilia sunt

A closer look at *Luke 18:27* reveals the following:
- The word-order in D agrees with that of most Greek witnesses, while the word-order in d is found in no other witness.
- Even though it is the reading of most Greek witnesses, the word-order of D is indeed unusual in Greek. In the Greek New Testament adverbial phrases like παρὰ θεῷ are usually placed *after* the verb (Robertson 1923:419; Blass-Debrunner 1975:259), unless they are emphasized (Jordaan 1980:103-106); furthermore, the Greek copulae, especially ἐστιν, are rarely found at the end of a sentence (Kieckers 1911:50ff; Blass-Debrunner 1975:248). There is good reason, however, to deviate from usual word-order in this passage. For the sake of antithesis between ἀδυνατὰ παρὰ ἀνθρώποις on the one hand, and δυνατὰ παρὰ θεῷ on the other hand, a figure of speech with unusual word-order is likely to have been employed (Moule 1953:194; Louw

1967:5). Whether the original figure of speech in the autographon was a parallelism as in D or a chiasm as in d, is impossible to determine on intrinsic grounds. External evidence would be decisive in this matter.

- The word-order in d is in line with the usual Latin word-order. In Latin the complement adheres very closely to the copulative verb, normally directly preceding it (Leumann *et al* 1965:405). The Latin Vulgate and the Itala have the word-order *possibilia sunt apud Deum*, a sequence which is even more usual in Latin: The Latin copulae are preferably placed somewhere in the middle of the sentence (Allen 1903:398).

How, then, can the word-order difference between D and d in this passage be explained? The following possible explanations have to be considered:

(1) It is possible that D was copied from a Greek archetype with the word-order δυνατὰ παρὰ θεῷ ἐστιν, and d from a Latin archetype with the word-order *apud Deum possibilia sunt*, and that the scribe failed to assimilate the word-order. If this had been the case, it has to be assumed that the Latin archetype of d and all other witnesses with the same word-order has since been lost.

(2) More probably is the possibility that the word-order variant in d originated in the copying process of Bezae itself. Most probably it happened in the following manner:

- The scribe used a Greek archetype with the word-order of most other Greek copies, viz. δυνατὰ παρὰ θεῷ ἐστιν. Since Greek was not the native tongue of the scribe, the word-order in the archetype did not strike him as irregular, and he reproduced it in D.

- Subsequently the scribe turned to the Latin archetype and found the reading *possibilia sunt apud Deum*, which is also the reading of most Latin manuscripts. In an effort to assimilate the Latin word-order to that of the Greek, he transposed the verb to a position after the adverbial phrase. Without noticing, however, he transposed not only the verb *sunt*, but also the complement *possibilia*. He did so almost instinctively, because Latin was his native tongue, and in Latin the complement usually directly precedes the copulative verb (Leumann *et al* 1965:405).

(3) A third possibility is that the scribe indeed tended to assimilate the word-order of D to that of d, but inattentively failed to do so in this passage. Before this explanation could be accepted, however, the following difficulties have to be dealt with satisfactorily:

- If, indeed, the word-order in D was brought in concordance with that of d, how did it happen that D agrees with most Greek witnesses and that d has a singular reading?

– If the scribe really wanted to assimilate the word-order of D to d, it can
be expected that *ordinary* word-order patterns in the Greek could have
gone unnoticed and consequently not assimilated to the Latin. But
such an unusual word-order as that of D should have caught his eye,
whether he was Greek or Latin-speaking: a Greek-speaking scribe
would have expected the word-order δυνατά ἐστιν παρὰ θεῷ; a Latin-
speaking scribe would have found it rather unusual that the complement was separated from the copulative verb, especially if he had just
copied d with *possibilia* directly preceding *sunt*. Why, then, did the
Greek word-order not catch his attention?

(4) The last possible explanation for the word-order difference is that
D was indeed *translated from d*, as Von Soden (1902:1340) believes, and
that in the process of translation the translator unintentionally deviated
from the word-order of d. This explanation is most improbable, because
it cannot possibly explain how it happened that the unusual word-order
of D which thus originated "by mistake", is in agreement with most
other Greek witnesses.

Everything considered, the most probable explanation for the word-
order difference between D and d in Luke 18:27 is the second of the four
possible explanations given above. Accordingly it seems probable that

– D was copied before d, from a Greek archetype;
— d was copied after D, and from a Latin archetype;
— the scribe of Bezae as a rule assimilated the word-order of d to that
of D; and
— the scribe was Latin-speaking.

As for the differences in Luke 5:14 and 11:9, it is obvious that in both
instances D has the verb and the adverbial phrase in an unusual order for
a Greek text, and d an unusual order for a Latin text. It is therefore difficult to make out a case for either D or d being dominant: any possible
explanation in favour of D could just as well be turned around and be explained in favour of d. The same accounts for the differences between D
and d in Luke 7:12, 8:39 and 10:40, where the word-order of neither D
nor d is anything out of the ordinary.

Thus it seems that the study of word-order differences is most pro-
fitably concentrated on those cases where either D or d has a usual word-
order, and the other an unusual word-order, as in the case of Luke 18:27
which has been discussed above. It is also profitable to determine
beforehand whether one of D or d presents a word-order which can be
regarded as a singular reading. Such information gives an indication of
the direction in which the assimilation between D and d possibly took
place.

2. *Differences in the order of the noun and the adjective*

In the Bezan text of Luke there are quite a number of instances where D and d differ regarding the order of the noun and the adjective.

Six of these instances concern the position of numerals:

Luke	1:26	εν δε τω εκτω μηνι	*in mense autem sexto*
	9:22	μεθ ημερας τρεις	*post tres dies*
	9:30	ανδρες δυο	*duo uiri*
	12:52	εν ενι οικω	*in domo una*
	18:33	τη ημερα τη τριτη	*tertia die*
	24:46	τη τριτη ημερα	*die tertia*

In twenty-two passages the position of the adnominal genitive is concerned:

— subjective genitives:

Luke	5:5	επι δε τω ρηματι σου	*in tuo autem uerbo*
	5:20	σου αι αμαρτιαι	*peccata tua*
	11:2	σου η βασιλεια	*regnum tuum*
	14:24	μου του δειπνου	*cena mea*
	15:13	εαυτου τον βιον	*substantiam suam*
	15:29	σου εντολην	*mandatum tuum*
	20:20	αυτου των λοφων	*uerborum eius*
		(both D and d have singular readings)	
	21:7	της σης ελευσεως	*aduentus tui*
	22:53	υμων η ωρα	*hora uestra*

— partitive genitives:

Luke	5:8	αυτου τοις ποσιν	*ad pedes eius*
		(both D and d have singular readings)	
	6:45	αυτου της καρδιας	*cordis sui*
	7:22	υμων οι οφθι	*oculi uestri*
		υμων τα ωτα	*aures uestri*
	12:35	υμων η οσφυς	*lumbus uester*

— genitives of relationship:

Luke	8:49	σου η θυγατηρ	*filia tua*
	9:60	τους εαυτων νεκρους	*mortuos suos*
	15:19	σου υιος	*filius tuus*
	15:21	σου υιος	*filius tuus*

— possessive genitives:

Luke	6:29	σου το ιματιον	*tunicam tuam*
	7:6	ινα μου υπο την στεγην	*ut sub tectum meum*
	7:44	σου εις την οικιαν	*in domum tuam*
	14:23	μου ο οικος	*domus mea*
	19:15	αυτου τους δουλους	*seruos suos*

In seven passages the demonstrative adjective is transposed:

Luke	4:6	της εξουσιαν ταυτην απασαν	*hanc potestatem omnem*
	4:36	ο λογος ουτος	*hic sermo*
	9:28	τους λογους τουτους	*haec uerba*
	14:21	παντα ταυτα	*haec omnia*
	20:34	του αιωνος τουτου	*huius saeculi*
	23:47	ο ανθρωπος ουτος	*hic homo*
	24:17	οι λογοι ουτοι	*ista uerba*

The differences between D and d as to the position of the demonstrative adjective are noteworthy. In all instances D has the demonstrative after the noun, while d has it before the noun. Postposition of the Greek demonstrative is not uncommon. According to Gehman (1951:211) the demonstrative adjective in biblical Greek is placed before the noun and after the noun with even frequency. In Latin on the other hand, the demonstrative adjective generally *precedes* the noun (Gildersleeve 1921:430; Woltjer 1924:518), and it is placed after the noun only for the sake of special prominence (Allen 1903:396; Sonnenschein 1914:256; Leumann *et al* 1965:407). Thus it is evident that in the seven cases of difference the word-order of both D and d is not unusual.

It has already been stated (see the final paragraphs of the section on the verb and adverbial phrases above) that a word-order difference between D and d which displays nothing unusual either in the Greek or in the Latin word-order, cannot reveal any evidence in connection with the direction in which the Bezan scribe assimilated the text. Such is the case with the seven instances of transposition of the demonstrative adjective.

Since D in all of the forementioned passages agrees with the word-order of most Greek witnesses, it is probable that the Greek archetype which the Bezan scribe consulted, had the same word-order as that of D. Likewise it is probable that the Latin archetype which the scribe consulted, had the same word-order as that of d. Because of an unintentional oversight the scribe failed to assimilate. Whether it had been his intention to assimilate to the Greek or to the Latin is impossible to determine from these passages.

Nevertheless, the study of these passages is not totally without profit. It produces evidence concerning the question whether D is a translation from d or not. If indeed D should be regarded as a translation from d, these instances of word-order difference between D and d have to be explained as unintentional errors in translation. If this had been the case, no reasonable explanation can be given why the translator would have transposed the demonstrative from a position before the noun to postposition, because the translator could easily have retained the demonstrative before the noun, since Greek word-order equally allows for pre-position and post-position of the demonstrative (Gehman 1951:211). Therefore these passages supply evidence against the theory that D is a translation from d.

3. *Differences regarding the position of the verb*

With regard to the position of the verb in the sentence, New Testament Greek differs from Latin.

In indirect speech the Greek verb is normally found first in the sentence, unless some other word has to be placed first for the sake of emphasis (Wellhausen 1911:10; Robertson 1923:417; Black 1946:50; Moulton *et al.* 1976:60). In the direct speech, however, the word-order is so often influenced by stylistic word-order patterns, emphasis and figures of speech that the verb is seldom found at the beginning of the sentence (Frisk 1932:6-7).

In Latin, on the other hand, the verb is usually placed at the end of the sentence (Woltjer 1924:510; Madvig 1859:415), often in the second to last position (Allen 1903:393), but in the initial position only for the sake of emphasis (Leumann *et al* 1965:403).

When therefore the position of the verb in Bezae is taken into account, it is obvious that the scribe throughout tried to achieve word-order similarity between D and d. Sometimes the verb of both D and d was placed in the typical Greek position, e.g. in Luke 7:36:

ηρωτησεν δε αυτον τις των φαρισαιων	*rogauit autem illum quidam*
	pharisaeorum

Sometimes the verb is in the typical Latin position, in both D and d, e.g. in Luke 6:1:

οι δε μαθηται αυτου ηρξατο τιλλειν	*discipuli autem illius <u>coeperunt uellere</u>*
τους σταχυας και ψυχοντες ταις	*spicas et fricantes*
χερσιν ησθιον	*manibus <u>manducabant</u>*

(mss gr: ἔτιλλον οἱ μαθηταὶ αὐτοῦ καὶ ἤσθιον τοὺς στάχυας ψώχοντες ταῖς χέρσιν)

In quite a number of instances, however, the scribe failed to assimilate the verb-position of D and d. Of these instances D is mostly in agreement with the Greek manuscripts and d with the Latin manuscripts, viz.

Luke	1:48	μακαριουσιν με	*beatam me dicent*
	4:2	και ουκ εφαγεν ουδεν	*et nihil manducauit*
	6:29	τω τυπτοντι σε	*qui te percutit*
	7:4	ω παρεξη τουτο	*cui hoc praestes*
	7:50	η πιστις σου σεσωχεν σε	*fides tua te salbam fecit*
	8:48	η πιστις σου σεσωχεν σε	*fides tua te salbam fecit*
	9:48	τον αποστειλαντα με	*qui me misit*
	10:16	του αποστειλαντος με	*qui me misit*

11:27	η βαστασα σε	qui te baiolauit
14:10	ο κεχληκως σε	qui te inuitauit
17:7	ποιμενοντα ος	oues pascentem
18:14	ο υφων αυτον	qui se exaltat
18:42	η πιστις σου σεσωχεν σε	fides tua salbum te fecit
19:28	και ειπων ταυτα	et haec cum dixisset
22:60	λαλουντος αυτου	eo loquente
22:64	ο παισας σε	qui te percussit

There are two instances where the word-order of all Latin and most of the Greek witnesses is found in d, while D has a word-order supported by only a few Greek manuscripts, viz.

Luke 7:12	χηρα ουση	cum esset uidua
14:17	παντα ετοιμα εστιν	parata sunt omnia

Sometimes the word-order of D is found in agreement with all Greek and Latin witnesses, while d stands alone with no support from any other witness, viz.

Luke 1:66	τι αρα το παιδιον τουτο εσται	quid utique erit infans haec
5:3	εδιδασκεν τους οχλους	turbas docebat
19:22	εγω ανθρωπος αυστηρος ειμι	ego homo sum austerus
21:22	ημεραι εκδικησεως αυται εισιν	dies uinctictae sunt istae
22:60	εφωνησεν αλεκτωρ	gallus cantauit

In most of the forementioned passages D displays the usual initial position of the Greek verb, and d the usual final position of the Latin verb. There are only a few instances where the verb is found in an unusual position in both D and d, e.g. Luke 16:11:

το αληθινον τις υμειν πιστευσει   quod uerum est quis credet uobis

Contrary to normal usage, the Greek verb in this passage is found in the final position, and the Latin verb in the middle of the clause. Why has the word-order not been assimilated? The following seems to have happened:

Since the word-order of D agrees with that of the Greek manuscripts, and the word-order of d with that of the Latin manuscripts, it can be accepted that D was copied from a Greek archetype, and d from a Latin archetype. In both archetypes the scribe found a proleptive word-order i.e. the object of the verb before the interrogative. This extraordinary word-order caught the attention and therefore he did not notice that the position of the verb in the Greek was different from the word-order in the Latin archetype. Consequently he failed to assimilate the verb-position of D and d.

This explanation supports the opinion that the Bezan scribe was Latin-speaking, for if he was of the *Greek* tongue, the unusual position of the

Greek verb at the end of the sentence is likely to have attracted his attention. As a result he would have noticed the word-order difference between the Greek and the Latin and he would have assimilated the word-order. If, on the other hand, the scribe was Latin-speaking, neither the final position (as in D) nor the second to last position (as in d) of the verb would have attracted his attention, because both positions are quite usual for the Latin verb (Woltjer 1924:510; Allen 1903:393). It therefore seems very probable that the scribe of Bezae was Latin-speaking.

In each of the instances discussed above, there is only one reconstruction of the scribal habits and the linguistic background of the Bezan scribe which satisfactorily explains the word-order differences between D and d, and which therefore seems acceptable, viz. the following:
* The scribe of Bezae copied D from a Greek archetype and d from a Latin archetype.
* The Greek was copied first, then the Latin, and while writing down the text of d, the scribe assimilated it to D.
* The scribe was Latin-speaking, and therefore
  – he sometimes made an unintentional copying error by writing a word or phrase in a typical Latin position, thus creating a singular word-order reading;
  – sometimes, where the word-order patterns of the Greek and that of the Latin archetypes were in disagreement, but neither was unusual to *Latin* word-order, the scribe did not notice the disagreement and failed to assimilate the word-order of D and d.
* From the Latin background of the scribe follows
  – that codex Bezae has probably been copied in the West;
  – that Latinisms in D should not necessarily be regarded as evidence of *translation* from a Latin text. It is much more probable that such Latinisms were the result of unintentional errors on the part of a Latin-speaking scribe.

This reconstruction of the background of the scribe of Bezae is of course only preliminary, awaiting a complete study of all the instances of word-order differences between D and d, not only in Luke, but also in the other Gospels. Nevertheless, this preliminary reconstruction of the scribal habits and linguistic background of the Bezan scribe amounts to the very probable conclusion that D, although heavily influenced by Latin, should be regarded as a distinct authority apart from d.

BIBLIOGRAPHY

ALLEN, H. H. & J. B. GREENOUGH 1903. *Allen and Greenough's new Latin Grammar for schools and colleges.* Boston: Ginn.

BLACK, M. 1954. *An Aramaic approach to the Gospels and Acts*. Oxford: University Press.

BLASS, F. & A. DEBRUNNER 1975. *A Greek grammar of the New Testament and other early Christian literature, tr. and rev. by R. W. Funk*. Chicago: University Press.

CLARK, A. C. 1899. *Codex Bezae Cantabrigiensis*. Cambridge: University Press.

CUENDET, G. 1929. *L'ordre des mots dans le texte grec et dans les versions gotiques des Evangiles*. Paris.

DENNISTON, J. D. 1952. *Greek prose style*. Oxford: Clarendon Press.

DOVER, K. J. 1960. *Greek word order*. Cambridge: University Press.

EPP, E. J. 1966. *The theological tendency of codex Bezae Cantabrigiensis in Acts*. Cambridge: University Press.

FRISK, H. 1932. *Studien zur griechischen Wortstellung*. Göteborg: Elander.

GEHMAN, H. S. 1951. The Hebraic character of Septuagint Greek. *VT* 1, 81-90.

GILDERSLEEVE, B. L. 1921. *Gildersleeve's Latin Grammar*. London: Macmillan.

HARRIS, J. R. 1893. *Codex Bezae; a study of the so-called Western text of the New Testament*. Cambridge: University Press. (Text and studies 2.)

JORDAAN, G. J. C. 1980. *Woordorde-variante in die Griekse Nuwe Testament*. Potchefstroom: Wesvalia.

KIECKERS, E. 1911. *Die stellung des Verbs im Griechischen*. Strassburg.

KLIJN, A. F. J. 1959. A survey of the researches into the Western text of the Gospels and Acts. *NT* 3, 161-173.

LEUMANN, J., J. B. HOFFMANN & A. SZANTYR 1965. *Lateinische Grammatik, II. Lateinische Syntax und Stilistik*. München: Beck. (Handbuch der Altertumswissenschaft 2.)

LOUW, J. P. 1967. *Stilistiese sinsboustrukture en Nuwe Testamentiese Grieks*. Bloemfontein: Universiteit van die Oranje-Vrystaat.

MADVIG, I. N. 1859. *A Latin grammar for the use of schools*. Oxford: Henry & Parker.

MIZZI, J. 1968. The African element in the Latin text of Mt 24 of cod. Cantabrigiensis. *RB* 78, 33-66.

MOHRMANN, Christine 1955. Problèmes stylistiques dans la littérature Latine Chrétienne. *VG* 9, 222-246.

MOULE, C. F. D. 1953. *An idiom book of New Testament Greek*. Cambridge: University Press.

MOULTON, J. H., W. F. HOWARD & N. TURNER 1976. *A grammar of New Testament Greek, IV. Style*. Edinburgh: T. & T. Clark.

RADEMACHER, L. 1909. Besonderheiten der Koine Syntax. *Wiener Studien*, 1909, 1-33.

ROBERTSON, A. T. 1923. *A grammar of the Greek New Testament in the light of historical research*. New York: Doran.

ROPES, J. H. 1926. The text of Acts, in F. J. Foakes-Jackson & K. Lake (eds), *The beginnings of Christianity, III,1. The Acts of the Apostles*. London: Macmillan.

ROSÉN, H. B. 1975. Gedanken zur Geschichte des griechischen Satzbaus. *Sprache* 21, 23-36.

SCHWYZER, E. 1950. *Griechische Grammatik auf der Grundlage von Karl Brugmans Griechischer Grammatik*. München: Beck. (Handbuch der Altertumswissenschaft 2.)

SCRIVENER, F. H. 1978. *Bezae Codex Cantabrigiensis*. Pittsburg: Pickwick Press. (Reprint of the 1864 edition.)

SONNENSCHEIN, E. A. 1914. *A new Latin grammar*. Oxford: Clarendon Press.

THRALL, Margaret E. 1962. *Greek particles in the New Testament; linguistic and exegetical studies*. Leiden: Brill. (New Testament tools and studies 3.)

WELLHAUSEN, J. 1911. *Einleitung in die drie ersten Evangelien*. Berlin: Reimer.

WESTCOTT, B. F. & F. J. A. HORT 1882. *The New Testament in the original Greek, II. Introduction and appendix*. New York: Harper.

WOLTJER, J. 1924. *Latijnische Grammatika*. Groningen: Den Haag.

YODER, J. D. 1959. Semitisms in codex Bezae. *JBL* 78, 317-321.

YODER, J. D. 1961. *Concordance to the distinctive Greek text of codex Bezae*. Leiden: Brill. (New Testament tools and studies 2.)

I. J. DU PLESSIS

CONTEXTUAL AID FOR AN IDENTITY CRISIS: AN ATTEMPT TO INTERPRET LUKE 7:35

Would it be an overstatement to say that Luke 7:35 is made up of a collection of *cruces interpretum*? Almost every word in this short verse presents difficulties. What, for instance, is meant by ἐδικαιώθη? Who is the σοφία referred to and why is it used and not θεός? And who are the τέχνα? We are faced in this short verse with problems of interpretation regarding both the subject and the object as well as the predicate of the sentence. So many dubieties in one verse weaken the position of any interpreter in taking a strong stand on any solution he may offer. If one of these words should be proved to be wrongly interpreted, it might upset the whole applecart. Our attempt to interpret this verse is therefore based on understanding the whole of the chapter in which it occurs. We will try to show how 7:35 becomes clear from what Luke has written in the whole unit comprising verses 1 to 50. The context will be scrutinized to see whether the themes and the various foci point to an understanding of 7:35. What is the point that Luke wished to make in this chapter which forms a unit on its own? Does the sumtotal of the foci in the various pericopes and episodes of this unit support the interpretation we offer for 7:35? What is the relation between the way Luke presents the identity of Jesus in the rest of the chapter and the identity of the σοφία and the τέχνα in 7:35? We are convinced that these questions can be answered when we look closely at the meaning of 7:35 within its context.

Earlier Bible translations give a very literal translation of the Greek text of Luke 7:35. It is typical of these translations to proceed in this fashion, but it does not really help us to identify the people to whom this text refers.

KJV: *But wisdom is justified of all her children.*
RSV: *Yet wisdom is justified by all her children.*
La Sainte Bible: *Mais la sagesse a été justifiée par tous ses enfants.*

In accordance with this kind of translation it does not become clear who "wisdom" is, neither is the identity of "her children" explained. What is meant by "justified" is not clear either.

The new Afrikaans translation (1979) comes closer to an acceptable solution with the following translation:

Maar God tree met wysheid op, en sy werke bewys dit.

Σοφία is explained here as referring to *God* and the noun is actually included in the translation as a quality ("met wysheid") of God's action. Τέχνα, again, is understood in this version as referring to the acts (deeds) of God. This, however, might have been influenced by the parallel in Matthew 11:19 ("But wisdom is proved right by her actions"). This translation, however, is closer to our own understanding of this verse. I would therefore like to offer the following translation as one which explains what Luke wants to say here and as being in correspondence with the context in which this verse is located:

> *But God is proved right by those who have become his children.*

In the remainder of this article I will argue why I believe that σοφία should be translated with "God" and why τέχνα refers to those who have accepted God's plan of salvation. I find support for this in various modern (recent) translations, e.g.:

> NIV: *But wisdom is proved right by all her children.*
> NEB: *And yet God's wisdom is proved right by all who are her children.*
> TEV: *God's wisdom, however, is shown to be true by all who accept it.*

The last translation (TEV) comes closest to our own approach and probably presents us with the best attempt to give a dynamic translation and at the same time reveals most of what can be found in the Greek text itself.

My reasoning in support of my translation is based on the way Luke has structured chapter 7 as a literary unit. The episodes he has included, his omissions and insertions, the themes which run through the various pericopes, the types of people who play the main roles in these episodes; all these aspects which are present in his composition of 7:1-50 add to our understanding of the point he wants to make. This applies to the total impression of 7:1-50 and to the main foci of attention in the various smaller segments.

Luke 7:1-50 within the framework of the Gospel

7:1-50 forms a unit on its own, the section dealing with Jesus' ministry in Galilee (4:14-9:50). The Galilee ministry commences with Jesus' ministry in Nazareth and Capernaum (4:14-5:16). This is followed by five controversies between Jesus and some Jewish spiritual leaders (5:17-6:11). This clash with the Pharisees and the scribes is interrupted by Luke with a description of Jesus calling the twelve apostles and his instruction of his disciples (6:12-49). Confrontation between Jesus and his opponents is taken up again in chapter 7. People are confronted to come to a decisive choice—for or against Jesus. From 7:1ff a definitely new literary unit within the Galilean ministry opens up. In the previous pericope Luke describes the so called sermon on the plain but in 7:1 the location moves to Capernaum again. Some miracles follow, as well as a discourse centering around John the Baptist, but involving Jesus himself. Included in this unit is also the controversy with Simon the Pharisee about a sinful woman. In 8:1ff Luke again describes Jesus on the move and in 8:4ff he switches back to Markan material. Luke 7:1-50 therefore forms a unit on its own which can be studied as such. Whereas the previous chapters are directed at the pious Jews, we see that his disciples are now increasingly drawn from the gentiles and the ordinary masses. In 7:1-50 we find a series of episodes describing how people respond to Jesus' actions. A decisive separation between the true Israel and Israel "after the flesh" becomes apparent (cf Schneider 1977:164, Schürmann 1969:386f).

Luke uses this confrontation to define the identity of Jesus. The first pericope (7:1-10) ironically presents the faith of a *gentile* Roman centurion as an example to Israel. The second pericope (7:11-17) demonstrates God's *care* for his people when the son of a widow is returned to her from death.

The *spiritual leaders* of the nation, however, *reject* God's purpose for them (7:30). This is accentuated in the last pericope (7:36-50) when God's *forgiveness* towards a sinner is illustrated. The whole unit (7:1-50) thus points to the fact that even though heathen, sinners and tax collectors have received and accepted God's grace in Jesus, those people in Israel who should have accepted him have not done so. In 7:31 Luke refers to "the people of this generation" who have actually rejected the offer of God. This would include everyone who has heard the preaching of John and Jesus, but in this passage it is the Pharisees and scribes, as the spiritual leaders of Israel, who are adressed. They symbolise those in Israel who should have accepted God's gift without hesitation. Ironically, they are the people who have rejected God's plan of salvation whereas the gentiles and the social outcasts are the people who gladly accept this gift. The spiritual leaders therefore are the target of Jesus' reproach, even though he might refer to "the people of this generation". Luke 7:1-50 could therefore be summarised under the theme:

> God has turned to his people but only some have accepted Him while Israel's leaders (and all who should have known better) have rejected Him.

This explains why Luke locates the pericope about John the Baptist (7:18-35) in the centre of this series of episodes, namely because the *identity of Jesus* is so clearly defined and accentuated in this passage. In this section John the Baptist fulfils the function of pinpointing the decisive stand of people towards Jesus. John's question and Jesus' reply give the answer as to whether Jesus is the one who has to come. Further, according to Luke it is evident that Jesus' witness concerning John and the contrast between the two identify Jesus as the Messiah.

The whole unit of 7:1-50 can thus be outlined as follows:

1. Two acts of mercy illustrating God's grace

7:1-10

7:11-17

2. Accusation against the spiritual leaders of Israel because they have rejected God's mercy

7:18-35

3. A demonstration of God's forgiveness which passes the spiritual leaders by and is offered to sinners

7:36-50

Number 2 (7:18-35) is the only negative reaction as against the two positive ones (1 and 3). The response to God's grace and mercy in this literary unit can thus be outlined as follows:

Positive   –   Gentiles and anyone who suffer

Negative   –   Israel and its spiritual leaders

Positive   –   Sinners

The negative reaction described in the central pericope seems to point to a focal attention by Luke. The way he has composed the whole chapter suggests that he intends this central pericope to receive the main emphasis. It stands in contrast to what we find in the positive reaction in the first and last pericope. This should allow us to consider the central pericope as of special importance.

Before we turn to pericope 7:18-35 let us first look at the main themes of the other pericopes in chapter 7. This should help us get a perspective on the significance of 7:18-35.

The faith of the centurion (7:1-10)

The first pericope (7:1-10) deals with a Roman officer whose servant is healed by Jesus. Luke makes use of Q material in this first pericope. When one compares it with Matthew's version (Mt 8:5-13) it seems as if vv 1a, 7a and 10a have been reworked redactionally by Luke and that he has added 3b-6d (cf Fitzmyer 1981:649). For the sake of our argument it is important to notice that Luke omits the fact that the centurion personally went to Jesus, while Matthew presents him as personally confronting Jesus (Mt 8:5-6). The reason why Luke presents the event in this way may indicate that he purposely wants to accentuate the *distance* between the *gentile* centurion and Jesus. This would remind his non-Jewish readers of the distance between the gentiles and God, but it also dramatizes the mercy of God as shown towards a gentile. The irony of the whole affair increases, however, when the delegation says of this officer: "This man deserves to have you do this..." (7:4). Jesus reacts in a sympathetic way by personally going to this man's house. Although the centurion confesses his unworthiness, this reference to his unworthiness is used as a literary technique to focus attention on Jesus' power and to demonstrate the centurion's faith. Jesus' reaction is one of amazement regarding this man's faith in Him. He exclaims: "I have not found such great faith even in Israel" (7:9). Verse 9c (τοσαύτην πίστιν) is the focus of this pericope: *the faith of a gentile in Jesus.*

This is not just a miracle-story. It is probably rather to be considered as an announcement story (cf Bultmann 1968:38), recorded here to accentuate the power of Jesus and the faith of a gentile centurion. He is held out as an example for Israel and his faith is contrasted to the lack of faith of Israel and its leaders.

The raising of the son of the widow at Nain (7:11-17)

This episode appears only in Luke and comes from his own material (L-source). Here Luke gives his readers another example of the power of Jesus. This is the first Lucan account of Jesus raising someone from the dead. He probably inserts this episode here to provide proof of Jesus' power to raise people from the dead as is claimed by Jesus in 7:22. This claim is a direct response to the question by John's disciples. Although not all the healing miracles mentioned in 7:22 are described previous to 7:22, the raising of a person from the dead might have been considered so important that Luke wants to furnish this proof before the claim of Jesus in 7:22.

Although this is an exceptional miracle the focus of this story is on the reaction of the audience. Their reaction to the miracle can be summarised as follows:
1. filled with awe
2. praised God
3. acknowledged Jesus as a prophet
4. acknowledged God's mercy.

The theme of their reaction should probably be sought in the praise of the people that "God has come to help his people" (v 16).

In contrast with the previous pericope where the *faith* of the centurion is stressed, it is the *mercy* of God in Jesus which predominates. The mercy shown by Jesus to a widow who has lost her son and her only support fits very well into the whole unit of 7:1-50 where a gentile, a socially under-privileged person and a sinner receive mercy at the hands of Jesus. These actions to various people, who were normally less esteemed in the social structure and the religious thinking of Jewish society, are bound together by Luke with the purpose of identifying Jesus as the Messiah and thus as a demonstration of Jesus' claim in 7:18-35.

This story has the typical form of a miracle-story (cf Bultmann 1968:215, 233-4). It reminds us of the raising of the son of the widow of Zarephath by Elijah in 1 Kings 17:8-24. In spite of a few differences most of the elements in the Elijah story agree with this Jesus miracle. This might indicate that Luke wants to picture Jesus as fulfilling the same role as Elijah. It is, of course, very likely that Luke found this in the source he is using (cf Fuller 1963:64).

In this specific miracle-story, *faith* in Jesus is not the main issue nor is it even required, because it is his *mercy* which is in the foreground. It is, however, Luke's purpose to identify Jesus as the one who has power over life and death. Therefore he records the exclamation of the bystanders: "A great prophet has appeared among us". From Luke's viewpoint this clearly contains christological undertones, if not a direct identification of Jesus as Messiah. The following pericope (7:18-35) will establish this more directly: Jesus' conduct in this act prepares the readers for the confession in the next episode (especially 7:22). The focus of 7:11-17 is therefore on the final words of the audience in 7:16: "God has come to help his people". This statement may be very significant and expresses this sentiment which is evident right through chapter 7. It makes the reader aware of the offer of God which can be either accepted and enjoyed or rejected. Every one who accepts this offer will understand and experience what God is doing in Jesus and "prove Him to be right" (ἐδικαιώθη - 7:35).

Pericope 7:18-35 which follows on the episode of the raising of the widow's son, forms the integration point of this whole chapter. But before we discuss the relevant material of 7:18-35, we first of all turn to the last pericope of chapter 7. In this way we can get perspective on the context of 7:18-35 before we deal with this central pericope.

Jesus forgives a sinful woman (7:36-50)

This is the last episode of this unit (7:1-50) and it again contains Luke's own material which does not occur in this form in the other Gospels. There are strong similarities with the other Gospels (cf Mk 14:3-9; Mt 26:6-13; Jn 12:1-8), but there are also real differences, so much so that we can rightly speak of this episode as material peculiar to Luke.

So far it has become evident that Luke wants to portray Jesus in Luke 7 as the miracle-worker who demonstrates God's merciful care for his own people, but also for others. The examples of the centurion (7:1-10) and the widow (7:11-17) prove this to be God's purpose. This theme is further illustrated in the episode of the sinful woman (7:36-50) who experiences God's forgiveness through Jesus. The third episode (7:18-35) receives the focus of the unit as a whole, but the claim in this episode is followed by a fourth (7:36-50) as a final proof of what has already been claimed in the third episode. It is altogether in line with Jewish and ancient reasoning to put the main point of an argument in the middle of the argument rather than at the end (cf Mt 7:6). The contrast between the sinners who accept God's plan of salvation and the Pharisees and scribes who reject it (cf 7:29-30) is concretely illustrated in the final episode dealing with Simon the Pharisee and the sinful woman.

Whereas the hero of the story in the first episode (the centurion) is contrasted with Israel, this sinful woman is contrasted with a Pharisee. This last contrast links up the readers' thoughts with what is said in 7:29-30 about "all the people" who comply with God's will as against "the Pharisees and experts in the law" who rejected God's purpose for themselves. This explains why Luke has included this pericope (7:36-50) *at this very point*, in comparison with the other evangelists who use a similar story within the *passion narrative* (cf Mk 14:3-9; Mt 26:6-13; Jn 12:1-8). Luke has separated his story from any connection with the passion narrative. He prefers to include it within this framework of 7:1-50 where the accent is on God's forgiveness and mercy.

The description by Luke of this woman's conduct is one of humility which is strongly contrasted with that of Simon the Pharisee. Her humility is dramatized in the description of how she kisses Jesus' feet. Whereas Mark records that the ointment was poured on Jesus' *head*, Luke speaks of the anointing of his *feet*. This intensifies her humility and her adoration of Jesus. The contrast is also endorsed by Simon's thought on Jesus and the woman. The words: "If this man were a prophet..." probably reflects on Jesus and John as prophets, as referred to in the previous pericope. In the story, the Pharisee's thoughts seem to be sarcastic, but Luke may have wished to provide an ironic touch. The Pharisee thinks that if Jesus is truly a prophet, he ought to know that this woman is a sinner. Luke, however, uses this turn of events for the benefit of his readers. His readers already know what is written in the previous pericope (7:18-35) and Luke therefore reasons as follows: Because Jesus is a prophet he knows that this woman is a sinner, but he allows her to touch him because it is exactly this kind of person who is eligible for forgiveness—as will be shown later on in this episode. This has already been pointed out in ironic fashion in 7:34-35. This rhetorical question by the Pharisee is used as a link with, or a preparation for, the parable which is to follow. The parable is used to accentuate the main thought in this pericope, namely: the person who has received most forgiveness will show most gratitude/love. Here "love" expresses gratitude for forgiveness. It refers to the forgiveness of Jesus and leads to the reaction of the bystanders in v 49: "Who is this who even forgives sins?"

Luke often uses this rhetorical question as a literary technique to draw the attention to Jesus' identity. He keeps up the tension of his story by repeatedly including this question in the course of his Gospel. He replies indirectly to this question from the bystanders by giving Jesus' last command to this woman: "Your faith has saved you; go in peace". Here, for the first time, we hear that it is her faith which has saved her. Although the main thrust of this pericope is to illustrate God's mercy in Jesus, Luke ends this pericope by pointing out that the groundrule of faith should not be lacking in any relationship with God.

This brings us to what we have already pointed out to be the main focus of the unit stretching from 7:1-50. We will now look at the third pericope in more detail, it being the narrower context within which our main problem occurs, namely: who are the τέχνα of v 35? and what is the meaning of v 35 as such?

Jesus and John the Baptist (7:18-35)

This third of the four pericopes in Luke 7:1-50 forms an integration point for the other three. This becomes clear only when one looks at the literary unit (7:1-50) as a whole. The action of Jesus towards a gentile centurion, a bereaved widow and a sinful woman and their reaction towards him, are used to demonstrate what is stated about God's actions in Jesus and John the Baptist. In 7:18-35 we have, on the one hand, the issue of Jesus' relationship to John the Baptist and, on the other hand, the attitude of people towards both of them. Luke 7:18-35 forms *one pericope* which concentrates on one topic, namely, the relationship between Jesus and John and the attitude of people towards them. The pericope can, however, be subdivided into three or four divisions depending on whether vv 29-30 is considered as a separate subsection or as part of the second or third subsection. Schürmann (1969:420) and Marshall (1978:297) take vv 29-30 as part of the last subsection, while Fitzmyer (1981:670) joins it to the second subsection and Schneider (1977:171) groups vv 24-35 together, thus dividing this pericope into only two subsections.

We prefer the following division:
1. 7:18-23 John's question and Jesus' reply.

2. 7:24-28   Jesus' witness regarding the role and identity of John.
3. 7:29-30   Reaction of the people to John.
4. 7:31-35   Jesus' judgement concerning the reaction of people towards John and himself.

Sections 1, 2 and 4 consist of Q material whereas section 3 contains a Lucan insertion.

This pericope being mainly Q-material, shows clear parallels with Matthew 11:1-19 with a few exceptions (cf Aland 1967:150-2). 7:20-21 was probably added by Luke. Matthew 11:2-4 omits these two verses and Matthew's version can probably be considered as containing the original Q. Matthew 11:12-13 also seems to contain the original Q while Luke uses these verses elsewhere (cf Lk 16:16). Luke 7:29-30 does not occur in Matthew and was probably never part of Q. Luke probably added these verses himself as comment on the reaction of people to John the Baptist. This fact is of significance for our understanding of v 35 and of the whole pericope, as we hope to demonstrate.

One last remark regarding the structure of this pericope as a whole: each of the subsections 1, 2 and 4 concludes with a special statement by Jesus in which the main point of this section is poignantly expressed. Thus:

section 1   *Blessed is the man who does not fall away on account of me* (v 23)
(vv 18-23)

section 2   *Among those born of women there is no one greater then John; yet the*
(vv 24-28)   *one who is least in the kingdom of God is greater than he* (v 28)

section 4   *But wisdom is proved right by all her children* (v 35) (NIV)
(vv 31-35)

These statements act as summary slogans to conclude each section. They also act as demarcations for the various subsections. There is no slogan in section 3 because here we have a Lucan comment on the previous section about John. This supports our suggestion that vv 29-30 are added by Luke and do not belong to either section 2 or 4. It also gives to section 3 a special significance within this pericope as a Lucan comment which summarises the response of both the ordinary people and the Pharisees and scribes to John and Jesus. It suggests the focal attention which this section deserves.

We now turn to detailed discussion of the various sections of this pericope.

1. *Luke 7:18-23*

The first section consists of a question and a reply. The question comes from the delegation which John has sent to ask Jesus: ''Are you the one who was to come, or should we expect someone else?'' (v 19). The repetition of this question in v 20 is only to be found in Luke and not in the parallel in Matthew 11:2-4. It is probably a Lucan addition to Q, stressing John's uncertainty regarding Jesus' identity. Neither does v 21 occur in Matthew 11:2-4 (but what of Q?) (see above). It is, however, characteristic of Luke to summarise events and true to his style to sum up the miracles of Jesus for the benefit of the delegation in the story. This should prove the power of Jesus to them. It also confirms ''all these things'' about which John has been informed (7:18).

The second part of this first section contains Jesus' answer to the delegation. They are ordered to tell John what they have seen and heard. Various healing miracles and the resurrection of the dead are referred to as proof. Added to this is mentioned the fact that the gospel is preached to the poor.

Finally they are called upon to report a macarism in which people are summoned to accept Jesus for what he is. This last summons appears to be a challenge to trust Jesus on the grounds of what he is doing.

A remarkable difference between the versions of Luke and Matthew is the fact that Luke omits the specific reference to Jesus as the *Christ* as found in the parallel in Matthew 11:2. This may be due to the fact that Luke wants to portray John as the one who really *doubts* whom Jesus is. We have already pointed out that this may also be the reason why Luke alone repeats the initial question put by John via his delegation.

Fitzmyer (1981:664) has put up a strong argument for the case that John actually sees Jesus as an *Elias redivivus*, a fiery reformer, who would be very much like John himself (cf Matthew 3:12). Jesus, however, does not conform to this expectation. The one who is coming is not Elijah in the sense of a preacher who begins and ends with preaching repentance— very much like John himself. He is rather one who blesses and brings salvation to people (cf 7:21-22). If Luke does think of Elijah as a parallel for Jesus it is more in line with the episode recorded in 7:11-17 which might find its model in the Old Testament story of Elijah and the widow of Zarephath (see above).

We generally infer from the text that Luke wants to present John in the right perspective. He presents him as the uncertain questioner compared with Jesus. Jesus' reply is a clear confession which calls upon people not to hold on to prejudiced ideas about him, but to accept him because of what he has done and preached publicly.

2. *Luke 7:24-28*

The confession of Jesus regarding himself is followed by his witness concerning John. This witness is expressed by means of a rhetorical question regarding John and is repeated three times: "What did you go out into the desert to see?" Three answers are given:

Not a reed swayed by the wind.

Not a man dressed in fine clothes.

But a prophet - yes.

The third answer is the correct one. However, this answer is immediately elaborated upon. John is more than a prophet. This is supported by a citation from the Old Testament which reminds one of Malachi 3:1:

> *I will send my messenger ahead of you,*
> *who will prepare your way before you.*

This second part gives further expression to the relationship between John and Jesus. This citation from Malachi 3:1 reminds one of the beginning of John's career in Luke 3:1ff where he is also described in a fashion characterising him as the one who prepares the way for the Lord. Although Jesus witnesses to John this witness is actually a statement about Jesus himself. John is the prophet who prepares the way for Jesus. This relationship between the two and their relative importance is underlined in the last statement from this section. Jesus claims the greatness of John (μείζων) but simultaneously stresses that even the smallest one (μιχρότερος) in the kingdom of God is greater than John. Jesus pays homage to John, but states unequivocally that one must progress beyond confidence in John. What Jesus has been preaching, namely the kingdom of God, offers much more than John. This last summarising statement of Jesus is his final comment on John and is presented here by Luke as the culminating statement of Jesus about him. As in the first section, this also concludes with a special statement of Jesus expressing the ultimate purpose of describing John the Baptist in this way.

3. *Luke 7:29-30*

These two verses have been inserted by Luke into the Q-material which he has in common with Matthew. It looks similar to a passage which Matthew uses elsewhere (Mt 21:31-32), but the fact that Luke makes a break in his Q-material just here, should suggest to us that he has good reason to do so. The remainder of the Q-material coincides so closely with that used by Matthew in a single block (Mt 11:1-19), that there must be a purpose in Luke's insertion of these two verses. Let us have a closer look at these two verses.

These two verses give us more information about John's ministry. They refer to people who accept and others who reject John's preaching. It could be considered as a summary of the success and failure of God's plan of salvation for Israel. We have previously pointed out that Luke is fond of summarising events in this way. Here, this summary prepares the reader for the following section where this attitude is illustrated as being applicable not only in the ministry of John, but also of Jesus.

Whereas the other three sections of this pericope end with a slogan in which the essence of the foregoing section is summarised (cf vv 23, 28 and 35), this insertion reveals nothing of that nature. It is, rather, a summary of the theological thrust of the whole of chapter 7:1-50. It gives in a nut-shell what is happening in this whole chapter. More specifically, it is a key for the understanding of the following section (vv 31-35).

These two verses could be considered as a parenthetical comment by Luke on the work of John which is meant to be a reflection on the whole passage (vv 18-35). The New International Version puts these two verses in brackets, not thereby indicating that it is based on a weak text, but probably to indicate its *insertion* character. The text reads as follows:

> *All the people, even the tax collectors, when they heard Jesus' words, acknowledged that God's way was right, because they had been baptized by John. But the Pharisees and experts in the law rejected God's purpose for themselves, because they had not been baptized by John.*

Luke's comment is therefore that there are two *reactions* to John's preaching, namely, those who accept it and those who reject it. These two groups can also be divided according to two categories of *people*: on the one hand, the ordinary people, including those who were considered social and theological outcasts, and, on the other hand, the spiritual leaders represented by the Pharisees and the scribes. The two categories can be seen in the *result* of their response to the preaching: those who were baptized and those who were not baptized.

Luke hereby prepares his readers for the application of this rule in the following section. The reaction of people to John's preaching is very much the same as their reaction to Jesus. In the case of Jesus, Luke has already described the reaction in the episode with the centurion (7:1-10) and the widow (7:11-17) and he will give a further example in the following episode of the sinful woman (7:36-50). In these three episodes he compares the faith of a gentile with that of Israel (7:1-10), the response of a sinner towards Jesus with that of a Pharisee (7:36-50) and also illustrates the mercy of God in Jesus (7:11-17) which is offered without any previous act of faith.

Luke's comment on the reaction of people to John also applies to their response to Jesus. In spite of the difference in style and preaching between John and Jesus—as will be demonstrated in the last episode—the indictment against the people remains the same: they reject the purpose of God for them.

This indictment is directed against the Pharisees and the scribes, who are representatives of those people in Israel who should have been the first to acknowledge God's purpose. The Pharisees were probably the people who disappointed Jesus the most, because they should have known better. No wonder that Luke includes the story about Simon in this context and that he refers to this man as a Pharisee, whereas the other evangelists call him by other names. To Luke this whole chapter is an indictment against those people who should have set the example by accepting John and Jesus.

4. *Luke 7:31-35*

This last section is connected to vv 29-30 by the use of οὖν which does not occur in the parallel in Matthew 11:16. This οὖν marks the connection of the parable with vv 29-30. In this section Jesus complains about the people who do not understand either John or himself. He again makes use of a comparison/parable and its explanation and concludes with a slogan which functions as a summary, not only of this section, but also of the whole literary unit which runs from 7:1 to 50.

The key to this section, which is offered in vv 29-30 in connection with people who either accept or reject John, is now illustrated in a parable. The parable refers not only to John but also to Jesus. Verse 30 is being elaborated chiastically in verses 31-34, as is verse 29 in verse 35 in the following way:

```
 ┌─v 29      All the people … acknowledged that God's way was right
 │ ┌─v 30      But the Pharisees … rejected God's purpose for themselves
 │ └─v 31-34   To what, then, can I compare the people of this generation
 └─v 35      But wisdom is proved right by all her children.
```

The special way in which these verses are connected with one another becomes clear in the use of ἐδιχαίωσαν (v 29) and ἐδιχαιώθη (v 35). Also in relation between πᾶς ὁ λαός ("all the people") (v 29) and the πάντων τῶν τέχνων ("all the children") (v 35).

The main features in verses 29 and 35 represent a balanced and even chiastic parallelism which can be clearly seen in the Greek text which follows.

v 29: χαὶ πᾶς ὁ λαός   …   ἐδιχαίωσαν τὸν θεόν

v 35: χαὶ ἐδιχαιώθη ἡ σοφία   …   πάντων τῶν τέχνων

The way θεός and σοφία are used in this parallel very strongly supports our suggestion that σοφία refers to God himself and not to the personified wisdom as was probably meant in the original Q-tradition. This point will be argued later.

Seen within the context of Luke 7 as a whole, we suggest that 7:35 should be understood as follows: From all the people, who included gentiles (7:1-10), tax collectors (7:29) and sinners (7:36-50) come the τέχνα of σοφία (7:35) who accepted God's purpose for them (7:30) and acknowledge that God's way is right (7:29). By acknowledging that God's way is right they recognise and acknowledge God's plan (βουλή) (v 30) which appears in both John and Jesus.

The Pharisees, however, reject both John and Jesus. John, who symbolises judgement and repentance, and who is presented here parabolically as the one who lives ascetically, is rejected. But Jesus also, who symbolises mercy, compassion and grace, and who is presented here as living a very sociable life, is rejected. Thus the Pharisees reject God's purpose for them. Whatever is offered them, whether by John by means of judgement and asceticism, or by Jesus by means of mercy and understanding, these are not acceptable and thus God's offer itself is rejected.

So far we have consistently referred to "God" as the ultimate author of these actions recorded in Luke 7:1-50. In 7:35, however, Luke uses σοφία in the Greek text. We take σοφία here as a paraphrasis for "God". Ellis' (1966:123) suggestion that it could refer to the Messiah is unacceptable within this context. It is much more congenial to Luke's style to quote Jesus' sayings from the source (= Q) which he uses. This is also suggested by the fact that Luke makes reasonably few inroads into the source he uses in 7:18-35. Furthermore, Jeremias (1980:167) has also pointed out that Luke usually changes the traditions he uses as little as possible when he quotes Jesus' own sayings.

It is well known that the Q-source, which Luke uses in this pericope, has a typical *wisdom* character. Probably, behind this saying in 7:35 lies the Jewish tradition concerning wisdom as a quasi-personal *hypostasis* who preaches to men and longs to dwell among them but is rejected by them (cf Fohrer & Wilckens 1964:465ff). If we accept that Luke quotes literally from his source and thus uses σοφία, it explains why he refers to the βουλή τοῦ θεοῦ in v 30 which he inserts into the Q-material. In v 30 he comments in his own words on the reactions of people to God's plan and therefore he refers to God with the ususal Greek term θεός. This supports the suggestion that vv 29-30 is a redactional insertion by Luke but not v 35 (cf Schürmann 1969:428). Luke includes his own comment in vv 29-30 because of what he has already found in his source as quoted in v 35. The σοφία therefore does not refer to wisdom as a personal being, but rather to God whose plan (βουλή) is proved to be the right one by those who accept it.

Luke stays true to his source in 7:35 and uses σοφία, but then as referring to God himself. Because of the connotation of σοφία it is justifiable to
understand verse 35 as including the idea of God's plan as a *wise* plan of
salvation. This plan is proved to be wise and is also experienced as a wise
plan by everyone who accepts it, thus demonstrating that they are truly
the children (τέκνα) of God.

7:35 thus forms a summarising accusation against the whole of Israel
who has rejected both John and Jesus. It simultaneously praises those
who have accepted God's offer in John and Jesus. On the one hand it
reflects the deep concern about the hopeless situation of Israel who has rejected the hope of redemption. On the other hand, however, it is a
demonstration of God's love and mercy for all mankind illustrated in the
way all his children are experiencing his gifts.

Conclusion

Luke 7:35, in our view, becomes clear if we accept that it should be interpreted not only from the direct context (7:18-35), but from the whole of
chapter 7 as wider context. Chapter 7 forms a structural unit on its own
within the larger structure of Luke's Gospel. Once we realize that 7:1-50
forms a unit on its own, the mutual relations and the main themes which
are displayed throughout this unit crystallise. This methodological approach helps us to see how the various pericopes and smaller episodes
within this unit relate towards one another. The context, whether in narrower or wider sense, gives us a perspective on the issues or issue at stake
in this unit. Luke 7:35 may be considered as an aphorism which draws
the details of the whole unit into a single statement and provides a focus
for the whole. What is given by means of a slogan in 7:35, is summarised
in the comment of Luke in 7:29-30. What Luke finds in his source (7:35)
he sums up in his own words in vv 29-30 as a comment on all the actions
of Jesus and the reactions of people. John's ministry is used as a catalyst
to identify Jesus as God's final offer to Jew and non-Jew.

It is thus considered that the problem of the identity of the σοφία and
the τέκνα has been solved and that the interpretation of ἐδικαιώθη has
been given. We therefore suggest the following dynamic translation of
Luke 7:35: *But God is proved right by all who experience his salvation.* ''Salvation'' could also be replaced by words like ''plan'', ''grace'', ''mercy'',
''kindness'', ''compassion''.

We have tried to solve the identity crisis of the σοφία and the τέκνα but
the solution we offer also sheds light on another identity, namely, that of
Jesus. Throughout chapter 7 the identity of Jesus is pointed out by Luke
as it is in the remainder of his Gospel. Although Luke never spells it out

in so many words, there remains little doubt that all the episodes point to Jesus as the ''one who was to come''. The question of John in the mouth of his disciples, is answered in the affirmative by Luke's presentation, not only in the key passage (7:18-35) in this chapter, but throughout Jesus' actions in the whole of this chapter. For Luke, therefore, there is no identity crisis. For him the answer is plain. Jesus is the one who demonstrates that God's way is right and therefore proves that he is indeed the ''one who was to come'' no matter how this phrase was understood or misunderstood. For Luke, it is not the people who decide who the one is who was to come or how he should behave, but it is God who sees to it that his will is done and his purpose fulfilled.

BIBLIOGRAPHY

Only works directly referred to are included in this list.

ALAND, K. 1967. *Synopsis Quattuor Evangeliorum*. Editio Septima. Stuttgart: Würtembergische Bibelanstalt.
BULTMANN, R. 1968. *History of the synoptic tradition*. Oxford: Blackwell.
ELLIS, E. E. 1966. *The Gospel of Luke*. London: Thomas Nelson.
FITZMYER, J. A. 1981. *The Gospel according to Luke (I-IX). Introduction, translation and notes*. New York: Doubleday.
FOHRER, G. & U. WILCKENS 1964. σοφία. TWNT.
FULLER, R. H. 1963. *Interpreting the miracles*. Philadelphia: Westminster
JEREMIAS, J. 1980. *Die Sprache des Lukasevangeliums*. Göttingen: Vandenhoeck & Ruprecht.
MARSHALL, I. H. 1978. *The Gospel of Luke. A commentary on the Greek text*. Exeter: Paternoster.
SCHNEIDER, G. 1977. *Das Evangelium nach Lukas Kapitel 1-10*. Gütersloh: Gerd Mohn.
SCHÜRMANN, H. 1969. *Das Lukasevangelium, Erster Teil. Kommentar zu Kapitel 1,1-9,50*. Freiburg: Herder.

J. P. LOUW

MACRO LEVELS OF MEANING IN LK 7:36-50

1. Language is often said to be a system of signs used to communicate messages. Yet language signs contribute but a smaller part in the total process of communication. Many other signs are involved to convey a message. In discourses para-linguistic signs such as intonation, pause, spelling, paragraphing, punctuation, literary forms such as prose or poetry, compositional structuring, etc. along with extra-linguistic signs such as body stance, the wink of an eye, clothing, hair style, context and setting of a situation, cultural presuppositions, the furniture in a room (office, kitchen, bedroom), pools of water along a highway, road signs, etc. all contribute towards an understanding of what an author wishes to convey by the words uttered. Written texts have numerous ways by which extra-linguistic signs can be incorporated into a text—the most obvious being descriptive notes to fill out the setting of an event.

These 'other' signs restrict the language signs, often even to the extent that an utterance can convey exactly the opposite of what the word and sentence level of an expression seems to convey. For example, the sentence 'you are a real friend' can be said within various contextual frameworks and with varying intonation stressing different terms of the utterance. A particular context and intonation may communicate approval and appreciation. Or, within a given context one may stress the word 'real' to disapprove of what has been done, even to censure. The same sentence can be uttered by stressing the word 'you' and addressing one of two persons present in order to tell the other one that what has been done was not at all what one would expect from a friend. Extra-linguistic and para-linguistic features signal how an utterance is to be understood.

2. On returning from the city of Samaria to the well where Jesus was waiting, his disciples found him in conversation with a woman. In Jn 4:27 we read that the disciples were greatly surprised to find him talking with a woman. But none of them said to her 'What do you want?' or asked him 'Why are you talking to her?' The surprise was triggered by the cultural convention of the time. Men did not talk with women in public, at any rate not a Rabbi as Jesus was. The conversation was a semiotic sign of an unusual situation: Jesus breaking through a social convention. And later on in verse 39 we find Jesus breaking another

social convention by staying over with the Samaritans, a taboo for any orthodox Jew at the time. The cultural signs carry the essence of the incident recorded in Jn chapter 4: the ministry of Jesus sharply contrasts the Old and the New Order. The Gospel has no regard for petty human conventions. The disciples, however, knew Jesus for what he was and did not question his social behaviour. These conclusions come from extralinguistic information triggered by the text.

3. Language as such is but a part of a larger system of signs. To analyze a discourse, therefore, calls for going beyond the syntactic and semantic levels of the language code. A semiotic approach to discourse analysis is required since a discourse involves more than words and sentences. Using language involves a speech act, that is, language in context: a socio-linguistic event. As a matter of fact one can never use language except within a context. A semiotic approach to discourse analysis consequently involves recognition of multiple signs, interrelated and interacting, so that a particular utterance may have more than one level of meaning. For example, an utterance such as 'it's going to rain' can, in a given context, convey what the words as such signify, namely that 'rain is going to fall on the ground', but within another frame of reference it can also say that 'the crops will be saved', etc. The pragmatic situation, the context, determines how an utterance is to be interpreted. This means that on the word level an utterance conveys certain information, but *how* this word level information is *to be understood* in terms of its intention depends on the pragmatic situation. It involves language *in function*, that is to say: what is the author *doing* with the utterance, what speech act is the author performing. Thus the utterance 'it's going to rain' can be used to encourage and assure the receptor. Understanding an utterance involves far more than the lexical meanings of the words, or even their combination into sentences. Any utterance involves a complex network of layers, one of which would be the lexical level, another the syntax level, another the level of reference, another that of the context, etc. Multiple signs contribute towards the understanding of an utterance.

For example the term *New Baytown* as the name of a town is in itself a mere language sign to refer to a particular populated area, but the name can also, and at the same time, be a sign of an ultra-conservative community if such a town has acquired a reputation to that extent. In a discourse the mention of the name of the town can call up various connotations. For instance, in John Steinbeck's *The Winter of our Discontent* the sentence 'a lady does not wander—not in New Baytown', suggests that for *lady* the meaning 'a woman of refined habits' should be applied, and that in the particular community of New Baytown such a woman would not loiter the streets. In a different context in which New Baytown has been referred to as a suburb of villainy, the term *lady* would probably merely mean 'a female person' and *wander* would be understood as 'walking about' without any negative reference. The connotative features of meaning associated with New Baytown are suggested by the semiotic values attached to the town or suburb in question, and these connotative features stipulate our understanding of the utterance even to a larger extent than the meaning of the words themselves.

As a matter of fact, the same utterance may be used to convey quite divergent intentions. A sentence such as 'do you eat strawberries' may be understood as a question asking information about a person's likes or dislikes of certain foods. It may also be said to voice a reproach: 'you eat strawberries all by yourself, what about sharing with me'. But the same sentence may also be used to give a warning: 'what on earth are you doing, you know eating strawberries is not allowed'. The latter may be said in a warehouse to a packer of fruit, or to a person known to be allergic to strawberries. Multiple semiotic signs contribute towards our understanding of an utterance.

4. In oral discourse facial expressions, gestures, intonation, silence, etc. are semiotic signs conveying important information. In written texts descriptive notes, referred to above, as well as choice of words, allusions, punctuation, etc. supply the necessary background. These are semiotic signs determining our frame of reference. Another extract from John Steinbeck's *The Winter of our Discontent* may illustrate the point:

> Margie said, ''Hi! You're busy. I'll come back later.''
> She crossed the alley mouth and went into the bank.   2
> Joey Morphy lighted up the whole barred square of his tel-
> ler's window when he saw her. What a smile, what a good   4
> playmate, and what a lousy prospect as a husband. Margie
> properly appraised him as a born bachelor who would die   6
> fighting to remain one.
>   She said, ''Please, sir, do you have any fresh   8
> unsalted money?''
>   ''Excuse me, ma'am, I'll see. How much would you like?''   10
>   ''About six ounces, m'sieur.'' She took a folding
> book from her white kid bag and wrote a cheque for twenty   12
> dollars.
>   Joey laughed. He liked Margie. He turned her   14
> cheque round. ''Do you want this in twenties, fifties
> or hundreds?''

To appreciate the significance of this little conversation one has to know the context in which it took place. The context provides the signs by which the meanings of the words and sentences can be understood. In line one Margie addressed the grocer whose shop is next to the bank. In terms of this information the phrases 'fresh unsalted money' and 'six ounces' in lines 9 and 11 become significant of the lighthearted relationship between Margie and Joey Morphy. Without this setting such expressions in a bank situation would seem very strange and out of place. This lighthearted relationship is also suggested by Joey Morphy's jovial reaction in line 3 when Margie enters the bank, as well as Margie's opinion of Joey Morphy as a friend (line 5). In fact, the novel occasionally describes the relationship between Joey and Margie as that of very close friends but without any further pretensions. They like to be playing in their relationship as is also indicated in line 14. The same attitude is signalled within such a frame of reference by the words 'bachelor' and 'like' in lines 6 and 14. Even the emphatic descriptive phrase 'who would die fighting to remain one' in line 6 along with 'a lousy prospect as a husband' in line 5, indicate that in the relationship between Joey Morphy and Margie serious considerations are not at all envisaged. It is remarkable how many signals Steinbeck has built into the passage to clearly mark the essence of what he wanted to convey. Reading this passage without the contextual background would result in a fairly awkward impression of the events. The semiotic signs condition our understanding of the written text.

5. A Semiotic approach to a discourse takes cognizance of all possible signs, linguistic, para-linguistic and extra-linguistic, that may be relevant to understand and to interpret a text. These signs function as multiple layers which may be conveniently grouped into three significant macro levels: (a) the *declarative level*, that is the level of the mere statement, the bare facts as they are lexically and syntactically predicated, (b) *the structural level*, that is the compositional features suggesting particular groupings and bundles or clusters of information along with their interrelationship to one another by which the focus of the discourse is signified, and (c) *the intentional level*, the purpose of the discourse, that is what the author, or perhaps rather what the text seems to convey within a particular frame of reference—in short, what is the message. Though each level communicates a seemingly different set of features, the first leads to the second, and the second to the third to convey the real purpose and sense of what a text has to say.

Very often discourse analysis concerns itself mainly with the second level because discourse analysis developed within a structural approach to linguistics. The methodology suggested by the present discussion stresses the necessity for acknowledging all three levels in terms of a semiotic approach. This, in fact, contends that discourse analysis involves a wider scope.

The following discourse (Lk 7:36-50) clearly shows the relevance of the three levels of interpretation signified by the semiotic features of the text.

The first level of reading a text, the declarative level, deals with the bare facts of the communication. In the case of Lk 7:36-50 we find the following: A Pharisee invited Jesus to have dinner with him. During the meal a woman known for her sinful life entered the room, stood behind Jesus by his feet crying and wetting his feet with her tears. Then she dried his feet with her hair, kissed them and poured expensive perfume on them. The Pharisee now concludes that if Jesus were a prophet he would not have allowed the woman to touch him. Then Jesus spoke to the Pharisee telling him a little story about two men who owed money, the one 500 silver coins, the other 50. The moneylender cancelled the debt of both. 'Which one', Jesus asked, 'will love him more?' Simon had to answer that it would be the one who was forgiven more. Turning to the woman Jesus reminded the Pharisee that the woman did what the Pharisee himself should have done. The woman who had more to be forgiven than the Pharisee, showed more love. Then Jesus forgave her sins to the surprise of the other people sitting at the table.

On the first level a number of semiotic signs are apparent. The story ends rather abruptly and the woman never spoke a word. This immediately suggests that the story was not told by the author to merely jot down what happened at a particular dinner but that the author selected certain events to suit a purpose. The story is a vehicle for some message. This possible judgment becomes more probable when one considers that the story told by Jesus about the two men who owed money is applied to the woman and to the Pharisee. One feels that there must be more behind the events than what meets the eye. This is strengthened by certain cultural signs: the woman managed to get into the room without anyone stopping her. She was apparently no stranger in the household. She could even have been acquainted to the Pharisee. What she did to Jesus corresponded exactly to the customary tokens of hospitality at the time: wash, kiss, anoint—factors referred to later in the story: she did what the Pharisee should have done. His lack in performing such regular acts of showing hospitality suggests that his invitation to Jesus was not one of friendship, but that there were other reasons involved. This is signalled by his thoughts, explicitly mentioned, namely that the Pharisee had doubts about whether Jesus was a real prophet. Perhaps the Pharisee invited Jesus to have dinner with him, not because he treasured his company, but rather to have Jesus at hand to question him, or rather to examine him.

A structural analysis of the story reveals how the focus of the discourse is on the Pharisee and his own selfrighteousness, a fact which might have even more significance if he was indeed acquainted with this woman.

Structurally the story has two main sections: a narrative (7:36-39) and a dialogue (7:40-50). The Greek text of the narrative section has 7 sentence construction units, numbers 1-7 of the following outline:

1. A Pharisee invited Jesus to have dinner with him
2. Jesus went to his house and sat down to eat
3. In that town was a woman who lived a sinful life
4. When she heard that Jesus was eating in the Pharisee's house, she brought an alabaster jar full of perfume and stood behind Jesus, by his feet, crying and wetting his feet with her tears and drying his feet with her hair.
5. And she kissed his feet
6. And she anointed his feet with perfume
7. When the Pharisee who invited him saw this, he said to himself: If this man really were a prophet he would know who this woman is who is touching him; he would know that she is a sinner.

Structurally we have the following:

1. Pharisee
2. Jesus ———————————> introduced as the main actors
3. Woman

4-6. The woman ——— 4. washes his feet
                ——— 5. kisses his feet
                ——— 6. anoints his feet
7. The Pharisee judges: he is no prophet.

Then the story changes to a dialogue between Jesus and the Pharisee, called Simon, followed by a short dialogue between Jesus and the woman (although only Jesus talks) which in turn is interrupted by a response from the other guests, numbers 8-16 of the following outline:

8. Jesus spoke up and said to him: Simon, I have something to tell you
9. He said: Teacher, tell me
10. (Jesus said:) There were two men who owed money to a moneylender. The one owed 500 silver coins, the other 50. Neither of them could pay him back, so he cancelled the debts of both. Which of them will love him more?
11. Simon answered: I suppose that it would be the one who was forgiven more
12. Jesus said: You are right
13. Then he turned to the woman and said to Simon: Do you see this woman?
    I came into your home and you gave me no water
    for my feet
    She washed my feet with her tears and dried them
    with her hair
    You did not give me a kiss
    She did not stop kissing my feet since I came
    You did not anoint my head with olive oil
    She anointed my feet with perfume
    Therefore I tell you: her many sins have been
    forgiven because she has loved much
    Whoever has been forgiven little, loves
    a little

14. Jesus said to her: Your sins are forgiven
15. The others at the table began to say to themselves: Who is this man who even forgives sins?
16. Jesus said to the woman: Your faith has saved you, go in peace

Structurally we have the following:

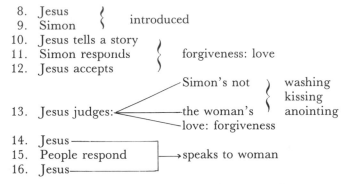

Note that in the first section (1-7) the woman and the Pharisee react towards Jesus. The Pharisee and the woman are the protagonists of the story. Jesus is in the background. In the second section (8-16), however, Jesus takes the initiative and reacts toward the Pharisee and the woman. Jesus now becomes the protagonist. In the first section the Pharisee finally dominates the scene, in the second section Jesus takes over vindicating the woman and denouncing the Pharisee. The second section also indicates structurally that the opposition forgiveness: love is the pivot point of the story. The Pharisee's answer in colon 11 contains the essence of the story: forgiveness stands in a direct relationship to love. This is the theme of the story.

    This brings us to the third level of interpretation, the intentional level. It seems that Luke uses the events to convey a message of utter irony: Jesus and his preaching is not for people (like the Pharisee) who regard themselves as righteous. Jesus came to minister unto the underdogs, the outcasts, the sinners. His message is understood by these very people, while the respected of society, the privileged, the powerful, stand aloof. Those who can be expected to appraise the preaching of Jesus do not understand his message at all, while the despised and rejected really comprehend the essence of the message. The story illustrates the paradoxical impact of Jesus on our everyday life. He shatters our existence and breaks through the clichés of our value systems. He uncovers our distorted world. We are shocked like the people at the dinner to experience how Jesus works. Because we do not love, we also do not experience the peace and amity of forgiveness. The story becomes a symbol of our own world. We see ourselves in the actors and events of the story.

6. Translating a text such as Lk 7:36-50 may involve a decision to render either one or more of these levels of meanings. Or perhaps rather to test the translation in terms of how people in the target language would respond to the translated text. Would they be able to recognize the structural relationships along with the other semiotic signs which enabled us to read the text as we have just done? It seems more and more feasible that Bible translations for the modern reader should have at least some footnotes suggesting how the meanings of certain words and phrases are to be understood in terms of their contextual and cultural reference in order to enable the reader to grasp what a text is saying. It is imperative to recognize that understanding comes from a wider area than that provided by the mere linguistic signs. Translation is not rendering one language into another language, but rather one discourse into another discourse by means of a particular language substituting for the source language.

Significant structural clusters may, for example, be suggested to the reader by means of the layout of the translated text. Even the order of sentences (and for that matter also of verses) ought to be changed if such a change would afford the reader a proper understanding of what the text is saying. Extensive research is needed to know exactly what are the general discourse patterns favoured by a particular language or even a particular community using such a language.

The closest natural equivalents of word or phrase meanings have been in focus for some time already and with considerable positive results. The same should be done for discourses. That is to say, what would be the closest natural discourse pattern to render Lk 7:36-50 into, say, language Z. This should be done along with due attention to all other semiotic signs by which a reader understands a text. Translation requires a semiotic approach.

P. J. DU PLESSIS

THE LAMB OF GOD IN THE FOURTH GOSPEL

Much has been written on this enigmatic expression in John 1:29,33 (Burrows 1973). Despite the abundance of thought given to the matter we have the uncomfortable feeling that we still do not know what the expression means. The reconstruction of what the historical background could be is varied (Du Plessis 1978:120-124).

There is not much point in reviewing and discussing at length, all these views yet once more. It does however serve our purpose to give an indication of the main streams of thought. For Barrett (1954/55) and many others (Roberts 1968:42) John 1:29 should be primarily interpreted as an allusion to the Passover Lamb. Related to this point of view is the interpretation of *agnos* against the background of the *tamid* (daily temple sacrifices) or other cultic sacrifices mentioned in Numbers 29:1-4, 8-10; Lv 1:10; 3:7-9; 4:32; 5:6; 14:12 and others (Negoitsa & Daniel 1971:26ff). Foremost among these sacrificial interpretations is the acceptance of Is 53:7 as the origin of the expression in John (Mealand 1978:457). Dodd in his own unique way developed the original idea of Spitta into an estimable theory that the Apocalyptic usage could account for John's employment of the word (Dodd 1965:237): "The Lamb of God in John 1:29 would be like the Lamb in many passages in Revelation, the horned Lamb, the bell-wether of the flock" (cf Barrett 1954/55: 210). Another such a beacon is Cullmann (1966:70). Jesus as ὁ ἀμνὸς τοῦ θεοῦ would be the Suffering Servant (Son) of JHWH (Is 42:1-7; 53:7) as well as the Paschal Lamb. By combining these two notions he combines the best of two worlds but semantically overloads the concept in John. To mention only one more point of view: Negoitsa & Daniel see in the expression a reference to the divinity of Jesus. By linking John 1:14 to 1:36 their conclusion is that the expression "voilà l'agneau de Dieu" is to be understood as "voilà le verbe de Dieu".

My own stand in the article referred to (Du Plessis 1978:128-129) was that a structural analysis of John 1:29-39 taken in context with the whole of Chapter 1 leads us to the focal point of verse 14: καὶ ὁ λόγος σὰρξ ἐγένετο ... καὶ ἐθεασάμεθα δόξαν ὡς μονογενοῦς παρὰ πατρός. Accepting Jesus the μονογενής of the Father as concomitant with ὁ ἀμνὸς τοῦ θεοῦ made it a *terminus gloriae*. In my mind the case made for this interpretation still holds good. Since then however theological research has explored to a greater extent text analysis, literary forms, reader response, multiple reading of a text and other related avenues of inquiry. All of these methodological aids take as point of departure the text and its *intratextual* literary functions (Petersen 1984:5). These methodological issues as such are not relevant to this paper, but the question is whether fresh evidence can be found by examining the context of the text itself closer. It is becoming increasingly clear that despite their possibilities the historical-critical methods have decided limitations. Vorster is correct in his assumption that "historical explanations are normally built on hypotheses, but a hypothesis is something different than guess-work, and is very often replaced by a better one. It is often better to conclude with 'non licet' than to pretend to work with facts. One of the basic flaws of the underlying theory of traditional historical-critical interpretation is the assumption that texts are windows through which reality behind the text can be seen" (Vorster 1984:16). Historical construction, parallels, seeming references to biblical and extra-biblical literature can supply background material for comparison but it does not and cannot explain what a text means.

It is therefore no longer possible to collate, as Cullmann does, the *amnos* of John 1:29 with Is 42:1-7 and 53:7 and conclude on these grounds that John had the Paschal Lamb, the *Ebed JHWH* in mind when he wrote this. Neither is it possible to accept Barrett's statement of the historical background of the term: "John the Evangelist brought the resultant wealth of material together in a term which like many others he used, was at once Jewish and Hellenistic, apocalyptic, theological and liturgical" (Barrett 1954/55:218). It certainly does not mean that all these levels of interpretation, which represent various stages of historical development, are valid and relevant at the same time in one particular term or text.

The interpretation of texts is in a state of transition. It has been signified as the post-new criticism and post structuralism phase of literary criticism (Harrari, quoted by Combrink 1984:8). In effect it means a shift of emphasis from the *text* to the *reader*. No doubt it opens new venues for exploration but Combrink correctly remarks: "It seems that despite the conscious shift of emphasis from text to reader, the text as a stable and determinate structure often manages to intrude into the very heart of reception theory... At some level, both Iser and Jauss, as well as other reception theorists, call upon a determinate text (or sub-text) to prevent what threatens to be a totally subjective and arbitrary reader response" (Holub: 149f) (Combrink 1984).

What it thus means is that in the interpretation of texts we are compelled to take primary and secondary reading of a text and multiple meaning of a text into account. What it does not mean is that historical-criticism and structuralism have left the field in favour of a completely literary autonomous reading of a text with special emphasis on the receptor. All these interpretory approaches provide some answers to at least some aspects of interpretation. How we deal with these levels of meaning depends on the literary and other constraints in the text itself. There are multiple forces at work in a text, its interpretation and eventually its relevance and meaning.

Bearing these literary and semantic considerations in mind we now turn to John 1:29-34 (the microstructure). Finally we shall have to consider the macrostructure of the Fourth Gospel, and chapter 1 in particular.

Without going into detail, it appears that this pericope is constructed in a chiastic A-B-B-A pattern. It can be diagrammatically represented as follows:

> A. ἴδε ὁ ἀμνὸς τοῦ θεοῦ
> B. ὁ αἴρων τὴν ἁμαρτίαν τοῦ κόσμου
> B. οὗτός ἐστιν ὁ βαπτίζων ἐν πεύματι ἁγίῳ
> A. οὗτός ἐστιν ὁ υἱὸς τοῦ θεοῦ.

John 1:30-32 forms two clusters (C-C: not indicated above, as it need not concern us at this point). Both clusters have as its central theme the pre-existence of Jesus (v 29): the thought is taken up in v 30: οὗτος, and concludes the section, vv 33-34. This is not a conclusion of the Baptist as such. He states his ignorance of the true essence and identity of Jesus, the *amnos* (οὐκ ᾔδειν αὐτόν vv 31 and 33). For his statement he relies on 'a revelation of God' (ἐκεῖνός μοι εἶπεν (v 33)). In this context ἐκεῖνος can only refer to God. When, where and how this revelation occurred is not stated. The same applies to the Baptist's own conviction of his divine mission (ὁ πέμψας με ... μοι εἶπεν v 33).

The author's train of thought may be summarized as follows: Jesus is the ἀμνός of God (A); he takes away the sins of the world (B); he is the pre-existent One (vv 30-31); the One on whom the Spirit descended (v 33). He is the One who is to baptize with the Holy Spirit (B: v 33(b)); He is the Son of God (A: v 34)[1].

From the structural analysis it is clear that Jesus is given the title of *Amnos* which corresponds to the title of υἱός (cf the inclusio A-A). This

---

[1] There is no reason to accept Brown's view that "it is difficult to imagine that Christian scribes would change the 'Son of God' to 'God's Chosen One', while a change in the opposite direction would be quite plausible" (Brown 1982:57). One need not labour the point of weaker manuscript tradition. The theological impact of the first chapter of John would favour the reading ὁ υἱός (cf Metzger, B. M. 1971. A textual commentary on the Greek New Testament. 3. ed. United Bible Societies).

does not yet explain what the titles mean in respect to Jesus. The same is true of the christological titles in the first chapter. It does mean however that "Jesus Christ is the great subject of the Gospel and of the Prologue, and the Logos is the Predicate, and not the reverse" (Ridderbos 1966:198).

A similar correspondence is to be noted as far as the work of Jesus is concerned (B-B): He takes away the sins of the world and baptizes with the Holy Spirit. What these two qualifying phrases mean, is not clear from the statements as such. We need to know what is implied by calling Jesus (the amnos) ὁ αἴρων (v 29) and ὁ βαπτίζων (v 33b).

At this point it is necessary to bear in mind the connotation which various scholars attached to the *amnos* in John. Basically the question *is whether amnos* in this context is a sacrificial lamb (of whatever kind, Paschal or otherwise) or not (cf D. L. Mealand 1978:457, V. C. Pfitzner 1977:4). Barrett is correct in saying "that there is no simple explanation of the term" (1954/55:210). This is true also of Dodd's apocalyptic interpretation of the lamb as the horned lamb, the bell-wether of God's flock. Since Barrett's doubts (1954/55) no reconsideration of his explanation has led to any conviction that this is indeed probable. It is apparent that the *word lamb* immediately and almost automatically conjures up the vision of an animal being slaughtered for the remission of sin. This sort of associative response has dominated investigation of the term almost exclusively. Pfitzner's statements are symptomatic of this trend and therefore worth the trouble quoting: "Suffice to say at this point that John seems concerned to show that Jesus was, indeed, what John the Baptist had attested him to be: the Lamb of God sent to take away the sin of the world. Thus Jesus dies in John's Gospel on the same day on which the passover lambs were being slaughtered in the temple... What is clear is this: John is working with a clear theological conception of Jesus as the Pashal Lamb of God, the perfect Passover sacrifice. It is only to be expected that the Paschal motif should reappear in the actual passion narrative" (Pfitzner 1977:14). He then goes on to find Paschal allusions throughout the Fourth Gospel, "to certify Jesus as the perfect Paschal victim" (p 11). This way of doing is invalid. The passion narrative is in itself not a Paschal allusion or moulded on Paschal motifs.

To be sure, the Baptist is not saying that "Jesus is the Passover Lamb dying for the sin of the world" (Pfitzner 1977:21). While it is a fact that a lamb is slain and that its blood is shed, "it does not shepherd men (vii 17) ..." (Barrett 1954/55:216). Jesus is John's Good Shepherd who is willing to die for his sheep (John 10:7-17). He is not, despite whatever Paschal allusions we may seem to find, the sacrificial Lamb in the Fourth Gospel. His place is only in the first chapter of the Gospel. After that he disappears from the narrative and discourse of the Gospel. It seems perfectly valid to say that the term Lamb in the first chapter is used in a context which is completely devoid of sacrificial motifs. Quite the contrary is true. The main thrust of the chapter is to present Jesus from the outset in his full glory (δόξα).

It is as Hawkin says: "The Fourth Gospel shows little concern with history as the 'recovery of past particulars' and is thus perhaps the furthest removed of all the Gospels from the 'actualities' of history. The Christ of the Fourth Gospel is transposed from the realm of historicity to a realm that transcends the merely historical" (1980:89). The transcendent nature of the Johannine Christ is predominant in the first chapter. This has come to be called John's "high christology" (Neyrey 1982: 587ff).

We need not pursue the matter of John's christology at length. If we turn to the christological titles of the first chapter we are faced with an abundance of material. These titles are not randomly used but neatly arranged in a chiastic structure. Amidst these predicates of Jesus it becomes clear that whatever sacrificial connotation the term Lamb may have it is semantically void in this context, empty. *It clearly signifies* or points to something else which can only be extracted from the entire discourse. If we closely inspect the scheme we are able to identify the *Lamb* as a *terminus gloriae for the Son of God/Man*. Why the word *lamb* is used for this semantic function, or to signify this particular level of meaning becomes clear as we examine the structure:

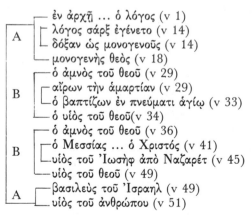

Only the focal points of the clusters are shown in the diagram. These focal points show the inner relationship of the terms and explain their significations. John 1:14 is the verse from which we take our cue: ὁ λόγος σὰρξ ἐγένετο ... καὶ ἐθεασάμεθα δόξαν ὡς μονογενοῦς παρὰ πατρός. This is a very important lead. Whatever our translation of μονογενής, its clear signification is the *special relationship between the Father and the Son*. The title or term expresses this unique relationship in much the same way as is spoken of in the OT of the first-born son of a father (De Kruijf 1970:111-113): "Every first-born male is to be dedicated to the Lord (Ex 13:2,12 cf Luke 2:23; cf also Amos 8:10; Judges 11:34; Micah 6:7; Jer 6:26).

This motif of the first-born is constitutive for the understanding of John 1:14. From the text as such we learn that Jesus is the recipient of God's special love and care. John uses the word five times in all: 1:14,18; 3:18,17.

As can be seen from the diagram of the structure, there is a certain progression in the use of the various titles, leading to an *inclusio*: From A to A the argumentation is as follows: λόγος ... σάρξ ... μονογενής ... ἀμνός ... ἀμνός ... υἱὸς τοῦ θεοῦ ... υἱὸς τοῦ ἀνθρώπου. In this way John testifies clearly to the *doksa* of Jesus as the μονογενής, the ἀμνός of God because he is *the Son of God*. Consequently *the term amnos* cannot be a sign of sacrifice and suffering. It is in fact a royal title like the Son of Man (Ridderbos 1975:32).

Returning to the question why John uses the term *amnos* to express this meaning, the answer is not that the word itself, in isolation has the linguistic meanings of tenderness, love, sonship and divine glory. It is given this meaning by the author in the structure and composition of his discourse. Although the word is not semantically 'empty' or purely a formal sign it is used by the author in such a way as suits his purpose because to some extent the semantic field of the word lends itself to appropriation in this way. This is important. The word *amnos* does not mean Son (or Son of the Father), it expresses this meaning in this context. The OT and other historical material are not the evidence to prove the use in John but the other way round. This historical background is not read into the text but out of the text. In this way it explains and illuminates historical parameters but it does not originate in any particular historical situation. It is because of these methodological considerations that we can no longer with ease accept either a paschal or any other connotation as apparently the concept the author had in mind when he wrote his discourse. The constraints in his text are sufficient to understand what he is driving at.

To summarize: the *amnos* in John 1:29,36 is a christological title of the Son of God. In its context there can be little doubt that the author gives these titles an *ontological dimension* (cf Neyrey 1982:595). The very fact that the *amnos* motif is included and enclosed within the boundaries of the titles son of God and son of Man (see the *inclusio* A-A in the diagram) is "an indication that Jesus' royal authority over Israel should be interpreted against the background of the unique relationship between Jesus the Son and God the Father. This is borne out by the fact that later on Jesus' knowledge of men is shown to have its roots in his special relationship with the Father. Here we may point again to 10:3,4,14,15,25-28 where the royal shepherd... is said to be known to the Father and to perform deeds in the name of the Father and in unity with the Father'' (De Jonge 1973:169).

The prominence in John of the transcendent Jesus need not deter us for fear of a "naive docetism" as Käsemann (1968:26) put it. The word 'docetism' itself is suspect. It is an old ecclesiastical relic from the heyday of gnostic controversies. Even though 1 John 4:23 and 2 John 7 seem to be ill at ease with some form of heterodoxy akin to what was later called 'docetism', the Gospel has its own proof of the humanity of Jesus (cf John 1:14; 1 John 4:2 and others). It falls beyond the purpose of this paper to pursue the discussion of these aspects any further.

Having indicated that John's use of *amnos* involved an *ontological* level of meaning the question still remains what the *functional* level of meaning is. It has already been pointed out that ὁ αἴρων (v29) and ὁ βαπτίζων (v 33) are to be read as qualifying attributes of the *amnos*. In this function (or functions) the concept receives its full validity. As I have discussed this aspect at length in my earlier paper (1978:131-137) a brief summary of results will suffice to bring the discussion to that point where briefly the community or readers of the Gospel should be considered. Only when that point is reached is justice done to the text's relevance and communication.

In John 1:14 the *amnos* is the one "who takes away the sin of the world". It is necessary at this stage to restate that there is no sacrificial background to the function αἴρων τὴν ἁμαρτίαν τοῦ κόσμου.

It corresponds closely to the βαπτίζων ἐν πνεύματι ἁγίῳ. (B-B in the diagram). To start with the latter expression, we know of no baptismal practice by Jesus. Jesus is not a Baptist (in the NT sense of the word): He is one who heals, performs miracles, proclaims the Gospel, and does works of all kind, not the least of which is to forgive sins. If therefore *amnos* is a christological title then ὁ βαπτίζων is a *soteriological* predicate. In other words, the baptism of Jesus is of a completely different type than baptism with water. His is the true (not symbolic) *purification from sin.* When one asks in what way he purifies people from sin the answer lies in his recreating activity. The Nicodemus conversation bears witness to this: "For God loved the world so much that he gave his only son, so that everyone who believes in him may not die but have eternal life. For God did not send his son into the world to be its judge, but to be its saviour''

(John 3:16-17). New life (cf John 3:5-6) means salvation and a life of faith in Jesus. Towards this end the miracles of Jesus serve their purpose (John 2:11). We may regard the 'purification of the temple' in the same light (John 2:13-21). (Compare αἴρων in 1:29 with ἄρατε ταῦτα 2:16.) In almost all the instances the aspect of faith is present, cf 2:23, 4:46-54; 5:1-18; 6:29,30,40,47; 9:38; 11:42.

These basic motifs of faith and new life are also present in the discourse material of the Gospel, cf John 5:19-47: "Indeed, just as the Father raises the dead and grants life, so also the Son grants life to those to whom he wishes (v 21)" (cf John 3:8). Other passages of this nature are John 6:22-59 (6:40); 7:29,37; 8:12; 10:11; 15:11. It is not possible (or necessary) to be exhaustive. From the above passages it is clear that the αἴρων τὴν ἁμαρτίαν of the Lamb of God is to be understood as a βαπτίζων ἐν πνεύματι ἁγίῳ in the forgiving of sin, the healing of people and the creation of a new life of faith.

It may be argued that quoting these passages goes beyond the limits of the context of the first chapter. This is true, but not entirely valid. In terms of the structure of John 1:29-34 (A B B A) the 'taking away of sins' corresponds to the 'baptism with the Holy Spirit' (1:29/1:33). This provides the link to consider the functional dimension of the Lamb in the context of the Gospel as macrostructure. Careful consideration shows that the *amnos predicate of Jesus is the only one of the Messianic titles of chapter one to which such a clear functional dimension is added.* It clearly indicates that 'baptism with the Spirit' is to be read in contrast to John the Baptist's 'baptism with water' (1:26; 1:29). There can be little doubt that a primary reader of the text understood this contrast. The idea is a wellknown OT one: "I will sprinkle *water* upon you, and you will be clean from all your impurities... A new heart will I give you and a *new spirit* will I put within you (Ezk 36:25-26 cf Brown 1982:51. Cf also Zch. 13:1-3 and 1 QS 4:20-21.). Equally clear is that that which is common to both forms of baptism is the concept of *purifying.*

The Baptist's literal immersion in water is symbolic of cleansing of impurity. The Lamb's purifying act is to take away sin, not symbolically but in reality. He does so by the baptism, or purifying act, of the Holy Spirit.

Thus, far from going beyond the limits of the context it is the text itself that suggests and signifies how it is to be understood. What follows in the Gospel beyond chapter one is a narration of the words and deeds of Jesus in which he does just this: to purify by creating new life in the Spirit. As an *inclusio* John 20:20-21 completes this circle of thought: "and when he had said this, he breathed on them, with the words: *Receive the Holy Spirit. If you forgive people's sins, they are forgiven*; if you do not forgive them they are not forgiven" (John 20:20-21).

On the other hand, if one doggedly accepts a Paschal reading of the *amnos* then one is compelled also accept at this point the concept of vicarious expiation. Given the setting of structure of the Gospel's first chapter, it is difficult to see how the imagery of the Paschal lamb could be associated with "the Lamb who takes away the sin of the world" (John 1:29). A lamb, in terms of imagery, does not sacrifice itself. He is the victim. Now, as for the Gospel of John, the passion narrative reveals just the opposite: Jesus is firmly in command from beginning to end. Even the so-called Paschal allusions in John offer no more than glimpses of lowliness, suffering and sacrifice, e.g. John 10:11, 19:26,36 and others. Käsemann's description of the passion of Jesus in the Fourth Gospel resembling "a triumphal procession" (Käsemann 1968:18) is not far wide of the mark.

How is it possible then that distinguished scholars are prepared to accept Paschal associations for the *amnos* in John on little more strength than the word itself, and their own reconstructed historical background? Reading their comments one senses their apprehension of their stand. Schnackenburg e.g. writes: "As regards the expiatory character of the Passover sacrifice, it is true that the annual killing of the Paschal lambs in Jerusalem was not considered an expiatory sacrifice; it seems, however, that this quality was attributed to the Passover of the exodus to that of the last days. But the question is not very important for the Christian interpretation" (1984:300). Strange words indeed for a matter as important as John's witness to Jesus and the meaning of his death.

Brown finds himself in a similar predicament but resolves the matter as follows: "One objection brought against interpreting the Lamb of God as the paschal lamb is that in Jewish thought the paschal lamb was not a sacrifice. This is true, although by Jesus' time the sacrificial aspect has begun to infiltrate the concept of the paschal lamb because the priests had arrogated to themselves the slaying of the lambs. In any case, the difference between the lambs' blood smeared on the doorpost as a sign of deliverance and the lambs' blood offered in sacrifice for deliverance is not very great" (1982:62). It seems that both these scholars offer historical considerations, which they construct extra-textually, to confirm their point of view. In any case these considerations represent a secondary reading and not a primary reading of the text. As such it is not necessarily invalid, but it is not original. All these sacrifical notions are alien to the structure, text and context of the words as spoken by the Baptist.

Summarizing the arguments, in conclusion, we are at least compelled to take seriously the possibility that the Lamb of God in the Fourth Gospel refers to the Son of God, his only begotten Son who takes away the sins of the world by and in the Holy Spirit. As God's Son, He is

God's ἀγαπητός (cf Matthew 3:17). Within this framework we look in vain for all manner of expiatory motifs in which Jesus' *doksa* is surrendered to a *via dolorosa* as in the Synoptics. It is more evident that the *doksa* of the Son of God is constitutive of the christological motifs in the Fourth Gospel. However, this does not mean that there are no expiatory and passion motifs in John. In John 2:21 the temple Jesus was speaking of was his own body and certainly a reference to his suffering and death. There are other passages in similar vein e.g. John 3:14; 10:11; 10:16; 10:18; 12:12,19,20-36; 13:31-35 to mention but a few. These passages are not 'Paschal allusions' but can only be understood in the specific perspective of the Fourth Gospel, which is the incarnate glory of the Son. It is not a question of priority, but of focus and integration. The suffering and dying of Jesus is integrated in John with the glory of the Son. For John, as Käsemann says, the cross is "Jesus' victory over the world" (Käsemann 1968:51). The author's own concluding words to his Gospel are indeed a fitting conclusion to what he started out to say in chapter one. Thus the macrostructure of the Gospel brings the ends together: "In his disciples' presence Jesus performed many other miracles. But these have been written in order that you may believe that Jesus is the Messiah, the Son of God, and through your faith in him you may live" (John 20:30-31).

It remains to survey briefly an aspect of the Fourth Gospel which may throw light on conclusions drawn in this paper. The questions of author, origin and addressees are not without relevance. It must be realized, however, that investigating such questions are by nature historical-critical and much of what we conclude are no more than historical construction. Despite this limitation it is nevertheless worthwhile to undertake such work. Some of the questions are e.g. whether the Gospel was written *to* a particular community (or communities) or a particular community. If author and reader is so closely related as to be almost identical then the question of reader response has to be viewed from a different angle. Within the scope of this paper it is possible only to give attention to this aspect and some related questions where necessary.

The main issue is the old one of the so-called Johannine community and the first recipients of the Gospel. To some extent this determines the character of the Gospel and in particular its christology. If the attempts of J. L. Martyn and R. E. Brown to reconstruct from the Gospel the historical situation of the Evangelist in relation to the conflict between the Jewish synagogue and his church at the end of the first century prove to be probable "it seems much easier to explain the reason why the Evangelist emphasized *seine Gottheit* (of Jesus) in the light of this historical and theological crush-and-split between Judaism and Christianity'' (N. Matsunaga 1981:124). Scholarship during the last decade or so has made a plausible case for the existence of a community from which the Fourth Gospel emanated. If we consider that the *pesher* on Habakkuk is unthinkable without the Qumran community it is not far-fetched to entertain the idea that there must have been such a Johannine community. Unfortunately we have no specific and direct information about the formation of this community. We are obliged to rely on deductions (cf Meaks 1972:69). Deductions are not guesswork, but it still remains a matter of weighing of probabilities. The existence of early Christian communities is well attested in the New Testament. In Acts 24:5 Jesus is called leader of a 'party' of the Nazarenes, while the Christians in Acts 9:2 are referred to as ''followers of the Way of the Lord''.

One prominent suggestion is that the development of a Christian community in Palestine with a Johannine type of christology is not improbable. This community would, so it is held, have regarded itself as alienated from the spiritual traditions of Jerusalem. Evidence seems to point to *Samaria* or *Samaria-Galilee* as the locale in which this community was centered. ''It makes little sense, therefore, to suggest that the Gospel of John was a missionizing tract designed to win Samaritan converts to unite Samaritans and Jews in Christ. The aims of the Gospel were essentially self-serving to the community which produced it, to re-inforce belief in Jesus as the Christ through whom one might have life (xx 31)'' (Purvis 1975:191; cf also Meeks 1972:70 & Hawkin 1980:98).

The object of such a community would obviously be to defend its faith in Jesus as the Christ. Without debating the point it does seem improbable that the Fourth Gospel is a missionary tract. It is rather more a document in which a community's faith is expressed. The Gospel creates the impression of a book which was written *from* and *for* some community. Whether the locality is to be sought in Samaria-Galilee is another matter. Although it is still very much an enigma there are scholars who favour Samaria (cf Matsunaga 1981:144 n. 22). If this view is correct the Gospel is directed at Jews not gentiles.

It is without doubt the most Jewish Gospel among the four. What relevance this has on the matter under discussion is not difficult to understand. For Jews and Jewish Christians the very idea of calling Jesus *theos* (or even implying something like this) would be a sensitive matter, because of their firmly-rooted monotheism. On balance of statements it seems obvious that the identification of Jesus with God is a unique feature of the Fourth Gospel. It has become custom to call this John's ''high Christology'' (Neyrey 1982:599). From John's point of view this was the major cause for Jesus' rejection by the Jews and his crucifixion (John 10:36; 19:7; cf the ἐγώ εἰμι formula in 8:24,28; 13:19 and others). It was also the cause for the final division between Judaism and Christianity. Obviously it was also the cause of a rift in the Christian community itself. In John 6:35-40 Jesus witnesses to his divinity. The formulation and context suggest an ontological level of meaning and not merely a functional one. In consequence "many of his followers... said, 'This teaching is too hard. Who can listen to it?' (v 60). Because of this, many of Jesus' followers turned back and would not go with him any more (6:66)''. The Jews, of course, faced expulsion from the synagogue if they accepted and believed in Jesus and his claims to divinity. The community did not cease to exist on account of these 'drop-outs' (Matsunaga), but could have developed and formulated its christology with and in words of Jesus which we now know as the Fourth Gospel.

At this point a word of caution is called for. What has been said is all very speculative and debateable. The origin of John's Gospel and the so-called Johannine community goes back a long way (cf Baldensberger 1898). Modern-day scholars who distinguish themselves as exponents of this stand are O. Cullmann, R. E. Brown (The Community of the Beloved Disciple, 1979) and others. J. L. Martyn distinguishes three stages in the history of the Johannine Community (1979) while Richter and Brown are able to identify four such stages (cf McPolin 1980:16ff). Despite Brown's careful 'detective work' in this regard his results are not convincing. What he presents is a highly ingenious historical construction, but like all historical constructions it is limited by its very nature. The matter as such does not concern us here. The question is whether or not the existence of any sort of Johannine community is suspect. Most scholars would agree that some form of community did exist but that its origin and boundaries are no longer to be reconstructed.

Returning to our theme, what bearing has this on the connotation of the Lamb of God in the context of the Fourth Gospel? We have seen that the title is a Messianic one and a *terminus gloriae*. Like the other titles it expresses, from a different angle, the Divine Sonship of Jesus. As such it is closely linked to the μονογενής concept in John 1:14. Given these analyses of the Gospel text viz that the historical background of a community in which a transcendant christology was prevalent, leading to the conclusion that John's *amnos* concept is of a sacrificial nature (of whatever kind) this has not been proved beyond doubt. If then a transcendant christology was the focus of a community linked in some way to the author and community of the Fourth Gospel then there is all the more validity for accepting *amnos* as referring to the Sonship of Jesus in an ontological sense.

BIBLIOGRAPHY

BARRETT, C. K. 1954/55. The Lamb of God. *NTS* 1:210ff.

BROWN, R. E. 1982. The Gospel according to John, in *The Anchor Bible*, vol. 1. London: MacMillan.

BURROWS, E. W. 1973. Did John the Baptist call Jesus "The Lamb of God"? *ET* 85, 245-249.

COMBRINK, H. J. B. 1984. Multiple meaning and/or multiple interpretation of a text. *Neotestamentica* 18.

CULLMANN, O. 1966. *Die Christologie des Neuen Testaments*. 4. ed. Tübingen.

DE JONGE, M. 1973. Jesus as Prophet and King in the Fourth Gospel. *ETL* 49, 161-177.

DE KRUIJF, T. C. 1970. The glory of the only Son (John 1:14), in *Studies in John, presented to J. N. Sevenster*. Leiden, 111-124.

DU PLESSIS, P. J. 1978. Zie het lam Gods. Overwegingen bij de Knechtsgestalte in het Evangelie van Johannes, in *Studies door collegas en oud-leerlingen aangeboden aan Prof. Dr. H. N. Ridderbos*. Kampen, 120ff.

HAWKIN, D. J. 1980. The Johannine transposition and Johannine theology. *Laval Theologique et Philosophique* 36, 88-98.

KÄSEMANN, E. 1968. *The Testament of Jesus. A study of the Gospel of John in the light of chapter 17*. London.

MATSUNAGA, K. 1975/76. The Galileans in the Fourth Gospel. *Annual of the Japanese Biblical Institute* 1-2, 139-158.

MCPOLIN, J. 1980. Studies in the Fourth Gospel. Some contemporary trends. *Irish Biblical Studies* 2, 4-26.

MEALAND, D. L. 1978. The christology of the Fourth Gospel. *SJT* 31, 449-467.

MEEKS, W. A. 1976. The Divine Agent and his counterfeit in Philo and the Fourth Gospel, in E. S. Fiorenza (ed), *Aspects of religious propaganda in Judaism and early Christianity*. London: Notre Dame, 43-67.

NEGOITSA, A. & C. DANIEL 1971. L'Agneau de Dieu est la Verbe de Dieu. *NT* 13, 24-36.

NEYREY, J. H. 1982. The Jacob allusions in John 1:51. *CBQ* 44.

PETERSEN, N. R. 1984. The reader in the Gospel. *Neotestamentica* 18.

PFITZNER, V. C. 1977. The coronation of the King - the passion in the Gospel of John. *Currents in Theology and Missions* 4, 10-21.

PURVIS, J. D. 1975. The Fourth Gospel and the Samaritans, *NT* 17, 161-198.

RIDDERBOS, H. N. 1966. The structure and scope of the prologue to the Gospel of John. *NT* 8, 180ff.

RIDDERBOS, H.N. 1972. Jezus en de apocalyptiek, in *Ad interim. Opstellen over eschatologie, apocalyptiek en ethiek aangeboden aan Prof. Dr. R. Schippers*. Kampen, 23-42.

ROBERTS, J. H. 1968. The Lamb of God. *Neotestamentica* 2, 41-52.

SCHNACKENBURG, R. 1984. *The Gospel according to St. John*, vol. 1. Burns and Oates.

VORSTER, W. S. 1984. The historical paradigm. It's possibilities and limitations. *Neotestamentica* 18.

J. A. DU RAND

PLOT AND POINT OF VIEW IN THE GOSPEL OF JOHN

It is a special privilege to be able to participate in these essays in honour of B. M. Metzger. His academic work and fascinating personality have always been an example and an inspiration to me.

The always recurring question, which captivates every exegete, is how a New Testament document such as the Gospel of John can still be made to speak after so many centuries so that people can be brought to action. Through the course of the centuries many have wrestled in the blast furnace of exegetical methodology in order to pour out instruments to enable them to exploit better the message of the New Testament. We could thus speak of an incomplete methodology with regard to New Testament interpretation of the Scriptures. Every academic age furnishes its own rewriting of the methodology which naturally can encompass moments of great gain, but there is also the possibility of all types of uncertainties. Therefore in 1980 F. F. Bruce said the following somewhat sceptically about Gospel research: "In the opinion of some students of the New Testament Gospel criticism has reached an impasse. Source criticism, form criticism, tradition criticism and redaction criticism have all been pursued as far as they are likely to take us, and the situation in which we now find ourselves is not encouraging" (1980:19).

The present article is part of that ongoing dialogue on exegetical method. Here I make use above all of the present results of general literary science with the eye on Gospel research. I have found very stimulating, among others, Alan Culpepper's work, *Anatomy of the Fourth Gospel* (1983).

1. *A shifting in paradigm*

Speaking methodologically, the Gospels were previously exploited in a onesided manner, much like an archaeological source. Layer by layer was removed of the different historical ages. In this way attention was given to the history of the existence of the writing, but not sufficient attention was given to the text as such, and as a whole. One has not sufficiently considered the effect of the text on the reader as well as the means by which the text itself is realised as an exegetical object of study.

According to Murray Krieger's figurative language (cf Culpepper 1983:3) the text of the Gospel of John is used, e.g. like a window. Through the window the exegete can touch and describe the history of the Johannine community. This means that the meaning of the text is situated on the other side of the window. Consequently, the reader must search for the meaning of the text in its history. The construction of parallels and agreements has led to ingenious analogies between the first century and the twentieth century, contexts which attempt to preserve the message of the Gospel of John in a living and applicable way (Culpepper 1983:4). This resulted in the fact that only the subject specialist was in a position to be able to read the Gospel because he is then equipped to reconstruct the contemporary parallels.

Although redaction criticism asked for attention to be given to the Gospel as a unity, the accent still fell in a one-sided way on the evangelist and not on the text as such. According to redaction criticism the evangelists were theologians and interpreters whose theology and goal can be determined through the study of the changes that they made to their sources. In such a way we have obtained an almost unbridgeable gulf between the original context of the biblical text and that of today. The view that we cannot understand a text unless we understand first the original author's intention, has in fact created more hermeneutical problems than it in fact solved. Yet, we must still take earnestly the fact of the author as the first sender of the message.

The shift from the more historical exegetical methods of investigation to the literary analysis of the text itself has shown that the meaning of the narrative text, such as the Gospels, does not just lie in the intention of the original author, but in the text itself. N. R. Petersen expresses it in this way: "...it is necessary to recover an appreciation of the text because it has become obscured by our greater appreciation of its context. Reader response criticism can help us to restore a critical balance because its frame of reference is based on the distinction between texts and contexts" (1984:4). We can whole-heartedly agree with this. In the context of the early church the meaning of the stories about Jesus were actualised every time by the process of reading and re-reading. Text and context may not be separated from each other.

We realise even more that meaning lies on this side of the text as the so-called window. This still does not mean that the text must be presented simply like a mirror to use Krieger's image (cf Culpepper 1983:4). Then, the meaning of the text would only be handed over to the projection of the reader. This would envelop the understanding process in a totally subjective atmosphere. In one or other ways controls must be established (cf Vorster 1984:8).

If the reading of the text can be presented as a communication process, we find that in the text speech acts take place. Thus, the accent falls on what must be done to the text and what language does (cf Van Rensburg & Van Coller 1982:218ff). Such a discussion between text and reader can be conducted in a meaningful and controlled way if certain speech maxims are met. The co-operative principle, where speaker and hearer work together in the discussion, leads among other things to the success of the discussion. The Gospel story can only be understood and its reader brought to action when the reader collaborates. A collaborating reader can be seen in such a way as a possible implied reader, that is to say the implied reader which the author had in mind when he began to write.

In a manner of speaking a person could say that the text as a window is coloured and painted. Light shines through from the other side, but the scenes and figures on this side are literarily (that is to say from the text) visible. This means that the Gospel story, as a literary text, must be lived by its reader (cf Van Rensburg & Van Coller 1982:215). Although extra-textual data concerns the reader, it is important to take account of the starting-point of faith as well as the Holy Spirit as part of the interpreting reader's hermeneutical framework.

To determine the point of view and plot, for example of the Gospel of John, means that we must analyse carefully the linguistic and cultural codes which themselves appear in the Gospel story. The author created a narrated world. The narrator, that is, the voice which tells the story to us, tries his best to involve us in the story. The narrator sketches the events and persons in certain relationships. By means of his commentary he foresees us in order to convince us to understand the story in the way in which he sees it. In such a way the narrator succeeds in creating in the reader the feeling of distance or of trust, which again leads to identification and engagement. We must keep clearly in mind that the narrated world of the Gospel story is not the same as that of Jesus or of the evangelist himself, but a literary world which is created by the author. Scholes and Kellogg explain this as follows: "Meaning in the work of narrative art is a function of the relationship between two worlds: the functional world, created by the author, and the 'real' world, the apprehendable universe. When we say we understand a narrative, we mean that we have found a satisfactory relationship or set of relationships between these two worlds" (1966:82, cf 84).

Within such a literary context the author succeeds in telling the story about Jesus in such a way that the reader is led to reveal different reactions: the reader can for example agree or differ, have sympathy or antipathy, be amazed or disappointed. From the faith-apriori, namely that the Bible is the inspired Word of God under the guidance of the Holy

Spirit, the reader is led from the text itself to perceive the sequence of events from a specific point of view. He receives information which the characters themselves do not share. The reader's vision is thus coloured. Outside the psychological observations and viewing of the narrated characters, the reader also has a special view giving insight to the role which space and time play in the Jesus-narrative according to the Gospel description. To read and to hear the Gospel story from all these interpretations from a specific point of view helps and compells the reader to understand Jesus anew and to come to a new orientation from the perspective of faith.

Historical research must always still provide necessary information in order to be able to read the Gospel story thoroughly. It cannot be simply described as complete interpretation. According to Petersen we must not simply throw away the historical and philological methods, but must "rethink and redesign so that it can deal with the neglected areas and complete what it was designed to do" (1984b:3).

The reader must be helped exegetically to grasp the signals which the text sends out, to rework them and to understand the point of view and the plot of the work. We must learn anew how to read a text. Through the Holy Spirit the Gospel story subjectively mediates to all the readers the redemptive work which objectively takes place in Jesus Christ's historical death and resurrection.

2. *The Gospel according to John as narrative*

Let us specify ourselves in the following by referring to the Gospel of John. It is an important and also a valid starting-point of literary criticism to examine the total structure of a writing such as the Gospel of John. No unanimity exists concerning the measures which must be used in order to determine and to describe the total position of the Gospel of John. Recently, M. Rissi emphasised the problem as follows: "Das Buch (=Johannesevangelium) als ganzes macht durchaus einen geschlossenen Eindruck und scheint einen sinnvollen Plan zu folgen. Und doch ist die Suche nach den leitenden Gesichtspunkten der Gesamtstruktur noch nicht zur Ende" (1983:55).

It is therefore important to place the structure of the Gospel of John in a wider framework and then to attempt to describe the Gospel story within a model of communication. It is not possible to see the Gospel of John constructed before you as a totality, as in the case of a piece of sculpture or a painting. The understanding of the whole from its parts and the parts from the whole has to do with the understanding of the artist's strategy of sequence (cf Du Rand 1982:18f). The author creates his own narrative scheme and therefore the Gospel of John must be read as a narrative rather than as just the final precipitation of a redactor. Actually, the evangelist's redactional work lies very close to his method of constructing the narrative (cf Tannehill 1980:58). The Gospel of John must be listened to as an authoritative witnessing narrative because it answers all the demands of a typical story. We find a message which is told and a narrative which hands it over to readers: "By definition, narrative art requires a story and a story teller. In the relation between the teller and the audience lies the essence of narrative art (Scholes 1966:240; cf Tannehill 1980:60). The narrative literary approach is not yet the only or final phase in the process of exegetical methodology, but only an earnest attempt to understand better the essence of the Scripture message according to the Gospel of John.

The narrator of the Jesus-story according to the Gospel of John observes the historical Jesus and witnesses to Him through the window of the gospel genre. As an ancient author the author did not arrange techniques such as chapter and paragraph divisions and therefore had to structure things in a different way (cf Perrin 1972:15). This is done in the text itself, namely through the composition of narrative, or the course and building up of the story. The narrative scheme of John also reflects, then, a logical unity in the sequence of events which also clearly come to the fore in the formal structure. The narrative course of the text is not yet the same as the story itself. It is further important to pay attention to the fact that, when we typify the Gospel of John as a narrative text, we must not just take earnestly the text itself, but also the cultural context in which it appears (cf Chatman 1978:24f). In the text as well as in the context we find the means by which the message is communicated. In the text, for example, the question about the 'how' of the narration is answered by means of all sorts of techniques, while the question about the 'what', that is its context, is determined by the unfolding of the plot in the story itself. Without enlarging upon it, among the textual techniques which indicate the 'how' of the Johannine narrative, the following can be indicated: chiasm (cf Jn 18:28-19:16), irony (cf 4:12; 7:35; 8:22), misunderstanding (cf Jn 7:4), the so-called double meaning (cf ἄνωθεν in Jn 3:3) and inclusion (cf 2:11; 4:46,54), to name but a few examples. A further characteristic technique of the Gospel of John is to join the narrative and discourse material by means of dialogue. This means, however, not that the Gospel of John is just a patchwork of narrative and discourse material from the Johannine traditions and thought complexes. The material is rather ingeniously integrated through his narration and his commentary on it. His narrative is, however, not as in the normal narrative so obvious as in a newspaper. It is a composed narrative with a certain plot in which different characters and roles are sketched. The author-narrator, John, tells his story of Jesus in a certain way from a specific point of view or perspective.

Without explaining it fully, I shall make use of the theoretical communication model of Culpepper with a few of my own adaptations. The model is chiefly borrowed from Seymour Chatman (1978:267) and Roman Jakobson (Culpepper 1983:6; cf Du Rand 1984:50f).

3. *Point of view in the Gospel of John*

The 'point of view' refers to the ways in which a narrator presents or structures his story. It is in other words the perspective or perspectives which the narrator creates and by means of which he presents for his reader the narrated characters and chronological and topographical details in the story (cf Scholes & Kellogg 1966:240f; Van Aarde 1982:34-37). The concept 'point of view' contains two components, namely the technical (angle of vision) from which the narrator observes the narrated world, and the ideological from which he evaluates the narrated world. Van Aarde defines it in this way: "Strictly spoken, the term point of view is ambivalent and comprises two components of referential meaning: the indicated technical perspective which corresponds with the emotive function in Jakobson's model (cf Petersen 1978:35) and the ideological perspective from which the narrator/implied author observes the story-stuff of the narrative world and evaluates (selects and combines) it with the result that the narrated world is arranged in a plot as an orchestration to the ideal/implied reader. The narrative point of view on the ideological plane corresponds on the one hand with Jakobson's 'poetic function' and on the other hand with his 'conative function'" (1984:2). Consequently, this causes the fact that the narrator's ideological perspective can be seen from his technical perspective (cf Lanser 1981:17).

The narrative is constructed from the interrelation among the perspectives of the author, the narrator, the implied reader and that out of which the characters are narrated. The author-narrator John tells his Jesus-story in a certain way from a certain angle or perspective and this narrative must be read against the background of the different perspectives such as, e.g. that perspective between the narrator and the implied reader, that perspective between the narrator and the different perspectives from which the characters are narrated, as well as that perspective of the different characters among themselves (cf Scholes 1966:207-39). The author observes the Jesus-events and sketches them not just literally, insensitively as a type of report, but offers a lively, interpreted narrative. The plan of the events or actions, i.e. the so-called plot of its narrative

determines, then, the arrangement of the material with an eye to unfolding the narrative (cf Vorster 1980:126).

Before we go further in trying to understand the place and function of
the point of view and plot in the Johannine narrative, one must
distinguish clearly among the real author, the implied author and the
narrator. It is also important to pay attention to the fact that the real
author and the real reader are extra-textual entities and must be taken
into account in the historical context of a written piece of literature. The
real author writes and makes certain decisions in his presentation of the
narrative. He constructs the story and so presents it through the narrator
that the narrative projects a certain image of the author which does not
necessarily agree with the identity of the real author (cf Culpepper
1983:6). In such a way we have to deal with the implied author. The latter is the literary artist who creatively determines the narrative, but who
is also determined by the narrative. Culpepper describes him in this way:
"The implied author is the sum of the choices made by the real author in
writing the narrative, but the implied author is neither the real author
(who wrote) nor the narrator (who tells)" (1983:16). The implied author
chooses consciously or unconsciously what we read. He is the literary
creation of the text itself, but must be very carefully distinguished from
the narrator who is the voice who tells the narrative. The narrator is the
rhetorical creation in the narrative who tells the story and introduces the
reader into the world of the narrative. The Johannine narrator is 'un-
dramatised, intrusive and omnicommunicative' (Culpepper 1983:21).
According to the Johannine narrative he narrated in the third person as
someone who adopts a position outside the events although one also has
in 1:14 and 16 and 21:24 the narrative 'we'. It is very difficult to say
precisely what is the relationship between the real author and the implied
author in the Gospel of John, but there is no difference between the point
of view of the narrator and that of the implied author as the text projects
him (Culpepper 1983:7). The implied author and the implied reader as
well as the narrator and the reader are literary functions within the text
itself.

The Johannine narrator is not unreliable. He does not keep information back purposely from the reader. The informative prologue bears
witness to this. It is an introduction of the protagonist, Jesus, who determines the further course of the narrative (cf 1:1-18). From the beginning
the narrator shares his omniscient perspective with the reader (cf Culpepper 1983:19). Consequently, the reader can follow the further course of
the narrative. The narrator gives explanations and information in the
prologue. He translates words and informs the reader about what
characters know or do not know. He helps and leads the reader to under-

stand the text (cf Petersen 1980:156; Booth 1961:273f). The Johannine
story of Jesus is itself composed of the mutual relationships of characters
and events to one another. As the conflict of powers unfolds among
characters and events the reader is involved in the narrative. The mean-
ingfulness of the plot of the Gospel of John also lies exactly in the fact that
it rests on events before and after Jesus' earthly ministry. His pre-
existence creates, e.g., an intensity which is of decisive hermeneutical importance in the rest of the narrative. The sequence and intention in which
events are narrated as well as the participation of the characters in them,
has an effect on the reader. In the Gospel narrative according to John the
reader is above all captivated by the sympathy or antipathy aroused by
the characters or as the characters are narrated. The readers' reaction is
also spurred and determined by the narrator's direct or indirect commentary as interpretation. We must above all pay attention to the implicit or
indirect commentary, i.e. irony or symbolism, because that is the way in
which the implied author communicates strategically and tactfully with
the implied reader. The implied reader is the reader whom the author
had in mind. "The implied reader is defined by the text as the one who
performs all the mental moves required to enter into the narrative world
and respond to it as the implied author intends" (Culpepper 1983:7).
The remarks, and explanations and elucidations of the narrator must be
examined to obtain the point of view (cf Tenney 1960:350-64, as well as
A'Rourke 1979:210-19).

The point of view manifests itself on several levels. Uspensky
distinguishes among all the following levels: phraseological (speech patterns), spatial (location of the narrative), temporal (the time of the narrative),psychological (internal and external to the characters) and
ideological (evaluation norms) (1973:6).

For the purpose of this article attention is above all focused on the
ideological point of view. The dominant perspective from which the
Johannine Gospel narrative is structured is his picture of Jesus. The narrator's point of view coincides with that of the protagonist Jesus as He is
presented by the narrator. I shall now briefly refer to the psychological,
spatial and temporal point of view and to a large extent I shall be making
use of Culpepper (cf 1983:21-34).

a. *Psychological point of view*
The narrator of the Gospel of John has an omniscient psychological
perspective. Culpepper presents it thus: "A narrator's psychological
point of view is determined by whether or not he or she is able to provide
inside-views of what a character is thinking, feeling or intending"
(Culpepper 1983:21). Thus, the narrator gives inside information which

cannot simply be observed by the recipient. He knows for example of the main character, Jesus' pre-existence as the Word (*Logos*) and he also knows what is going to happen before it does take place. The reader also receives the information from the narrator that Jesus Himself knew everything (cf 2:24). He interprets for us Jesus' thoughts and even His emotions (cf 11:33,38; 13:1,21; 16:19; 18:4; 19:28). It is clear that the narrator goes to work retrospectively, especially in what concerns the disciples as examples (cf 2:22; 12:16; 13:28,29; 20:9).

For the sake of the progression of the narrative the narrator has provided inside information about the characters, especially Judas (cf 12:4,6; 18:2). Yet, he has not laid bare completely the deeper psychological motivations of the characters.

b. *Spatial point of view*
The narrator has an omnipresent perspective. Confer, for example, chapter 4 when the narrator is present when Jesus and the woman are at the well; at the same time he is also present in the Samaritan town when the woman comes to tell them about Jesus (4:28-29). He is again present when Jesus and the disciples hold a discussion at the well (4:31f). Another example illustrates his omnipresence. The narrator is presumed to be present when Peter denies Jesus before the servantgirl (18:25-27), while he is at the same time also present when Pilate questions Jesus (18:28-31). The impression that one gains following the Gospel of John is that the narrator is part of a group or community which does not necessarily co-incide with the group of disciples, especially when he uses the expression 'we' (cf 1:14,16; 21:24-25). It appears from the use of ἐχεῖ (22 times), ἐχεῖθεν (twice) as well as ὅ-δε (5 times) that the narrator's spatial position in the Gospel does not contribute much, e.g. to determine the spatial position of the author.

The narrator is presupposed by the narrative to be everywhere omnipresent.

c. *Temporal point of view*
The narrator has a retrospective temporal point of view. This means that the narrator presents his narrative retrospectively by telling the reader what is going to happen before it happens and before the characters know it (cf Uspensky 1973:65).

The retrospective point of view of the narrator gives illuminating relief to the understanding of his ideological point of view. The most well known reference to the retrospective point of view of the narrative is 7:39: "As yet the Spirit had not been given, because Jesus was not yet glorified". The narrator interprets Jesus from a future perspective. The present observer of the Jesus narrative was not in a position to do this in such a way. What is above all striking are the references to the disciples, who at that stage did not understand, but will understand for the first time after Jesus' resurrection (cf 2:22; 12:16; 13:7; 20:9). The Jesus events are placed by the Johannine community in perspective after the resurrection of Jesus (Culpepper 1983:28; cf Van Aarde 1982:130f).

The narrator does not wish to present purely historical facts, but an interpreted story of Jesus. This helps the reader to make his own orientation with regard to Jesus. The retrospective point of view is well illustrated in 12:16: "His disciples did not understand this at first; but when Jesus was glorified, then they remembered that this had been written of Him and had been done to Him". A reporter who was actually present in time and space could not have given a commentary on the entry into Jerusalem as is given here. It is only possible from the retrospective point of view. It is further important to note that the narrator describes the Jesus-events from a post-resurrection point of view. Culpepper has described the retrospective view of the Johannine Gospel so clearly: "In this broad sense, the Johannine narrator, who presumably expresses the perspective of the author, tells the story from a point of view which in its retrospection is informed by memory, interpretation of Scripture, the coalescing of traditions with the post-Easter experience of the early church, consciousness of the presence of the Spirit, a reading of the glory of the risen Christ back into the days of His ministry, and an acute sensitivity to the history and struggles of the Johannine community" (1983:30; cf Wilder 1971:69f).

d. *Ideological point of view*

The narrator's point of view is in the literary sense reliable. He influences his readers and is not clinically impartial. This does not mean that the narrator of the Gospel of John wishes to be simply historically trustworthy, but he wishes rather to challenge his hearers to an orientation which affects their faith. In 20:31 the ideological purpose of the narrator is put into words: "But these (signs) are written that you may believe that Jesus is the Christ, the Son of God, and that believing you may have life in His name". Consequently, he has a faith-perspective. The impression that one gains is that the Gospel of John is directed to a group or community whose faith has to be strengthened (cf Du Rand 1982:16f; 1983:386f; 1984:54f).

The narrator also accompanies the reader with regard to the origin and destiny of the protagonist. His origin is that of the pre-existent Logos and his destiny is that of the glorified Son of God with the Father (cf Du Rand 1982:31f). He comes from the Father, and is on the road back to the

Father. It is from the ideological perspective that we must read and understand the Johannine Gospel. The narrator knows the main protagonist, Jesus, and he participates in what Jesus knows (cf 11:11; 6:6,71; 13:11; 18:32; 21:23). Jesus comes to continue the creation work of the *Logos* by making the blind see and raising the dead and giving life to the lifeless (cf Culpepper 1983:34).

From the ideological point of view the effect of John's Gospel narrative on his readers is death or life. What is decisive is the faith-acceptance of Jesus' origin and destiny as Son of God. This is the narrator's perspective according to which the readers must establish and rectify their perspective on Jesus. The disciples did not understand Jesus' words and deeds during His ministry, but they did indeed understand them later (cf 12:16; 13:17). The retrospective ideological point of view gives to the reader the necessary insight, e.g. to understand the Gospel of John. The two observation corners in the ideological point of view in the Gospel of John can be described as 'from above' (ἄνωθεν) and 'from below'. To think 'from below' involves total misunderstanding of the protagonist, Jesus. It is only those who think 'from above' who can grasp Jesus' identity. The narrator tries then to influence his readers from his 'from above' perspective.

4. *The plot of the Fourth Gospel*

The ideological 'from above' point of view of the narrator of the Gospel of John unfolds further in the plot of the Gospel narrative.

But what is the plot of the narrative? In the sequence of events in the Gospel of John it is not difficult to trace a certain plot; but to give a definition of the plot as such, is not so easy. Scholes and Kellogg speak of "an articulation of the skeleton of narrative, the dynamic, sequential element in narratives" (cf 1966:121,207 as quoted by Culpepper 1983:79). Culpepper (1983:80) also quotes the definition of E. M. Forster (1962:470): "A plot is also a narrative of events, the emphasis falling on causality 'The king died, and then the queen died' is a story. 'The king died and then the queen died of grief' is a plot. The time-sequence is preserved, but the sense of causality overshadows it". The definition of M. H. Abrams (1971:127) is elucidating: "The plot in a dramatic or narrative work is the structure of its actions, as these are ordered and rendered toward achieving particular emotional and artistic effects".

In the footsteps of Aristotle's *Poetica* (1450-1451) Crane divided plots into three categories, namely plots of action, plots of character and plots of thought (1966:239). It is still further expanded and refined, e.g. by N. Friedman (1967) and N. Frye (1957:33-34).

Through the plot of the narrative the reader is led to a purposeful and freely chosen reaction which can consist in satisfaction or discontentment, or sympathy or antipathy, or even faith, just to name a few examples. This does not mean, however, that one must view the Gospel of John simply as a piece of fiction in which the protagonist is the hero. Jesus is rather the revealer of the Father and not just the hero. The events which the Gospel of John narrate have meaning precisely because they are part of a story which is leading somewhere. The narrative has a starting-point and an end. The end, namely the death and resurrection of the protagonist Jesus, greatly determines the unfolding of the story. The unity of the course of the story is therefore important. The unity of the course of the narrative lies in the unfolding of the Johannine plot, exactly where Jesus as the Son of God accomplishes the mission of His Father.

The plot of the narrative manages and interprets events by placing them in a certain sequence and context. In such a manner the events become secondary because they are then simply the bearer of interpreted meaning. The message of the narrative gives meaning to the events, and the succession of events must play out the meaning. Each Gospel tells the same narrative, yet each differs from the other. One could ask what causes this difference. Several factors contribute to it, such as among others, the difference in plot, interpretations of the evangelists and also the circumstances of the implied readers (cf Du Rand 1984:54f). The interpretative reformulation of the traditional material leads to a distinctive plot in each of the Gospels. The interpretation of the Jesus-events and characterisation produces the distinctiveness of the Johannine plot according to his Gospel narrative.

Different literary characteristics contribute to the formation of the Johannine plot (cf Culpepper 1983:86f). The sequence of events differs for example from that of the other Gospels. Jesus' first public appearance is, for example, in the Temple. In the Synoptics Jesus ends His public appearance in the Temple. A further literary characteristic in the Gospel of John is that the events and discourses are coupled by dialogue in which so-called misunderstandings are an important tendency (cf 2:1-12; 4:19-20; 6:15,22-40). An important stylistic characteristic of the Gospel of John is the effect of repetition. We find for example themes such as life which is repeated, certain images, statements about Jesus' identity, conflict discussions with the Jewish authorities. If all these repetitions were to be analysed, we would find in the Gospel of John unifying lines which bind it to a central plot. The beginning and the end of the Jesus narrative according to John contributes largely to the unity of the Johannine plot.

The Gospel narrative according to John begins with an extended introduction on the protagonist Jesus around which the rest of the plot revolves. An understanding of the prologue presents, in my opinion, the basis for the understanding of the rest of John's Gospel (cf Hooker 1975:42f; Du Rand 1984:19f). In 1:14 we find the focus of the Johannine plot, namely the protagonist's coming into the world: "And the Word became flesh and dwelt among us, full of grace and truth, we have beheld His glory, glory as of the only Son from the Father". The protagonist Jesus is sent by the Father (1:18), who came to His own possession, and yet His own people did not accept Him. To those who did, however, accept Him, He gave them the right to become children of God (1:11-12). This outlines the focus and presents the starting point for the further framework of the Johannine plot.

The protagonist Jesus came to make His Father known (cf 17:6,26) by also taking away the sins of the world (cf 1:29). In the accomplishment of the task the Son of God has to deal with opposition in the form of the Jewish authorities and disbelief (cf 16:8-9). Belief consists, then, in the acceptance of the *Logos* as the Son of God. The making known of the Father as well as the truth culminates in Jesus' crucifixion. Therefore, Jesus' cross and resurrection are rightly His glorification which finally demonstrates His δόξα (cf Culpepper 1983:88).

The clearer Jesus' mission penetrated mankind, the greater became the hostility and opposition. The opposition which Jesus experienced served to illustrate the difference between those who believe and those who do not believe. The apparent victory of Jesus' opponents, namely when the protagonist must die, is actually the fulfilment of Jesus' mission from the Father.

The unfolding of the plot by means of the events obtains momentum through the proscription of the protagonist (11:57). This gives to the course of the narrative a sharper direction. The protagonist is on His way to His death. It is, however, a voluntary death (10:18) for the sake of His own (13:1).

Jesus' identity becomes all the clearer in proportion to the choice made for or against Him. In this regard the prologue offers an accompanying introduction to help the reader identify with the protagonist from the side of faith. It is, consequently, not difficult for the reader to agree at the end of the narrative that Jesus is the Christ, the Son of God (cf 20:30) in the light of the prologue that Jesus is the *Logos* of God. In the plot of the Gospel of John taken as a whole Jesus' mission from His Father is in the forefront. Parallel to the line of service of Jesus, namely His accomplishment of his mission, runs that mission of the disciples (cf Tannehill 1980:60f). The disciples were called already in chapter 1 (verses 35-51); in chapter 6 they were confronted with a choice (cf verses 60-71); in chapters 13 to 17 they were equipped with the assurance of the support of the Holy Spirit. In 17:18 this parallel is made explicit when Jesus prays to His Father: "As thou didst send me into the world, so I have sent them into the world". In 17:20 there is also express mention of those who will come to belief in Jesus through the disciples' words. The appearances in chapter 21 to the disciples brings to an end the one narrative line, namely Jesus' service as fulfilment of the mission by the Father but it serves precisely as the basis for the progress of the disciple's mission. The threefold re-affirmation of Peter in chapter 21 serves as a powerful acceleration for the disciple's further mission. Even Peter's concern for the disciple whom Jesus loved was received with the expression: "Follow me" (21:22). Chapter 21 exercises a function *par excellence* of giving a powerfull stimulus to the disciple's mission.

The identity of Jesus as the Son of God who was pre-existent with God and who was on the road to be glorified by His death and resurrection offers the central line around which the plot of John's Gospel is entangled. Jesus' origin and His destiny can only be understood from the ideological point of view. Only those who think 'from above' can understand it and can orientate themselves with regard to Jesus. Therefore the narrator of John's Gospel attempts to bring home the plot concerning Jesus' identity from this point of view.

5. *Development of plot in the Fourth Gospel*

The designation of identity and the decision with regard to the protagonist Jesus, runs throughout the Johannine plot. It concerns the faith which leads to life. It brings conflict between the protagonist and the opponents, but also solidarity between Jesus and His disciples. The plot of the Johannine Jesus narrative unfolds as follows:

Setting	1:1-51:	Christological inventory as making known the protagonist Jesus, the Son of God.
Complication	2:1-17:26:	Appearance of the protagonist through signs and discourse and the reaction of the helpers and opponents.
Resolution	18:1-21:25:	Christological end: climax events concerning the protagonist Jesus, the Son of God.

1. *Setting (1:1-51)*

In everything that Jesus would narrate, He is the bearer of glory; therefore the prologue serves as an introduction to explain the incarnation of the Divine *Logos*. The mission of the *Logos* is to make known the Father. The prologue would not have had so much meaning if the rest of the Gospel narration was missing. Whoever understands and accepts the *Logos* as protagonist finds life, but whoever does not accept Him remains blind (cf ch. 9). In the prologue as inventory the narrator makes mention of a number of themes which expand his plot and repeatedly appear, for example life (1:14), the opposition of light and darkness (1:5), world (1:10f), his possession, his own people (1:11), the glory of Jesus (1:14), the Fatherhood of God (1:13) and the role of revelation or making known (1:18). The narrator of the Fourth Gospel places the protagonist Jesus in a framework of glory.

The narrator does not give the reader the full narrative of John the Baptist. The latter is described as a figure parallel to the protagonist, Jesus. Mention is made only of his witness in 1:6-8, his identity crisis in 1:22f, and the unravelling of it with the focus on the protagonist, Jesus in 3:2f. In the rest of chapter 1 the reader's attention is directed to the plot through the narrator's commentary, namely that the Old Testament is entering into fulfilment (1:21). Even the so called christological titles fulfil an important function: Lamb of God (1:29), Son of God (1:34,49), Messiah (1:41), King of Israel (1:49) and the Son of man (1:51). The official acceptance by Jesus of His office as Son of God (1:32-34) and the direction of His personnel, His disciples as helpers, establishes the protagonist in the Johannine narrative as the person from whom the readers can still cherish great expectations.

2. *Complication* (2:1-17:26)

The middle section of the Jesus-narrative consists of chapters 2-17. The protagonist, Jesus appears in His public ministry (2:1-12:50) as well as in His private discussions and instruction with the disciples (13.1-17.26). The plot unfolds and arouses opposition which ultimately resulted in the final resolution. The narration tied chapters 2-12 together by narrating Jesus' miracles. In this way he emphasised once again Jesus' identity as the real Son of God. In a way which is different from the Synoptics the narrator does not present Jesus' miracles as manifestations of the eschatological rupture of the kingdom. They are rather the making known of the identity of the protagonist Himself. The miracles are so narrated that they must be kept by faith. They have however a spiritual character and strengthen faith. Only those who think 'from above' can understand. They also bring, however, people to faith (cf 2:23). Attention has already been focused on the importance of 1:14 for the development of plot of the Johannine Jesus-narrative. It describes the incarnation of the *Logos* and that He lived among us: "We have beheld His glory..." It is precisely in the miracles that the protagonist visibly performs His Father's work (cf 5:17).

The protagonist brings life (from above). The sign at the wedding of
Cana (2:1-12) by which Jesus wins the trust of His disciples is followed by
the narrative of the purification of the Temple (2:13-22). This emphasises
that Jesus introduces a new era and has brought a new dispensation. The
subsequent discourse with Nicodemus (3:1-21) explains once again that
the protagonist is the spiritual giver of new life 'from above'. The discussion also explains that the real opponent of the protagonist is not the
Jewish authorities, but the underworld. Nicodemus (from the Jews) and ‹
the Samaritan woman (from the non-Jews) do not know from where
Jesus comes because the concept of a birth 'from above' is lacking among
them. It is striking how the narrator follows the discussion with
Nicodemus with the witness of John the Baptist who was precisely convinced of Jesus' divine origin (3:22f). While it says that the Samaritans
come to faith (4:27-42), it is actually the Jews who do not understand
Jesus' words (cf 6:41-59). The Jews do not think 'from above'.

The first four chapters of John's gospel narrative describe very little
opposition towards the protagonist, Jesus. The first impression which the
readers of the protagonist obtain is that as the Son of God He is also the
Messiah who performs miracles. The reader is convinced to accept the
narrator's perspective of Jesus.

The acknowledgement of Jesus' identity through the faith-decision of
the disciples in 6:60-71 is presented as a contrast to the disbelief of those
who left Him, as well as of Judas (6;71) and Jesus' brothers (7:1-9). Jesus
is sketched as the fulfilment of the Old Testament (6:1; 16:21). From
chapters 5-10 Jesus appears at the great Jewish feasts and He is presented
as the new tabernacle and the new Temple, the One who replaces the
waters of the Jewish ritual.

The readers of the Jesus-narrative according to John are constantly
conscious of the growing conflict and confrontation with the Jewish
authorities as a consequence of their disbelief (cf 7:45; 8:21; 9:13). In
7:25 the narrator succeeds brilliantly in lighting up the role of the Jews as
opponents when the inhabitants of Jerusalem ask if the Jewish leaders
have not perhaps come to the conviction that Jesus is the Christ. This
forces them, the Jewish leaders, to send officers to arrest Jesus (7:32ff).

The narrator uses the events and discourses of 7:1-52 as a summary to
place the focus on the central plot in his narrative. The Jews wish to kill
Him (7:1); His brothers mock Him (7:3-5); the crowd waver (7:44); the
Pharisees wish to arrest Him because of their disbelief (7:47-49). Within
this framework of strife between faith and disbelief with reference to the
life-giving Jesus, Jesus' identity is precisely placed in relief. When the
Jewish leaders were exposed to public contempt, it in fact strengthened
the position of the protagonist. In 7:33ff the narrator succeeds in causing

an acceleration in the journey of the narrative composition when the protagonist announces that He is leaving. Among the readers the expectation is aroused: where is He going, when and how? In a tense way this couples the further course of the narrative with what has already happened. The narrator also stresses that the arguments of Jesus' opponents do not hold much weight (7:20; cf 8:48,49,52; 10:20-21).

In chapter 8 the conflict between Jesus and the Jews reaches its breaking point. The Jews wish to know forcibly who Jesus' Father is (8:19). They also lay claim to being the children of Abraham (8:33). To which the protagonist stresses that the Jews do not act as children of Abraham (8:39-40). The fury of the Jews is expressed in 8:41 when they say: "...We were not born of fornication; we have one Father, even God". The protagonist's counter argument draws attention in a striking way to His identity when He says: "...If God were your Father, you would love me, for I proceeded and came forth from God". The Jewish leaders were blind as regards Jesus' true identity because they do not wish to see. Therefore they are also guilty (9:35-41).

As regards the plot, chapter 9 and the first part of chapter 10 form an interpretative interlude (cf Culpepper 1983:93). In place of a further accumulation of enmity the accent falls rather on the development of the function of the protagonist, Jesus. He, who is the light of the world (8:12), is now busy healing a blind person. The blind also receive spiritual sight and as a consequence the blindness of the Pharisees is exposed to public contempt (9:39-41). The protagonist cares for His sheep (10:11) and the Jewish leaders are the false shepherd (the hireling) who flees when faced with danger (10:12). Jesus' claim to unity with His Father aroused disagreeable venom (10:30,31). One again the efforts to take Jesus captive failed (10:39).

The description of the resurrection of Lazarus is presented as an illustration of Jesus' word that He is the resurrection and the life, but it is also narrated as a foreshadowing of His own resurrection. In an explanatory way it reaches forward to chapters 13-21. According to 11:57 it appears that the protagonist, as a result of His identity as the Son of God, will have to pay the highest tribute. The reader is prepared for it and in chapter 12 he is reminded of it as a result of Jesus' anointing with nard oil in Bethany (12:1-8). Chapter 12 is a transition chapter. Jesus' public ministry is coming to an end. This is the hinge which allows the whole plot to swing open on to His approaching death and resurrection. In such a way chapters 11 and 13 are bound together in the course of the narrative. Pay attention especially to 12:7 where Jesus expressly says that the woman has anointed His body for His burial. On His entry into

Jerusalem Jesus is honoured as king. In 12:23 the plot of the narrative discovers another acceleration point when Jesus says "...the hour has come for the Son of man to be glorified". Death has now such a great reality for the protagonist that He also experiences the affliction of it (12:27-28). He accepts it because He fulfills by means of it the mission of His Father and He conquers the devil. The public ministry of Jesus is rounded off in a summary form in 12:44-50 by laying the emphasis again on Jesus' origin and on the purpose of His mission: He comes from the Father as the light for mankind so that those who believe in Him will not remain in darkness (12:46). His words bring decisions with regard to eternal life (12:50). Together with the prologue (1:1-18) it offers a perspective for the reader of the total Jesus events.

The narrative composition of the so-called farewell speeches centres around the unity motif between Jesus and His disciples. We could call it the inner unfolding of the plot alongside the two narrative lines, namely the mission of Jesus as well as the mission of the disciples. The disciples wrestle with the identity question although the reader is brought under the impression that it no longer happens as a result of hostility, as was the case of the Jewish leaders. The unifying line is still the question of where Jesus is going and from where he comes (cf 13:36 and 16:30). The farewell discourses are narrated as an interpretation of Jesus' death and resurrection in order to prepare the readers. They offer a retrospective image. The reader is also involved (cf 17:20). What is typical of the Johannine narrative is that the 'hour' of the suffering and death of the protagonist, Jesus, is also the 'hour' of His glorification. This is the 'hour' of His return to the Father (13:1). By means of the farewell discourses the narrator wishes to create an interpretative framework of reassuring trust in order to make as meaningful as possible remaining behind and the task of the disciples in their unity. In order to make meaningful their remaining behind, especially with regard to the hostile world, the disciples receive the assistance of the Holy Spirit (cf 14:15-17, 25-26; 15:26-27; 16:4-11,12-15). The Holy Spirit will always allow the light to fall on the protagonist, Jesus. The functional place of Jesus' prayer (ch. 17) in John's narrative composition cannot be sufficiently emphasised. Through the reproduction of Jesus' prayer for His own glorification (17:1-5), for the believers who were eyewitnesses (17:6-19), as well as for those who believe on the basis of the testimony of the eyewitnesses (17:20-26), the narrator succeeds in allowing the Jesus narrative to be more universal and actual. The readers are made aware that through their faith they are solidly united with the latter group for whom the prayer was offered and that they must identify themselves with them.

3. *Resolution* (*18:1-21:25*)

In the course of the Johannine Jesus-narrative the protagonist's suffering and death, as well as His resurrection, are narrated. This is the price which He must pay to make His Father known, but also to take away sins. The role of the opponents, who until now have chiefly come from the Jewish authorities, is now embodied, for example, in persons such as Annas and Caiaphas. Even Judas appears to be in the service of the High Priest and Pharisees by betraying Jesus. Even Peter takes on the role of an opponent through his express denial of Jesus. All this gives more relief to the protagonist. The readers realise now that in the unravelling of the Johannine Jesus narrative, Jesus' opponents are going to overpower Him. The narrator allows the question of Jesus' origin to surface again during the trial before Pilate. Although Pilate finds Jesus innocent, he gives in to the pressure of the opponents (the Jews). Yet, the narrator explains to the reader that Pilate allowed a placard to be erected above Jesus' head to add support to Jesus' true identity. When the narrator comes to the kernel of the narrative, namely Jesus' death, the milieu is such that the protagonist stands out as the bearer of glory. His whole narrative indicates that Jesus must die and that it is part of His glorification (1:29). In this way the Scriptures are also fulfilled and Jesus dies obedient to His own decision (cf 10:18). The protagonist's death is not sketched as a failure, but as a triumphant glorification. Jesus dies, then, also according to the Johannine account with a forceful expression: "It is finished" (19:30). After that the narrator of the Gospel of John adds a commentary by saying that he is witness to the events and that his witness is true, and that he knows that he speaks the truth so that the reader can believe (19:35). The resurrection of Jesus is narrated within the framework of the appearances. Thomas calls out with an acknowledgement of Jesus' identity: "My Lord and my God". The full restoration of Peter as the helper of the protagonist is strikingly narrated in chapter 21. The narration of the miraculous sign of the catch of fish rounds off the Johannine miracles. Chapter 21 rounds off the Johannine Jesus narrative. The characterisation of Peter and the disciple whom Jesus loved has great importance for giving a direction for the future. The Johannine narrative does not end with Jesus' ascension. The Holy Spirit will accompany the disciples in their continued mission. In a certain way the gap is bridged between the reader and the narrative by the emphasis on the function of the Holy Spirit.

Conclusion

The unifying plot, which runs throughout the construction of the narrative of John's Gospel, is really the witness to the identity of Jesus. He is the bearer of the divine glory as incarnate Son of God. This is continuously made known through His person and work. The reader is fascinated by the effect which Jesus' identity has on different roles. An answer must be given to His revelation. Some roles react with disbelief and hostility (for example the Jewish authorities), others again with faith and acceptance (e.g. the Samaritan woman). Underlying the decision for faith or disbelief, is the understanding of Jesus' origin and goal. The latter are not hidden but are only understandable by those who can think 'from above' i.e. those who have a divine perspective. Those are still blind, despite the miraculous signs and words of Jesus, still think 'from below'; they do not understand Jesus' actual identity. The narrator gives the essence of Jesus' identity by situating his narrative, namely the prologue as the key to understanding the rest. In the middle section, the plot, that is in Jesus' public appearance and private discussion, the reader can visibly experience that some understand and accept Jesus, but that others reject Him because they do not understand His origin nor His goal. In the final section everything is unravelled when the protagonist triumphantly dies and rises as an accomplishment of His Father's mission. The mission of the disciples carries forward this mission.

The witnessing Johannine narrative about Jesus' identity calls on the reader for identification.

BIBLIOGRAPHY

ABRAMS, M. H. 1971. *A glossary of literary terms.* 3. ed. New York: Holt.

BOOTH, W. C. 1961. Distance and point of view: an essay in classification. *Essays in Criticism* 11, 60-79.

BRUCE, F. F. 1980. Charting new directions for New Testament studies. *Christianity Today* 24, 19-22.

CHATMAN, S. 1978. *Story and discourse: narrative structure in fiction and film.* Ithaca: Cornell University Press.

CULPEPPER, R. A. 1983. *Anatomy of the Fourth Gospel. A study in literary design.* Philadelphia: Fortress Press.

CRANE, R. S. 1966. The concept of plot, in R. Scholes (ed), *Approaches to the novel.* San Francisco: Chandler.

DU RAND, J. A. 1982. *Die struktuur van die christologie van die Evangelie van Johannes - metodologiese oorwegings.* Bloemfontein: Universiteit van die Oranje-Vrystaat.

DU RAND, J. A. 1983. Die Evangelie van Johannes as getuigende vertelling. *NGTT* 24, 383-97.

DU RAND, J. A. 1984. Die leser in die Evangelie volgens Johannes. *Fax Theologica* 4, 45-63.

FACKRE, G. 1983. Narrative theology. An overview. *Interp* 37, 340-52.

FRYE, N. 1957. *Anatomy of criticism: four essays.* Princeton: Princeton University Press.

HOOKER, M. D. 1975. The Johannine prologue and the Messianic secret. *NTS* 21, 40-48.

JAKOBSON, R. 1981. Linguistics and poetics, in S. Rudy (ed), *Selected writing* III. Den Haag, 22ff.

KYSAR, R. 1975. *The Fourth Evangelist and his Gospel: an examination of contemporary scholarship.* Minneapolis: Augsburg Publishing House.

LANSER, S. S. 1981. *The narrative act. Point of view in prose fiction.* Princeton: University Press.

MINEAR, P. 1977. The audience of the Fourth Gospel. *Interp* 31, 339-45.

PERRIN, N. 1974. *The New Testament: an introduction. Proclamation and parenesis, myth and history.* New York.

PETERSEN, N. R. 1978. *Literary criticism for New Testament critics.* Philadelphia: Fortress Press.

PETERSEN, N. R. 1980. When is the end not the end? Literary reflections on the ending of Mark's narrative. *Interp* 34, 151-66.

PETERSEN, N. R. 1984a. The reader in the Gospel. (Paper read at NTSSA 1984. To be published in *Neotestamentica* 18.)

PETERSEN, N. R. 1984b. Toward a literary-sociological method. (Paper read at University of the Orange Free State, 1984.)

RABINOWITZ, P. J. 1977. Truth and fiction. A re-examination of audiences. *Critical Inquiry* 4, 121-41.

RISSI, M. 1983. Der Aufbau des vierten Evangeliums. *NTS* 29, 55-61.

SCHOLES R. & R. KELLOGG 1966. *The nature of narrative.* London: Oxford University Press.

TANNEHILL, R. C. 1980. The Gospel of Mark as narrative christology. *Semeia* 16, 57-95.

VAN AARDE, A. G. 1982. *God met ons. Dié teologiese perspektief van die Matteusevangelie.* Petoria: Unpublished diss, University of Pretoria.

VAN AARDE, A. G. 1984. Plot as mediated through point of view. Mt 22:1-14 - a case study. (Paper read at NTSSA 1984.)

VAN RENSBURG, M. C. J. & H. P. VAN COLLER 1982. Van mond tot oor, in G. J. van Jaarsveld (ed), *Wat sê jy? Studies oor taalhandelinge in Afrikaans.* Johannesburg: McGraw-Hill, 215-33.

VORSTER, W. S. 1980. Die Evangelie volgens Markus, in A. B. du Toit (ed), *Handleiding by die Nuwe Testament* IV. Pretoria: NG Kerkboekhandel, 109-155.

VORSTER, W. S. 1982. Mark: collector, redactor, author, narrator? *Journal of Theology of South Africa* 31, 46-61.

VORSTER, W. S. 1983. Kerygma/history and the Gospel genre. *NTS* 29, 87-95.

VORSTER, W. S. 1984. The historical paradigm - its possibilities and limitations *Neotestamentica* 18.

WILDER, A. N. 1971. *Early Christian rhetoric: The language of the Gospel.* Cambridge Mass: Harvard University Press.

ADDITIONAL NOTE

Compare the following publications as part of the fast growing flood which put the exegetical emphasis on the text:

RHOADS, D. 1982. Narrative criticism and the Gospel of Mark. *Journal of the American Academy of Religion* 50, 411-34; RHOADS, D. & D. MICHIE 1982. *Mark as story: an introduction to the narrative of a Gospel.* Philadelphia: Fortress Press; KELBER, W. 1979. *Mark's story of Jesus.* Philadelphia: Fortress Press; KYSAR, R. 1984. *John's story of Jesus.* Philadelphia: Fortress Press; TALBERT, C. H. 1982. *Reading Luke: a literary and theological commentary on the Third Gospel.* New York: Crossroads; CULPEPPER, A. 1983. *Anatomy of the Fourth Gospel: a study in literary design.* Philadelphia: Fortress Press; FRYE, N. 1982. *The great code: the Bible and literature.* New York: Harcourt; VORSTER, W. S. 1984. Reader-response, redescription and reference. "You are that man" (2 Sm 12:7), in B. C. Lategan & W. S. Vorster 1984. *Text and reality: aspects of reference in biblical texts.* Philadelphia: Fortress Press (Semeia sup); VAN AARDE, A. G. 1982. *God met ons. Dié teologiese perspektief van die Matteusevangelie* (Unpublished Dissertation, University of Pretoria); Combrink, H. J. B. 1982. The structure of the Gospel of Matthew as narrative. *Tyndale Bulletin* 1982; DU RAND, J. A. 1983. Die Evangelie van Johannes as getuigende vertelling. *NGTT* 24, 383-97; 1984. Die leser in die Evangelie volgens Johannes. *Fax Theologica* 4, 45-63.

J. C. COETZEE

JESUS' REVELATION IN THE *EGO EIMI* SAYINGS IN JN 8 AND 9

1. *Introductory notes*

Since the 1950's a radical change in the historico-exegetical reading of the Gospel of John occurred. J. A. T. Robinson (1962:94) called it "The New Look on the Fourth Gospel".

This is in no way meant to be an article on literature evaluation. It wants to be a direct and straightforward exegetical study. Still it does have its clearcut presuppositions in the field of Johannine studies: as opposed to so many decades of "hellenistic-gnostic" reading of John it supports the increasing and intensifying reading of John as a Jewish-Christian writing solidly built on the revelation and prophecies of the Old Testament.

Undoubtedly one of the most intriguing and theologically controversial issues in the Johannine debate has been the wellknown "I AM" or *EGO EIMI* utterances of Jesus in this Gospel. They are not unknown to the Synoptics; cf Mt 14:27; Mk 6:50; Mk 15:6; Lk 21:8. Still, they are quite characteristic of John.

In this Gospel they occur as a wonderful compendium of the overflowing richness of God's grace given to us in Jesus Christ, both the Word and the Good Shepherd (cf 1:14; 10:10). According to Schnackenburg (1971:59-60) *EGO EIMI* occurs 26 times in the mouth of Jesus as distributed between Jn 4 and 19; 13 times used absolutely and 13 times used in connection with a predicate.

This brings us to an important point of delimitation of this article: we want to confine ourselves to a short exegetical investigation into the absolute *EGO EIMI* utterances in Jn 8 and 9—with special attention, as stated previously, to the Old Testament background(s) of these sayings. The absolute use, being the shortest and most essential—that is: concerning the Being, the Essence, of Jesus Christ—utterances are regarded as being the primary motif that should therefore be studied first.

2. *Relationship between Jn 8-9 and Is 42-43*

2.1 *Statement*

When one makes an intensive comparison in the original New Testament Greek and the Old Testament Hebrew as well as in the Septuagint translation between the teaching of Jesus in Jn 8 with the coinciding sign in Jn 9 on the one hand, and the prophetic preaching of Isaiah on the Lord Jahweh as Saviour-God through his unique and elected Servant of the Lord (עֶבֶד וְהֹוָה) in Is 42-43 on the other hand the similarity is striking. To such an extent that it exhibits to our mind unquestionably the fact that Jesus' absolute *EGO EIMI* utterances in Jn 8 *deliberately refer to the prophecies of Is 42-43*—the same may probably be said to be true of his ''I AM the light'' sayings in these two chapters!

2.2 *A synoptic comparison between Jn 8(-9) and Is 42-43*

This brings us to what may be regarded as the fundamental part of this paper. By way of a synopsis we shall deal in the left hand column with the relevant issue, with the Old Testamental, Isaian witness in the middle column, and with the Jesus-Johannine references in the right hand column:

The Issue	Is 42-43	Jn 8(-9)
1. Absolute - I AM sayings	Is 42-43 is marked by an accumulation of I AM sayings, with *Jahweh* always as subject. Kernel-saying: BH 43:10 ''…so that you may know, and believe me and understand כִּי־אֲנִי הוּא (that I AM)''; LXX 43:10 ''…καὶ συνῆτε ὅτι ἐγώ εἰμι (and understand that I AM)''. See also 42:8; 43:3,11,12 (BH), 15 (LXX).	Also Jn 8-9 is marked by an accumulation of I AM-sayings, with *Jesus* now always as subject. See 8:12 and 8:18… 8:24: ''ἐὰν γὰρ μὴ πιστεύσητε ὅτι ἐγώ εἰμι, ἀποθανεῖσθε…'' 8:28: ''…τότε γνώσεσθε ὅτι ἐγώ εἰμι''. 8:58: ''…πρὶν Ἀβραὰμ γενέσθαι ἐγώ εἰμι''.
2. The Light-motif	The *Ebed Jahweh* as Light for the world or the nations: 42:4, 6-7,16 (εἰς φῶς ἐθνῶν - LXX; לְאֹור גֹּויִם)	Jesus as Light for the world: 8:12; 9:5 (τὸ φῶς τοῦ κοσμοῦ).
3. Both sections formulated in terms of a lawsuit (or in the atmosphere of a court-room).	(i) A lawsuit between Jahweh and all the unbelieving *gojim* (כָּל־הַגֹּויִם). See especially Is 43:9-12. (ii) Bearing witness in the lawsuit: 43:9b,10,12 (LXX: μάρτυς, μάρτυρες). (iii) Jahweh's two or three witnesses (according to the Law of Moses - Dt 19:15): BH 43:10: ''You are my witnesses … and my servant whom I have	(i) A lawsuit between Jesus and the unbelieving Jews. See especially Jn 8:13-18. (ii) Bearing witness in the lawsuit: 8:13,14,17-18 (μαρτυρεῖς, ἡ μαρτυρία, μαρτυρῶ, ὁ μαρτυρῶν). (iii) Jesus' two (or three) witnesses (according to ''your law'' - 8:17): ἐγώ εἰμι ὁ μαρτυρῶν περὶ ἐμαυτοῦ καὶ μαρτυρεῖ περὶ ἐμοῦ ὁ πέμψας με πατήρ

The Issue	Is 42-43	Jn 8(-9)

<table>
<tr><td></td><td>chosen (thus *two* witnesses)''; LXX: Γένεσθέ μοι μάρτυρες, καὶ ἐγὼ μάρτυς ... καὶ ὁ παῖς μου ὃν ἐξελέξαμην (thus three witnesses: the people of God, Jahweh Himself ánd the *Ebed Jahweh.* (See also 43:12).)</td><td>(and where are your witness, o people of God?!)</td></tr>
<tr><td></td><td>(iv) Jahweh Himself witnesses (and the *gojim* will have to agree to that!) the Truth - 43:9b BH: אֱמֶת; LXX: ἀληθῆ.</td><td>(iv) Jesus Himself witnesses the Truth - 8:13-14, 32, 40, 45, 46 (ἀληθής, ἡ ἀλήθεια).</td></tr>
</table>

4. The essential contents of the message of the two (or three) witnesses.

Jahweh witnesses (as *must* be confirmed by the other witnesses):	Jesus witnesses (as is confirmed by his Father, and ought to be confirmed by his people):
(i) With regard to *his own Person* (Essence: WHO He is): BH 43:10: ''so that you may know (תֵּרְעוּ) that I AM (כִּי־אֲנִי הוּא). LXX 43:10 ἵνα γνῶτε καὶ πιστεύσητε, καὶ συνῆτε ὅτι ἐγώ εἰμι.	(i) With regard to *his own Person* (Essence, WHO He is): 8:24: ἐὰν γὰρ μὴ πιστεύσητε ὅτι ἐγώ εἰμι 8:28: ''..., τότε γνώσεσθε ὅτι ἐγώ εἰμι...''
(ii) With regard to *Jahweh's saving activity*: BH 43:3: ''I Am the Lord, your God ... your Saviour'' (כִּי אֲנִי יְהוָה אֱלֹהֶיךָ ... מוֹשִׁיעֶךָ). BH 43:11: ''I AM, even I, the Lord, and apart from Me there is no saviour'' (אָנֹכִי אָנֹכִי יְהוָה ... מוֹשִׁיעַ)	(ii) With regard to *Jesus' saving activity* 8:24: ''If you do not believe that I AM, you will indeed die in your sins'' (ἐὰν γὰρ μὴ πιστεύσητε ὅτι 'ΕΓΩ 'ΕΙΜΙ ἀποθανεῖσθε ἐν ταῖς ἁμαρτίαις ὑμῶν). Thus, as Jahweh claimed in Is 43:3, 11 so Jesus as *EGO EIMI* now claims to be the one and only Saviour!
	8:32 ''And you will know (γνώσεσθε) the truth, and the truth will set you free'' (καὶ γνώσεσθε τὴν ἀλήθειαν, καὶ ἡ ἀλήθεια ἐλευθερώσει ὑμᾶς).
	8:36: ''so if the Son sets you free, you will be free indeed'' (ἐὰν οὖν ὁ υἱὸς ὑμᾶς ἐλευθερώσῃ, ὄντως ἐλεύθεροι ἔσεσθε).
Thus: Jahweh, He who is I AM, is the only true Redeemer.	Thus: Jesus, He who is I AM, is the only true Redeemer!

The Issue	Is 42-43	Jn 8(-9)
5. This witness MUST be acknowledged (more than be known) and MUST be believed.	LXX 43:10b "so that you may *know* and *believe* me and understand that I AM he": ἵνα γνῶτε καὶ πιστεύσητε, καὶ συνῆτε ὅτι ἐγώ εἰμι.	8:24: "for, if you do not believe: I AM ..." and 8:28: "then will you know: I AM" (8:24: ἐὰν γὰρ μὴ πιστεύσητε ὅτι 'ΕΓΩ 'ΕΙΜΙ...; and 8:28: τότε γνώσεσθε ὅτι 'ΕΓΩ 'ΕΙΜΙ...)
6. Through Whom and in which way the Freedom or Redemption occurs.	(i) *Jahweh* calls his Servant, his *Ebed*, as Covenant for his people and as Light for the nations:..."אֲנִי יְהוָה. BH 42:6 לְבְרִית עָם לְאוֹר גּוֹיִם" LXX 42:6: "'Εγὼ κύριος ὁ θεός... ἔδωκά σε εἰς διαθήκην γένους, εἰς φῶς ἐθνῶν ..."	(i) *Jesus* announces Himself to be the one and only Light to (for) the world, the Light towards eternal life: 8:12(9:5): "'Εγώ εἰμι τὸ φῶς τοῦ κοσμοῦ... τὸ φῶς τῆς ζωῆς".
	(ii) Where will The Servant of the Lord primarily operate? The *Ebed Jahweh* will primarily operate in the midst of the blind and a blindness-stricken people (42:7,16,18-20; 43:8).	(ii) Where does Jesus operate as The Light? With regard to a man blind from birth (9:1) and over against an unbelieving Phariseism who is spiritually blind (9:39-41).
	(iii) The Servant, and thus Jahweh Himself, will open the eyes of the blind. LXX 42:7: "ἀνοῖξαι ὀφθαλμοὺς τυφλῶν".	(iii) Jesus confirms his original assumptive statement that He truly is The Servant Who really can heal the blind: 9:5-7, 25-26,39.
	(iv) As Light for the nations the Servant will lead people out of the darkness into the light. LXX 42:16: ποιήσω αὐτοῖς τὸ σκότος εἰς φῶς (cf 42:7).	(iv) Jesus declares Himself as the Light for the world who leads people out of the darkness into the light of life. 8:12: ὁ ἀκολουθῶν ἐμοί οὐ μὴ περιπατήσῃ ἐν τῇ σκοτίᾳ, ἀλλ' ἕξει τὸ φῶς τῆς ζωῆς.

2.3 *Conclusions drawn from the above synopsis*

Through the synopsis the following became evident:

2.3.1 Jesus uses the absolute *EGO EIMI* as a technical term which carries exclusive claims with regard to both his own Person and his messianic work.

2.3.2 Beyond all doubt Jesus makes the radical claim in Jn 8(-9) of his unique unity with Jahweh, the God of the Covenant. By *EGO EIMI* Jesus does not only claim to be a very special "I", but that in Him is personified the very unique divine "I AM" (the אֲנִי הוּא or ἐγώ εἰμι of Is 43:10-11).

In the following section this conclusion will be checked by way of comparison between Jn 8(-9) and Ex 3:13-17.

2.3.3 By way of his *EGO EIMI* sayings in Jn 8(-9) Jesus clearly in a very special way identifies Himself to be the long awaited messianic Servant of the Lord (the *Ebed Jahweh*) prophesied in Is 42-43 (even in 40-55).

3. *Relationship between the absolute EGO EIMI in Jn 8(-9) and Ex 3:13-17*

In Jn 8:58 Jesus claims: "before Abraham was born, I AM" (πρὶν Ἀβραὰμ γενέσθαι ἐγώ εἰμί) with the result that the Jews immediately picked up stones to stone Him. This clearly shows that they regarded his claim as utterly blasphemous. This is, when seen from their viewpoint and with their vivid knowledge of Ex 3, especially 3:6 and 13-17, highly understandable:

(a) In Jn 8:51-59 Jesus claims that whoever keeps his word, will for ever not see death (v 51).

(b) The Jews who do not believe, compare Him contemptuously with Father Abraham: "Abraham died ... Are you greater than our Father Abraham?" (vv 52-53).

(c) They then dare Him to identify his true personality or rather, "his (mad) idea" of his true personality: "Who do you think you are?" (τίνα σεαυτὸν ποιεῖς; - v 53).

(d) Jesus then firmly declares: "Your father Abraham rejoiced at the thought of seeing my day, and he saw it and was glad" (v 56). Now Jesus had directly put Himself above Abraham - that was as close to blasphemy as can be, without involving the Lord God Himself.

(e) But then at last Jesus adds a final fully blasphemous (if He was not what He really claims!) word: "Truly, truly, I say unto you, before Abraham was, I AM" (Ἀμὴν ἀμὴν λέγω ὑμῖν, πρὶν Ἀβραὰμ γενέσθαι ἐγώ εἰμί v 58).

The intimate correlation between Jn 8(-9) and Ex 3:13-17 ought to be evident:

(a) Direct comparison between Jn 8:58 (in its context) and Ex 3:14-15 (in their contexts) reveals how closely Jesus in Jn 8 relates to Ex 3:14-15 (or 3:13-17) and its revelation of the holy and covenantal Name of the Lord God, of יְהוָה אֱלֹהִים.

(b) Jesus promises salvation (liberation) from the slavery of sin, just as Jahweh promised liberation (salvation) from the slavery of Egypt (Jn 8:31-36; Ex 3:12,16-17).

(c) In Ex 3:13 Moses, in the name of Israel, confronts the Lord with the key-question: "...if they ask me: What is his Name? - Then what shall I tell them?"

This, explicitly, calls for a personal identification. And this the Lord God provides in Ex 3:14:

אֶהְיֶה אֲשֶׁר אֶהְיֶה - BH;

ἐγώ εἰμι ὁ ὤν - LXX.

In the same way the Jews confront Jesus twice (in Jn 8:25 and 53) with calls for personal identification. The first time in 8:25 the Jews react by saying "Who are you?" (Σὺ τὶς εἶ;) to Jesus' first *EGO EIMI* saying of 8:24. In answer He simply states: "Just what I have been claiming all along" (τὴν ἀρχήν ὅ τι καὶ λαλῶ ὑμῖν - 8:25b). Implicitly, therefore, He reiterates his *EGO EIMI* claim, building up to his second explicit claim in 8:28. The second time, much later in their discussions, the Jews ask in more aggressive fashion: "Who do you think you are?", or more literally: "whom do you make yourself into?" (τίνα σεαυτὸν ποιεῖς;) - comparing Jesus, to his discredit, to "our father Abraham" (8:52-53). And now finally Jesus makes an explicit personal identification in line with Jahweh's personal identification in Ex 3:14. He answers: "Amen, amen ... before Abraham was born, I AM!" ('Αμὴν ἀμὴν λέγω ὑμῖν, πρὶν 'Αβραὰμ γενέυθαι ἐγώ εἰμί-8:58).

(d) In Jn 8:24 and 28 Jesus repeats his *EGO EIMI* title or name in much the same way as did Jahweh in Ex 3:14a,14b, and 15:

In Jn 8:24 Jesus claims to be *EGO EIMI.* Yet in 8:25 the Jews again ask: "Who are you?" To this Jesus reacts almost in frustration in 8:26 as to all the things He could have said about *them,* but He refrains from that and rather emphatically repeats in 8:28 who *He* is: -"then (after my resurrection) you will come to know (or: to acknowledge) 'I AM!'" Finally, for a third time, He repeats in 8:58: "*EGO EIMI!*"

The same emphatical repetition of God's Covenant-name is to be found in Ex 3:14-15. Revealing Himself to Moses He, "the God of your father, the God of Abraham..." (Ex 3:6) declares in 3:14(a): "I AM WHO I AM" (אֶהְיֶה אֲשֶׁר אֶהְיֶה). In 3:14(b) He repeats: "This is what you are to say to the Israelites: "I AM (אֶהְיֶה) has sent me to you". And in 3:15 He finally for a third time, repeats: "Say to the Israelites, Jahweh (יְהֹוָה) ... has sent me to you".

(e) Jahweh, when revealing Himself to Moses declares that He as I AM, is "the God of Abraham (the God of Isaac and the God of Jacob)". Jahweh, I AM, was there before Abraham (Ex 3:6,16)! He is *greater* than Abraham—He is "the God of Abraham".

And now the Jews finally challenge Jesus: "Are you greater than our father Abraham? ... Who do you think you are?"

And Jesus dramatically, and finally, declares in Jn 8:58:

"Before Abraham was, I AM (EGO EIMI)".

Yes. I am greater than Abraham!

I am one with the God of Abraham!

I am *I AM*!

Conclusion

From our study it has become clear that the absolute *EGO EIMI* in Jn 8 is definitely a technical expression in the mouth of Jesus whereby He explicitly claims: (i) his identification with the messianic Servant of the Lord (*Ebed Jahweh*) of Is 42-43 (40-55);

(ii) his essential unity with Jahweh, the Covenant-god of the Old Testament, both in terms of Ex 3:13-17 and Is 42-43.

BIBLIOGRAPHY

As stated at the beginning this paper does NOT intend to discuss theological literature on *EGO EIMI* in Jn 8(-9). Therefore this short-list also does not in any way pretend to be exhaustive. For further references see the authors referred to.

BROWN, R. E. 1966. The Gospel according to John (1-12), in *The Anchor Bible*. New York: Doubleday and Company, Appendix IV, 533-538.

BULTMANN, R. 1964. *Das Evangelium des Johannes*. Göttingen: Vandenhoeck & Ruprecht, 161-177.

DAUBE, D. 1956. The 'I Am' of the Messianic presence, in *The New Testament and Rabbinic Judaism*. London: Athlone, 325-329.

DODD, C. H. 1965. *The Interpretation of the Fourth Gospel*. Cambridge: University Press, 93-96, 349-362.

DODD, C. H. 1965. *Historical Tradition in the Fourth Gospel*. Cambridge: University Press, 315-387.

FEUILLET, A. 1966. Les Ego eimi christologies du quatr. Evangile. - *RSR* 54, 5-22, 213-240.

KUNDZINŠ, K. 1939. Charakter und Ursprung der johanneischen Reden, in *Acta Universitatis Latviensis* I, 4. Rega, 185-293.

KUNDZINŠ, K. 1954. Zur Diskussion über die Ego-eimi-sprüche des Johannes-Evangeliums, in J. Köpp (ed.), *Charisteria*. Stockholm, 95-107.

MORRIS, L. 1971. *The Gospel according to John*. London: Marshall, Morgan and Scott, 350f. (The New London Commentary on the New Testament).

NORDEN, E. 1956. *Agnostos Theos* (originally 1913). Leipzig/Stuttgart, 177-201.

RICHTER, J. 1956. *Ani Hu und Ego eimi*. Erlangen: ungedr Diss.

SCHNACKENBURG, R. 1971. *Das Johannesevangelium, II Teil. Kommentar zur Kap 5-12*. Freiburg: Herder, 59-71. (Herders Theologische Kommentar zum Neuen Testament.)

SCHNACKENBURG, R. 1984. *Das Johannesevangelium, IV Teil. Ergänzende Auslegungen und Exkurse*. Freiburg: Herder, 84-86. (Herders Theologische Kommentar zum Neuen Testament.)

SCHULZ, S. 1960. *Komposition und Herkunft der Johanneischen Reden.* Stuttgart: Kohlhammer, 70-131.

SCHWEIZER, E. 1939. EGO EIMI ... Die religionsgeschichtliche Herkunft und theologische Bedeutung der johanneischen Bildreden, zugleich ein Beitrag zur Quellenfrage des vierten Evangeliums, in R. Bultmann (ed.), *Forschungen zur Religion und Literatur des Alten und Neuen Testaments* 56. Göttingen: Vandenhoeck & Ruprecht.

STAUFFER, E. 1957 (1939). Ego *eimi. TWNT* II, 350-360.

WETTER, G. P. 1915. 'Ich bin es'. Eine johanneische Formel. *Theologische Studien und Kritiken* 88, 224ff.

ZIMMERMANN, H. 1960. Das absolute 'Ego eimi' als die neutestamentliche Offenbarungsformel. *BZ* 4, 54-69, 266-276.

A. B. DU TOIT

HYPERBOLICAL CONTRASTS: A NEGLECTED ASPECT OF PAUL'S STYLE

1. *Orientational remarks*

The term 'hyperbolical contrast' is used here for a specific group of relational sayings, the two constituents of which appear to be exclusive (A and definitely not B, A vs. B) or at least strongly contrastive (A in contrast to B), but which, viewed semantically, are really comparatives (A rather than B), or, at least, less strongly contrastive than a superficial reading suggests (A $\neq$ B).

Like so many other stylistic aspects of biblical language, this feature is often overlooked. This may cause the exegete considerable problems[1]. On the other hand, its recognition may serve to solve more than one exegetical enigma. Although known by different names and treated under various headings, this figure was already known to grammarians of previous centuries. In our own era Hommel[2], Vaccari[3], Kuschke[4] and Kruse[5] have paid attention to it, but in recent literature it has largely been neglected[6].

As I shall try to point out below, we can distinguish two kinds of hyperbolical contrasts[7], but the characteristic common to both is that *the mean-*

---

[1] When hyperbolical expressions, for instance, are taken at face value, they may cause serious dogmatic puzzles, cf e.g. 1 Cor 1:17 which is discussed later on.

[2] E. Hommel, with his article, A rhetorical figure in the Old Testament, *ET* 11 (1900), 439-41, started a whole discussion (cf *idem*, 517-9, 564). He was supported by scholars like Eb. Nestle and James Moffatt, but criticized (in my opinion unconvincingly) by E. König. It must, however, be conceded that not all Hommel's examples were equally conclusive.

[3] A. Vaccari, Antica e nuova interpretazione del Salmo 16 (15), *Biblica* 14 (1933), 408-34. Kruse (cf *infra* n.5) also mentions two other publications of Vaccari which were inaccessible to me.

[4] A. KUSCHKE, Das Idiom der 'relativen Negation' im Neuen Testament, *ZNW* 43 (1950/1), 263.

[5] H. Kruse, Die 'dialektische Negation' als semitisches Idiom, *VT* 4 (1954), 385-400. I wish to express my gratitude to one of my Old Testament colleagues, Prof. Dr. A. P. B. Breytenbach, for his valuable remarks on this phenomenon and for drawing my attention to Kruse's article.

[6] Even F. Blass, A. Debrunner, F. Rehkopf, *Grammatik des neutestamentlichen Griechisch*, Göttingen [14]1976, only find room for this figure in a short note (§ 488 n. 1).

[7] The designation 'exaggerated contrast' for this figure appears in Eb. Nestlé's comment on Hommel's article, viz. in *ET* 11 (1900), 518. It is, however, not clear whether it was Nestlé himself or Prof. Lucien Gautier, to whom he refers, who coined this term.

ing of the exaggerated element (which they all contain) should not be absolutized. It should be understood dialectically, i.e., in its relation to the contrasted part of the saying.

1.1 The dialectical negation

The 'dialectical negation', as Kruse designates this first and most important kind of hyperbolical contrast, seems to be common to all Semitic languages. It does, however, also appear in Greek writers[8] and Nestle surmises that it will probably be found in all languages[9]. But it would be fair to say that it is a more strongly Semitic characteristic.

From Socin Kruse[10] cites the following Arab idiom:

An egg today and not a chicken tomorrow.

At face value we have here an exclusive contrast. But the real meaning is: "*Much rather* an egg today (of which one can be sure), *than* a chicken tomorrow (of which one cannot be so sure)".

Let us examine some Old Testament examples. We start with Ex 16:8[11]:

וַיֹּאמֶר מֹשֶׁה בְּתֵת יְהוָה לָכֶם בָּעֶרֶב בָּשָׂר לֶאֱכֹל וְלֶחֶם בַּבֹּקֶר לִשְׂבֹּעַ
בִּשְׁמֹעַ יְהוָה אֶת-תְּלֻנֹּתֵיכֶם אֲשֶׁר-אַתֶּם מַלִּינִם עָלָיו
וְנַחְנוּ מָה
לֹא-עָלֵינוּ תְלֻנֹּתֵיכֶם כִּי עַל-יְהוָה

A direct translation of the final part of this saying would be: "Your murmurings are not against us but against the Lord".

Once again, at first sight this relational saying is totally exclusive. But if the intention is actually to deny that the congregation murmurs against Moses and Aaron, it would simply not be true. That has already been stated quite emphatically (v 2f). For the real sense of this saying we should look, then, to the dialectical relationship of its constituents: "It is not so much against us that you murmur; you are rather murmuring against Jahweh himself".

How this kind of expression actually works may now be apparent. It seeks to express, not an absolute contrast, but a comparison. But why, then, this hyperbolic formulation? Why this choice of an apparent clash between surface structure and semantic deep structure? The motivation behind this stylistic device is the desire to drive home the overriding importance (greater desirability, superior quality, etc.) of B in comparison with A (or *vice versa*). Sometimes A represents a *status quo*, a situation, a

---

[8] G. B. Winer, *Grammatik des neutestamentlichen Sprachidioms*, Leipzig [6]1855, 439-41.
[9] Art. cit., 518.
[10] Art. cit., 399.
[11] Cf also Kruse, art. cit., 389.

thought pattern which should, in the opinion of the author, be played down as effectively as possible. Winer describes this figure as follows: "In andern Stellen (he had just discussed the fullfledged negation) ist aus *rhetorischem* Grunde die absolute Negation statt der bedingten (relativen) gewählt, nicht um reell (logisch) die erste Vorstellung aufzuheben, sondern um alle Aufmerksamkeit ungetheilt auf die zweite hinzulenken, so dass die erste gegen sie verschwinde"[12]. He could have added that the reason for applying this kind of rhetoric was the intention to persuade. Rhetoric is here indeed an *art of persuasion*.

Many more instances of the use of the comparative *lo'* in the Old Testament could be cited[13]. In this context two more examples, one from the wisdom literature, and one from the prophetic literature, must suffice: Literally translated, Pr 8:10 reads:

> Receive my instruction and not silver;
> and knowledge rather than gold.

Surely the author's intention is not a blunt prohibition to accept silver in contrast to a concession to accept gold. His real aim is to drive home the point that instruction is worth much more than silver. The comparative *min* in the second part of the parallelism serves to confirm that this is the correct interpretation[14].

An example from the prophets (there are more) would certainly be Hs 6:6:

> Since what I want is love, not sacrifice;
> knowledge of God rather than holocausts.

Grammatically this saying is exactly parallel to Pr 8:10, and in spite of the protests of König[15] and others (many of whom want to safeguard certain a priori's, e.g., about a late dating for the priestly codex), we must obviously interpret it in the same way as the verse from Proverbs. God does not reject sacrifice, but he prefers love to sacrifice: "I want love rather than sacrifice".

In view of the Semitic background of many New Testament sayings, it is not surprising that we find there a substantial number of dialectical negations, especially in the Gospels. But it is not always easy to deter-

---

[12] G. B. Winer, op. cit., 440. Winer is, of course, referring to this figure in the New Testament.

[13] Cf e.g. H. Kruse, op. cit., although not all his suggested texts can stand the test (a possibility which he himself readily concedes).

[14] Cf Pr 3:14 and V. Hamp, *Das Buch der Sprüche*, Echter Bibel, Würzburg 1954, 25 who *i.a.* refers to Pr 17:12, Eccl 9:4 and Sir 25:13. Pr 27:2 is not a case in point.

[15] *Inter alia* in *ET* 11(1900), 519 ("what a danger to any certainty in exegesis might arise, if the negatives 'not' and 'no' are not meant to signify 'not' and 'no'!").

mine whether what we have is this figure and not a real absolute contrast[16]. And we must be very careful not to relativize an utterance which was intended absolutely[17]. The golden rule remains that each passage is interpreted on its own within its unique context. Once again only a few instances must suffice. The first one, chosen almost at random, is Lk 10:20.

> Nevertheless do not rejoice in the fact that the spirits are subject to you; rejoice because your names are written in heaven.

Surely Jesus did not want to inhibit the joy of his followers at the subjugation of the devils. But this injunction *is* a forceful challenge to see things in their right perspective: what is by far the most important thing is to rejoice in one's heavenly destination.

Another well-known example is Mark 9:37b:

καὶ ὃς ἂν ἐμὲ δέχηται, οὐκ ἐμὲ δέχεται ἀλλὰ τὸν ἀποστείλαντά με.

This should be understood in the sense of: "and who receives me does not so much receive me, but rather him who sent me" or, alternatively (but less probably): "and who receives me receives not only me, but also him who sent me." The *varia lectio* of the codex Koridethi and a few other manuscripts show how some early copyists already had problems with this figure.

A muchloved example is Acts 5:4:

οὐκ ἐψεύσω ἀνθρώποις ἀλλὰ τῷ θεῷ.

Clearly Ananias did try to beguile the apostles. The words of Peter are not intended to deny that, but to shock him into realizing that much more is at stake. The forceful hyperbolical language makes one feel, as Tannehill has put it aptly, the "bite of the text"[18].

Before we turn our attention to the dialectical negation in Paul, there remains one other group of hyperbolical contrasts to survey briefly.

1.2 *Normal hyperbolical contrasts*

In common with the first (and larger) group, the hyperbolical element in these sayings has to be understood dialectically in the light of the rest of their content. It likewise intends a weaker contrast than indicated on the surface level. But in this case it does not designate a comparative *non tam*

---

[16] How should one for instance interpret Mt 6:19f?

[17] This is the important element of truth in the warnings of König and also of Winer, op. cit., 439f.

[18] R. C. Tannehill, *The Sword of his Mouth.* SBL, Semeia Sup 1, Philadelphia: Missoula 1975, 30.

... *quam*. And also no 'shock treatment' is intended. Here we often have to do with contrasting pairs like 'love-hate', 'many-few', etc. Negations can also function within this group.

No one would dispute that, when in the Old Testament the verb 'to hate' is coupled with the verb 'to love', it can mean: 'to love less'. This is quite clear in Gn 29:30f:

> and he (i.e. Jacob) *loved* Rachel *more than Leah* (מִלֵּאָה) ...
> When the Lord saw that Leah was *hated* (שְׂנוּאָה) ... (cf v 33).

This will also hold true of Dt 21:15-17:

> If a man has two wives, the one *loved* and the other one *hated*...

There is no suggestion that here שְׂנוּאָה could mean anything other than 'less loved' or 'not loved'[19].

When we come to Ml 1:2d-3a we should, however, take care. In the light of the passages already quoted we should be inclined to understand this statement in the sense of: 'I have loved Jacob more than Esau' or: 'I have loved Jacob, but Esau I did not love'. This certainly removes the sharp edges to some extent. But apologetics should not determine how we interpret a text. The rest of the pericope makes it more than probable that in this case the verb 'hate' should carry its full force: Jahweh elaborates on his drastic actions against Esau.

The milder use of the verb 'to hate' when contrasted with 'to love' is also found in the New Testament. In Mt 6:24 (par. Lk 16:13) the contrast between μισεῖν and ἀγαπᾶν should not be taken in its plenary sense. It indicates rather that the servant will be *more* attached to the one master than to the other[20]. In these same verses the verbs ἀντέχειν and καταφρονεῖν, coupled chiastically with the two previous verbs, also form a rhetorical contrast pair[21].

Lk 14:26 (par. Mt 10:37) presents us with an interesting case. The Lucan wording of the first part of this statement, which, due to its Semitic colouring, offers the more original formulation, does not contain the love-hate contrast. It contains only μισεῖν. The contrasting concept of loving Jesus is missing. But this is only superficially the case. At the semantic deep level it is present, as is shown by Matthew. Moreover, the Lucan presentation certainly implies that one's love for Jesus should take precedence over family ties.

---

[19] See also Pr 13:24.

[20] G. B. Caird, *The language and imagery of the Bible*, London 1980, 112 paraphrases: "No man can take service under two masters without giving one of them preferential treatment".

[21] The love-hate contrast also occurs in Jn 12:25; 1 Jn 2:9 and Rm 9:13. This last verse is discussed below.

Another interesting example of this kind of exaggerated contrast is the 'many-few' contradiction in Mt 22:14: "For many are called, but few are chosen". It seems more than probable that this saying is not meant to indicate the very limited number of the elect, but rather that those who are called (invited) are substantially more than those actually chosen[22].

2. *Hyperbolical contrasts in Paul*

After this rather lengthy but necessary orientation we turn our attention to some of the more prominent cases of exaggerated contrast in Paul[23]. We find a text-book example of dialectical negation, which even the cautious Winer[24] accepts, in 1 Th 4:8:

> Therefore whoever rejects (this teaching which I have delivered to you - *vide* v 1ff) is not rejecting man but God..."

Undoubtedly anyone who rejected Paul's teaching by implication also rejected Paul the apostle and Paul the man. The semantic level of his statement therefore indicates that whoever rejects Paul's teaching rejects not so much the apostle as God who gave him his commission. But this is not expressed in a bland comparative. Paul applies the technique of verbal shock in order to counter the possibility of unholy living.

The Corinthian correspondence provides us with some interesting examples. At first reading 1 Cor 1:17 gives the impression that Paul's commission excludes the charge to baptize. When we realize that here we have an exaggerated contrast, it becomes clear that no such denial is intended. Paul simply wishes to stress the most important aspect of his charge. 1 Cor 7:10 is almost always interpreted as exclusive: "not I but the Lord", thus indicating that Paul is not only interrupting but also correcting himself. He has started to say: "To the married I give charge", and suddenly he breaks off to add that it is not his command but the Lord's. It seems more logical to accept that this is a dialectical negation: "To the married I give charge, but rather not I, the Lord himself..." In this way Paul does not contradict himself, and no real contrast between his command and the Lord's is implied.

1 Cor 15:10 is another fine example in point:

> But by the grace of God I am what I am, and his grace towards me was not in vain. On the contrary, I have worked harder than them all; and yet *not I, but the grace of God which is with me.*

---

[22] The same distinction would apply to Luke 12:47f.

[23] I restrict myself to some prominent examples in the Pauline *homologoumena*.

[24] Op. cit., 440f.

Again Paul does not wish to posit a contrast between his labour and the grace of God working through him. But he wants to have things in the right perspective: *Not so much* I, *but rather* the grace of God which is with me[25].

In conclusion we shall examine some intriguing passages in Romans. It seems apposite at this stage to quote a remark of Heinz Kruse. In discussing the characteristics of the dialectical negation he makes the observation "dass die in Frage stehende stilistische Eigentümlichkeit besonders in der direkten Rede, im Gespräch und in der Dichtung verwendet wird, wo durch die paradoxale Redeweise die Lebhaftigkeit des gesprochenen Wortes eine Verstärkung erfährt"[26]. We should expect, then, to encounter this figure fairly frequently in Romans (with its characteristic *diatribe* style). On the other hand, the dialectical negation tends to occur more often in passages where some kind of 'existential wrestling' is involved. This would be one reason why we find fewer specimens of this kind of rhetorical contrast in Romans than, say, in 1 Corinthians. As a matter of fact I have found only two probable examples. Characteristically enough both appear in the highly personal and existential Rm 7:14ff. The two occurrences are in vv 17 and 20. The content of these two verses agree substantially:

17. νυνὶ δὲ   οὐκέτι ἐγὼ κατεργάζομαι αὐτὸ
20. εἰ δὲ ὅ οὐ θέλω (ἐγὼ) τοῦτο ποιῶ οὐκέτι ἐγὼ κατεργάζομαι αὐτὸ

17. ἀλλὰ ἡ οἰκοῦσα ἐν ἐμοὶ ἁμαρτία.
20. ἀλλὰ ἡ οἰκοῦσα ἐν ἐμοὶ ἁμαρτία.

The literal translation of these two verses has provided a strong argument for the traditional view that Paul is dealing here with the Christian, torn apart in the battle between his converted ego and his sinful inclinations: he can at least console himself that it is not his ego, his real self, that breaks the law, but indwelling sin. But if these two sayings are taken as dialectical negations, which they probably should be, the situation changes[27]. It should be noted that in v 15f Paul actually states that it is

---

[25] Other instances in the Corinthian letters are 1 Cor 9:9f and 2 Cor 2:5. I do not consider 1 Cor 10:24 (cf Phlp 2:4) an instance of dialectical negation. The contrast seems to be absolute. The same applies to the Philippian passage, although the harshness of the contrast is here softened by καί

[26] Art. cit., 391.

[27] I am of opinion that this passage does not have either the pre-conversion or the post-conversion situation one-sidedly in view, but *concentrates on man's inability to fulfil the law on his own.* This is especially true of the pre-Christian who desires to conform to God's will, but it can also be true of the Christian who relies on his own strength and will-power. The real solution lies in Rm 8: Only through the Spirit is true obedience possible. In this sense I agree with O. Michel, *Der Brief an die Römer*, Meyers kritisch-exegetischer Kommentar über das Neue Testament, Göttingen [14]1978, 225ff, who stresses strongly that the main thrust of Rm 7:7ff is man's confrontation with the law of God.

"he"[28] who does the sinning, so that a flat denial of this fact in v 17 seems inconsistent. It would suit the context much better if we accepted that we have here a dialectical negation. Paul is really saying: "But now it is not so much I who am doing this, but rather sin which dwells within me". He does not exonerate himself, but points to the deeper cause of his misery: indwelling sin. The same reasoning applies to vv 18-20. In v 18f Paul again declares that it is "he" who is doing the evil which he does not want. In line with v 17, v 20 should therefore also be understood as stating: "But if I do what I do not want, it is not so much I who am doing this, but rather sin which dwells in me". In this regard it is worth pointing out that there is a strong structural resemblance between 1 Cor 15:10, which we have identified as a dialectical negation, and our two verses:

οὐκ   ἐγὼ δὲ   ἀλλὰ ἡ χάρις τοῦ θεοῦ (ἡ) σὺν ἐμοί.
οὐκέτι ἐγὼ κατεργάζομαι αὐτὸ ἀλλὰ ἡ οἰκοῦσα ἐν ἐμοὶ ἁμαρτία.

Do we find any normal hyperbolical contrasts in Romans?
Some three passages deserve our attention.
The most obvious will certainly be 9:13:

καθὼς γέγραπται· τὸν Ἰακὼβ ἠγάπησα, τὸν δὲ Ἡσαῦ ἐμίσησα.

This is a citation from Ml 1:2f (LXX). When we were discussing whether Ml 1:2f should be identified as a hyperbolical contrast, in view of the context of Ml 1:1-5 we came to a negative conclusion. But we cannot mechanically transfer this decision to Rm 9:13. It may well be that here, in line with the other New Testament passages we have mentioned, we do indeed have a rhetorical contrast and should therefore interpret: "God loved Jacob, but Esau he loved less/not". If at all possible, we should allow the Pauline context to decide the issue. (Apologetical considerations might entice us to settle for the less harsh option, but that would not be honest exegesis). Unfortunately the context does not help us any further. We could argue that in these verses the stress is on the positive aspect of God's favour towards Jacob, and that his attitude towards Esau should be seen only as the absence of such favour. But v 17ff refer not merely to the absence of God's favour but to an active hardening of the heart. It seems wisest, then, to leave the matter undecided. If a decision must be made, the strong emphasis on God's mercy tips the scale in favour of hyperbolical contrast.

An equally difficult decision confronts us in v 21 of the same chapter: The potter makes different vessels from the same clay

ὃ μὲν εἰς τιμὴν σκεῦος ὃ δὲ εἰς ἀτιμίαν.

---

[28] The ἐγώ of this passage is rhetorical, but that, of course, does not exclude Paul.

The question is whether we should translate: "the one (vessel) for decorative, the other for ordinary (menial) use" or rather "the one for noble (decorative), the other for ignoble use". A comparison with 2 Tm 2:20 or with the pottery imagery in the Old Testament and in late Judaism really does not help us much. We might be inclined to opt for the former alternative and agree with Cranfield that ἀτιμίαν "implies menial use, not reprobation or destruction"[29], if this did not conflict with the rest of the context (v 22f) where "the vessels of punishment made for destruction" (sic) (σκεύη ὀργῆς κατηρτισμένα εἰς ἀπώλειαν) are contrasted with the "vessels of mercy" (σκεύη ἐλέους ἅ προητοίμασεν εἰς δόξαν). We have therefore no choice but to decide for the second possibility.

There remains one passage which has caused some exegetical headaches in the past, viz. Rm 5:13

ἄχρι γὰρ νόμου ἁμαρτία ἦν ἐν κόσμῳ, ἁμαρτία δὲ οὐκ ἐλλογεῖται μὴ ὄντος νόμου.

In what sense can Paul say that "sin is not counted where there is no law?"[30] Has he not just stated that through Adam's sin death, which cannot be interpreted otherwise than as a penalty for his sin, has come over the whole of the human race? With unerring exegetical intuition Cranfield has concluded that οὐκ ἐλλογεῖται "must be understood in a relative sense: only in comparison with what takes place when the law is present can it be said that, in the law's absence, sin οὐκ ἐλλογεῖται". V 13b should certainly be understood as one part of an implied exaggerated contrast[31]. The objection that the other part of the saying is missing is not unsurmountable. As was the case with Luke 14:26[32], that part of the contrast is not really absent: it lies hidden in the semantic deep structure of the text, as is shown by the fact that it can readily be provided from the context. V 13b should therefore be translated: "But sin is reckoned less stringently when there is no law"[33].

---

[29] C. E. B. Cranfield, *Romans*, The International Critical Commentary Vol. II, Edinburgh 1979, 492 n. 2. Likewise many new translations.

[30] Cranfield, op. cit., I, Edinburgh 1975, 282.

[31] It is not impossible that also Rom 4:15 is an example in point. In that case v 15b should be understood as meaning: "But where there is no law, transgression is less clearly identified". On the other hand C. K. Barrett, *A Commentary on the Epistle to the Romans*, Black's New Testament Commentaries, London ²1962, 112 may be correct in accepting that Paul makes a distinction between 'sin' and 'transgression'. The former existed before the law was given; the latter, however, is associated with the promulgation of the law: "Sin is turned into transgression, and becomes visible and assessable, only when a law is given" (Barrett, op. cit., 112). And yet it should be noted that Paul speaks also of Adam's *parabásis* (5:14).

[32] Cf above p. 7f.

[33] I would not favour each and every rhetorical contrast being removed in translation, since that would cause impoverishment through the loss of the stylistic effect this figure provides. In many instances even a modern reader can supply the correct meaning from the context itself. But in instances where a misunderstanding is likely a clear formulation of the correct meaning is to be preferred.

J. H. ROBERTS

TRANSITIONAL TECHNIQUES TO THE LETTER BODY IN THE *CORPUS PAULINUM*

Studies on the formal aspects of the New Testament letters have not held the centre of the field of interest, but have nonetheless appeared regularly throughout this century. Next to the information provided in the more general works of Wendland (1912) and Deismann (1923), and the very detailed and comprehensive work by Exler (1923), as well as that by Meecham (1923) and Koskenniemi (1956) on the form of the Greek letter as seen especially in the papyri, specific studies on the New Testament letters began to appear in a constant, though shallow, stream.

The article on the Pauline greetings (Briefliche Grussüberschriften) by Lohmeyer (1927) was followed by Roller's study (1933) on the formal structure (das Formular) of the Pauline letter. In addition to a more general discussion of the form and function of Paul's letters (1939b), Schubert (1939a) made a detailed analysis of the form and function of the Pauline thanksgiving. He was later followed in this by O'Brien (1974/75; 1977; 1980). Alongside this should be placed the analysis of Paul's intercessory prayer passages by Wiles (1974). Work on the formal aspects of the body of the Pauline letter was by this time undertaken by White (1971a; 1971b; 1975). Kim (1972) studied the familiar Greek letter of recommendation, finding, on comparing Paul's recommendations, that Paul used his own typical forms.

General surveys of the letter form are to be found in Funk (1966), Van Roon (1969), Doty (1973) and Du Toit (1984b). Funk (1967) followed his overview with a study on a detail of the letter form, called by him the apostolic *parousia*. Another study on detail, viz. the use of *parakalō* as a formal element was presented by Bjerkelund (1967). Meanwhile a number of small literary forms within the Pauline letters—sometimes also appearing in other New Testament books and indeed outside the New Testament—were studied by Mullins (1962; 1964; 1968; 1972; 1972/73; 1980).

Further studies worth mentioning here are those by Boers (1975/76) who applied form critical findings to 1 Thessalonians arguing the point that the second thanksgiving (2:13-16) is an interpolation. Berger (1974), taking a different tack argues that Paul's letters should not be studied solely from the view point of letter form. In actual fact these letters are, according to him, apostolic speeches which show forth the typical form of such speeches. In line, perhaps, with this we find Galatians being read from the view point of ancient rhetoric by Betz (1974/75; 1979), and Philemon in the same way by Church (1978). Mention should also be made of the volume of contributions pertaining to various aspects of biblical letter writing, published in *Semeia* 22 under the editorship of White (1982).

In looking for definite results accruing from this intensive research, one could perhaps, somewhat simplistically, summarise the more or less accepted viewpoint with Du Toit (1984b:8,9) as follows, although one should take greater cognizance of the distinctions made by Exler (1923): (1) Letter opening containing the elements of sender, recipients and greeting; (2) *Formula valetudinis*; (3) Body opening; (4) Body; (5) Body closing; (6) Letter ending.

This analysis of the Pauline letter structure in particular, and some of the assumptions lying behind it can be criticised on various points. One can question whether the Greek *chairein*-greeting is equatable with the Pauline thanksgiving; whether thanksgiving and prayer sections should not be distinguished and whether the prayer sections are to be equated with the *proskunēma* formulae of the Greek letter; whether more attention should not be paid to the distinction between the thanksgiving form and the *berachah* form of 2 Corinthians, Ephesians (and 1 Peter); whether body openings and body closings—if these are indeed to be distinguished —should be treated as separate elements of the letter structure; and also, whether this kind of structuring in any way helps us to understand the relationship between the argument of a letter and the parenesis as well as the relationship between the opening sections of Paul's letters and the body. In addition more attention should definitely be paid to the various Aramaic letters found in biblical literature and outside it, in which the typical background to the Pauline letter conventions may be found.

To conclude this section we now have to return to the early sixties when, according to my knowledge, the first study to concern itself particularly with the transitional material which led from the letter opening into the body of the letter was published. This study by Sanders (1962) dealt with the "transition from opening epistolary thanksgiving to body in the letters of the Pauline corpus". His contribution is directly related to that of Schubert. Schubert had observed an eschatological climax at the end of the thanksgiving period. This was followed directly by the body matter—the reader finding himself in *medias res* once the eschatological climax was reached. According to Sanders the body itself was introduced by a formal phrase, either παρακαλῶ δέ, ἐρωτῶμεν δέ, or γινώσκειν δέ.

From these observations it follows that *at least two* transitory techniques are to be discerned: (1) the end of the thanksgiving period contains an *eschatological climax* marking the transition to the letter body; (2) the letter *body itself opens with a formal introduction*, again marking the transition into the body matter.

In addition to these Sanders noted three others. First he argued that thanksgiving (the Jewish *hodaya* form) is sometimes replaced by the *berachah* form (2 Corinthians, Ephesians, 1 Peter) which is doxological in nature and is in Jewish custom often concluded by a doxology. This implies that a doxology may form a *third transitional technique.* Such a doxology may however, be replaced by surrogate expressions. Thus the πιστός ὁ θεός expressions (as in 1 Cor 1:9) are to be understood as *surrogate doxologies*, again functioning as *a fourth transition* to the body matter. In the same way the *oblique petitions* in the second thanksgiving of 1 Thessalonians (3:11,12) was understood to be related to the *berachah*, indeed a surrogate of this form, denoting the end of the thanksgiving and forming *a fifth transition* to the body matter.

As far as transitional material in the body opening is concerned, White (1971) contributed five additional "formulae" to the already stated "request formula". He tabulates the following: a disclosure formula—the "you should know", or "I want you to know" type of expression; a request formula—e.g. the *parakalō* type; an expression of joy; an expression of astonishment; a statement of compliance—either reminding the readers that they have not yet complied or a statement that the writer has complied with previously given command(s) or request(s); and a formulaic use of a verb of hearing or learning.

The above analyses result in the following state of affairs: Transitional techniques are encountered in two sections of the Pauline letters: in the thanksgiving and in the body openings.

Within the thanksgiving may be encountered:

1) an eschatological climax at the end of the thanksgiving period;
2) a doxology;
3) a surrogate *berachah* in the form πιστός ὁ θεός;
4) an oblique petition functioning as a surrogate of the *berachah* form.

In addition, within the body opening the following may be encountered:

5) a disclosure formula;
6) a request formula;
7) an expression of joy;
8) an expression of astonishment;
9) a statement of compliance; and
10) a formulaic use of a verb of hearing or learning.

Generally speaking Sanders' strict adherence to the idea of a thanksgiving section being followed directly by the body, and the resulting attempt to define the encountered material in terms of thanksgiving, led to his circuitous argument regarding doxologies as elements of *berachoth* (true in itself) which can then be expected to form part of the thanksgiving; *berachoth* as substitutable for thanksgiving proper; and πιστός ὁ θεός as well as an oblique petition as surrogates for a *berachah*.

This reasoning is not only unconvincing, but also leads to a much too complicated picture of Paul's techniques of effecting a transition into his main topic or topics to be discussed. As will be seen later our analysis of the material leads to a much clearer picture once one no longer accepts that all material directly preceding the body must *per se* be defined as thanksgiving. Furthermore, the distinctive formal differences between *eucharistō* periods and *berachoth* should be borne in mind much more clearly than is here the case. The one is not simply a part of the other, and even if it should prove to be the case, then the tracing of this historical development can be of no help in determining either the techniques used to effect a transition into the body of the letters, or the function these techniques fulfilled within a particular letter.

As far as White's work on transitions within the body opening is concerned, one may, again generally speaking, question his use of the term "formula". In a thorough investigation of this matter Mullins (1972: 384-6) comes to the conclusion that the evidence for joy expressions as fixed forms is insufficient, and that it is lacking for statements of compliance and the so called formulaic use of verbs of hearing or learning, whereas the situation with expressions of astonishment is more complicated than White realized since a formal use only comes into focus where the verb is used ironically. Also "the characterization of these forms as 'introductory formulae' is inaccurate" (386). Rather they "punctuate a break in the writer's thought" (387).

In essence Mullins' criticism maintains that some of White's introductory formulae are not formulae and secondly that they do not fulfil an introductory function but rather serve to punctuate a break in the author's thought. Mullins certainly appears to have the right on his side. Does this, however, imply that the phenomena to which White had drawn attention (or at least some of them) have no epistolary function? I would suggest that the question whether these phenomena are formulae or not, is of no consequence to this question, and, furthermore, that their punctuating a break in the author's thought could point towards a transitional function between letter opening and letter body. In view of this I would suggest that we speak rather of techniques than of formulae, recognising that some of these techniques may very well have formulaic character—

this, however, being a totally different matter from the one we are treating here. Furthermore, I would suggest that we stress the transitional function of these techniques rather than the possible introductory role that some of them may also fulfil with regard to the body opening.

Bearing the foregoing in mind we can now turn to an analysis of the Pauline material. Before, however, paying attention to the transitional techniques themselves, one other question has to be resolved. Above, I referred to the fact that in the Pauline letters thanksgivings and prayer periods should be distinguished. In the literature this fact has mostly been overlooked (however, see Wiles 1974). In fact no less than three distinct patterns can be discerned in connection with thanksgivings and/or eulogies (*berachoth*) and prayer periods. This quite clearly will have specific bearing on the question of the collocation of transitional techniques within the letter opening. If my perception should prove to be correct, this means that one cannot simply speak of transitions from thanksgivings to body but should be much more precise with regard to the exact occurrence of the transitional techniques. This in turn will point to a more detailed set of epistolary conventions in the letter openings than is e.g. recognised in existing overviews of the Pauline letter form (cf above p. 188).

If a thanksgiving section is not the sole or distinctive element preceding the body opening, what then is the situation? In this connection the following should be borne in mind. *First*, a clear cut thanksgiving section does precede the body opening in 1 Cor 1:4-7. *Second*, combined thanksgivings/prayer periods which comprise a strongly formalised mixture of thanksgiving and prayer appear in Phlm 4-6; Eph 1:16-21; Col 1:3-8 and 2 Tm 1:3. *Third*, in some cases we find that the letter opening contains two separate periods consisting of a thanksgivings and a prayer section. This happens in Rm 1:8,9 and 1:9,10; Phlp 1:3-7 and 1:(8)9-11; 2 Th 1:3-10 and 1:11,12. In Colossians we find a combined thanksgivings/prayer period (Col 1:3-8, see above) followed by a prayer period (1:9-12). *Fourth*, in the case of 2 Corinthians and Ephesians the second epistolary element is not a thanksgiving but an eulogy in the form of a *berachah*. In 2 Corinthians the *berachah* (in the simplest form: call to praise God, followed by the reason for praising Him - 1:3-5) is followed by discrete periods of transition to the body (1:6-11). In Ephesians the first three chapters contain the elements of a complicated *berachah*. Here the call to praise God and its *accompanying* reasons (1:3-14) is followed by a combined thanksgivings/prayer period (1:15-21) and this in turn by a discrete period of transition (1:22,23).

The abovementioned clearly indicates that thanksgivings and prayer sections should be distinguished. The periods differ in form and in content as they differ from the combined thanksgivings/prayer periods found in Phlm 4-6; Eph 1:16-21; Col 1:3-8; 2 Tm 1:3. Once this has been recognised it becomes untenable to speak of transitions from thanksgiving to body of the letters. It should, instead, be recognised that transitions could occur in any of the forms referred to above. This means that, in addition to various transitional techniques used in the body opening itself, transitions may occur in the simple thanksgiving, in the combined thanksgivings/prayer period, and in the prayer period following on a thanksgiving. In the last case one should also be on the look out for transitional techniques that may already have been applied in the thanksgiving preceding the prayer period. In the same way one should look for such devices in the opening eulogies of 2 Corinthians and Ephesians.

To summarise—transitions may occur within a thanksgiving, an eulogy, a combined thanksgivings/prayer period, a prayer period, and in the body opening itself. The question now remains whether the available material corroborates this statement, and whether these were the only ways by which transitions were effected. As will be shown below, the Pauline letters indeed point towards an additional, yet unexplored, practice, viz. that transitional techniques were often grouped together in a clearly distinguishable, discrete period of transition situated directly before the body opening, and following on either one of the three thanksgivings/prayer or eulogy arrangements in the letter openings— whether a simple thanksgiving, or an eulogy, a combined thanksgivings/ prayer, or a thanksgiving plus separate prayer period. A careful analysis of the corpus of Pauline letters proves that such discrete transitional periods occur in Romans, 1 Corinthians, 2 Corinthians, Philippians, 1 Thessalonians, Philemon, as well as in Ephesians, Colossians, 1 Timothy and perhaps 2 Timothy (cf Rm 1:11-17; 1 Cor 1:8,9; 2 Cor 1:6-11; Eph 1:22,23; Phlp 1:12-30; Col 1:13-2:5; 1 Th 2:1-12; 1 Tm 1:15-17; 2 Tm 1:3b-5; 1:15-18; Phlm 7).

The picture relating to these statements, as well as the proof thereof, should become clear as we now turn our attention to the techniques of transition themselves and the various places they occupy within the letters.

To facilitate our ordering of the material I would suggest *first* that matters such as the so called disclosure formula and White's expressions of joy and astonishment, statements of compliance and formulaic use of verbs of hearing and learning all belong together under the heading: *"Expressions of a personal nature"*. These personal matters serve to bridge

the gap between the formal letter opening and body and therefore appear, with only one exception, in discrete periods. There appear to be
three kinds of such personal expressions, the *first* containing a desire dealing with knowledge, the *second* a feeling or statement regarding the
author's situation, and the *third*, used once only, a desire to visit the recipients.

The second and very important group of techniques have, as far as I
can see, up till now not been recognised for their transitional function.
These are all statements regarding aspects of faith or belief and may be
labelled: *Credal statements*. They all appear in discrete periods.

Table 1
Pauline transitions to the letter body - the various techniques and the letters in which they appear

Techniques	Number of occurrences	Source	Place within source
1. *Expressions of a personal nature*	14		
1.1 Desire dealing with knowledge	6	Rm 1:13-15	Discrete period
		2 Cor 1:8-11	Discrete period
		Phlp 1:12-30	Discrete period
		Col 2:1-4	Discrete period
		1 Th 2:1-12	Discrete period
		2 Tm 1:15-18	Discrete period
1.2 Feeling or state-ment regarding his situation	7	2 Cor 1:6,7	Discrete period
		Gl 1:6	Body opening
		Col 1:24-29	Discrete period
		Col 2:5	Discrete period
		1 Th 1:4-10	Thanksgiving period
		2 Tm 1:4	Discrete period
		Phlm 7	Discrete period
1.3 Desire to visit recipients	1	Rm 1:11,12	Discrete period
2. *Credal statement*	5	Rm 1:16,17	Discrete period
		1 Cor 1:8,9	Discrete period
		Eph 1:22,23	Discrete period
		Col 1:13-20	Discrete period
		1 Tm 1:15	Discrete period
3. *Doxology or doxological expression*	5	Gl 1:5	Letter opening
		Phlp 1:11	Prayer period
		2 Th 1:9,10	Thanksgiving period
		2 Th 1:12	Prayer period
		1 Tm 1:17	Discrete period
4. *Eschatological reference or climax*	4	1 Cor 1:7,8	Thanksgiving period
		Phlp 1:10	Prayer period
		1 Th 1:10	Thanksgiving period
		2 Th 1:6-10	Thanksgiving period
5. *Statement of a request*	3	2 Th 2:1	Body opening
		Phlm 8,9	Body opening
		Phlm 10	Body opening

As a third group we can distinguish either *doxologies* or *doxological expressions*. They can be found in almost any element at the start of the letters, ranging from formal letter opening, to thanksgiving period, to prayer period, to a discrete period of transition.

The fourth group consists of the well known *eschatological climaxes* or *references*. They seem to occupy a place in the thanksgiving or prayer sections.

The fifth and last group, found in the body opening is what has been called the disclosure formula and what I would rather designate as *the statement of a request*.

In the following diagram (table 1) the 31 occurrences of transitional techniques are tabulated under the five main headings mentioned above. It will be noticed that we are dealing with seven techniques in all.

Relating to the way in which they were used, the following remarks may be made:

1. It is noticeable that in 18 cases the techniques used occupy a more-or-less independent position in a discrete period at the beginning of the letter, i.e. a position not identical with the thanksgivings/prayer periods nor with the body opening.

2. The most popular techniques are those to do with personal feelings or matters, being applied 14 out of the 31 cases.

2.1 Among these the desire in connection with knowledge and a feeling or statement regarding the author's situation are the most important, taking first place among all occurrences, respectively six times in six letters, and seven times in six letters.

2.2 A desire to visit the recipients (the apostolic *parousia*) occurs only once.

2.3 Almost all these cases on the personal level occur in a separate period whose function lies in its transitional value—the only exceptions being Galatians, and 1 Thessalonians.

3. Combinations of various techniques are the rule and single occurrences rather the exception.

The following diagram points out the way in which techniques were combined:

As can be seen from the above table 30 out of the 31 occurrences of transitional techniques are used in combination with one or more other techniques, leaving only one case from the entire *corpus Paulinum* where only one technique is utilised.

In addition to this conclusion it remains to state explicitly that solely in the case of Titus no transitional technique is to be found.

Table 2
Single and combined use of transitional techniques

Number of techniques used	Count	Source		Total occurrences
Only one technique	Once	Eph	1	1
Two techniques used	5 times	1 Cor	2	
		2 Cor	2	
		Gl	2	
		1 Tm	2	
		2 Tm	2	10
Three techniques used	4 times	Rm	3	
		Phlp	3	
		1 Th	3	
		Phlm	3	12
Four techniques used	2 times	Col	4	
		2 Th	4	8
Total				31

Table 3
Number and nature of techniques used in each individual letter and its place within the letter

Source	Count	Technique	Place within letter
Rm 1:11-16	3	1. Desire to visit (1:11,12) 2. Readers should know (1:13-15) 3. Credal statement (1:16,17)	1-3. Discrete period(s) in between prayer period (1:9,10) and body opening (1:18ff)
1 Cor 1:7-9	2	1. Eschatological climax (1:7,8) 2. Credal statement (1:8,9)	1. End of thanksgiving (1·4-7) 2. Discrete period in between thanksgiving and body opening (1:10ff)
2 Cor 1:6-11	2	1. Personal statement on suffering and encouragement (1:6,7) 2. Readers should know (1:8-11)	1-2. Discrete periods in between *berachah* (1:3-5) and body opening (1:12ff)
Gl 1:5,6	2	1. Doxological expression (1:5) 2. Personal statement of astonishment (1:6)	1. Affixed to letter opening (1:1-5) 2. Body opening (1:6ff)
Eph 1:22,23	1	1. Credal statement (1:22,23)	1. Discrete period in between a combined thanksgiving-prayer section (1:15-22) and three explanations of the confession's meaning (2:1ff) which already forms part of the body
Phlp 1:10-30	3	1. Eschatological climax (1:10) 2. Doxology (1:11) 3. Readers should know (1:12-30)	1-2. End of prayer period (1:9-11) 3. Discrete period in between prayer period (1:9-11) and body (2:1ff)

Col 1:13-2:5	4	1. Credal statement (1:13-20) plus affixed period on its meaning (1:21-23) 2. Personal feeling of joy in tribulations (1:24-29) 3. Readers should know (2:1-4) 4. Personal feeling of joy and assurance (2:5)	1-4. Discrete periods in between prayer period (1:9-12) and body (2:6ff)
1 Th 1:4-2:12	3	1. Personal statements (1:4-10) 2. Eschatological climax (1:10) 3. Readers should know (2:1-12) with affixed second thanksgiving based on what is to be known (2:13-16)	1-2. Thanksgiving period 3. Discrete period in between a combined thanksgiving-prayer period (1:2-10) and body (2:17ff) (The personal desire to visit in this case is not a transitional device but the body matter itself.)
2 Th 1:6-2:1ff	4	1. Eschatological climax (1:6-10) 2. Doxological expression (1:9,10) 3. Doxological expression (1:12) 4. Request statement (2:1)	1-2. Thanksgiving period (1:3-10) 3. Prayer period (1:11,12) 4. Body opening (2:1ff)
1 Tm 1:15-17	2	1. Credal statement (1:15) plus reminiscence of personal experience of salvation (1:16) 2. Doxology (1:17)	1-2. Discrete period(s) following after thanksgiving period on initial direct opening of body which is resumed after this period (1:3-11,18ff)
2 Tm 1:4-18	2	1. Personal feeling of longing (1:4) coupled with various statements of personal nature and eschatological perspective (1:5-14) 2. Reader should know (1:15-18)	1-2. Discrete periods in between a combined thanksgiving-prayer period (1:3) and body (2:1ff)
Tt	–	–	–
Phlm 7-10	3	1. Personal feeling of joy (7) 2. Request statement (8,9) 3. Request statement (10)	1. Discrete period following on a combined thanksgiving-prayer period (4-6) 2-3. Body opening (8-10)

In view of table 1 and 2 we can now look at the results from the perspective of the various letters. Table 3 tabulates the results for each letter. Space will not allow us to discuss all these, but a few examples will suffice to show how the traditional techniques may function to highlight the main thrust of a letter.

Romans: In Rm 1:8 we find a thanksgiving dealing with the recipients' faith. This is followed in 1:9,10 by a prayer period. The content of the prayer was Paul's desire to be granted the opportunity to visit the recipients. Verse 11 no longer forms part of the prayer although it gives a motivation for the prayer. By means of an independent colon starting with γάρ Paul explains his personal longing to see them. This verse can not be construed as belonging to the prayer report. Paul is here addressing his readers. If it is not part of the prayer, it can only be taken as the start of a discrete period effecting a transition to the body, and therefore to the main purpose of the letter. Its function is to effect a feeling of friendliness (φιλοφρονησις - cf Koskenniemi 1956), to establish a close-felt relationship between author and readers. This is further clarified by stressing the reciprocal service to one another's faith that his visit would enhance (1:11,12).

The period is continued and brought to an end by 1:13-15. The litotes emphasises the author's desire for his readers. He definitely wants them to know how often he had thought to visit them and bring them the fruits of his service. Again this "readers-should-know-technique" here functions as a means of effecting a transition into the main reason for writing. On the one hand it further assures the reader's sympathy towards the author. On the other hand it establishes the fact that the author has a claim to them: they belong to the heathen communities among whom he has found his field of work; he is under an obligation towards them as towards all Greeks and *barbaroi* to bring them the gospel message. Since he can not be with them his letter will substitute for him as bearer of his message.

A new period consisting of 1:16-17 contains the third technique applied here to lead into the body. The litotes of verse 16 stresses Paul's pride in preaching the gospel. This in itself is a personal confession and leads into a credal statement regarding the gospel message: it is a powerful medium for the salvation of all men; it leads to the right relationship with God which is true life; it attains its effect where men put their trust in God.

Whereas it was the function of the previous two techniques to establish an experience of a friendly and close relationship between author and readers and to ensure a correct understanding of Paul's interest in them, the credal statement has the function of determining the essential core of the argument to be made by the letter.

1 Corinthians: The thanksgiving of 1 Cor 1:4-7 mentions that God is thanked for his gracious gift bestowed on them in Christ, for the richness given them, for their steadfastness in the message concerning Christ, for the fact that they abound in spiritual gifts (*charismata*). To top all this they are expecting the revelation, the *parousia*, of Christ.

Since the eschatological climax concludes the thanksgiving it has a formal transitional function. Content wise, however, it functions with the rest of the thanksgiving to relate the readers to the message of the letter. They are a richly blessed community with a wonderfully high expectation of the future. This determines the answers to their problems, the way they live their lives. Also, it establishes a foundation upon which later admonitions can be built, thus performing a rhetorical function.

The thanksgiving period is followed by a discrete period containing a credal statement (1:8,9). The fact that the statement is introduced by the relative ὅς does not imply that the sentence following is a subordinate relative clause, defining Christ as that Christ who .... As so often happens it introduces an independent colon which contains new information about the one to which v 7 refers: This Jesus Christ will keep firm to the end (TEV) at the day of the Lord. Following on this renewed eschatological reference, the second part of the credal statement moves to God, the Father: He who called them to communion with Jesus Christ his Son, is the trustworthy God upon whom they can depend.

Again, the transitional function of this credal statement should be clear: it states the essential saving work of God in Christ which ensures for the readers their dependable future; it thus enables Paul to grapple with their problems from this perspective.

Galatians: In the case of this letter Paul dispensed with both the thanksgiving and/or prayer forms which typify his letters. A doxological expression is affixed directly onto the greetings period which has been extended to include references to the fact that Christ had given himself to save us, and that this was in accordance with the will of God—to whom belongs everlasting glory. The extension as such, and particularly the fact that it stresses the glory of God who planned it all, contrasts strongly with the ironical θαυμάζω with which the letter body opens. Seeing that God should be glorified for the deliverance brought about in Christ, how could the author but be astonished that they have turned to some other message of "good news"? By means of this he directly enters into the main topic of his letter.

Ephesians: After the opening sender-addressees-greetings, the first three chapters of this letter contain the elements of a *berachah*, chiastically structured as a palindrome revolving around the credal statement in 1:22,23. First we find the call to praise God and the reasons for praising

Him (1:3-14) (a); then a combined thanksgivings/prayer period (1:15-21) (b); next the credal statement (1:22,23), followed by three pericopae explaining what this confession meant to the recipients (2:1-10; 2:11-18; 2:19-22) (c); now a renewed prayer period follows (3:1,14-19 with an interruption 3:2-13) (b¹); the whole section is concluded by a doxology (3:20,21) (a¹).

From the perspective of the letter form these elements could all be fitted into the Pauline letter pattern without any difficulty, the only exceptional feature being the fact that it also contains an opening *berachah* (as in 2 Corinthians) and an opening combined thanksgivings/prayer period. Again, looked at from the perspective of the letter form, the actual information which the author wishes his readers to understand clearly, is contained in the three explanatory passages of chapter 2. On the other hand 1:22,23 clearly no longer forms part of the foregoing prayer. These verses represent a credal statement situated as a discrete period in between the combined thanksgivings/prayer period and the letter body. As such it functions as a transition into the body. It provides the basis for the main argument of the letter provided by the three pericopae of chapter 2.

Philemon: Following on the greeting this letter has an intricately woven combined thanksgivings/prayer period (4-6). His thanking God is on account of reports he had heard to the effect that they put their trust in the Lord Jesus and that they love all God's people. His prayer is to the effect that others may start to partake of their trust in the Lord, i.e. may begin to trust Him as they do, when they perceive the good things Christians do for each other for the sake of Christ.

Structurally the thanksgivings/prayer period ends here. Structurally as well as contents-wise verse 7 does not belong to this period. Also it does not belong to the section starting with verse 8 since the request formulas in 8 and 10 point to the body opening, the request being the reason for writing.

Verse 7 thus forms a discrete period whose function lies in the transition it effects into the body material. It expresses the author's personal feeling of joy on account of the recipient's loving relationship to God's people who in turn were strengthened by his service. The author's joy for what Philemon did for other Christians leads into his request concerning Philemon's responsibility towards Onesimus who had now also become a Christian.

It would appear that, with the exception of the request verb in the body opening whose function is simply to state the request, the functions of the transitory techniques are to create a sympathetic relationship between author and reader which will allow successful communication and to lay a foundation for the argument/s or admonition/s to follow.

BIBLIOGRAPHY

BERGER, K. 1974. Apostelbrief und Apostolische Rede - zum Formular frühchristlicher Briefe. *ZNW* 65, 190-232.

BETZ, H. D. 1974/75. The literary composition and function of Paul's letter to the Galatians. *NTS* 21, 353-79.

BETZ, H. D. 1979. *Galatians*. Philadelphia: Fortress.

BJERKELUND, C. J. 1967. *Parakalô - Form, Funktion und Sinn der parakalô-Sätze in den paulinischen Briefen*. Oslo: Universitetsforlaget.

BOERS, H. 1975/76. The form critical study of Paul's letters. I Thessalonians as a case study. *NTS* 22, 140-58.

BRADLEY, D. G. 1953. The *topos* as a form in the Pauline paraenesis. *JBL* 72, 238-46.

CHURCH, F. F. 1978. Rhetorical structure and design in Paul's letter to Philemon. *HThR* 71, 17-33.

DEISMANN, A. 1923. *Licht vom Osten - das Neue Testament und die neuentdeckten Texte der hellenistisch-römischen Welt.* 4. ed. Tübingen: Mohr, 116-213.

DOTY, W. G. 1973. *Letters in primitive Christianity*. Philadelphia: Fortress.

DU TOIT, A. B. (ed) 1984a. *Handleiding by die Nuwe Testament, Band V: Die Pauliniese Briewe: Inleiding en Teologie*. Pretoria: N.G. Kerkboekhandel.

DU TOIT, A. B. 1984b. Oriënterende opmerkings oor die Pauliniese briefliteratuur, in Du Toit (ed) 1984a, 1-22.

EXLER, F. 1923. The form of the ancient Greek letter. A study in Greek epistolography. Washington DC: Catholic University of America.

FITZMYER, J. A. 1974. Some notes on Aramaic epistolography. *JBL* 93, 201-25.

FRIEDRICH, G. 1956. Lohmeyers These über das paulinische Briefpräskript kritisch beleuchtet. *ThLZ* 81, 343-46.

FUNK, R. W. 1966. *Language, hermeneutic, and Word of God - the problem of language in the New Testament and contemporary theology*. New York: Harper & Row.

FUNK, R. W. 1967. The apostolic parousia: form and significance, in W. R. Farmer, C. F. D. Moule & R. R. Niebuhr (eds), *Christian history and interpretation - studies presented to John Knox*. Cambridge: University Press, 249-68.

JEWETT, R. 1970. The epistolary thanksgiving and the integrity of Philippians. *NT* 12, 40-53.

KIM, C. H. 1972. *Form and structure of the familiar Greek letter of recommendation*. [Missoula]: SBL dissertation series 4.

KOSKENNIEMI, H. 1956. *Studien zur Idee und Phräseologie des griechischen Briefes bis 400 n Chr.* Helsinki: Akateeminen Kirjakauppa.

LOHMEYER, E. 1927. Probleme paulinischer Theologie I. Briefliche Grussüberschriften. *ZNW* 26, 158-73 = Briefliche Grussüberschriften, in *Probleme paulinischer Theologie*. Stuttgart: Kohlhammer (s.a.), 7-29.

MEECHAM, H. G. 1923. *Light from ancient letters - private correspondence in the non-literary papyri of Oxyrhynchus of the first four centuries, and its bearing on New Testament language and thought*. London: Allen & Unwin.

MULLINS, T. Y. 1962. Petition as a literary form. *NT* 5, 46-54.

MULLINS, T. Y. 1964. Disclosure. A literary form in the New Testament. *NT* 7, 44-50.

MULLINS, T. Y. 1968. Greeting as a New Testament form. *JBL* 87, 418-26.

MULLINS, T. Y. 1972. Formulas in New Testament epistles. *JBL* 91, 380-90.

MULLINS, T. Y. 1972/73. Ascription as a literary form. *NTS* 19, 194-205.

MULLINS, T. Y. 1980. Topos as a New Testament form. *JBL* 99, 541-7.

O'BRIEN, P. T. 1974/75. Thanksgiving and the gospel in Paul. *NTS* 21, 144-55.

O'BRIEN, P. T. 1977. *Introductory thanksgiving in the letters of Paul*. Leiden: Brill.

O'BRIEN, P. T. 1980. Thanksgiving within the structure of Pauline theology, in D. A. Hagner & M. J. Harris, *Pauline studies - essays to Professor F. F. Bruce on his 70th birthday*. Grand Rapids: Eerdmans, 50-79.

PARDEE, D. 1978. An overview of ancient Hebrew epistolography. *JBL* 97, 321-46.

PARUNAK, H. V. D. 1983. Transitional techniques in the Bible. *JBL* 102, 525-48.

ROBERTS, J. H. 1978. De knechtsgestalte van de kerk in de brief aan de Efeziërs, in *De knechtsgestalte van Christus - studies door collega's en oud-leerlingen aangeboden aan Prof. Dr. H. N. Ridderbos*. Kampen: Kok, 166-77.

ROBERTS, J. H. 1983. *Die Brief aan die Efesiërs*. Kaapstad: N. G. Kerk-Uitgewers.

ROBERTS, J. H. 1984. Die Gevangenskapsbriewe, in Du Toit (ed), 1984a, 114-57.

ROETZEL, C. 1969. The judgement form in Paul's letters. *JBL* 88, 305-12.

ROLLER, O. 1933. *Das Formular der paulinischen Briefe*. Stuttgart: Kohlhammer.

SANDERS, J. T. 1962. The transition from opening epistolary thanksgiving to body in the letters of the Pauline corpus. *JBL* 81, 348-62.

SCHUBERT, P. 1939a. *Form and function of the Pauline thanksgivings*. Berlin: Töpelmann.

SCHUBERT, P. 1939b. Form and function of the Pauline letters. *JR* 19, 365-77.

VAN ROON, A. 1969. *Een onderzoek naar de authenticiteit van de brief aan de Epheziërs*. Delft: Meinema.

WENDLAND, P. 1912. *Die hellenistisch-römische Kultur in ihren Beziehungen zu Judentum und Christentum - Die urchristlichen Literaturformen*. Tübingen: Mohr. (Handbuch zum Neuen Testament I.2.3, resp. 2. & 3. ed.)

WHITE, J. L. 1971a. The structural analysis of Philemon: a point of departure in the formal analysis of the Pauline letter, in *SBL one hundred seventh annual meeting seminar papers*, 1-47.

WHITE, J. L. 1971b. Introductory formulae in the body of the Pauline letter. *JBL* 90, 91-7.

WHITE, J. L. 1975. *The form and function of the body of the Greek letter - a study of the letter-body in the non-literary papyri and in Paul the apostle*. 2. cor ed. Missoula: Scholars Press/SBL.

WHITE, J. L. (ed) 1982. *Studies in ancient letter writing*. [Missoula]: SBL. (Semeia 22.)

WICKERT, U. 1961. Der Philemonbrief - Privatbrief oder apostolisches Schreiben? *ZNW* 52, 230-8.

WILES, G. P. 1974. *Paul's intercessory prayers - the significance of the intercessory prayer passages in the letters of St Paul*. Cambridge: University Press.

WUELLNER, W. H. 1976. Paul's rhetoric of argumentation in Romans. *CBQ* 38, 330-51.

A. H. SNYMAN

REMARKS ON THE STYLISTIC PARALLELISMS
IN I CORINTHIANS 13

ABSTRACT

The long history of research on Paul's style has neglected to a large extent the question of the (semiotic) meaning of the various rhetorical devices used in his letters. Instead of merely listing and classifying the rhetórical devices, an attempt is made in the present article to define their meanings in respect of two relations which they serve to mark, namely
— the relationship of parts of a text to one another, and
— the relationship of the text to the participants in the communication.

I Corinthians 13 is analyzed according to a method of stylistic analysis which takes into account the broader and more inclusive units normally related semantically, as well as the rhetorical features which serve to increase the impact and appeal of these broader units. In determining the meanings of these rhetorical devices, rhetorical principles in Hellenistic times are considered, as well as certain techniques used in modern literary analysis.

I Corinthians 13 has always been regarded as a jewel among the writings of Paul, mainly owing to the subject discussed. The aim of the present article is to add to such appreciation by drawing attention to an aspect of style in the said chapter: the parallelisms and their meaning, especially in view of certain theories on this literary mechanism in the hellenistic period.

In order to study the parallelisms within a comprehensive approach to style, the subject will be discussed under the following headings:
1. Methodological considerations in any stylistic analysis of the Greek New Testament;
2. An analysis of I Corinthians 13;
3. Possible meanings of the stylistic parallelisms identified in the chapter;
4. Conclusion.

1. *Methodological considerations*

The relation between rhetoric and style is not clear-cut. The two fields of study overlap and interact and applications of the terms are often very confusing. It is therefore advisable to clarify their relation in advance, before moving on to describe a specific method for stylistic analysis.

The classical distinction is that rhetoric is the wider subject including argumentation and the divisions of a speech—introduction, statement of the case, the proofs and the conclusion—while style is the technique employed in practice when the author expresses himself in language. Style is thus only a part of the whole rhetorical process and not identical with it (Louw 1982:6). Kennedy (1963:3-4), however, has a wider view of rhetoric and speaks of the rhetoric of sculpture and other arts in so far as they aim to change the attitudes of people, while Turner goes to the other extreme by restricting style to the syntactic level of language when he writes: "...style, in our view, involves the same considerations as syntax". (Moulton 1976:1). Zmijewski (1978:40-48) presents us with no less than seven different definitions of style and their representatives, apart from his own proposal. It seems as if the dispute concerning the relation between, and the definitions of, rhetoric and style is not to be resolved easily.

I wish to observe the subject from a different angle. In this approach, which forms part of the publication *Style and discourse*, no attempt is made to evaluate or classify the various definitions of rhetoric and style. Instead, attention will be paid to the way in which the concepts and thoughts in a discourse are arranged on two distinct levels: the macro- and the microlevel of rhetorical structure. The former deals primarily with the broader and more inclusive units which are normally related semantically, while rhetorical features on the microlevel serve to relate units on the macrolevel or to increase their impact and appeal by means of various formal devices. These rhetorical features must be classified in terms of processes, for the process is the actual key to the semiotic meaning of such features.

This brings us to the function or meaning of the rhetorical features. These features are signs which have meaning for the receptors. Anything that serves as a sign of something else, has meaning in the broad semiotic sense. It is in this sense that the term 'meaning' is used in the present article.

Turning now to the specific method for stylistic analysis proposed in *Style and discourse* (cf especially pp. 11-18 and 22-45) the following summary will suffice:

1.1. *The macrolevel of rhetorical structure*

The two elements on the macrolevel are progression and cohesion. Progression involves four discourse types:

– The first consists of a set of related events, essentially organized in terms of temporal progression;

– The second type consists of the description of certain objects or events. The description may be given in terms of space or in terms of categories;

– The third involves a set of discourse elements mainly related by virtue of certain logical connections between the parts. These logical relations may be classified as dependent, qualificational and dyadic (for more detail, see also Nida 1975:50ff);

– The fourth consists of dialogue in the sense that an author anticipates the objections of his readers and provides them with solutions in advance.

So much for progression. The second major element on the macrolevel is cohesion, which is attained by the following means:
– The thematic unity within a pericope or chapter;
– The unfolding nature of a sequence;
– Situational markers on the microlevel such as *here, now, there,* as well as referential markers including personal pronouns, relative pronouns and so on.

Progression accounts for the diversity of elements within a discourse, cohesion for its unity.

1.2. *The microlevel of rhetorical structure*

The significant rhetorical processes on this level include repetition, omission, a shift in expectancies and compactness:
– Repetitions may involve almost any unit of discourse from sounds to series of propositions and are classified in terms of sounds, grammatical constructions, lexical units and propositions;
– As with repetition, there are numerous possibilities for omission. They are of two main types: Omissions that can readily be supplied from the context, and those which cannot;
– Shifts in expectancies account for some of the more effective rhetorical features. The shift may be on the level of word order, of sentence structure or of lexical meaning;
– Compactness involves packing the maximum amount of meaning into the fewest possible words. It is typical of discourse formulae and credal formulations.

Just as important as—perhaps more important than—the identification of the rhetorical structures on the macro and microlevels, are their (semiotic) *meanings*. These can best be understood in terms of the five most important relations which the rhetorical features serve to mark:
– The interrelationship of parts of a text (cohesion);
– The relationship of a text to the participants in the communication (traditionally called the functions of a communication: informative, emotive, performative and the rest);
– The relationship of the text to the setting in terms of time and place;
– The relationship of the text to the real world;
– The relationship of the text to other, similar texts.

The specific method employed in the analysis of a text depends upon the type of text and the purpose of the analysis. In the case of I Corinthians 13 we have an example of poetic structure in the Greek New Testament. The main purpose of the analysis is to determine the (semiotic) meanings of the various repetitions used. To achieve this goal, the following method will be employed: Firstly the sentences will be broken up into their nuclear structures; secondly, the progression in the chapter in terms of the logical relations between the nuclear structures will be described; thirdly, attention will be paid to the cohesion of the chapter by studying its thematic unity. This will complete the description of the rhetorical structure on the macrolevel, dealing with the units which are normally related semantically.

The fourth step will be to identify the rhetorical features on the microlevel in terms of the repetition of, and balance between, sounds, lexical units and clauses.

The analysis will be concluded by a discussion of the possible meanings of the repetitions described in step four. In determining these meanings, only two relations in which they figure will be considered, namely the relationship of parts of the text to one another, and the relationship of the text to the reader.

2. The analysis of I Corinthians 13

1 Corinthians 13 may be divided into the following nuclear structures:

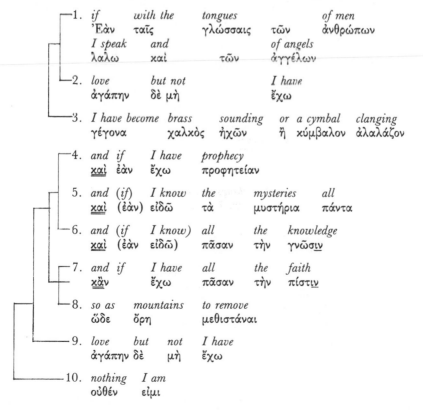

1. *if*   *with the*   *tongues*   *of men*
   Ἐὰν   ταῖς   γλώσσαις   τῶν   ἀνθρώπων
   I speak   *and*   *of angels*
   λαλῶ   καὶ   τῶν   ἀγγέλων

2. *love*   *but not*   *I have*
   ἀγάπην   δὲ μὴ   ἔχω

3. *I have become brass*   *sounding*   *or a cymbal*   *clanging*
   γέγονα   χαλκὸς ἠχῶν   ἢ   κύμβαλον   ἀλαλάζον

4. *and if*   *I have*   *prophecy*
   <u>καὶ</u> ἐὰν   ἔχω   προφητείαν

5. *and (if)*   *I know*   *the*   *mysteries*   *all*
   <u>καὶ</u> (ἐὰν) εἰδῶ   τὰ   μυστήρια   πάντα

6. *and (if*   *I know)*   *all*   *the*   *knowledge*
   <u>καὶ</u> (ἐὰν εἰδῶ)   πᾶσαν   τὴν   γνῶσι<u>ν</u>

7. *and if*   *I have*   *all*   *the*   *faith*
   <u>κἂν</u>   ἔχω   πᾶσαν   τὴν   πίστι<u>ν</u>

8. *so as*   *mountains*   *to remove*
   ὧδε   ὄρη   μεθιστάναι

9. *love*   *but*   *not*   *I have*
   ἀγάπην δὲ   μὴ   ἔχω

10. *nothing*   *I am*
    οὐθέν   εἰμι

11. *and* *if*   *I give away* *all*   *the*   *goods*   *of me*
    χἂν   ψωμίσα   πάντα   τὰ   ὑπάρχοντά   μου

12. *and* *if*   *I deliver up* *the*   *body*   *of me*
    καὶ ἐὰν παραδῶ   τὸ   σῶμά   μου.

13. *that*   *I may be burned*
    ἵνα   καυχήσομαι

14. *love*   *but*   *not*   *I have*
    ἀγάπην   δὲ   μὴ   ἔχω

15. *nothing*   *I am profited*
    οὐδὲν   ὠφελοῦμαι

16. *love*   *has patience*
    ἡ ἀγάπη   μακροθυμεῖ +

17. *it is kind*   *love*
    χρηστεύει   ἡ ἀγάπη

18. *not*   *it is envious*
    οὐ   ζήλοι
    1   2

19. *not*   *it is vain-glorious*
    οὐ   περπερεύεται +
    1   2

20. *not*   *it is puffed up*
    οὐ   φυσιοῦται   +
    1   2

21. *not*   *it acts unseemly*
    οὐχ   ἀσχημονεῖ
    1   2

22. *not*   *it seeks*   *the*   *things of its own*
    οὐ   ζητεῖ   τὰ   ἑαυτῆς   +

23. *not*   *it reckons*   *the*   *evil*
    οὐ   λογίζεται   τὸ   κακόν

24. *not*   *it rejoices*   *at*   *unrighteousness*
    οὐ   χαίρει   ἐπὶ   τῇ ἀδικίᾳ +

25. *it rejoices with* *but*   *the*   *truth*
    συγχαίρει   δὲ   τῇ   ἀληθείᾳ

26. *all things*   *it covers*
    πάντα   στέγει
    1   2

27. *all things*   *it believes*
    <u>πάντα</u>   <u>πιστεύει</u> +
    1   2

28. *all things*   *it hopes*
    <u>πάντα</u>   <u>ἐλπίζει</u>
    1   2

29. *all things*   *it endures*
    <u>πάντα</u>   <u>ὑπομένει</u>
    1   2

30.   *love*   *never*   *fails*
    ἡ ἀγάπη οὐδέποτε <u>πίπτει</u>

31. *whether* *but* *prophecies*
    εἴτε   δὲ   <u>προφητεῖαι</u>

32. *they shall be done away*
    <u>καταργηθήσονται</u>

33. *whether* *tongues*
    εἴτε   <u>γλῶσσαι</u>

34. *they shall cease*
    <u>παύσονται</u>

35. *whether* *knowledge*
    εἴτε   γνῶσις

36. *it shall be done away*
    <u>καταργηθήσεται</u>

37. *in part* *for* *we know*
    <u>ἐκ μέρους</u> γὰρ <u>γινώσκομεν</u>

38. *and* *in* *part*   *we prophesy*
    (καὶ) <u>ἐκ</u> <u>μέρους</u> <u>προφητεύομεν</u>

39. *when* *but it* *may come* *the* *perfect*
    <u>ὅταν</u> δὲ <u>ἔλθῃ</u> τὸ <u>τέλειον</u>

40. *that* *in part*   *shall be done away*
    τὸ <u>ἐκ μέρους</u> <u>καταργηθήσεται</u>

41. *when* *I was* *an infant*
    ὅτε <u>ἤμην</u> <u>νήπιος</u> +

42. *I spoke*   *as* *an infant*
    <u>ἐλάλουν</u>   <u>ὡς</u> <u>νήπιος</u> +
    1   2   3

43. *I thought* *as* *an infant*
    <u>ἐφρόνουν</u> <u>ὡς</u> <u>νήπιος</u>
    1   2   3

44. *I reasoned   as   an infant*
    ἐλογιζόμην   ὡς   νήπιος
    1   2   3

45. *when   I became   a man*
    ὅτε   γέγονα   ἀνήρ

46. *I did away with   the things   of the   infant*
    κατήργηκα   τὰ   τοῦ   νηπίου

47. *we see   for   now   through   a glass*
    βλέπομεν   γὰρ   ἄρτι   δί'   ἐσόπτρου   ἐν
    obscurely
    αἰνίγματι

48. *then   but   (we shall see)   face   to   face*
    τότε   δὲ   (βλέψομεν)   πρόσωπον   πρὸς   πρόσωπον

49. *now   I know   in   part*
    ἄρτι   γινώσκω   ἐκ   μέρους   +

50. *then   but   I shall know*
    τότε   δὲ   ἐπιγνώσομαι   +

51. *according   as also   I have been known*
    καθὼς   καὶ   ἐπεγνώσθην

52. *now   but   abides   faith*
    νυνὶ   δὲ   μένει   πίστις

53. *(now   but   abides)   hope*
    (νυνὶ   δὲ   μένει)   ἐλπίς

54. *(now   but   abides)   love*
    (νυνὶ   δὲ   μένει)   ἀγάπη

55. *(now   but   abides)   these   three   things*
    (νυνὶ   δὲ   μένει)   τὰ   τρία   ταῦτα

56. *the greater   but   of these   (is)   love*
    μείζων   δὲ   τούτων   ἡ   ἀγάπη

Before describing the relations between the nuclear structures it is necessary to make some remarks on the syntactic structure of the pericope. The syntactic structure is indicated by the couplings on the left-hand side of the text and consists of 56 nuclear structures (if the divisions between 31-36 and 52-55 are accepted), embedded into 34 cola (for a definition of a nuclear structure, see Nida 1983:93ff; for a colon, see Louw 1979:24ff). The three cola with which the chapter begins (items 1-3, 4-10 and 11-15), have a parallel structure:

ἐάν-clause	: 1	4-8	11-13
Statement	: 2	9	14
'Then'-clause	: 3	10	15

The statement is the matrix, bracketed in each case by an ἐάν-clause and a 'then'-clause, and each time the wording is identical: ἀγάπην δὲ μὴ ἔχω (2, 9 and 14). In items 3, 10 and 15 we have a repetition of the same 'then'-clause, stated positively in item 3, and negatively in items 10 and 15. Semantically, however, all three are negatives, because item 3 means the same as οὐθέν εἰμι (10) and οὐδὲν ὠφελοῦμαι (15). (The possible meanings of these repetitions will be discussed below).

The logical relations between the nuclear structures are as follows: Item 2 is in contrast with item 1, and together they form the concession for item 3. Item 3 is the result of items 1 and 2. Items 4-7 are additive-different, while item 8 is the result of 7, with 7 the means for item 8. Item 9 is in contrast with items 4-8, and items 4-9 are the concession for 10. Item 10 is the result of 4-9. The same pattern repeats itself in items 11-15. Items 11-12 are additive-different, while 13 is the purpose of 12, with 12 the means for 13. Item 14 is in contrast with items 11-13, and items 11-14 the concession for 15. Item 15 is the result of items 11-14.

Items 16-29 are all characterizations of love and additive-different. Item 30 is also a characterization of love, with 31-36 in contrast with 30. Items 31-32, 33-34 and 35-36 are additive-different. Items 37-40 are the reason for 30-36, with 37 and 38 additive-different, 39-40 in contrast with 37-38 and 39 temporal in relation to 40.

Item 41 is temporal with regard to items 42, 43 and 44, and items 42, 43 and 44 are additive-different. Item 41 is also generic, with 42-44 specific. Items 45-46 are in contrast with 41-44, while 45 is temporal with regard to 46. Item 48 is in contrast with 47, just as 50-51 are in contrast with 49. Items 52-55 are also in contrast with the whole preceding section, i.e. items 30-51. Item 55 is generic, with items 52-54 specific. Item 56 stands in comparative relation to 52-55.

It is certainly possible to describe the logical relations in more detail, but this brief exposition gives an idea of the progression in the chapter. Cohesion is the next element on the macrolevel of rhetorical structure, and is mainly brought about by the thematic unity of I Corinthians 13. The theme of the chapter is love, as is shown by the word ἀγάπη in items 2, 9, 14, 16, 17, 30, 54 and 56, and by the third person singular ending with all the verbs in items 16-29 referring to love. Cohesion on the macrolevel is also brought about by the repetition of the same syntactic structures in items 1-3, 4-10 and 11-15 (as indicated above). The same thoughts in 1-15 are repeated towards the end of the chapter, namely in 52-56: love is the supreme gift of the Spirit. All these repetitions strengthen the thematic unity within the discourse. Our discussion thus far will suffice for the description of the rhetorical structure on the macrolevel.

A. H. SNYMAN

With reference to the rhetorical features on the microlevel, observations will be limited to the process of repetition of, and balance between, sounds, lexical units and clauses. The parallelisms are marked on the Greek text above as follows:

Antithesis: ⌐ ͞ ͞ ⌐
                  ⌞ ͏ ͏ ⌟

Sound or word similarities at the beginning
of successive items: ═══

Sound or word similarities at the end
of successive items: ─────

Agreement in the number of syllables: ═ ═ ═ +

Parallel sentence structure: 1   2   3
                                1   2   3

A cursory view shows that most figures of style occur in items 16-29, where love is characterized, with a considerable number also in items 31-51, where the permanent nature of love is described by referring to the transient nature of the other gifts of the Spirit - especially knowledge. The following features are worth mentioning:
- The antitheses between 24 and 25, 37-38 and 39-40, 49 and 50-51;
- The sound or word similarities at the beginning of 18-24, 24 and 25, 26-29, 37-38, 42-44;
- The sound or word similarities at the end of 19 and 20, 24 and 25, 26-30, 31-34, 37-38, 41-44;
- The agreement in number of syllables in items 16 and 17, in 19, 20 and 21, in 22 and 23, in 24 and 25, in 27 and 28, in 37 and 38, in 39 and 40, in 41, 42 and 43, and in 49, 50 and 51;
- Parallel sentence structures in items 18, 19, 20 and 21, in 26, 27, 28, 29 and in 42, 43 and 44.

3. *Possible meanings for these stylistic parallelisms*

It is clear from the previous section that there is a very high frequency of parallelisms in I Corinthians 13. What could be the semiotic meanings of these rhetorical markers?

In answering this question, two scholarly viewpoints will be taken into account. The first is the broad framework of modern literary analysis in which rhetorical features are studied and described in terms of their semiotic meanings. The second is a study of the theoretical works of the Hellenistic period, dealing with the notion of repetition. Special attention will be focused on the influential work of Demetrius entitled περὶ

ἑρμηνείας, in which several meanings of stylistic parallelisms are discussed in detail. These meanings will be described in just two relations which they serve to mark, namely:
– the relationship of parts of the text to one another; and
– that of the text to the reader.
The former is actually an aspect of cohesion. Repetition is the most important way in which cohesion is attained. The following examples will show how this process strengthens the ties between the nuclear structures on the macrolevel: The additive relation between items 16 and 17 is reinforced by the fact that both have the same number of syllables (and the words are also arranged chiastically); the negative οὐ at the beginning of items 18-24 enhances the additive relation between them; πάντα at the beginning of items 26-29, plus -ει at the end of each, strengthen the ties between them; the additive relation between 42-44 gains strength by each beginning with ε-, ending on νήπιος and having the same sentence structure, with νήπιος linking them to 41.

The cohesion of the whole chapter is strengthened by the same kind of rhetorical markers, distributed evenly throughout the discourse. Agreement in number of syllables is for example used as rhetorical marker in items 16 and 17, in 19, 20 and 21, in 22 and 23, in 24 and 25, in 27 and 28, in 37 and 38, in 39 and 40, in 41-43, and finally in 49-51. The repeated use of the same kind of rhetorical marker on this broad level also serves a cohesive function.

Demetrius suggests a further possible meaning of these parallelisms. In paragraph 154 of his περὶ ἑρμηνείας he stresses that similarity in the members of a sentence is one of the sources of graceful composition. The numerous similarities in I Corinthians 13 may thus characterize the discourse as graceful. At the same time Paul is obeying one of the most important principles of style in Hellenistic times: that of τὸ πρέπον (appropriateness). The charm of his subject, Love, is in harmony with the graceful expression of his thoughts.

The three possible meanings of the parallelisms discerned so far may thus be summarized as
– strengthening the ties between the nuclear structures on the macrolevel,
– strengthening cohesion in the chapter as a whole, and
– characterizing the discourse as graceful.
In what way do the parallelisms mark the relationship of the text to the reader?

Firstly, they create a gracious effect. Paragraphs 27-29 of the first, and 154, 247 and 250 of the second part of the περὶ ἑρμηνείας deal with the functions or meanings of the socalled Gorgianic figures (stylistic parallelisms). In these paragraphs Demetrius emphasises that the use of cola, at once antithetical and symmetrical, are ill-suited in passages expressing honest indignation (par. 250), or in outbursts of passion (ἐν πάθεσιν). They are, however, very useful to produce a pleasant effect (par. 29).

A second possible meaning results from the previous one. By a gracious appeal to his readers' emotions, Paul attracts them to his subject and persuades them at the same time to share his sentiments on love as the supreme gift of the Spirit. The motive of persuasion in the stirring up of emotions was an important and well-known one from the time of Gorgias up to Quintilian. Both the poet and the orator were ψυχαγωγοί, that is, people who ''lead the souls'' of other people by appealing to their emotions (Kennedy 1963:63). Emotive persuasion was one of Gorgias' original aims, and it is possible that we should also reckon with this motive in determining the meanings of the stylistic parallelisms in I Corinthians 13.

Regarding the relationship of the text to the reader, the parallelisms in our chapter may thus signal either or both of the following:
– a gracious effect;
– persuasion.

4. *Conclusion*

In the introduction to this article the purpose of my investigation was described as an attempt to determine the meanings of the stylistic parallelisms in I Corinthians 13 by means of a comprehensive approach to stylistic analysis. The proposed analytic method is not content with the mere listing or classification of stylistic devices, but aims at defining their meanings in terms of certain processes. Several meanings were identified for the parallelisms by applying techniques used in modern literary analysis and also by studying the meanings of rhetorical features as defined in theoretical works of the Hellenistic period. There may be more, but those mentioned above seem to be the most obvious ones in view of the subject under discussion and the poetic nature of the chapter.

Certain problems, however, require further investigation. The first is the relation between progression and cohesion. Must we regard them as two distinct elements on the macrolevel of rhetorical structure, or is progression just an aspect of cohesion? Another problem of a more serious nature is the relation between stylistic studies like the one presented here, and sociolinguistics. The method used in our analysis does not treat the communication event in its totality, but restricts itself to the linguistic features of the text. It ought to be extended to include also the extra-linguistic or social context in which Paul has written his letter. Such an extension will enable us to determine the meanings of the stylistic devices with greater certainty.

BIBLIOGRAPHY

DEMETRIUS 1965. *On style*, tr by W. R. Roberts. London: Heinemann. (Loeb Classical Library.)

KENNEDY, G. 1963. *The art of persuasion in Greece*. Princeton: Princeton University Press.

LOUW, J. P. 1979. *A semantic discourse analysis of Romans*, Vols. I and II. Pretoria: University of Pretoria (Dept. of Greek).

LOUW, J. P. 1982. *Rhetoric and style in ancient Greek education, with special emphasis on style*. Unpublished contribution to a seminar on style, University of Pretoria.

MOULTON, J. H. 1976. *A Grammar of New Testament Greek, Vol. IV, Style*. Edinburgh: Clark.

NIDA, E. A. 1975. *Exploring semantic structures*. München: Fink.

NIDA, E. A., J. P. LOUW, A. H. SNYMAN & J. v. W. CRONJE 1983. *Style and discourse (with special reference to the text of the Greek New Testament)*. Cape Town: Bible Society.

ZMIJEWSKI, J. 1978. *Der Stil der paulinischen ''Narrenrede''. Analyse der Sprachgestaltung in 2 Kor 11,1-12,10 als Beitrag zur Methodik von Stiluntersuchungen neutestamentlicher Texte*. Köln-Bonn: Peter Hanstein. (Bonner Biblische Beiträge.)

J. VAN W. CRONJÉ

DEFAMILIARIZATION IN THE LETTER
TO THE GALATIANS

Reading the *Letter to the Galatians* from a stylistic point of view, one is struck by the impact achieved by various stylistic devices or techniques. The object of this paper is to show that the special effect of this letter is achieved due to the fact that most of its special stylistic features have one common denominator: the unexpected.

The first part of the paper will be devoted to the theory concerning the element of the unexpected in general and in literature in particular; in the second part this theory will be applied to the letter to the Galatians.

In 1919 an essay of the Russian formalist, Victor Shklovsky, *Iskusstvo kak priem*, was published, translated by L. T. Lemon and M. J. Reis in 1965, with the title "Art as Device". In this essay Shklovsky dealt with the problem of the distinctive nature of literature. Disputing the prevailing view that the distinctive characteristic quality of literature is imagery (Visser 1982:17), he turns to what he believes to be the function and effect of art: *ostranenie*, defamiliarization.

How is this to be understood?

Ostranenie can only be understood in relation to its counterpart, *automatization*, habitualization. According to him perception becomes habitual to the point of being merely automatic: "perception becomes habitual, it becomes automatic" (Shklovsky 1965:11).

This quality of habitualization involves the whole spectrum of life, destroying the essence of sensation of life. This is where art comes in: the object of art is to restore this sensation: "And art exists that one may recover the sensation of life; it exists to make one feel things, to make the stone *stony*" (Shklovsky 1965:12).

The way in which art accomplishes this object, is by making familiar objects unfamiliar, by presenting familiar objects in an unfamiliar way, thus overcoming the automatic quality of familiar perception. This is the technique, device of art, and so far as literature is concerned, the very distinctive nature of literariness; this is what Shklovsky called *ostranenie* and what has been translated by "defamiliarization", "estrangement", "alienation" (Stacy 1977:3), "foregrounding" (Mukařovský 1964:19).

There are numerous ways in which this defamiliarization can be brought about as will be explained in due time; but the interesting point is that all these techniques have the same effect upon the reader: the difficulty and length of perception are increased (Shklovsky 1965:12) causing a definite "retardation" in perception. The reader is forced to reconsider, "re-think" the meaning of a word, phrase or sentence, which is exactly what the author would have liked him to do. To Shklovsky this effect of the technique of *ostranenie* will enable the reader to experience art in itself, for to him the process of perception is an aesthetic end in itself and must be prolonged. "Art is a way of experiencing the artfulness of an object: the object is not important".

For the purpose of this paper it is likewise of crucial importance, but for another reason: the reader's attention is captivated by the unfamiliar way a familiar subject is presented.

According to Shklovsky and Jan Mukařovský (1964:19) the reader's attention will thus be drawn to the "act of expression" itself in the case of literature—not to the content. In the case of non-literary texts, however, the purpose of foregrounding is to attract the reader's (listener's) attention to the subject-matter expressed by foregrounded means of expression (Mukařovský 1964:19).

The Russian Formalist soon realized that a work of art had to be more than the sum total of all the devices applied in a work, a view proposed by Shklovsky in 1921 (Erlich 1969:20). They proceeded to a more advanced view of a literary work, seeing it as "an integrated, structured system" (Visser 1982:29).

At the same time R. Jakobson introduced the concept of the *dominant*. This became an important concept among structuralists. It is used to distinguish literary from non-literary texts[1], to distinguish one genre from another and one mode from another. As a matter of fact, recently J. Mukařovský even applied this concept to every individual work of art. Many components are involved in a work of art: the phonetic structure, lexical selection, sentence structure, etc. However, not all components are equally foregrounded. In every work of art all the components are interrelated, but one component emerges as the most important. This is the *dominant*, the one component which determines the interpretation and position of the other components, thus creating the unity of a work of art (Mukařovský 1964:21).

The dominant determines the relative functional position of all the other components in a work. Some components will converge towards the dominant, thus creating a "unity in variety", a dynamic unity, while others will diverge from this trend, forming the unforegrounded background.

---

[1] Considering all literature, i.e. literary as well as non-literary works, Jakobson claims that the dominant feature of literary works is the "aesthetic function" (Visser 1982:21).

From this it follows that a foregrounding of all components would be impossible and in any case undesirable, the reason being that the foregrounding of a component would not be possible without the relative less foregrounded position of other elements. As a matter of fact, a simultaneous general foregrounding, had it been possible, would create the exact opposite effect than desired: automatization (Mukařovský 1964:20).

Furthermore, the presence of automatization in a work should not be regarded as weak spots. On the contrary, without them foregrounding would not be possible: "they constitute the background against which the distortion of the other components is reflected" (Mukařovský 1964:19).

So far as the linguistic components of a literary work are concerned, foregrounding occurs when distortion of the norms of the standard language occurs, but also when the literary tradition is violated, e.g. concerning fixed rules concerning a genre or sub-genre. This is especially true of the times in which genres were regarded as fixed, distinctive types, and so far as the standard language is concerned, the more the norms of the standard are stabilized in a given language, the more varied can be their violation (Mukařovský 1964:18).

Turning to the devices by means of which *ostranenie* can be effectuated, Shklovsky gives a general principle: "all techniques whereby the artist portrays or describes—and thereby causes us to see—something familiar in a fresh, defamiliarized way" (Stacy 1977:39). In antiquity these devices were known as figures of speech (σχήματα) and were subdivided in two major categories, i.e. figures of thought (σχήματα διανοίας) and figures of diction (σχήματα λέξεως). Other classifications were also proposed, e.g. between grammatical and syntactical figures on the one hand, and rhetorical figures on the other, or poetic vs. rhetorical in other cases. These distinctions have proven to be untenable, due to overlapping and inconsistencies.

A new classification was proposed by A. H. Snyman and J. van W. Cronjé in 1983 in cooperation with dr. E. A. Nida en prof. J. P. Louw (cf. Snyman & Cronjé 1983:172-191). All figures were classified according to four basic principles, i.e. repetition, omission, shift in expectancies and measurement of units. Comparing the devices of estrangement by Stacy with this classification, it is interesting to note that they coincide to a great extent with the devices classified under "shift in expectancies", and quite understandable too, for "shift in expectancies" is basically the same as the principle involved in *ostranenie*. For the sake of clarity this category can be sub-divided into five sub-sections, according to 1. word-order; 2. syntax; 3. propositions; 4. communication function; 5. meaning and referent. A further sub-division is possible, but not necessary. A synopsis of this category amounts to the following scheme:

Shift in expectancies

A. *Shifts in expectancies of word-order*

    1. Unusual position in a clause: Hyperbaton.
    2. Unusual position outside the clause: Prolepsis.
    3. Insertion: Parenthesis and Dihorthosis.

B. *Shifts in expectancies of the syntax*

    Anacoluthon.
    Synecdoche.

C. *Shifts in propositions*

    1. Apparent contradictions: Oxumoron and Paradoxon.
    2. Contradiction in content and intent: Eironeia, Litotes, Hyperbole and Paraleipsis (to proceed contrary to statement).

D. *Shifts with regard to the communication function*

    1. Rhetorical question: Erotema.
    2. Question and answer: Dialektikon.
    3. Literal and figurative meaning: Metaphora, Metonumia and Prosopopoiia.

E. *Shifts between meaning and referent*

    Periphrasis and Antonomasia.

In principle all figures of speech—and not only these—could be classified under "shifts in expectancies", for all figures in fact deviate from what could be regarded as the standard, normal.

In this sense the classification by Snyman and Cronjé is not altogether consistent. Many figures, however, have additional formal features which are in fact more conspicuous than their being "ab-normal". That is the reason why a classification according to these conspicuous features (repetition, omission, measurement of units) is quite justified. Furthermore, it goes without saying that not all figures would have the same estranging effect. Thus not all types of repetition would have the same striking effect: for example, all repetitions involving structurally significant positions would have more effect than repetitions in structurally non-significant positions, but would not be as effective in terms of estrangement as e.g. a Metaphora. But then, many Metaphoras have become so common, that they have indeed lost all estranging effect and have become automatized.

Before proceeding to the application of this theory of *ostranenie* to the *Letter of Paul to the Galatians*, one final remark: figures of speech are not the only technique by means of which *ostranenie* can be brought about; any deviation from the customary, whatsoever, will effectuate *estrangement*. That goes for the use of rare, archaic, obsolete words (ἄπαξ λεγόμενα) (Stacy 1977:56), as well as for any deviation from literary convention, e.g. with regard to a specific genre or sub-genre (Mukařovský 1977:21).

Turning to the *Letter to the Galatians*, one is struck by the fact that figures of repetition are virtually non-existent; a few chiasms have been applied (e.g. in 5:16), but the highly artificial Gorgianic figures (Isocolon, Parison, Parhomoiosis) have not been used once. Paul does, however, make use of Antitheses of content, e.g. in 5:13-26. So far as figures of omission are concerned, only some Elleipses can be annotated, but they are purely grammatical and need not be considered. No example of Gnomes or Aphorisms ("measurement of units") can be provided.

In contrast to this, virtually all figures present in this letter are figures involving a "shift in expectancies". Of virtually every figure of this category examples can be supplied, but some figures should receive special attention, e.g. the use of rhetorical questions (ἐρωτήματα) Metaphors, Anacoluthons and Paradoxes.

In Gl 1:6 Paul states his disappointment in the Galatians in deserting the gospel being taught them by himself:

Θαυμάζω ὅτι οὕτως ταχέως μετατίθεσθε ἀπὸ τοῦ καλέσαντος ὑμᾶς ἐν χάριτι (Χριστοῦ) εἰς ἕτερον εὐαγγέλιον

("I am surprised at you! In no time you are deserting the one who called you by the grace of Christ, and are going to another gospel") (TEV).

In Gl 3:1-5 Paul is really showing his disappointment in this sin of the Galatians, but instead of using straight forward statements, he expresses the intensity of his emotions concerning this matter in six consecutive questions:

1. ῏Ω ἀνόητοι Γαλάται, τίς ὑμᾶς ἐβάσκανεν, οἷς κατ᾽
   ὀφθαλμοὺς Ἰησοῦς Χριστὸς προεγράφη ἐσταυρωμένος;
2. τοῦτο μόνον θέλω μαθεῖν ἀφ᾽ ὑμῶν, ἐξ ἔργων νόμου
   τὸ πνεῦμα ἐλάβετε ἢ ἐξ ἀκοῆς πίστεως;
3. οὕτως ἀνόητοί ἐστε; ἐναρξάμενοι πνεύματι νῦν σαρκὶ
   ἐπιτελεῖσθε;
4. τοσαῦτα ἐπάθετε εἰκῇ; εἴ γε καὶ εἰκῇ.
5. ὁ οὖν ἐπιχορηγῶν ὑμῖν τὸ πνεῦμα καὶ ἐνεργῶν δυνάμεις
   ἐν ὑμῖν ἐξ ἔργων νόμου ἢ ἐξ ἀκοῆς πίστεως;

1. "You foolish Galatians! Who put a spell on you? Right before your eyes you had a plain description of the death of Jesus Christ on the cross!
2. Tell me just this one thing: did you receive God's Spirit by doing what the Law requires, or by hearing and believing the gospel?
3. How can you be so foolish? You began by God's Spirit; do you now want to finish by your own power?

4. Did all your experience mean nothing at all? Surely it meant nothing!
5. When God gives you the Spirit and works miracles among you, does he do it because you do what the Law requires, or because you hear and believe the gospel?'' (TEV).

Paul is not really asking any questions; he is making statements by means of questions—rhetorical questions (ἐρωτήματα). All these questions are asked in such a way, that there can be just one answer to every question: Although the reader/listener has a choice to answer each question in his own way, this choice is only a theoretical one; the way in which the questions are asked, forces the reader/listener to give the answer intended by the author.[2]

This highly unconventional way of making a statement is forceful, has tremendous impact, and has been recognized by Antiquity (e.g. by Demetrius) as one of the means of creating forceful style. It has been used in 4:9, 4:15,21 and in 5:7 as well as in much the same way as discussed above and as a means of conveying the same subject-matter in the same intensive, forceful way.

The full meaning of the use of this unconventional way of making a statement comes to the fore when the issue of this letter is taken into consideration. In all these cases where the rhetorical questions have been used, Paul is discussing the heart of the problem: the desertion of the true gospel by the Galatians. The questions enable the apostle to drive home his alarm more forcefully than by merely exhorting them not to do that again, as in ch 5:1-5.

There is amply evidence that Paul reserves the use of rhetorical questions virtually exclusively to moments of intense upset.[3] The only rhetorical questions being used in his letter to the Colossians occur in 2:20-21, where he is criticizing these christians for their Judaistic tendencies; in 1 Cor 1:13 and 3:3-5, where the forming of factions in this congregation is discussed and in Rm 2:3-4,21,22,26 and 27 (hypocrisy among Jews). Contrary to these, no rhetorical question has been used in his letters to the Ephesians, the Philippians and his second letter to the Thessalonians.

The next device of estrangement applied in the letter to the Galatians is the Metaphor. Metaphors are very common (even in colloquial speech)

---

[2] The rhetorical question should not be confused with the διαλέκτικον, where the writer argues by means of a question immediately followed by an answer, e.g. in 1:10, 2:17, 3:19, 3:21 and 4:30. This technique is also one of those recognized as contrary to expectations, but not having the same impact as the rhetorical question due to its popularity in the Pauline writings (especially in his letter to the christians in Rome). The technique as such must have become automatized to an extent for this very reason.

[3] ''Intense upset'' would not suit 1 Th 2:19 and 3:9-10, where one can clearly discern emotion, but no upset. Paul is rejoicing in the christians of Thessalonica.

and although the danger of automatization is valid for all techniques of estrangement, it is especially true in the case of Metaphors and even more so in religious language. Thus, the only Metaphors which will be considered, are those which evidently would have been experienced as striking, non-static, not yet automatized. The Metaphors in 3:23-25, 4:19 and 5:15 are of this kind. Calling the Law our instructor (παιδαγωγὸς ἡμῶν) (3:24,25) must have been quite striking; the idea of a παιδαγωγός was familiar to all, but not the Law being called that. This is confirmed by the fact that this is being done nowhere else in the Bible and, as a matter of fact, neither in the LXX nor any other Greek version of the OT, including the Apocrypha (Moulton & Geden 1963:745).

In 4:19 Paul expresses the intense painful feelings he has for the Galatians with reference to the pain of a mother in labour. Most extraordinary, and thus striking. (Nowhere else in the NT has this word been used to express pain experienced by a man (by a woman: Gl 4:27; Rv 12:2)). As a matter of fact, he does not use a comparison, but a direct Metaphor (ὠδίνω), which has more estranging effect than a comparison.

One last example: In Gl 5:15 Paul again describes mutual strife in a striking metaphorical way with reference to fighting animals: εἰ δὲ ἀλλήλους δάκνετε καὶ κατεσθίετε, βλέπετε μὴ ὑπ' ἀλλήλων ἀναλωθῆτε. Comparing the TEV with the KJV the impact of this Metaphor really comes to the fore: ''But if you act like animals, hurting and harming each other, then watch out, or you will completely destroy one another'' (TEV); ''But if ye bite and devour one another, take heed that ye be not consumed one of another'' (KJV). Further examples are present in 2:19 and 5:4.

The following technique of estrangement applied in the letter under discussion, is the Anacoluthon. In Gl 2:4-5 as well as Gl 2:6 Anacolutha can be detected. In 2:4 the main clause starts with διὰ δὲ τοὺς παρεισάκτους ψευδαδέλφους (''And because of false brothers unawares brought in''), but is never completed. After the relative clause (οἵτινες) the reader expects to return to the rest of the half-completed clause in a periodic fashion, but the sentence simply stops dead.

The next sentence commences with a relative (οἷς), referring to the same antecedent (ψευδαδέλφους), thus effectuating the same expectation of a periodic return to the rest of the uncompleted clause, and again the same thing happens: no return, no καμπή.

Instead, a new idea is expressed in the next sentence (2:6), and again a distortion of sentence-structure and syntax occurs. The main clause, starting with ἀπὸ δὲ τῶν δοκούντων εἶναί τι (''But of those who seem to be the leaders''), is interrupted by an insertion, a Parenthesis, made up of two short sentences: ὁποῖοί ποτε ἦσαν οὐδέν μοι διαφέρει· πρόσωπον (ὁ) θεὸς ἀνθρώπου οὐ λαμβάνει ("It makes no difference to me what they were; God does not judge by outward appearances"). After the Parenthesis the main clause is again taken up, but now the Genitive, τῶν δοκούντων, is changed to Nominative, thus becoming the subject of the sentence: ἐμοὶ γάρ οἱ δοκοῦντες.

Unlike the Anacoluthon in 2:4, this one produced no difficulties so far as the meaning of the sentence is concerned. But whether it is a transparent Anacoluthon or an obscure one, the effect produced by the syntactical distortion is in both cases the same: a retardation in the reading process for the very reason that the meaning is not as self-evident as in normal constructed sentences: "Intentional anacolutha (like unintentional ones) can, by disrupting the syntax, alert the reader or complicate or retard his perceptive process and introduce an element of discontinuity" (Stacy 1977:61).

In the case of non-literal texts (like this letter) the reader's attention is thus focused on the subject-matter (in these two cases on τοὺς παρεισάκτους ψευδαδέλφους (2:4) and on οἱ δοκοῦντες (2:6)). In the case of τοὺς παρεισάκτους ψευδαδέλφους it is striking how this stylistic device focused the attention on one of the major themes in this letter. That goes for the second Anacoluthon as well, for οἱ δοκοῦντες is directly related to a major theme in this letter, viz. the authority of Paul as apostle (ch 1:1 and 1:11ff).

Closely related to the Anacoluthon is the Parenthesis, which has already been mentioned in the discussion above. The distorting effect of this technique is actually two-fold, and even more so when combined with other techniques as in 2:6, as illustrated above. So far as the Parenthesis itself is concerned, the attention of the reader/listener is deliberately diverted to the content of the insertion.

The importance of this feature is sometimes exploited when the writer uses the insertion to communicate important subject-matter. This is clearly the case in Gl 2:8, when the heavenly origin of Paul's apostleship, the basis of Paul's criticism of the Galatians, is foregrounded and brought in direct relation to that of Peter: ὁ γὰρ ἐνεργήσας Πέτρῳ εἰς ἀποστολὴν τῆς περιτομῆς ἐνήργησεν καὶ ἐμοί εἰς τὰ ἔθνη ("For by God's power I was made an apostle to the Gentiles, just as Peter was made an apostle to the Jews") (TEV).

On the other hand, the content need not be so important, as could be argued in the case of the insertion in 2:6: ἀπὸ δὲ τῶν δοκούντων εἶναί τι — ὁποῖοί ποτε ἦσαν οὐδέν μοι διαφέρει· πρόσωπον (ὁ) θεὸς ἀνθρώπου οὐ λαμβάνει — In this case, however, the Parenthesis causes so much distortion, that an Anacoluthon resulted at the resuming of the main clause (οἱ δοκοῦντες).

Thus one could say that, although this Parenthesis did not attract the attention to subject-matter of equal importance as in 2:8, it did that indirectly by being the means by which the Anacoluthon was brought about.

The next estranging device to be considered, is the Paradox: In Gl 1:6-7 the reader/listener is struck by a seemingly contradictory expression: Θαυμάζω ὅτι οὕτως ταχέως μετατίθεσθε ἀπὸ τοῦ καλέσαντος ὑμᾶς ἐν χάριτι (Χριστοῦ) εἰς ἕτερον εὐαγγέλιον, ὃ οὐκ ἔστιν ἄλλο.

Now, if one could talk about retarded perception, intensified perception due to distortion of some kind, due to deautomatization, estrangement, this is one place where it most certainly would have occurred. ἕτερον εὐαγγέλιον, ὃ οὐκ ἔστιν ἄλλο seems to mean "another gospel, which is no other (gospel)". Grammatically, this seems the obvious translation and probably also the reason why so many of the traditional versions have this translation (e.g. KJV, and 1933 Afrikaans equivalent version) (cf discussion by Hendriksen 1969:39f). However, would Paul be annoyed at the Galatians for going to another gospel which is actually not another but the same gospel? The context points in another direction: this ἕτερον εὐαγγέλιον of the detractors is in fact not an ἄλλο εὐαγγέλιον, for it does not deserve the name εὐαγγέλιον. There is no other Gospel than the one the Galatians received by Paul.

An example of this interpretation is seen in the TEV: "I am surprised at you! In no time at all you are deserting the one who called you by the grace of Christ, and are going to another gospel. Actually, there is no 'other gospel' ..." (cf also Hendriksen 1969:37).

The ambiguity must have caused intensification of perception, thus foregrounding the important theme of the "other Gospel".

Another technique of defamiliarization applied in *Galatians* is the Hyperbole.

In Gl 4:14-15 Paul reminds his readers of the extraordinary relation that used to be between them: They received him as they would receive an angel of God or even as Christ Himself: ὡς ἄγγελον θεοῦ ἐδέξασθέ με, ὡς Χριστὸν ᾿Ιησοῦν. Their feelings for him were of such a kind, that they would have taken out their own eyes, if they could, and given them to him: εἰ δυνατὸν τοὺς ὀφθαλμοὺς ὑμῶν ἐξορύξαντες ἐδώκατέ μοι. These words are so passionate that they must have struck the Galatians in their hearts. Paul is not merely condemning the Galatians for their desertion in this letter. In an electrified passage (Gl 4:8-20) he not only reminds them of his love for them (4:19), but also of their love for him (4:14-15).

The last technique to be considered, is the Hyperbaton, distortion of word-order.

This technique was popular in antiquity and, according to Demetrius, very effective in producing forceful style. In the *Galatians* a few examples of minor distortion can be quoted, e.g. in 2:15-16, 4:12, 4:14 and 5:13, with notably less estranging effect as the other devices discussed above. In 3:28, however, the word-order of the short sentence ensures that the main points of his argument in 3:26-28 are highlighted. In these sentences he wishes to stress the *unity* of *all* Christians in *Christ*. Now consider 2:28b: πάντες γὰρ ὑμεῖς εἷς ἐστε ἐν Χριστῷ 'Ιησοῦ. πάντες and ἐν Χριστῷ 'Ιησοῦ are foregrounded by virtue of their occupation of the extreme positions of the sentence; the placing of εἷς between ὑμεῖς and ἐστε causes a discontinuity which highlights both ὑμεῖς and εἷς. Thus πάντες, ὑμεῖς, εἷς and ἐν Χριστῷ 'Ιησοῦ, the main elements of the foregoing argument, are all stylistically highlighted by the manipulation of the word-order.

At this point of the argument it must have become clear that Paul has abundantly applied techniques of defamiliarization. This is indeed the overwhelming impression the reader has when reading this letter. In presenting the letter in this uniform way, Paul has succeeded in maintaining a high degree of effectiveness for two reasons.

Firstly, although virtually all techniques applied are techniques with a high degree of estranging effect, Paul carefully honoured the principle of variety, ἡ μεταβολή, one of the indispensable virtues of good style in antiquity (cf Cronjé 1984:139ff). He did not use only one or two striking devices repeatedly, but a great variety. By doing this he avoided the danger of automatization of techniques of defamiliarization.

The principle of μεταβολή has also been applied in another way: the emotional or passionate sections have been alternated by less emotional (passionate) sections. Thus the emotional or passionate section, Gl 1:6-10, in which the θαυμάζω (1:6), the Paradox concerning the "other gospel" (1:7), the two curses (1:8 and 1:9) and two rhetorical questions (1:10) occur, is preceded by the less emotional introduction (1:1-5) and followed by the statement of the theme concerning his authority as an apostle (1:11-12). Likewise the passionate section concerning Paul's deep feelings for the Galatians and their previous feelings for him (4:8-20) is surrounded by sections of rational argumentation. That goes for the emotional six consecutive rhetorical questions (3:1-6) within a section (3:1-14) as well. By organizing the material in this way, the emotional passages would have the best impact.[4]

Closely related to this application of μεταβολή is the constant balance between foregrounding (by means of defamiliarization) and background-

---

[4] The arrangement of material was regarded as the most important aspect of style in Hellenistic times, cf Dionysius of Halicarnassus, *De Demosthene*, 56.

ing or automatization. Simultaneous foregrounding of all components is not possible, for all components would thus be on the same plane. This would then result in general automatization (Mukařovský 1964:20).

A unit is only in the foreground when considering its relative position to other elements which need to be in the background. This principle has been constantly applied in the letter under discussion. Comparing greater units (pericopes), it will be observed that some exhibit more features of estrangement than other (e.g. the passionate sections discussed above); in the paraenetic section (6:1-10) *ostranenie* is virtually non-existent (cf the Paronomasia in 6:6)—for at least one obvious reason: the inclusion of a list of exhortations was a convention; its content had no relation with the rest of the letter, so why foreground such an ''unimportant'' conventional element?

The principle is also applied within each section on the micro-level. The Anacolutha in 2:6 and 2:7-9 are even more foregrounded by the fact that they have been placed within a narrative section with simple, paratactic sentences. Had they been placed in a section with intricate, hypotactic sentences, all the elements would have been foregrounded (from the perspective of sentence-structure), resulting in the automatization of *all* the elements. For the same reason 1:15-17 is foregrounded: this is the only hypotactic sentence in a narrative section constructed in paratactic sentences (1:13-24). The sudden distortion of the pattern attracts the attention to the content of 1:15-17. In the same way the use of extremely short sentences (or clauses) is foregrounded by the presence of sentences of average length. Consider the impact of the extremely short sentence in 2:19b: Χριστῷ συνεσταύρωμαι (cf also 4:7 and 5:7-9).

In the same way it could be argued that all the techniques of estrangement are highlighted by the presence of automatization.

The second reason has to be treated more extensively. Paul did not only rely on special recognised devices in effectuating an estranging effect. The *total* stylistic presentation involving all aspects of style was adapted to a certain degree, ranging from words, phrases and sentences to paragraphs, sub-genres and genre.

So far as words are concerned, a number of ἅπαξ λεγόμενα ensures an estranging effect. παρεισάκτος (secretly brought in) in 2:4 is not only an ἅπαξ λεγόμενον; it could even possibly have the same effect as a newly coined word, for it is absent in the LXX, the Apocrypha, other Greek versions of the OT and even any Greek writings before the Christian era. βασκαίνω (to bewitch) in 3:1 is another example: ῏Ω ἀνόητοι Γαλάται, τίς ὑμᾶς ἐβάσκανεν... (''You foolish Galations! Who put a spell on you?'') (TEV). Although βασκαίνω is used nowhere else in the Bible, the Galatians must have been quite shocked to hear that they have been

bewitched into a "new Gospel". Whether βασκαίνω is used metaphorically or not, whether the deceivers are magicians or not, at least one thing
seems to be sure: the Galatians behaved like people who have been bewitched: they had access to the true Gospel (3:1b: οἷς κατ' ὀφθαλμοὺς Ἰησοῦς
Χριστὸς προεγράφη ἀσταθρωμένος) and yet they deserted it. (Cf the discussion of Hendriksen 1968:111f and the article of Delling on βασκαίνω in
TDNT 1:594ff. Both scholars, however, are too explicit and thus
speculative in their views.)

In addition to *bona fide* ἅπαξ λεγόμενα, some words have been used in a
striking, extraordinary way, thus causing impact. In Gl 5:12 a common
word, ἀποκόπτω, has been used in the sense of "to castrate" and
ἐπιστρέφω in 4:9 not in the common sense of "to turn" to God (intr.: "to
be converted") (cf Bertram 1971:726-729), but of "to turn from God".
To be converted to a false gospel! Again, the choice of words must have
produced a striking effect.

Proceeding to expressions, groups of words, a few have been used
which must have caused considerable retardation of perception. Of these
the most puzzling must have been τὸν Ἰσραὴλ τοῦ θεοῦ (Gl 6:16), a phrase
found nowhere else in the Bible: καὶ ὅσοι τῷ κανόνι τούτῳ στοιχήσουσιν,
εἰρήνη ἐπ' αὐτοὺς καὶ ἔλεος, καὶ ἐπὶ τὸν Ἰσραὴλ τοῦ θεοῦ. It is clear that the
meaning has been made more obscure by the καί (καὶ ἐπί) when taken as
"and". It does not make sense and would not be in harmony with the
rest of the letter to wish the Christians ("those who follow this rule")
peace and mercy *and also* a group which are not part of Christianity, i.e.
"the Israel of God". Taking καί as "even" would be more acceptable (cf
Hendriksen 1969:247) when "the Israel of God" is included in the ὅσοι:
May peace and mercy be upon all (even the Israel of God) who will follow
this rule" (i.e. "also upon the Israel of God when they will follow this
rule"). However, nowhere in the Bible has Israel been described in this
way. Another possibility seems to be more acceptable: by taking καί as
epexegetical, "the Israel of God" becomes the "*title*" of "all those who
will follow this rule". They, then, are the real Israel of God, not the
Israel of the Judaistic intruders. Thus: "And all that will follow this
rule—the true Israel of God—may peace and mercy be with them!"

This discussion clearly shows how much retardation this sentence must
have caused.

Similar instances of striking phrases occur in 6:2 (τὸν νόμον τοῦ
Χριστοῦ), which must have sounded contradictory to what Paul had to say
about the Law, e.g. in 5:4, and in 4:6 (τὸ πνεῦμα τοῦ υἱοῦ αὐτοῦ), an unique and strange way of referring to the Holy Ghost.

So far as sentences are concerned, the curse in 1:8, repeated in 1:9,
deserves special attention. Paul expresses his strong feelings towards the

Judaistic intruders with a curse: ἀνάθημα ἔστω: "Let him be accursed!" Stronger condemnation of a false prophet can hardly be possible.

Finally, even the conventions of letters were used as automatized background against which a deviation would attract special attention. In all but two of the letters of Paul to parishes, the introduction is immediately followed by an expression of thanks to God for the faith of the addressees: Rm 1:8; 1 Cor 1:4; Col 1:3; 1 Th 1:2 and 2 Th 1:3. (In his letter to the Ephesians this happens a bit later: 1:16.)

In the second letter to the Corinthians as well as the letter to the Ephesians this is replaced by an eulogy to God: 2 Cor 1:3 and Eph 1:3. This pattern points in the direction of a convention, which was deliberately distorted in the letter to the Galatians. The first element after the introduction was expected to be something positive, most probably Paul thanking God for the faith of the Galatians. Instead, they were struck by an unexpected denouncement concerning their faith. Instead of the usual εὐχαριστῶ τῷ θεῷ, or εὐλογητός ὁ θεός, an unexpected θαυμάζω: θαυμάζω ὅτι οὕτως ταχέως μετατίθεσθε ἀπὸ τοῦ καλέσαντος ὑμᾶς, ἐν χάριτι (Χριστοῦ) εἰς ἕτερον εὐαγγέλιον ("I am surprised at you! In no time at all you are deserting the one who called you by the grace of Christ, and are going to another Gospel").

Conclusion

In the letter of Paul to the Galatians a great number of devices has been applied which can all be described as devices of estrangement. This is the dominant feature of the letter from a stylistic point of view. These devices all effectuate a retardation in the reading process and consequently an intensified perception. In general, the devices have been skilfully applied in such a way that the subject-matter (which is in every case, one of the main themes of the letter) is highlighted. In other words, the retardation and consequent intensified perception occur on occasions when the writer really wants his readers to pay attention to what he has to say. A careful balance between estrangement and automatization has been maintained. In addition to all this, most of these devices were regarded as forceful by Hellenistic rhetoricians and are thus most suitable for communicating the subject-matter of this emotional letter.

BIBLIOGRAPHY

ALAND, K., M. BLACK, C. M. MARTINI, B. M. METZGER & A. WIKGREN (eds) 1968. *The Greek New Testament*. 2. ed. New York: American Bible Society.
BERTRAM, G. 1971. ἐπιστρέφω. *TDNT* 7, 714-729.
CRONJÉ, J. v. W. 1984. *Dionysius of Halicarnassus: De Demosthene: A critical appraisal of the status quaestionis, followed by a glossary of the technical terms*. Bloemfontein: Diss.

DELLING, G. 1969. Βασκαίνω. *TDNT* 1, 594-595.

DEMETRIUS 1973. *On style.* London: Heinemann. (Loeb Classical Library.)

DIONYSIUS OF HALICARNASSUS 1974. De Demosthene, in S. Usher (ed), *The critical essays I.* London: Heinemann. (Loeb Classical Library.)

DRIJEPONDT, H. L. F. 1979. Die antike Theorie der *varietas*, in *Spudasmata* 37. Hildesheim: Georg Olms.

ERLICH, V. 1969. *Russian Formalism: history-doctrine.* 3. ed. The Hague: Mouton.

HAVRÁNEK, B. 1964. The functional differentiation of the standard language, in P. L. Garvin (ed), *A Prague school reader on esthetics, literary structure, and style.* Washington, D.C.: Georgetown University Press, 3-16.

HENDRIKSEN, W. 1969. *A commentary on Galatians.* London: Banner of Truth Trust.

MOULTON, W. F. & A. S. GEDEN 1963. *A concordance to the Greek Testament.* 4. rev. ed. Edinburgh: T. & T. Clark.

MUKAŘOVSKÝ, J. 1964. Standard language and poetic language, in P. L. Garvin (ed), *A Prague school reader on esthetics, literary structure, and style.* Washington, D.C.: Georgetown University Press, 17-30.

NIDA, E. A., J. P. LOUW, A. H. SNYMAN & J. v. W. CRONJÉ 1983. *Style and discourse.* Cape Town: Bible Society.

SHKLOVSKY, V. 1965. *Russian Formalist criticism: four essays,* tr by L. T. Lemon & M. J. Reiss.

SNYMAN, A. H. & J. v. W. CRONJÉ 1983. Towards a new classification of the figures (σχήματα) in the Greek New Testament, in E. A. Nida *et al., Style and discourse.* Cape Town: Bible Society, 172-191.

STACY, R. H. 1977. *Defamiliarization in language and literature.* Syracuse University Press.

VISSER, N. W. 1982. Structuralism, in R. Ryan & S. van Zyl (ed), *An introduction to contemporary literary theory.* Johannesburg: Jonker, 53-65.

Bible translations.

KJV
TEV

P. J. HARTIN

ΑΝΑΚΕΦΑΛΑΙΩΣΑΣΘΑΙ ΤΑ ΠΑΝΤΑ ΕΝ ΤΩ ΧΡΙΣΤΩ (Eph 1:10)

1. *Introduction*

The aim of this article is to give an exegesis of the phrase ἀνακεφαλαιώσασθαι τὰ πάντα ἐν τῷ Χριστῷ. At the outset a word is needed to explain the method of procedure adopted here. To understand this phrase correctly it is necessary first of all to place it within the thought process of the whole epistle, as well as within the immediate context of 1:10. An examination of each one of the words of this phrase will be undertaken in order to come to a clearer perception of the whole phrase. Finally, some reflections will be given on the meaning of this phrase for today.

It is not possible to consider the question of authorship here, but I presuppose the fact that this letter does come from Paul either directly or indirectly: It bears witness to a further development of Paul's thought.

2. *The context of this phrase within the Letter to the Ephesians*

2.1 *The basic theme and thought process of Ephesians*

The central theme of this letter revolves around the mystery of Christ who has united the two groups of Jews and Pagans in Himself. This mystery is God's plan of salvation which brings an end to divisions among mankind as well as all divisions within the world and reunites all things in Christ.

The letter treats this theme in two main sections, one doctrinal, the other hortatory. Chapters 1-3 (the doctrinal section) announce this plan of God and explain its meaning, while chapters 4-6 (the hortatory section) draw out its implications for the Christian life.

The doctrinal section (chapters 1-3) begins with an eulogy or praise of God (1:1-14) because He has blessed the members of the church with many gifts, especially that of eternal pre-determination to divine sonship. Paul states that the plan of God to reunite all things in Christ had been kept hidden, but now was revealed in Christ. Jews and pagans are now united in sharing in these blessings of salvation.

"Chapters 1-3 announce God's great plan, hidden from the beginning of the world, to create a messianic people of God, a new community of men uniting in Christ both Jew and Gentile and erasing the impenetrable social and religious barriers that had previously divided mankind" (Grassi 1970:343).

Paul then passes on to a prayer (1:15-23) that his readers may be given wisdom and the ability to understand this great mystery. This great act of God's salvation has been accomplished in Christ who was raised from the dead and who has now authority over all things. To Christians has been granted a share in the destiny of Christ (2:1-10). They were at first dead because of their sins, but they have now been made alive by God in Christ. Paul recalls their history (2:11-22) of how Christ has forgiven the two opposing human groups of Jews and Pagans and has united them together in His body, the church. Paul gives himself as an example of how God has worked in him (3:1-12): to Paul and to the other apostles and prophets, God has revealed His mystery of uniting in one body, Jews and pagans. To Paul belongs the task of bringing a knowledge of this revelation to others. In 3:13-21 Paul prays once more that the Christians may experience the love of Christ and that they "may be filled with all the fullness of God" (3:19).

In the hortatory-section (chapters 4-6) Paul draws conclusions for their daily life. He appeals to his readers to live in such a way that their unity will always be preserved. It commences with advice to unity (4:1-6) and the different services are outlined (4:7-16) which work together for building up the church. They are not to revert to their previous ways, but are to put off their old nature and to put on the new nature (4:17-32). They are called to imitate God (5:1-7) and to struggle against all evil. Now united in Christ they are children of light and are to put off the works of darkness (5:8-14). Because of the gift of unity they have received, they are to join together in songs of praise to the Lord (5:15-20). A long section follows, (5:21-6:9), in which unity and love are stressed in family relationship. In 6:10-20 Paul speaks of the armament which is needed in order to persevere in this unity, and he ends off in his usual way with his final greetings and blessing.

2.2 *1:10 in the context of this thought-process*

1:10 forms part of an eulogy which is used to introduce the epistle and operates in a way similar to that of the prologue of the Gospel of John (cf Schlier 1965:38). The eulogy has the task of laying the foundation for the whole writing by stating what God has done for the community. It must be seen as an *ad hoc* creation for which Paul is responsible, based upon liturgical traditions (cf Gnilka 1971:59-60). Within this eulogy, and from the above outline of the main thoughts running throughout the letter, one can see that without doubt 1:10 is the central verse of the whole letter: the plan of God for the fullness of time, which is to reunite all things in Christ. In this verse Paul succinctly states the theme and throughout the rest of the letter he elaborates upon this, either by explaining its doctrinal implications or by drawing out its practical consequences for daily life. As E. F. Scott says, the verse is "the key to the whole Epistle" (Scott 1952:125).

3. ἀνακεφαλαιώσασθαι τὰ πάντα ἐν τῷ Χριστῷ

3.1 The plan of God

1:10 begins by referring to the plan which God had established for the fullness of time (εἰς οἰκονομίαν τοῦ πληρώματος τῶν καιρῶν). God had made this decision before time in Christ. This fullness of time is a frequent concept in the New Testament (cf Gl 4:4). Here it does not indicate that the fullness of history has been brought to an end, but that the fullness of time is something which endures and the divine decision is to see that it does continue (cf Gnilka 1971:79).

God is the one who governs the ages of history in their totality and sees that they come to completion or fullness. The determination of this plan of God, which He has established in Christ, is determined by what follows: to reunite all things in Christ (ἀνακεφαλαιώσασθαι τὰ πάντα ἐν τῷ Χριστῷ). The mystery of His plan is to see that the totality is brought together in Christ.

3.2 ἀνακεφαλαιώσασθαι

This infinitive is to be derived from the word κεφάλαιον and literally means "to sum up" or "to divide into main portions" (Schlier 1972:681). Liddell and Scott give the meaning for this word in the following way:

> "to sum up the argument: Pass. to be summed up, NT" (Liddell & Scott 1968:57).

It is not to be derived from the word κεφαλή. The word κεφάλαιον belongs predominantly to the realm of rhetoric, where a speaker puts his speech together, where he sums it up or unites it.

> "Das Wort hat—so seltsam das klingen mag—seine Heimat in der Rhetorik: Ein Redner faßt seine Rede zusammen, d.h. wiederholt sie mit Beschränkung auf die Hauptsache, 'rekapituliert' sie" (Gnilka 1971:80).

Paul used this word in his letter to the Romans (Rm 13:9) in the rhetorical sense when he said that the commandments of the second table of the Decalogue "are summed up" (ἀνακεφαλαιοῦται) in the commandment of brotherly love.

Because every summing up implies a repetition it can have the meaning of "to repeat". This repetitive aspect is indicated by the prefix ἀνα. Here the aorist infinitive is used which must indicate that the event as referred to has taken place. In order to be able to explain the fuller significance of this word, it is necessary to take it in conjunction with τὰ πάντα ἐν τῷ Χριστῷ to which it refers.

3.3 τὰ πάντα

Here the object of the event of summing up, or re-uniting, is indicated. This word is neuter plural from the word πᾶς, used as a noun. In the New Testament, this term is very common, being used 1228 times (cf Reicke 1970:893). It is an attempt to express the notion of totality, which is further determined in 1:10 by the explanation τὰ ἐπὶ τοῖς οὐρανοῖς καὶ τὰ ἐπὶ τῆς γῆς. Thus the word τὰ πάντα refers to the totality of all things in our sense of the universe or the cosmos. The designation "heaven and earth" corresponds to the Old Testament usage of referring to the universe in this way (Reicke 1970:889-890). In the New Testament usage the τὰ πάντα is referred to the context of creation and salvation and is a means of expressing the universality of God's activity.

> "The uniqueness of the NT view, (with regard to the non-biblical world) is that here all ideas of totality relate to a specific history of creation and salvation. As compared with the OT the NT is distinguished especially by a richer soteriology" (Reicke 1970:893).

As a result of the death and resurrection of Christ, all power over the universe is communicated to Him. "ἐδόθη μοι πᾶσα ἐξουσία ἐν οὐρανῷ καὶ ἐπὶ (τῆς) γῆς" (Mt 28:18). This universal power of Christ is not acknowledged by all men, so the mission of the church is needed to bring about this recognition in order that He will be all in all (Eph 1:22).

3.4 ἐν τῷ Χριστῷ

This formula is a very frequent one in the writings of Paul where it occurs 164 times (excluding Colossians, Ephesians and the Pastorals). In Ephesians it appears 34 times (cf Allan 1958:54), though its form does change between ἐν τῷ Χριστῷ, ἐν Χριστῷ, ἐν αυτῷ, ἐν τῷ κυριῷ. The title Χριστός in Paul has a personal designation, but it must also be seen as referring to *the function* which Jesus of Nazareth possesses. It refers to the Jewish hopes of the Old Testament in an "Anointed One or Messiah". In Ephesians it is used to emphasise the messianic function of Jesus, and this is supported here by the use of the article together with the noun. The title refers to Jesus, who is now enthroned as Messiah and exercises His power as Messiah with regard to the universe.

Gnilka points out that the use of the expression ἐν τῷ Χριστῷ in Ephesians usually shows a three-cornered scheme encompassing God, Christ and the community.

> "Sie läßt sich vereinfacht so ausdrücken: Gott handelt in Christus im Hinblick auf uns" (Gnilka 1971:67).

This three-fold relationship is characteristic of Ephesians, but is not found in the earlier letters of Paul. By means of this title, Ephesians expressed that the actions of God are communicated to the community through Christ. This enables Paul to emphasise the christological aspect of the work of salvation. In our verse a new aspect in the three-fold relationship of God-Christ-community is introduced, namely the all, the universe. Here God is acting through Christ for the sake of the entire creation, the universe.

3.5 The meaning of this expression ἀνακεφαλαιώσασθαι τὰ πάντα ἐν τῷ Χριστῷ

The task of summing up or uniting the totality has been granted to Christ. This presupposes that the totality has become divided; the unity of the all-reality has become broken. No reflection is passed upon this break in the creation: it is presupposed. Christ's task is to gather together, to sum up all things in Himself. In what way is this achieved? This can be seen from the wider context of the letter itself. In 1:22 Paul says: "καὶ πάντα ὑπέταξεν ὑπὸ τοὺς πόδας αὐτοῦ καὶ αὐτὸν ἔδωκεν κεφαλὴν ὑπὲρ πάντα τῇ ἐκκλησίᾳ".

The function which Christ exercises here is that of the Head which subjects all things to Himself. The ἀνακεφαλαιώσασθαι must therefore be seen as being exercised in this function as Head.

The summing up of the totality, its unification, takes place in so far as the totality is subjected to Christ, its Head. Although the word ἀνακεφαλαιώσασθαι is not to be derived from the word κεφαλή, nevertheless from the context of the letter this ἀνακεφαλαιώσασθαι does exercise a relationship to the function which Christ performs as Head. It was probably this connection which suggested this word to Paul in the first place (cf Schlier 1972:682).

Schlier expresses this again very well when he says:

"Dann ist aber deutlich, dass der Apostel in ἀνακεφαλαιώσασθαι obwohl es nicht von κεφαλή sondern von κεφάλαιον abzuleiten ist, einen Begriff sah, in dem er das mit einem Wort wiedergeben konnte, was in 1:22 so umschrieben ist: αὐτὸν ἔδωκεν κεφαλὴν ὑπὲρ πάντα τῇ ἐκκλησίᾳ.
Das ἀνακεφαλαιώσασθαι des Alls in Christus ist dies, dass Gott dem All in Christus ein übergeordnetes Haupt gibt, unter dem es geeint und aufgerichtet wird" (Schlier 1965:65).

In the letter to the Ephesians Christ appears as κεφαλή in two senses: first of all He is Head of His body, the church, and in a second sense, He is Head of all reality, of all creation. It is probable that this powerful position of Christ with regard to all things, described by the concept of Head, was derived through an analogy of Christ's position with regard to the community (cf Ridderbos 1973:85). However, while the church is referred to as the body of Christ, this is never applied in Ephesians to "all things", to the creation. Thus, in dealing with Christ as Head over all things, one is dealing with the image of Head, and the further, second image of body is not associated with it at all. As Ridderbos says:

"Evenzo, als in Eph 1:22 Christus het Hoofd over alle dingen en in Kol 2:10 het Hoofd over alle heerschappij en macht wordt genoemd, houdt dit niet in, dat 'alle dingen', alle heerschappij en macht nu ook zijn lichaam zouden zijn of tot zijn lichaam zouden behoren. *De qualificatie 'hoofd' heeft haar eigen zelfstandige betekenis, ongeacht of daarmee het overdrachtelijk spreken van een 'lichaam' verbonden wordt*" (Ridderbos 1973:425-426).

Many have tried to interpret Christ as Head in reference to the gnostic myths and the belief in the anthropos myth (e.g. Schlier 1965:60ff), but as W. D. Davies has shown it is best to see the connection of Paul's concept of Head as stemming from his idea of Christ as the second Adam, which has its foundations in Jewish rabbinic speculation at that time in reference to Adam (Davies 1970:56-57). Davies shows how the rabbis conceived the unity of humanity as coming from the body of Adam, which included all humanity:

"Was it not natural then, that Paul, when he thought of the new humanity being incorporated 'in Christ' should have conceived of it as the 'body' of the second Adam, where there was neither Jew nor Greek, male nor female, bond nor free" (Davies 1970:57).

Thus, in Paul's proclamation he shows how what was lost in the first Adam, has now been re-won by the second Adam. Christ, as the second Adam refers back to the beginning of time and He now appears in a much more glorious way as the image of God and the first-born of all creation which restores unity to mankind and to the whole world. The choice of the word ἀνακεφαλαιώσασθαι which has a repetitive sense in the prefix ἀνα- shows also that Paul is thinking of a renewal of what took place at the beginning of creation.

Christ as head over all things, means that all things are in a special relationship to Christ as the first-born of all creation (cf Ridderbos 1973:426-427). As a result of this Christ exercises a dominating position over all things and in this way He exercises His blessing over them. This title of Head expresses Christ's superiority over everything which is subjected to Him. This power was already His at the creation of the world (Col 1:16), but through His exaltation all powers have once more been placed under Him (Eph 1:22) and He begins to exercise this power which has as its goal the re-unification of all things under Him.

From this one can see more clearly what is meant by this expression ἀνακεφαλαιώσασθαι τὰ πάντα ἐν τῷ Χριστῷ. In Christ all things are to be subjected to His dominion as Head and once more the essential oneness, the essential unity of all things is achieved, just as it was at the very beginning of the world in Adam according to the rabbinic speculations. The bringing-together of all things in Himself is a restoration of the old order in a new manner. The whole world has Christ as its Head, and it is both united and directed to Him.

This position and function of Christ is very similar to that of Phlp 2:9ff. Here Christ is established as Lord over all the universe, and the whole universe acknowledges this position of Christ.

It has been pointed out that ἀνακεφαλαιώσασθαι is an aorist infinitive referring to the fact that the event has taken place (Gnilka 1971:81). Through the exaltation of Christ all reality has come under the power and dominion of Christ. All reality is the place where Christ exercises His rule, and in exercising His rule over it, it is being brought into a closer unity both within itself and with Christ Himself.

3.6 Conclusion

By means of this expression ἀνακεφαλαιώσασθαι τὰ πάντα ἐν τῷ Χριστῷ the purpose of the plan of God has been determined. It is a plan which aims at summing up, uniting all things in Christ as Head. All things have been subjected to Christ, but the creation does not yet know of this position of Christ, which aims at bringing the creation to acknowledge Christ as its Head, and with this the new creation is realised. In this dynamic movement of bringing the creation to acknowledge Christ as its Head, the church too has a special function. Its task is to co-operate in bringing a knowledge of the revelation of this mystery to all creation.

4. *The meaning of* ἀνακεφαλαιώσασθαι τὰ πάντα ἐν τῷ Χριστῷ *for today*

It is often said that the thought concepts and problems with which Paul is preoccupied are far different from our own. But behind these concepts and these problems lies a teaching which is as relevant today as it was at the time of Paul. The teaching of Paul in this phrase has, I feel, an importance for today which can be seen in two ways.

4.1 *Its importance with regard to science*

In this verse Paul has stated that it was God's plan to unite and subject all things under Christ as Head. But today we see especially in the realm of science, that science has declared its autonomy from religion, and has developed a system of laws, forces and theories in which the universe is understood and accounted for and which makes no reference to God or to the position of Christ. In this process man too is tending to become dehumanized, to lose his freedom, and is becoming subservient to physical laws and mechanical processes.

Paul had to attack a situation in which man was seen as subservient to angelic powers and principalities. Our situation is that man too has lost his freedom and is subservient to physical laws of the universe and the mechanical processes which he himself has invented. In both situations the message remains the same. It is the task of the church, it is our task, to bring a knowledge of God's plan to the men of our day. It is our task to show them the liberating power of the gospel in which man accepts Christ as his Head and in which Christ is seen as the Head of the universe. Christ must once more be restored to his true position in the universe in the minds of men. This does not mean that science and religion must be seen as having two opposing conceptions of the universe. Rather the teaching of Eph 1:10 should be seen as giving a deeper unifying dimension to the understanding which science give to the universe, and in this way it will achieve the liberation of man. His freedom in Christ, his Head, will once more be established.

4.2 *Its importance with regard to the relationship between men*

Not only is the creation subjected and brought to unity in Christ as Head, but mankind itself is also part of this creation and is also called to participate in this subjection and unity. Differences and tensions among classes, races, nations, religions are a characteristic feature of our world. In Paul's day the differences and tensions among Jews and Pagans were a characteristic feature. Here again the message remains the same: all men are called to unity in Christ.

It is the task of the church, the task of the individual Christian, to make this teaching of Christ actual. The church and the individual must strive to bring about and promote unity among all men and to show that this unity is not just something to be experienced among themselves, but is a unity which is experienced in Christ, the Head of the Universe, the Head of all believers. This should be the guiding force and principle behind the ecumenical movement.

4.3 Conclusion

From this it appears clearly that this teaching of Paul is as vital today as it was in Paul's own day.

> "In this epistle, therefore, Paul seeks to correlate his Christian faith with his outlook of the universe. His modes of thinking are different from ours, but he is grappling with our problems, and his ideas are of permanent value" (Scott 1952:135).

As Christians we are called upon to bring mankind to a realisation of this mystery, this plan of God, just as Paul was called to preach this mystery (Eph 3:1ff). In this way peace and harmony will be established in the world and the plan of God will be brought to fulfilment: all things, the whole universe will be brought to a realisation of its unity under Christ, its Head.

BIBLIOGRAPHY

ABBOT, T. 1964. *A critical and exegetical commentary on the Epistles to the Ephesians and to the Colossians.* Edinburgh: Clark. (International Critical Commentary of the Holy Scriptures of the Old and New Testament.)

ALLAN, J. A. 1958. The 'In Christ' formula in Ephesians. *NTS* 5, 54-62.

ALLAN, J. A. 1963. The 'In Christ' formula in the Pastoral Epistles. *NTS* 10, 115-121.

ARNDT, W. F. & F. W. GINGRICH 1952. *A Greek-English lexicon of the New Testament and other early Christian literature.* Chicago: University of Chicago Press.

BRUCE, F. F. 1968. *The Epistle to the Ephesians.* London: Pickering and Inglis.

DAVIES, W. D. 1970. *Paul and Rabbinic Judaism.* London: SPCK.

GNILKA, J. 1971. *Der Epheserbrief.* Freiburg: Herder. (Herders Theologischer Kommentar zum Neuen Testament.)

GRASSI, J. A. 1970. The Letter to the Ephesians, in R. E. Brown (ed), *The Jerome biblical commentary.* London: Geoffrey Chapman, 341-349.

GRUNDMANN, W. 1974. Χριστός. *TDNT* IX, 527-572.

JOHNSTON, G. 1962. Ephesians, in G. Buttrick (ed), *The interpreter's dictionary of the Bible.* vol. 2. New York: Abingdon Press, 108-114.

LIDDELL AND SCOTT'S GREEK-ENGLISH LEXICON 1968. *An intermediate Greek-English lexicon.* Oxford: Clarendon Press.

MOULE, C. F. D. 1971. *An idiom book of New Testament Greek.* London: Cambridge University Press.

REICKE, B. 1970. πᾶς, ἅπας. *TDNT* V, 886-896.

RIDDERBOS, H. 1973. *Paulus ontwerp van zijn theologie.* Kampen: J. H. Kok.

Roberts, J. H. 1963. *Die opbou van die kerk volgens die Efese-brief.* Kampen: Theologische Academie.
Rowley, H. H. (ed) 1962. *Ephesians.* London: Nelson. (Peake's commentary on the Bible.)
Schlier, H. 1972. κεφαλή, ἀνακεφαλαιώσασθαι. *TDNT* III, 673-682.
Schlier, H. 1965. *Der Brief an die Epheser.* Freiburg: Herder. (Herders Theologischer Kommentar zum Neuen Testament.)
Scott, E. F. 1952. *The Epistles of Paul to the Colossians, to Philemon and to the Ephesians.* London: Hodder and Stoughton. (The Moffatt New Testament Commentary.)
Swain, L. 1969. Ephesians, in *A new Catholic commentary on Holy Scripture.* London: Nelson, 1181-1191.
Zerwick, M. 1966. *Analysis philologica Novi Testamenti Graeci.* Rome: Pontificii Instituti Biblici.

J. BOTHA

A STYLISTIC ANALYSIS OF THE CHRIST HYMN
(COLOSSIANS 1:15-20)

A striking stylistic pattern in Col 1:15-20 is easily recognizable: it consists of two strophae, in each case introduced by the typical hymnic introductory phrase ὅς ... (cf Phlp 2:6; 1 Pt 2:22; 1 Tm 3:16). In each strophe the introductory phrase is followed by what Bruce (1984:100) calls "key words", namely, πρωτότοκος, ὅτι ἐν αὐτῷ, δι' αὐτοῦ and τὰ πάντα. According to Delling (1972:501) Col 1:15-20 exhibits a "lofty speech and integrated structure" and it is "distinctively stylised".

Furthermore, there is a fair degree of consensus among scholars that Col 1:15-20 is a *hymn*:

— "Der hymnische charakter von Kol 1:15-20 ist längst erkannt und allgemein anerkannt" (Käsemann 1965:34).
— "It is no longer a matter for dispute that we have in these verses a hymn..." (Schweizer 1982:55).

Because of the peculiar content of this passage—it is one of the key passages for the Pauline christology (cf Du Plessis 1984:226-228)—and because of its unique style, a vast amount of scholarly research was focused on it. Problems concerning the *origin*, *authorship* and *structure* of the hymn were in most instances of special interest for scholars, who have diverse opinions on these matters. With regard to authorship arguments are put forward for a Pauline as well as a non-Pauline authorship, and regarding the origin arguments are put forward to prove a stoic, Judaistic, Gnostic or Christian origin[1].

As far as the structure of the hymn is concerned, there is also no general consensus among scholars (cf Hendriksen 1964:67: "Whatever be their (= the two strophae - J. B.) origin, they share a definite stylistic pattern, a strophic arrangement. But just what was this *strophic* arrangement?" and McCown 1979:157: "...we are confronted with a number of differing analyses of the hymn itself").

However, these matters as such are not the primary concern of this article. Instead of simply attempting to put forward another structural analysis of the hymn, the purpose of this article is to try to determine the

---

[1] Cf Norden (1913:250-254); Lohmeyer (1930:40-68); Robinson (1957:270-287); Ridderbos (1960:131-151); Bammel (1961:88-95); Hendriksen (1964:66-82); Martin (1964:195-205); Käsemann (1965:34-50); Schille (1965); Craddock (1965:78-80); Gabathuler (1965); Deichgräber (1967:143-155); Kehl (1967); Louw (1967); Sanders (1971); Lohse (1971:41-61); Martin (1972:40-55); Pöhlmann (1973:55-74); O'Brien (1974:45-53); McCown (1979:156-162); Schweizer (1982: 55-88) and Bruce (1984:99-111).

function(s) of the stylistic features as they occur in the final redaction of the hymn.

Louw (1975:108) maintains that it is noteworthy that commentaries on classical authors, when they do say something on the rhetoric seldom try to point out its meaning—the reason for this is probably that rhetorical elements are seen as purely aesthetical material. This is also true of many commentaries on this hymn. For instance, Hendriksen (1964:73) identifies the chiasm ἐν τοῖς οὐρανοῖς (a), καὶ ἐπὶ τῆς γῆς (b) and τὰ ὁρατά (b), καὶ τὰ ἀόρατα (a) in Col 1:16, but he fails to point out the *meaning* or the *function* of the σχῆμα in this particular context.

According to Nida *et al* (1983:11) the meaning of rhetorical elements cannot be explicated in the same manner as one defines lexical meanings, viz. through componential features. The signification of these rhetorical elements should be treated in a semiotic sense: "In order to grasp the significance of rhetorical features it is therefore preferable to classify these features in terms of processes, for the nature of the process is really the key to the semiotic significance of such features" (Nida *et al* 1983:12).

With this in mind, the purpose of this article can be stated more explicitly, namely, to try to determine the processes caused by the rhetorical features of the hymn in the relationship of parts of a text to one another and to try to determine on this basis the possible meaning(s) of the rhetorical features of the hymn for the reader. Furthermore, a detailed analysis of the style of this passage may be a confirmation of its generally recognized hymnic character.

In order to accomplish this purpose, the methodology proposed by Nida *et al* (1983) for stylistic analysis of New Testament passages is followed. The basic procedures of this methodology are summarised by A. H. Snyman in his contribution to this *Festschrift* and therefore it is not repeated here.

1. *Demarcation of nuclear structures*

(1) ὅς ἐστιν εἰκὼν
(2) τοῦ θεοῦ τοῦ ἀοράτου
(3) πρωτότοκος πάσης κτίσεως
(4) ὅτι ἐν αὐτῷ ἐκτίσθη τὰ πάντα
   ἐν τοῖς οὐρανοῖς
   καὶ ἐπὶ τῆς γῆς

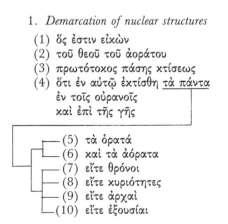

(5) τὰ ὁρατά
(6) καὶ τὰ ἀόρατα
(7) εἴτε θρόνοι
(8) εἴτε κυριότητες
(9) εἴτε ἀρχαὶ
(10) εἴτε ἐξουσίαι

(11) τὰ πάντα δι' αὐτοῦ καὶ εἰς αὐτὸν ἔκτισται
(12) καὶ αὐτός ἐστιν πρὸ πάντων
(13) καὶ τὰ πάντα ἐν αὐτῷ συνέστηκεν
(14) καὶ αὐτός ἐστιν ἡ κεφαλὴ τοῦ σώματος τῆς ἐκκλησίας
(15) ὅς ἐστιν ἀρχή
(16) πρωτότοκος ἐκ τῶν νεκρῶν
(17) ἵνα γένηται ἐν πᾶσιν αὐτὸς πρωτεύων
(18) ὅτι ἐν αὐτῷ εὐδόκησεν πᾶν τὸ πλήρωμα κατοικῆσαι
(19) καὶ δι' αὐτοῦ ἀποκαταλλάξαι τὰ πάντα εἰς αὐτόν
(20) εἰρηνοποιήσας
(21) διὰ τοῦ αἵματος
(22) τοῦ σταυροῦ αὐτοῦ (δι' αὐτοῦ)
     (19b) εἴτε τὰ ἐπὶ τῆς γῆς
     (19c) εἴτε τὰ ἐν τοῖς οὐρανοῖς

Certain items in the above analysis have to be motivated briefly before proceeding to discuss the macrolevel of the rhetorical structure according to this analysis.

The nuclear structure is delimited around the events in the surface structure. Here it should be kept in mind that the purpose of this division of the text is not to make a semantic structural analysis as such, but to get an idea of the progression in the hymn, which is an aspect of its style.

The event in item 1 is εἰκών = He *depicts*. In item 2 the event is ἀόρατου = He *is invisible*. Item 3 expresses the event/state of *being first* (πρωτότοκος). It is here concerned with *order of rank* and not with chronological order. It is the priority and sovereignty of Christ which is expressed here (Du Plessis 1984:227). Although κτίσεως is an event, it is not taken as a separate nuclear unit because in this context it refers in the first instance to the object *creation* and not the event *create*.

Items 5-10 are all demarcated around events in the surface structure and therefore are all taken as separate nuclear structures. In classical Greek events can be expressed in the surface structure by five different morphological formations: verbs, substantives, infinitives, adjectives and participles (Louw 1979:21). Louw (1979:27) calls the nominalization of events a distinctive stylistic feature of classical Greek. In the case of the items under discussion, the events in items 5 and 6 are expressed by adjectives and in items 7, 8, 9, 10 by substantives.

Item 11 consists of a normal nuclear structure, built up around the event to *create*, expressed by the verb ἔκτισται in the surface structure. In the deep structure the event is repeated twice: *to create through him* and *to create for him*. But, because it is expressed only once in the surface structure, the entirety is seen as one nuclear structure.

The event *being first* is in item 12 expressed by ἐστιν in combination with the phrase πρὸ πάντων. Thus, with regard to the event they express, items 3 and 12 are parallel.

The event in item 13 is *held together* and it is expressed in the surface structure by the verb συνέστηκεν.

Although the word ἐκκλησίας in item 14 can be transformed into the event *to gather*, it is not taken as a separate nuclear unit, since in the context of the hymn it refers in the first place to the object the *congregation* and not the event *to gather*. This transpires clearly from the fact that τῆς ἐκκλησίας is used here in an epexegetical construction with the object τοῦ σώματος. The event in item 14 is expressed by the ἐστιν in combination with ἡ κεφαλή = He *rules*.

The nucleus of item 15 is expressed by the verb ἐστιν in combination with ἀρχή and this represents the event/state He *is first*.

Item 16 can be transformed into the following two sentences in the deep structure, (a) *He is first* and (b) *people rise from death*. Since the event *rise* is presumed in the surface structure, the entirety is taken as one nuclear structure. In this context, the event of νεκρῶν (= *to die*) is not in focus. In combination with the preposition ἐκ, the word νεκρῶν here refers to an *object*, namely a particular kind of *people*. The kernel sentence expressed in this context by this nuclear structure is, *He rises from death first.* In contrast to item 3 where the πρωτότοκος refers to order of rank and *not* to chronological order as well, πρωτότοκος in item 16 refers to both order of rank and chronological order: in importance or rank, Christ is the first of the people rising from death, but in chronological sense He is also first (cf Ridderbos 1960:143).

In item 17 the event πρωτεύων is the nucleus of the structure = *being first*. Although γένηται is a verbal form in the surface structure it cannot be taken separately as a nucleus. It is merely a surface structure construction which expresses in combination with πρωτεύων only *one* event.

As in the case of item 17, the event in item 18 is primarily κατοικῆσαι and the finite verb εὐδόκησεν forms *part* of the event expressed by κατοικῆσαι. Nida *et al* (1983:100-117) deals with this phenomenon by pointing out that the event in the phrase κατεργάζεται ὑπομονήν in James 1:3 is situated in the word ὑπομονήν while the verb κατεργάζεται simply serves as a ''marker of causative relationship...''. Thus the phrase can be rendered as *to cause perseverance*. Analogous to this, the phrase in item 18 can be rendered as *to desire inhabitance* = *to inhabit*.

In item 19 εὐδόκησεν is omitted in the surface structure, but the nucleus which is situated in the word ἀποκαταλλάξαι presumes it to be part of the event. Thus the event in item 19 can be rendered as *to desire reconciliation* = *to reconcile*.

The event expressed by item 20 is clear: *He makes peace*. (The principle which applies to the word *makes* in the English is the same as the one that applies to εὐδόκησεν in items 18 and 19 in the Greek phrase – it is part of one event.)

The nucleus in item 21 is αἵματος. In semiotic theory this type of sign is called an *index*. Indices are signs based on some or other form of *association* (cf Nida *et al* 1983:87). One associates blood with the event *to die*. Therefore *die* is the event represented by this nuclear structure.

In item 22 σταυροῦ acts as an index for the event *to die*.

The fact that three events occur in the surface structure between the elements of nuclear structure 19, namely items 20-22, causes the last elements of item 19 to be separated from the rest of the structure. In the surface structure of 19b and 19c the event *reconcile* is not repeated. The unity of the nuclear structure is broken by items 20-22. However, it is given in this analysis in the broken form because of the importance of retaining the original word order in a stylistic analysis.

2. The macrolevel of rhetorical structure

2.1 Progression

To get an idea of the progression in the hymn seems to be the most difficult part of the analysis. Depending on the kind of factors one deals with, the progression can be described in different ways and it is possible to give a sound motivation in each case.

Robinson (1957:286) divides the hymn in his analysis into *two* strophae. The factors indicating this binary division are obvious and in many other analyses of the hymn, a form of binary division is proposed (cf Lohse 1971:45; Sanders 1971:12; Schweizer 1982:63-81; Martin 1972:45-46; 1964:195 and Bammel 1961:95). Strophe 1 deals with Christ and creation and strophe 2 with Christ and the church (Martin 1964:196).

But this leaves an important problem: Although the phrases καὶ αὐτός ἐστιν πρὸ πάντων, καὶ τὰ πάντα ἐν αὐτῷ συνέστηκεν, αὐτός ἐστιν ἡ κεφαλὴ τοῦ σώματος τῆς ἐκκλησίας are structurally part of strophe 1, they occur in the hymn before the second ὅς ἐστιν which introduces the second strophe —this being semantically part of strophe 2. For this reason Bruce (1984:100,104,10) proposes a division of two strophae, each beginning with the phrase ὅς ἐστιν, but with the above-mentioned three phrases as a transitional link in the middle. McCown (1979:161-162) has the same thing in mind when he calls the phrases under discussion a refrain. The refrain is written only once at the end of strophe 1—the normal practice of writing down a song. But McCown offers no solution for the question as to whether this modern way of writing down a song has already been practised in the ancient world.

In the light of the discussion so far, it seems to be evident that the hymn's progression on the macrolevel of rhetorical structure, can be seen in more than one way. For the purpose of this analysis, however, the word order is left unchanged and an attempt is made to point out the logical relations between the nuclear structures.

Logical relations:

— Item 2 is the content of item 1: He depicts the invisible.

— Item 3 is the effect of item 4, the cause: *Create* causes *being first in order of rank*. Remove the cause and the effect also vanishes.

— Items 5-10 characterize τὰ πάντα in item 4.

— Items 5-6 are additive different non-consequentials: *see* and *not see*.

— Items 7-10 are additive equivalents: *rule* and *rule* and *rule* and *rule*.

— Items 5-6 and 7-10 are generic-specific.

— Item 11 is the cause of item 12, the effect. Thus, items 3 and 4 occur in the same logical relation to each other as items 11 and 12 do, although in reversed order:

    3 – being first α
    4 – create   β
    11 – create   β
    12 – being first α

Since items 5-10 are semantically subordinate to item 4, they can be regarded as part of item 4. Thus, between items 3-10 and 11-12 the logical relation is additive-equivalent. Because of the semantic chiasm existing between them, items 3-12 should be seen as in a closer relationship to each other, as for instance the relationship between 2 and 3 or 12 and 13.

Item 13 is the effect of item 14, the cause: the fact that everything *holds together* in him is the effect of his recreation, the cause of that.

Thus, between items 11 and 13 and 13 and 14 similar logical relations exist, and seeing it in this way, items 11-12 and 13-14 form a semantic parallelism:

    11 – effect   α
    12 – cause   β
    13 – effect   α
    14 – cause   β

The last two legs of the chiasm, items 11 and 12, form at the same time the first two legs of the immediately following parallelism.

Items 3-12 (the chiasm) and items 13-14 are additive-different consequentials: *create - hold together*.

Items 1-2 and 3-14 are generic-specific: *depicts - create/hold together*.

The logical relation between items 15 and 16-22 is generic-specific.

Item 16 is the means of item 17, the purpose: *first rise* (means) has *being first* in everything as purpose.

Items 16-17 are the effect of item 18, the cause: *inhabit* is the cause of *first rise/being first*, the effect.

Items 16-18 are the cause of items 19-22, the effect: *inhabit/(first rise/being first)* is the cause which has *reconcile* as effect.

Items 20-22 are the manner of item 19: *makes peace* is the manner of *to reconcile*.

Item 20 is the result of items 21-22, the means: *to die* is the means of the result *to make peace*.

Items 21 and 22 are generic-specific: *to die* in general (21) is generic but *to die on a cross* (22) is a specific way of dying.

Items 1-14 are generic with items 15-20 specific: *depicting through creation and holding together* is generic with *first rising from death* and everything in connection with that (= recreate) specific.

While progression focuses upon the diversities which occur in a sequence, cohesion focuses upon the way in which they are tied together (Nida *et al* 1983:16).

2.2 *Cohesion*

The cohesion in the hymn is especially accomplished by the different means of repetition occurring in it. Repetition is an important instrument of cohesion (Nida *et al* 1983:16).

The same *themes* are frequently repeated: Christ is the first of the creation (items 3 and 12) and also the first of the recreation (items 16 and 17). Everything in the heavens and on earth is created through Christ and holds together in Him. The Aorist ἐκτίσθη in item 4 is replaced by the Perfectum ἔκτισται in item 11 and this emphasizes the continuing existence of the creation. Everything is reconciled through Christ (items 4, 13, 19). The following remark of Lohse (1971:42) is a good summary of the theme: ''... creation and reconciliation, cosmology and soteriology are dealt with in order to praise Christ as the Lord of the cosmos, who is head of the body and whose reign encompasses all things''.

The same *lexical units* are repeated: ὅς ἐστιν (items 1 and 15); κτίσεως/ἐκτίσθη/ἔκτισται (items 3, 4, 11); τὰ πάντα/πάντων/πᾶσιν (items 4, 11, 12, 13, 17, 19); πρωτότοκος (items 3 and 16); οὐρανοῖς (items 4 and 19c); ἐπὶ τῆς γῆς (items 4 and 19b); ὅς and αὐτός in its declined forms (items 1, 4, 11, 12, 13, 14, 15, 17, 18, 19, 22).

The same *syntactical structure* is repeated: a relative phrase (items 1 and 15), followed by a ὅτι + Indicative-phrase (items 4 and 18), followed by proposition(s) introduced by καί + Indicative (items 12, 13, 14, 19).

Propositions identical or nearly identical in meaning are repeated: items 4, 11, 12, 13.

In addition to all these cases of repetition, certain *transitional devices* are also used to mark cohesion: items 4 and 18 are introduced by ὅτι; items 12, 13, 14, 19 by καί and item 17 by ἵνα.

With this in mind one gets a good idea of the strong unity of the hymn. Yet, the cohesion (as well as the progression) is further marked by certain features on the microlevel of rhetorical structure.

3. *The microlevel of rhetorical structure*

According to the classification of the figures (σχήματα) in the Greek New Testament, proposed by Snyman and Cronjé (1983:172-191), all the σχήματα are classified in terms of three processes, namely, repetition, omission and shifts in expectancy. By way of *identifying*, *naming* and *classifying* the σχήματα occurring in the hymn, the microlevel of rhetorical structure is discussed. The system of Snyman and Cronjé is followed and each σχήμα is numbered for the sake of further reference.

3.1 *Repetition*

Repetition of single items in structural significant positions with reference to the linguistic world:

Identical bound forms with the same meaning in analogous positions:

(i)	Homoeoteleuton	–	(5) τὰ ὁρατά
			(6) καὶ τὰ ἀόρατα
(ii)		–	(9) εἴτε ἀρχαί
			(10) εἴτε ἐξουσίαι
(iii)		–	(16) νεκρῶν
			(17) πρωτεύων
(iv)	Alliteration	–	(3) πρωτότοκος πάσης κτίσεως
(v)		–	(16) πρωτότοκος ἐκ τῶν νεκρῶν
(vi)		–	(2) τοῦ θεοῦ τοῦ ἀοράτου
(vii)		–	(22) τοῦ σταυροῦ αὐτοῦ (δι' αὐτοῦ)

Repetition of single items in non-structurally significant positions:
1. With reference to the non-linguistic world:

(viii)	Anaphora	–	(3) κτίσεως, (4) ἐκτίσθη, (11) ἔκτισται
(ix)		–	ὅς (1, 15)
(x)		–	αὐτός (4, 11, 11, 12, 13, 14, 18, 19, 22, 22)
(xi)		–	πρωτότοκος (3, 16)
(xii)		–	πάντα (4, 11, 12, 13, 17, 19)
(xiii)		–	ἐστι(ν) (1, 14, 15, implicit in 3 and 16).

(This definition of Snyman and Cronjé (1983:177) differs from that of Smyth (1956:673) and Lausberg (1960:318) who both see the anaphora as a repetition *at the beginning* of a colon or comma (/x.../x...).)

2. With reference to the linguistic world:

(xiv) Polysundeton - εἴτε (7, 8, 9, 10)
(xv)   - καί   (12, 13, 14)
(xvi)   - εἴτε (19b, 19c)

Repetition of two or more items in structurally significant positions in the same text:

1. The same lexical units:

(xvii) Chiasm - (12) καὶ αὐτός ἐστιν πρὸ πάντων
                   (13) καὶ τὰ πάντα ἐν αὐτῷ συνέστηκεν
(xviii) Mixed   - (only certain lexical units correspond but the syntactical structure of both phrases is the same):

(1) ὅς ἐστιν...   (15) ὅς ἐστιν...
(3) πρωτότοκος...   (16) πρωτότοκος...
(4) ὅτι ἐν αὐτῷ...   (18) ὅτι ἐν αὐτῷ...
(14) καὶ αὐτός...   (19) καὶ δι' αὐτοῦ...

2. Different lexical units:

(xix) Parallel - (11) τὰ πάντα δι' αὐτοῦ καὶ εἰς αὐτόν ἔκτισται   (A)
                   (12) καὶ αὐτός ἐστιν πρὸ πάντων   (B)
                   (13) καὶ τὰ πάντα ἐν αὐτῷ συνέστηκεν   (A)
                   (14) καὶ αὐτός ἐστιν ἡ κεφαλὴ τοῦ σώματος τῆς ἐκκλησίας (B)
(xx)   Reversed (Semantic chiasm):
                   (4) ἐν τοῖς οὐρανοῖς   (A)
                       καὶ ἐπὶ τῆς γῆς   (B)
                   (19) εἴτε τὰ ἐπὶ τῆς γῆς   (B)
                        εἴτε τὰ ἐν τοῖς οὐρανοῖς   (A)
(xxi)   (4) ἐν τοῖς οὐρανοῖς   (A)
                       καὶ ἐπὶ τῆς γῆς   (B)
                   (5) τὰ ὁρατά   (B)
                   (6) καὶ τὰ ἀόρατα   (A)
(xxii) Since the words in items 7-10 are semantically closely related, the semantic chiasm in these items is not easily recognizable. But, according to Bammel (1961:90-92) θρόνοι and ἐξουσίαι refer in most instances to *earthly* powers and κυριότητες and ἀρχαί on the other hand, to *heavenly* powers. Thus, the chiasm in items 4-6 (xxi) is immediately followed by another chiasm with a reversed arrangement:

(7) εἴτε θρόνοι   (B)
(8) εἴτε κυριότητες   (A)
(9) εἴτε ἀρχαί   (A)
(10) εἴτε ἐξουσίαι   (B)

(xxiii) (3) πρωτότοκος πάσης κτίσεως   (A)
        (4) ὅτι ἐν αὐτῷ ἐκτίσθη   (B)
        (11) τὰ πάντα δι' αὐτοῦ καί εἰς αὐτόν ἔκτισται (B)
        (12) καὶ αὐτός ἐστιν πρὸ πάντων   (A)

Repetition of identical forms with different meanings:

(xxiv) Diaphora   (3) πρωτότοκος πάσης κτίσεως
                  (first in order of rank)
           (16) πρωτότοκος ἐκ τῶν νεκρῶν
                  (first in chronological order)

Repetitions of different forms with the same meaning:

(xxv)   Pleonasm – (7) εἴτε θρόνοι
                   (8) εἴτε κυριότητες
                   (9) εἴτε ἀρχαί
                (10) εἴτε ἐξουσίαι
(xxvi)   – (3) πρωτότοκος πάσης κτίσεως
                (12) καὶ αὐτός ἐστιν πρὸ πάντων
(xxvii)   – (4) ... ἐν αὐτῷ ἐκτίσθη τὰ πάντα...
                (11) ... τὰ πάντα δι' αὐτοῦ καί εἰς αὐτόν ἔκτισται

Repetition of different forms with opposite meanings:

(xxviii) Antithesis – (4) ἐν τοῖς οὐρανοῖς
                    καὶ ἐπὶ τῆς γῆς
(xxix)   (5) τὰ ὁρατὰ
                 (6) καὶ τὰ ἀόρατα
(xxx)   (19b) εἴτε τὰ ἔπὶ τῆς γῆς
              (19c) εἴτε τὰ ἐν τοῖς οὐρανοῖς

3.2 *Omission*

Omission of words important for the referential context in analogous positions:

(xxxi)   Sulleipsis (1) ὅς ἐστιν εἰκὼν (2) τοῦ θεοῦ τοῦ ἀοράτου
                (15) ὅς ἐστιν ἀρχή [_____]

Omission of words important to the linguistic context:

(xxxii)   Elleipsis – ἐκτίσθη in items 5, 6, 7, 8, 9, 10.
(xxxiii)   – ἐστι(ν) in items 3 and 16.
(xxxiv)   – εὐδόκησεν in item 19.

Deep structure omissions of taboo forms:

(xxxv)   ὁ θέος in items 4 and 11.

3.3 *Forms involving a shift in expectancies*

Shifts in expectancies of the word-order:

(xxxvi)   Unusual position in a clause (Hyperbaton): δι' αὐτοῦ in item 22.
(xxxvii)   Unusual position outside the clause (Prolepsis): items 19b and
               19c.
(xxxviii) Insertion (Parenthesis): items 20-22.

Shifts in propositions:

> (xxxix)   Apparent contradictions (Parodoxon): items 1 and 2.
> εἰκών — ἀοράτου: to depict the invisible.

Shifts with regard to the communication function: literal and figurative meaning:

> (xl)   Metaphora   – (14)   αὐτός ἐστιν ἡ κεφαλή
> (xli)   Metonumia   – (14)   σώματος (referring to *congregation*)
> (xlii)   (21)   διά τοῦ αἵματος
>   (referring to *to die*)
> (xliii)   (22)   τοῦ σταυροῦ
>   (referring to *to die*)

4. The possible meaning(s) of the rhetorical features of the hymn

4.1 In the relationship of parts of the text to one another

This discussion of the processes caused by the rhetorical features in the relationship of parts of the text to one another, is a fuller discussion of the cohesion in the hymn, already touched on in 2.2.

By far the most rhetorical features on the microlevel of rhetorical structure cause a process of repetition. Of the 44 σχήματα identified in the hymn, 30 cause a process of repetition. This repetition occurs between elements which occur next to or near each other, but also between elements not near each other. This causes the hymn to be closely bound together regarding its internal structure and it motivates the demarcation of the different units in the hymn as well as their connection to each other.

Because of the semantic chiasm in items 3, 4, 11, 12 (xxiii), the whole section is linked together as a unit. The middle elements (4 and 11) are further linked to each other by the pleonasm (xxvii) and the outer elements of the chiasm (3 and 12) are also pleonastic-propositions (xxvi). For this reason items 3-12 as a whole are in a closer relationship as for instance the relationship between items 2 and 3 or 12 and 13. The unit 3-12 is then bound to the unit 13-14 by the chiasm in items 12 and 13 (xvii).

As far as logical relations are concerned, items 11 and 12 and 13 and 14 are parallel (xix). The first two legs of this parallelism are also the last two legs of the preceding chiasm (xxiii). Therefore, items 3-14 as a whole are in a closer relationship, as in the case of items 2-3.

Items 5-10 are qualificational nuclear structures of πάντα in item 4. The following σχήματα are occurring in these items: homoeoteleuton (i) and (ii), polysundeton (xiv), two successive chiasms (xxi and xxii), pleonasm (xxv) and antithesis (xxviii and xxix). All these features serve to bind items 5-10 to a unit and thereby to qualify πάντα in item 4 in a striking manner. The absolute totality of the concept signified by πάντα is emphasized by the accumulation of all these σχήματα.

The obvious demarcation of items 1-14 and 15-22 as two separate units is further motivated by the anaphora in items 1 and 15 (ix), the repetition of the same syntactical structure in both units (xviii) and the diaphora in items 3 and 16 (xxiv).

The chiasm in items 4a-4b and 19b-19c which consists of two antitheses (xxviii and xxx) serves to link the two bigger units (items 1-14 and 15-22) and mark the end of the hymn in item 19c.

A special feature of the hymn is that all the major thematic units are repeated anaphorically (viii-xiii). This is a very striking means of reinforcing cohesion in the hymn.

On the basis of these possible meanings of the rhetorical features on the microlevel of rhetorical structure, it can be concluded that the demarcation of the units in the hymn as well as the relationship between these units, as it was pointed out in the discussion of the progression (2.1), is further motivated and confirmed by the rhetorical features on microlevel.

4.1 In the relationship text to receptor

Two major propositions can be made here:
1) this analysis confirms the general consensus of scholars on the hymnic character of these verses, and
2) the possible meaning(s) of poetry as a socio-semiotic sign, proposed by Nida et al (1983:66), is also confirmed.

To distinguish between "prose" and "poetry" is one of the much-debated issues in literary theory. Jakobson (1960) has made a number of insightful comments concerning poetry as being essentially based upon parallelism. There are many instances of parallelism in the hymn. Furthermore, the large number of σχήματα (43 identified) in this relatively short passage is a sure sign of its aesthetic and emotional quality and confirms its hymnic character.

With regard to the function of poetry, Nida et al (1983:66) name five important contributions which poetic structure makes to a text—all applicable to the function of this hymn under discussion:
1. Poetic language highlights and emphasizes the significance of the theme. The very unusualness of the structure of the hymn adds impact and therefore calls attention to the lexical content.
2. The poetic structure no doubt makes the passage more aesthetically attractive. The balance, symmetry and rhythm in the hymn, make it more pleasurable to read (and/or sing).

3. The use of poetic structures permits the grouping of ideas in ways which defy normal logical formulations but which express important insights and relations which people can feel but not necessarily explain. The idea of something being overwhelming because of the majestic concepts dealt with—Christ, creation, recreation—is successfully communicated (cf e.g. the very striking sulleipsis in item 15).

4. The use of poetic structure certainly *identifies* this hymn as a passage having some supernatural basis and implication. Utterances having important theological implications—as in the case of Col 1:15-20—frequently occur in hymnic/poetic structure in the Bible (e.g. Phlp 2:6-11).

5. The poetic structure of the hymn provides a high degree of emotive impact. In the Bible, this emotive impact is even more enhanced by the association of poetic features with divine authority.

BIBLIOGRAPHY

BAMMEL, E. 1961. Versuch zu Col 1:15-20. *ZNW* 52, 88-95.

BRUCE, F. F. 1984. The "Christ hymn" of Colossians 1:15-20. *BS* 141, 99-111.

CRADDOCK, F. B. 1965. 'All things in Him': a critical note on Col 1:15-20. *NTS* 12, 78-80.

DEICHGRÄBER, R. 1967. *Gotteshymnus und Christushymnus in der früher Christenheit. Untersuchungen zu Form, Sprache und Stil der frühchristlichen Hymnen.* Göttingen: Vandenhoeck & Ruprecht.

DELLING, G. 1972. ὕμνος, ὑμνέω, ψάλλω, ψαλμός. *TDNT* VIII, 489-503.

DU PLESSIS, I. J. 1984. Die Pauliniese Christologie, in A. B. du Toit (ed), *Handleiding by die Nuwe Testament* V. Pretoria: N. G. Kerkboekhandel Transvaal, 213-233.

GABATHULER, H. J. 1965. *Jesus Christus. Haupt der Kirche - Haupt der Welt. Der Christushymnus Colosser 1:15-20 in der theologischen Forschung der letzten 130 Jahre.* Stuttgart: Zwingli.

HENDRIKSEN, W. 1964. *Colossians and Philemon.* Edinburgh: Banner of Truth Trust.

JAKOBSON, R. 1960. Linguistics and poetics, in A. Sebeok (ed), *Style in language.* Cambridge, Mass: Technology Press, 350-377.

KÄSEMANN, E. 1965. Eine urchristliche Taufliturgie, in *Exegetische Versuche und Besinnungen.* Göttingen: Vandenhoeck & Ruprecht, 34-50.

KEHL, N. 1967. *Der Christushymnus in Kolosserbrief. Eine motivgeschichtliche Untersuchung zu Kol 1:12-20.* Stuttgart: Katholisches Bibelwerk. (Stuttgarter Biblische Monographien.)

LAUSBERG, H. 1960. *Handbuch der Literarischen Rhetorik. Eine Grundlegung der Literaturwissenschaft.* München: Max Heuber.

LOHMEYER, E. 1930. *Die Briefe an die Kolosser und an Philemon.* Göttingen: Vandenhoeck & Ruprecht (Kritisch-exegetischer Kommentar über das Neue Testament.)

LOHSE, E. 1971. *Colossians and Philemon*, tr by W. R. Poehlman & R. J. Karris. Philadelphia: Fortress. (Hermeneia-series.)

LOUW, J. P. 1967. *Stilistiese sinsboustrukture en Nuwe-Testamentiese Grieks.* Bloemfontein: Universiteit van die Oranje-Vrystaat.

LOUW, J. P. 1975. Semantiek en Antieke Retoriek. *Acta Classica* 17, 99-108.

LOUW, J. P. 1979. Nominalisering van gebeure as stylkenmerk in antieke Grieks. *Taalfasette* 26, 21-27.

MAN, R. E. 1984. The value of chiasm for New Testament interpretation. *BS* 141, 146-157.

MARTIN, R. P. 1964. An early Christian hymn (Col 1:15-20). *EQ* 36, 195-205.

MARTIN, R. P. 1972. *Colossians: The church's Lord and the christian's liberty. An expository commentary with a present-day application.* Grand Rapids: Zondervan.

McCOWN, W. 1979. The hymnic structure of Colossians 1:15-20. *EQ* 51, 156-162.

NORDEN, E. 1913. *Agnostos Theos. Untersuchungen zur Formengeschichte Religiöser Rede.* Stuttgart: Teubner.

NIDA, E. A., J. P. LOUW, A. H. SNYMAN & J. v. W. CRONJÉ 1983. *Style and discourse.* Cape Town: Bible Society.

O'BRIEN, P. T. 1974. Col 1:20 and the reconciliation of all things. *Reformed Theological Review* 33, 45-53.

POHLMANN, W. 1973. Die hymnischen All-Prädikationem in Kol 1:15-20. *ZNW* 64, 55-74.

RIDDERBOS, H. 1960. *Aan de Kolossenzen.* Kampen: Kok. (Commentaar op het Nieuwe Testament.)

ROBINSON, J. M. 1957. A formal analysis of Colossians 1:15-20. *JBL* 76, 270-287.

SANDERS, J. T. 1971. *The New Testament christological hymns. Their historical religious background.* Cambridge: Cambridge University Press. (SNTSMS 15.)

SCHILLE, G. 1965. *Frühchristliche Hymnen.* Berlin: Evangelische Verlagsanstalt.

SCHWEIZER, E. 1982. *The letter to the Colossians. A Commentary,* tr by Andrew Chester. Minneapolis: Augsburg Publishing House.

SMYTH, H. W. 1956. *Greek grammar.* Cambridge, Mass: Harvard University Press.

SNYMAN, A. H. & J. v. W. CRONJÉ 1983. Toward a new classification of the figures (σχήματα) in the Greek New Testament, in E. A. Nida, J. P. Louw, A. H. Snyman a J. v. W. Cronjé 1983. *Style and discourse.* Cape Town. Bible Society, 172-191.

SNYMAN, A. H. 1984. Style and meaning in Romans 8:31-39. *Neotestamentica* 18, 94-103.

VAWTER, B. 1971. The Colossian hymn and the principle of redaction. *CBQ* 33, 62-81.

J. J. JANSE VAN RENSBURG

AN ARGUMENT FOR READING νήπιοι IN I THESSALONIANS 2:7

In the third corrected edition of *The Greek New Testament* of the United Bible Societies (1983:705-6) 1 Thessalonians 2:6-8 is printed as follows:

6 οὔτε ζητοῦντες ἐξ ἀνθρώπων δόξαν οὔτε ἀφ' ὑμῶν οὔτε ἀπ' ἄλλων, 7 δυνάμενοι ἐν βάρει εἶναι ὡς Χριστοῦ ἀπόστολοι. ἀλλὰ ἐγενήθημεν νήπιοι ἐν μέσῳ ὑμῶν, ὡς ἐὰν τροφὸς θάλπῃ τὰ ἑαυτῆς τέκνα, 8 οὕτως ὁμειρόμενοι ὑμῶν εὐδοκοῦμεν μεταδοῦναι ὑμῖν οὐ μόνον τὸ εὐαγγέλιον τοῦ θεοῦ ἀλλὰ καὶ τὰς ἑαυτῶν ψυχάς, διότι ἀγαπητοὶ ἡμῖν ἐγενήθητε.

Thus the reading adopted as the text in v 7 is νήπιοι, and the Committee has indicated their relative degree of certainty with a (C), which means that there is a considerable degree of doubt whether the text or the apparatus contains the superior reading. In his *A textual commentary on the Greek New Testament* Metzger (1971: 630) comments:

"In the absence of any strong argument based on internal probabilities, a majority of the Committee preferred to follow what is admittedly the stronger external attestation and to adopt νήπιοι."

Metzger (1971:630) then adds the following on behalf of himself and Allen Wikgren:

"Despite the weight of external evidence, only ἤπιοι seems to suit the context, where the apostle's gentleness makes an appropriate sequence disclaimed in ver. 6."

Bertram (1967:919) shares this view: "But though this reading is well attested, the reading with ἤπιοι is to be preferred."

In this article I am proposing an argument based on internal probabilities in support of the stronger external attestation for νήπιοι.

1. *1 Th 2:1-12 as a thought unit*

The UBS (1983) prints 1 Th 2:1-12 as a separate pericope, as does the NEB. The contents of 2:1-12 compels such a demarcation.

In ch 1 Paul refers to the success of their visit to the Thessalonians (v 9). In ch 2 Paul resumes the theme of his and his fellow workers' visit to the Thessalonians. In 1:9 he states "All those people speak about how you received us when we visited you and how you turned away from idols to God, to serve the true and living God..." In 2:1 Paul motivates (cf the γάρ in 2:1) his previous statement concerning their visit to the Thessalonians:

"You know for yourselves, brothers, that our visit to you was not fruitless".

In both instances the word translated with 'visit' is εἴσοδος.

In 2:1-12 Paul explicates the nature of his and his fellow workers' εἴσοδος, and uses this explication to defend himself against the slanderous accusations, probably instigated by Jewish opponents.

2. The flow of thought in 1 Th 2:1-11

2.1 Vv 1,2: Theme announced

In vv 1,2 Paul announces the theme of the pericope under discussion, viz. the assertion of the nature of his and his fellow workers' 'visit' to the Thessalonians.

Paul points to the fact that the believers in Thessalonica know the nature of the visit (v 1a). He first states the nature of the visit in the negative: It was not fruitless (v 1b). Then—contrastively (cf the conjunction ἀλλά)—he states it in the positive: We declared the Gospel of God to you frankly and fearlessly (v 2).

2.2 Vv 3,4: Motivation for the statement in vv 1,2

In vv 3,4 Paul motivates (cf the γάρ in v 3, rendered by the NEB with "Indeed, ...") his statement in vv 1,2. This he does by explicating the most characteristic activity of their εἴσοδος, viz. their παράκλησις, rendered by the NEB as "...the appeal we make...". Paul uses παράκλησις here for missionary proclamation (Schmitz 1967:795). ἡ παράκλησις ἡμῶν is thus used parallel to λαλῆσαι ... τὸ εὐαγγέλιον τοῦ θεοῦ- in v 2.

In vv 3,4 Paul is thus motivating the assertion made in vv 1,2, and in doing this he describes the character of his and his fellow workers' "declaration of the gospel of God".

In v 3 Paul describes this character negatively, and in v 4 positively.

The negative description is threefold: 1) οὐκ ἐκ πλάνης; 2) οὐδὲ ἐξ ἀκαθαρσίας; 3) οὐδὲ ἐν δόλῳ. These three negative qualifications of their παράκλησις are rendered by the NEB as: "Indeed, the appeal we make never springs from *error* or *base motive*; there is no *attempt to deceive*".

The main thrust of the positive description (v 4) is the statement of the fact that in their declaration of the gospel, they sought only the favour of

God. The NEB's rendering of v 4 is: "...but God has approved us fit to
be entrusted with the gospel, and on these terms we speak. We do not
curry favour with men; we seek only the favour of God, who is continual-
ly testing our hearts".

2.3 Vv 5-7a: Threefold negative motivation of the statement in v 3

In vv 5-7a Paul motivates (cf the γάρ introducing v 5) the preceding
verses with a threefold negative statement:

1) οὔτε ... γάρ ποτε ἐν λόγῳ κολακείας ἐγενήθημεν. (v 5a)
2) οὔτε ἐν προφάσει πλεονεξίας. (v 5b)
3) οὔτε ζητοῦντες ἐξ ἀνθρώπων δόξαν οὔτε ἀφ' ὑμων οὔτε ἀπ' ἄλλων, δυνάμενοι
ἐν βάρει εἶναι ὡς Χριστοῦ ἀπόστολοι. (vv 6-7a)

A closer examination of this threefold motivation shows that Paul uses it
to demarcate and pinpoint his threefold negative characterization of his
παράκλησις in v 3. The first of the threefold motivation (v 5a) demarcates
and pinpoints the first of the threefold negative characterization of
παράκλησις in v 3, the second of the threefold motivation (v 5b) demarcates the second of the threefold negative characterization in v 3, and the
third demarcates the third:

2.3.1 V 5a: The demarcation of παράκλησις οὐκ ἐκ πλάνης

In v 3a Paul states that their preaching was not ἐκ πλάνης. The Greek
word πλάνη can be rendered in English as "deceit, deception, delusion"
(Newman 1971:143). In v 5a Paul demarcates and pinpoints ἡ παράκλησις
ἡμῶν οὐκ ἐκ πλάνης with οὔτε ποτε ἐν λόγῳ κολακείας ἐγενήθημεν. What he
actually says, is: We have not *deceived* (cf KJV's translation of v 3, and cf
Braun 1968:250) you in our preaching by *flattering* you. "Deception" (v
3) is demarcated and pinpointed as "flattering" (v 5).

2.3.2 V 5b: The demarcation of παράκλησις οὐδὲ ἐξ ἀκαθαρσίας

In v 3b Paul states that their preaching was not ἐξ ἀκαθαρσίας. The Greek
word ἀκαθαρσία can be rendered in English as "impurity, immorality;
impure motive" (Newman 1971:6). In v 5b Paul demarcates and pinpoints ἡ παράκλησις ἡμων ... οὐδὲ ἐξ ἀκαθαρσίας with οὔτε ἐν προφάσει
πλεονεξίας. Paul thus says that their preaching does not have a *base motive*
(v 3), pinpointed as "nor have our words ever been a cloak for *greed*" (v
5b, NEB). "Base motive" (v 3) is demarcated as "a cloak for greed" (v
5).

2.3.3 V 6-7a: The demarcation of παράκλησις οὐδὲ ἐν δόλῳ

In v 3c Paul states that their preaching was not ἐν δόλῳ. The Greek word δόλος can be rendered in English as "deceit, treachery" (Newman 1971:48). In v 6 Paul demarcates and pinpoints ἡ παράκλησις ἡμῶν ... οὐδὲ ἐν δόλῳ with οὔτε ζητοῦντες ἐξ ἀνθρώπων δόξαν. Paul thus says that their preaching is no attempt to *trick* anyone (v 3), pinpointed as "we have never sought *honour* from men" (v 6a, the NEB). "Attempt to trick" (v 3) is demarcated as "seeking honour from men" (v 6).

2.4 Vv 7b-12: Threefold positive inverted counterpart of vv 5-7a

The following punctuational changes are made in v 7: A minor after ἀπόστολοι, and a major after ὑμῶν.

Vv 7b-12 is interpreted to be made up of three thought units, viz.:

1. V 7b: ἀλλὰ ... ἐν μέσῳ ὑμῶν;
2. Vv 7c-9: ὡς ἐὰν τροφὸς ... τὸ εὐαγγέλιον τοῦ θεοῦ;
3. Vv 10-12: ὑμεῖς ... καὶ δόξαν.

The three thought units v 7b, vv 7c-9 and vv 10-12 are a positive inverted counterpart of the three negative motivations in vv 5-7a, which are—as has been argued in 2.3—a threefold demarcation of the threefold characterization of Paul's and his fellow workers' παράκλησις in v 3.

2.4.1 V 7b: Positive counterpart of vv 6-7a

In v 3c Paul states that their preaching is no attempt to trick or deceive anyone. He pinpoints what he means, and he does this with the demarcation in vv 6-7a: "We have never sought honour from men, from you or from anyone else" (NEB). With this statement Paul says that they did not make use of any tricks or pretences in order to be praised by *men*.

In v 7b Paul then states the positive counterpart: ἀλλὰ ἐγενήθημεν νήπιοι ἐν μέσῳ ὑμῶν. His argument is more or less the following: "Our preaching is no attempt to trick or deceive anyone; from men we have never sought honour. But—we were babies among you". The meaning of the baby metaphor becomes clear: A baby has no pretence and uses no tricks in an attempt to gain praise; a baby shows his actual feelings. Paul claims this characteristic of a baby for his and his fellow workers' work in Thessalonica.

2.4.2. Vv 7c-9: Positive counterpart for v 5b

In v 3b Paul states that their preaching does not have a base motive. He pinpoints what he means, and he does this with the demarcation in v 5b: "Our words have never been a cloak for greed" (NEB).

Paul says that they did not have the covert base motive of financial enrichment.

In v 7c-9 Paul then states the positive counterpart. In vv 7c, 8 Paul again uses a metaphor, this time of a mother/nurse taking care of her children: "As a mother (or: nurse) caring fondly for her children—with such yearning we love you—we chose to impart to you not only the gospel of God but our very selves, so dear had you become to us" (my modification of the NEB). It is immediately clear what Paul is arguing: Instead of having a covert, base motive of financial enrichment, Paul's argument is: Like a mother who not only gives her milk and everything she has for the benefit of her children, but who is also willing to give her very self, in the same way Paul and his fellow workers were willing not only to impart the gospel of God to the Thessalonians, but also themselves.

In v 9 Paul motivates (cf the introductory γάρ) why his statement in vv 7c,8 is justified: "Surely you remember, our brothers, how we worked and toiled! We worked day and night so that we would not be any trouble to you as we preached to you the Good News from God" (GNB).

2.4.3 Vv 10-12: Positive counterpart for v 5a

In v 3a Paul states that their preaching has in no way been a deception. He pinpoints what he means, and he does this with the demarcation in v 5a: "Our words have never been flattering words" (NEB). With this statement Paul says that they have not abused their preaching to deceive the Thessalonians by flattering them.

In vv 10-12 Paul then states the positive counterpart. This positive counterpart consists of two parallel constructions, viz. v 10 en vv 11,12, each introduced by ὡς. In v 10 Paul appeals to a more general characteristic of their παράκλησις to the Thessalonians: "We call you to witness, yes and God himself, how devout and just and blameless was our behaviour towards you who are believers" (NEB). After this more general characteristic Paul actually comes to the point in vv 11,12: In their preaching they did not deceive the Thessalonians by using flattering words; instead—"As you well know, we dealt with you one by one, as a father deals with his children, appealing to you by encouragement, as well as by solemn injunctions, to live lives worthy of God who call you into his kingdom and glory" (NEB). The meaning of this father-children metaphor is clear. As a father does not deceive his children by using flattering words, but in love deals with them directly, in the same way Paul and his fellow workers *urged* the believers to live the kind of life that pleases God.

2.4.4 Recapitulation

In vv 7b-12 Paul uses three metaphors, viz. the νήπιοι metaphor (v 7b), the τρόφος-τέχνα metaphor (vv 7c-9) and the πατήρ-τέχνα metaphor (vv

10-12) to give the positive counterpart—in inverted order—of the threefold negative demarcation in vv 5-7a.

2.5 *A synopsis of the flow of thought in 1 Th 2:1-12*

In vv 1,2 Paul asserts the nature of their visit (εἴσοδος) to the Thessalonians, viz. that the gospel of God was declared frankly and fearlessly. In vv 3,4 Paul motivates this assertion by stating the character of their proclamation (παράκλησις), first in the negative with a threefold statement (v 3), and then generally in the positive (v 4). In vv 5-12 he motivates the statement in v 3,4, first in the negative with a threefold statement (vv 5-7b) in the same order as the threefold statement in v 3, then in the positive with a threefold statement (vv 7c-12) in the reverse order of the threefold statement in v 3.

Represented visually:

Vv 1,2: The theme announced: An assertion of the nature of their εἴσοδος

* V 1b. Negative: The visit was not fruitless
* V 2: Positive: The gospel of God was declared frankly and fearlessly

Vv 3,4: Paul motivates vv 1,2 by stating the character of their παράκλησις

*   V 3. Negative. 1. It is not based on deception (οὐκ ἐκ πλάνης)
2. It does not spring from a base motive (οὐδὲ ἐξ ἀκαθαρσίας)
3. It is no attempt to deceive (οὐδὲ ἐν δόλῳ)
*   V 4: Positive: Approved by God and under his testing of the heart

Vv 5-12: Paul motivates vv 3,4 by explaining the character of their παράκλησις more fully

* Vv 5-7a: A threefold negative demarcation of the three negative characteristics in v 3, in the same order:
1. No flattering words (v 5a)
2. No cloak for greed (v 5b)
3. No seeking for honour from men (v 6-7a)
* Vv 7b-12: A threefold positive counterpart in reverse order:
1. We were non-pretentious, like babies (v 7b)
2. We gave our very selves, like a mother to her children (vv 7c-9)
3. We urged you, like a father does his children (vv 10-12)

2.6 *Relevant characteristics of the flow of thought in 1 Th 2:1-12*

1Th 2:1-12 has three pairs of positive-negative statements, as becomes evident from the visual representation of the thought structure. The following summarises this fact:

First pair: v 1   :   Negative
                 v 2   :   Positive
Second pair: v 3   :   Negative
                 v 4   :   Positive
Third pair: vv 5-7a :   Negative
                 vv 7b-12 : Positive

The relation between the three pairs is the following: The first pair asserts the nature of the εἴσοδος (vv 1,2); the second pair motivates this assertion by stating the character of the παράκλησις (vv 3,4); and the third pair motivates this statement by first negatively demarcating the character of the παράκλησις (vv 5-7a), and then giving the positive counterpart of this demarcation (vv 7b-12).

The visual representation of the thought structure makes evident a very definite structural pattern in the second and third pairs, summarised by the following representation:

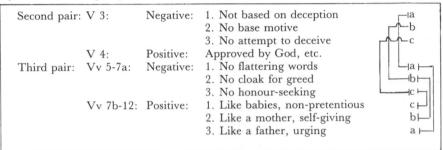

Second pair: V 3:	Negative:	1. Not based on deception
		2. No base motive
		3. No attempt to deceive
V 4:	Positive:	Approved by God, etc.
Third pair: Vv 5-7a:	Negative:	1. No flattering words
		2. No cloak for greed
		3. No honour-seeking
Vv 7b-12:	Positive:	1. Like babies, non-pretentious
		2. Like a mother, self-giving
		3. Like a father, urging

3. Conclusion

It becomes evident that νήπιοι fits the context. If ἤπιοι is adopted as the text of 1 Th 2:7, the very logical thought structure of the pericope is changed: V 7b would then no longer be a positive counterpart of vv 6-7a's negative demarcation of ἡ παράκλησις ἡμῶν ... οὐδὲ ἐν δόλῳ in v 3, and this fact will break the evident structural pattern of vv 3-12.

I thus maintain that internal probabilities are in support of the stronger external attestation for adopting νήπιοι as the text in 1 Th 2:7, and that the following punctuational changes in v 7 be made: A minor after ἀπόστολοι and a major after ὑμῶν.

BIBLIOGRAPHY

ALAND, K., M. BLACK, C. M. MARTINI, B. M. METZGER & A. WIKGREN (eds) 1983. *The Greek New Testament*. 3. cor ed. Stuttgart: United Bible Societies.
BERTMAN, G. 1967. νήπιος, νηπιάζω. *TDNT IV*, 912-923.
BRAUN, H. 1968. πλανάω etc. *TDNT VI*, 228-253.
METZGER, B. M. 1968. *The text of the New Testament; its transmission, corruption and restoration*. Oxford: Clarendon Press.

METZGER, B. M. 1971. *A textual commentary on the Greek New Testament.* London: United Bible Societies.

NEWMAN, B. M. 1971. *A concise Greek-English dictionary of the New Testament.* London: United Bible Societies.

SCHMITZ, O. 1967. παρακαλέω, παράκλησις. *TDNT V*, 773-799.

Bible translations:
   GNB
   KJV
   NEB

J. H. L. DIJKMAN

"OTI AS AN INTRODUCTORY FORMULA TO CATECHETICAL REFERENCES IN I PETER

The pioneering studies of B. M. Metzger first drew my attention to the fascinating subject of introductory formulae to quotations of Scripture in the New Testament.[1] A study of 1 Peter in this regard reveals that the author has a particular approach in his use of the scriptures of his day and the standard teaching material of his church.

His letter includes many and sometimes lengthy quotations from the LXX, but only a few of them are introduced by an acknowledgement like γάρ, γράφει or διότι. For example, γάρ introduces his quotation from Ps 34:12-16 in 3:10-12. διότι γέγραπται in 1:16 leads into a combination of texts from Lv 11:44; 19:2; 20:7; while in 2:6-8 a mosaic of Is 28:16; Ps 118:22 and Is 8:14 is preceded by διότι περιέχει ἐν γραφῇ. διότι is used on its own to introduce Is 40:6-8 in 1:24. A number of fairly lengthy LXX quotations in 1 Peter have no introductory formula whatsoever. They are in 2:9-10 (Is 43:20-21; Ex 19:5-6; 23:22[2]; Hs 1:6,8-9; 2:1,23), 2:22,24-25 (Is 53:9,12,6) and 4:18 (Pr 11:31). Hence 1 Peter uses very few introductory formulae in comparison with the rest of the New Testament's variety of introductory terms ranging from γέγραπται, λέγει, εἶπεν, φησίν to πληροῦν. Moreover, he never refers to a particular part of the Scriptures as the Law, the Prophets[3], or the Writings, nor does he quote his scriptural authorities like Moses, Isaiah, Jeremiah, Hosea, Joel, Daniel or Enoch by name. Neither does he introduce a text with such customary verbs as πληροῦν, ἀναπληροῦν or τελειοῦν, which occur relatively often in the rest of the New Testament, particularly in Matthew and John. Even James 2:23 has ἐπληρώθη ἡ γραφή ...

Against this background 1 Peter's use of ὅτι in 4:8 and 5:5 is quite remarkable. It introduces quotations from Pr 10:12 and 3:34, but in both instances the text varies from that of the LXX, the author's usual source.

---

[1] See B. M. Metzger, "The formulas introducing quotations of Scripture in the New Testament and the Mishna", *JBL* 70:297-307, 1951; Idem, *Historical and literary studies, Pagan, Jewish, and Christian*, Leiden: Brill, 1968:52-63. Cf D. A. Hagner, *The use of the Old and New Testaments in Clement of Rome*, NTSup 34, Leiden: Brill, 1973; R. H. Gundry, *The use of the Old Testament in St Matthew's Gospel*, NTSup 18, 1967.

[2] Cf Ml 3:17.

[3] His reference to the prophets in 1:10 is not within the context of a LXX quotation.

1 Peter 4:8

In reinforcing his teaching in 4:8 he quotes Pr 10:12 in a form which is much closer to the Hebrew[4] than to the LXX version, "love covers all those who do not love strife"[5]. The same is true of James 5:20 at this point. This raises a problem. Why would James and 1 Peter suddenly translate from the Hebrew text when they normally use the LXX? Possibly, the answer is to be found in the view that this aphorism did not come to them by way of LXX, but was already included in the early Judean Christian paraenetic tradition which they are both using to instruct the Greek speaking Jewish believers they are addressing. The saying is reproduced in its Petrine form in some of the early Fathers[6], while Clement of Alexandria[7], Origen[8] and the Didascalia[9] ascribe it to Christ. Origen[10] cites it in connection with Lk 7:47, where Jesus' teaching about the woman whose sins are forgiven parallels the admonition of 1 Peter and could even be understood as a paraphrase of the aphorism in Pr 10:12. Thus it is quite possible that the saying was included in some early collection of Jesus logia, or at least became proverbial in the Jerusalem church from whence it was passed on in its catechetical instruction. Then, like many proverbial expressions, it was interpreted and adapted to suit the varying contexts where it was applied, as is done in James 5:20. Interestingly, when on rare occasions the rabbis comment on Pr 10:12, they interpret it in the same way as 1 Peter[11]. It is also important to note that neither he nor James gives any indication that by introducing this aphorism they are quoting or even alluding to authoritative scripture. This lends further support to the view that for this saying they are both indebted not to scripture, but to a current corpus of teaching like an early Jerusalem catechism.

1 Peter 5:5

Among the many parallels between 1 Pt 5:5-9 and writings of the New Testament, those with James 4:6-10 appear to be the most significant and may best be examined by setting them out as follows:

---

[4] ועל כל-פשעים תכסה אהבה – καλύπτει πλῆθος ἁμαρτιῶν.
[5] πάντας δὲ τοὺς μὴ φιλονεικοῦντας καλύπτει φιλία.
[6] See 1 Clem 44:5; 2 Clem 16:4; Tert Scorp 6:11; Clem Alex Quis Div 38.
[7] Paed 3:12.91.
[8] Hom in Lv 2:4.
[9] Didasc II 3:3.
[10] Op. cit.
[11] See Str-B III:766.

<table>
<tr><td>

1 Peter 5:5-9

5 Ὁμοίως, νεώτεροι, ὑποτάγητε
πρεσβυτέροις. πάντες δὲ ἀλλήλοις τὴν
ταπεινοφροσύνην ἐγκομβώσασθε, ὅτι
ὁ Θεὸς ὑπερηφάνοις ἀντιτάσσεται,
ταπεινοῖς δὲ δίδωσιν χάριν.

6 Ταπεινώθητε οὖν ὑπὸ τὴν κραταιὰν
χεῖρα τοῦ Θεοῦ, ἵνα ὑμᾶς ὑψώσῃ ἐν
καιρῷ,

7 πᾶσαν τὴν μέριμναν ὑμῶν ἐπιρίψαντες
ἐπ' αὐτόν, ὅτι αὐτῷ μέλει περὶ ὑμῶν.

8 Νήψατε, γρηγορήσατε. ὁ ἀντίδικος
ὑμῶν διάβολος ὡς λέων ὠρυόμενος
περιπατεῖ ζητῶν τινα καταπιεῖν.

9 ᾧ ἀντίστητε στερεοὶ τῇ πίστει, εἰδότες
τὰ αὐτὰ τῶν παθημάτων τῇ ἐν τῷ
κόσμῳ ὑμῶν ἀδελφότητι ἐπιτελεῖσθαι.

</td><td>

James 4:6-10

6 Μείζονα δὲ δίδωσιν χάριν. διὸ λέγει,
Ὁ Θεὸς ὑπερηφάνοις ἀντιτάσσεται,
ταπεινοῖς δὲ δίδωσιν χάριν.

7 ὑποτάγητε οὖν τῷ Θεῷ. ἀντίστητε δὲ
τῷ διαβόλῳ, καὶ φεύξεται ἀφ' ὑμῶν.

8 ἐγγίσατε τῷ Θεῷ, καὶ ἐγγίσει ὑμῖν.
καθαρίσατε χεῖρας, ἁμαρτωλοί, καὶ
ἁγνίσατε καρδίας, δίψυχοι.

9 ταλαιπωρήσατε καὶ πενθήσατε καὶ
κλαύσατε. ὁ γέλως ὑμῶν εἰς πένθος
μετατραπήτω καὶ ἡ χαρὰ εἰς
κατήφειαν.

10 ταπεινώθητε ἐνώπιον Κυρίου, καὶ
ὑψώσει ὑμᾶς.

</td></tr>
</table>

Both passages reflect a striking parallel of content and sequence of thought, namely, (i) a quotation of Pr 3:34; (ii) an exhortation to submit to God; (iii) a call to resist the devil.

The quotation from the LXX version of Pr 3:34, expresses an idea which is axiomatic to the Old Testament and is splendidly proclaimed in the Magnificat[12]. Notably in this citation ὁ Θεός is substituted for the original Κύριος and is paralleled in its Petrine form in Ja 4:6. This change is a notable characteristic of the early Judean church, for 1 Peter, James and Paul alike, always distinguish between ὁ Θεός and ὁ Κύριος ἡμῶν Ἰησοῦς Χριστός[13]. As this distinction faded after the first century in the Greek church, its presence in these two letters again indicates that they are drawing on paraenetical material emanating from the early Jerusalem church. Moreover, in both instances the quotation is followed by the injunction, "Submit then, to God"[14].

Boismard suggested that the parallels between these passages arose because both authors were using a common baptismal hymn[15]. The difficulty of that view soon becomes apparent when the passages are placed side by side as has been done above. If the writers both had the same hymn in mind, one might reasonably expect that the poetic rhythm of the hymn would have caused far more of the hymnodic language to have been kept intact, just as happened with the quotation from Pr 3:34,

---

[12] Lk 1:51-53.
[13] See Rm 5:1,11; 6:23; Ja 1:1; 1 Pt 1:3.
[14] ὑποτάγητε οὖν τῷ Θεῷ Ja 4:7.
[15] M.-E. Boismard, *Quatre hymnes baptismales dans la première Epître de Pierre*, LD 30, Paris: Cerf, 1961:133-163.

where both authors have emended the LXX version by replacing the original Κύριος with ὁ Θεός. Yet nothing of the sort happens in the subsequent verses. While the basic thought pattern is the same and similar phrases occur, there are differences in application and expression in a number of respects. In 1 Peter the quotation is adduced to reinforce his instruction to the younger members to submit to the elders for the good of the community, whereas in James it is used to illustrate the abundance of God's grace. While James simply claims that God will exalt them if they humble themselves and resist the devil, 1 Peter places this exhortation in an eschatological setting by adding ἐν καιρῷ in verse 6 and by connecting the devil with the suffering of the brotherhood throughout the world. He also omits James' claim that if they resist the devil he will flee from them, a claim which lacks any eschatological significance. Moreover, both writers add so much extraneous material, that it is improbable that they were inspired by a common hymn. What does emerge, however, is a common pattern of Judaeo-Christian teaching on resistance to the devil, despite the varied trials and persecutions to which their readers may have been subjected. Most likely the basic teaching and stock motifs on resistance to the devil formed part of the regular pre-baptismal catechetical instruction in view of the danger of persecution to which the members of the church might be liable. Indeed, the teaching here probably provided the seed-bed of the fully developed baptismal ceremony in later years, in which the solemn renunciation of Satan became a dramatic part[16].

The use of ὅτι to introduce catechetical teaching in these two remarkable passages suggests that its occurrence in other parts of the letter may also indicate references to a similar body of instruction emanating from the Jerusalem church[17].

1 Peter 1:18-21

1 Peter 1:18-21 begins with exactly the same expression, εἰδότες ὅτι, as that used by Paul in Rm 5:3; 6:9; 1 Cor 15:58; 2 Cor 1:7; 4:14 and 5:6[18], where in most cases it is also followed by pithy sentences. This suggests that the author is making use of standardized catechetical or liturgical material. As Goppelt[19] remarks, this section is marked by its poetic character. It also gives far more christological detail than a simple

---

[16] See Hippolytus, Trad Apost 21:9; Cyril of Jerusalem, Cat myst 1:2-9.

[17] For a full discussion of the probability of an early Jerusalem Catechism underlying the common paraenetic passages in 1 Peter and the other NT Epistles, see J. H. L. Dijkman, *The socio-religious condition of the recipients of 1 Peter*, unpublished PhD Thesis, University of the Witwatersrand, Johannesburg, 1984.

[18] Cf Eph 6:8-9.

[19] L. Goppelt, *Der erste Petrusbrief*, Göttingen: Vandenhoeck & Ruprecht, 1978:121.

reference to Christ's saving death, which the argument in hand would require. All of this further enhances the view that established credal, catechetical or liturgical material is being used.

Verse 18 is immediately reminiscent of Is 52:3, "You were sold for nothing, and not with silver shall you be ransomed"—καί οὐ μετὰ ἀργυρίου λυτρωθήσεσθε[20]. While λυτροῦσθαι and its derivatives are used extensively in the LXX for all kinds of redemption[21], the early church traditionally applied the concept to Jesus' death in terms of the Suffering Servant passages in Is 52:13-53:12. This strand of the tradition also appears at Mark 10:45 and Mt 20:28[22]. Elsewhere the same idea is expressed by ὑπὲρ ὑμῶν διδόμενον ... ὑπὲρ ὑμῶν ἐκχυννόμενον[23], ἐκχυννόμενον ὑπὲρ πολλῶν[24], and ἠγοράσθητε γὰρ τιμῆς[25]. In view of the importance of the concept in the Christian faith, it is surprising to find that the use of the actual words λυτρὸν, λυτρόω, λύτρωσις and λυτρωτής are restricted to so few passages. Closer scrutiny, however, reveals that most of these references appear in material with strong Judean associations, thus providing contributory evidence for the Jewish provenance of 1 Peter's quotation.

1 Peter 2:15

In 1 Peter 2:15 ὅτι again introduces an admonition to good works within the subordination theme of the social code in 2:13-17[26]. In discussing this teaching of good works, Van Unnik[27] laments the fact that the keyword of the passage, ἀγαθοποιεῖν is passed over without comment in many expositions, and that the short discussions by Grundmann[28] fail to give a full analysis and are quite unsatisfactory. To rectify this, he considers three possible interpretations (the Greek, Jewish and Christian) of "good works" to which 1 Peter's conception might be related.

He finds that it is decidedly different from the Jewish type like the גמילות חסדים   commended by the rabbis to assist the poor and others

---

[20] Cf Tt 2:14, where λυτρώσηται is used to describe the effect of Christ's passion.
[21] See Ex 4:6; 15:13; 21:30; 30:12; Dt 7:8; Lv 25:25-28; Nm 18:15; Ps 106:2; 129:8; Hs 13:14; Is 41:14; 43:1,14.
[22] Cf Lk 1:68; 2:38; 24:21; Ac 7:35; Tt 2:14; Hb 9:12. See also F. Büchsel, TDNT IV:340-356; V. Taylor, Jesus and his sacrifice, London: MacMillan, 1955:99-105; C. Bigg, The Epistles of St Peter and St Jude, ICC, 2. ed. Edinburgh: Clark, 1902:118.
[23] Lk 22:19 & 20. Cf Mt 26:28; 1 Cor 11:24.
[24] Mk 14:24.
[25] 1 Cor 6:20.
[26] Cf Rm 13:1-7.
[27] W. C. van Unnik, The Teaching of Good Works in 1 Peter, NTS 1, 92-110, 1954.
[28] W. Grundmann, TDNT I:17, and TDNT III:536-550.

unable to fulfil the Law's requirements[29]. Nor does the concept imply the good works of later Christian theology which would atone for post-baptismal faults. Instead it appears to Van Unnik that 1 Peter uses ἀγαθοποιεῖν with the same range of meaning as the Greeks. Yet its foundation is quite different from the Greek idea, for the "good deeds" are enjoined "not to earn glory for oneself, but to make the way free for the Gospel towards the disobedient"[30]. Further, Van Unnik argues that we must see ἀγαθοποιεῖν as part of the Christian's calling to holiness, as they follow the Lord's example. As their Redeemer, He did good in the midst of suffering. So must His followers. This thought is an echo of Peter's speech to Cornelius in Acts 10:38, which C. H. Dodd believes to be part of the Jerusalem Kerygma[31]. Hence Van Unnik concludes that for 1 Peter ἀγαθοποιεῖν was "a Greek word perfectly adequate to express how a Christian has to live with his fellow-men in love during this time of faith and hope"[32].

However, his analysis fails to take proper account of the Talmudic macaser Torah or מעשים טובים [33], "good works" or simply "works" for short as in James[34], by which contemporary pharisaism expressed the idea of doing the will (or Law) of God. In 1 Peter ἀγαθοποιεῖν is used to express this thought, not specifically to support the Imperial government, but rather to please God and to do His will. Thus those who falsely accuse them "will glorify God on the day of visitation"[35]. The Christians will be doing God's will when by doing right (ἀγαθοποιεῖν) they "put to silence the ignorance of foolish men"[36].

Confirmation of this Talmudic interpretation of ἀγαθοποιεῖν may be found in 1 Pt 2:19, where διὰ συνείδησιν Θεοῦ may be regarded as a synonym for "doing Torah" or "doing good works" in order to please God. Again in 3:10-12 the author quotes Ps 34:12-16 to justify his ethical stance. Lohse makes the point that 1 Peter exhorts his readers to cease from evil and *do good* precisely *because* the Lord favours the righteous and opposes those who *do evil*[37]. This use of ἀγαθοποιεῖν further substantiates the argument for a Judean origin of the paraenetic, and refutes W.

---

[29] For the relevant Talmudic references see Str-B III:505 & 161, and Str-B IV:559-561.

[30] W. C. van Unnik, op. cit., 108-109.

[31] C. H. Dodd, *The Apostolic preaching and its developments*, 2. ed. London: Hodder & Stoughton, 1951:27.

[32] Op. cit., 110.

[33] See M. Jastrow, *A dictionary of the Targumim, the Talmud Babli and Yerushalmi, and the Midrashic literature*, New York/Berlin: Choreb, 1926:820, who quotes Ber 32b.

[34] Ja 1:4; 2:14,17,22.

[35] 1 Pt 2:12.

[36] 1 Pt 2:15. Cf 1 Pt 4:3-6,12-19.

[37] E. Lohse, Paränese und Kerygma im 1 Petrusbrief, *ZNW* 45:68-89, 1954:86.

Munro's theory that the teaching of 1 Peter was aimed to elicit support for the Roman government[38].

1 Peter 2:21-25

ὅτι again introduces the thought of Christ as an example to οἰκέται in 1 Peter 2:21-25. It occurs in a lyrical passage which is sometimes seen as a "Song of the Suffering Servant", because it is based on Isaiah 53. Jesus, during His earthly ministry, was treated as a much-abused servant, thus setting an example to other οἰκέται. Therefore, they are urged to imitate Christ, for by His actions He has set the Christian free from ἁμαρτία to live for righteousness. Following in the steps of Jesus (ἐπακολουθήσητε) is also deeply ingrained in the Gospel tradition in Mark 8:34 (and parallels) and in John 13:15, while Paul quotes the Judean Christ-hymn in Phlp 2:5-11 as he encourages his readers to follow the example of Christ[39]. Similarly, 1 Tm 5:1 mentions the favourable effect a slave's good conduct will have on men's attitude to Christianity. The same thought is also applied to the good behaviour of young married women in Titus 2:5, and in the general passage in 1 Peter 2:1-2 which introduces the whole teaching of subjection.

J. Jeremias[40] suggests that in this poetic and didactic paraphrase of the Servant Song of Isaiah 53, 1 Peter is using a very ancient type of christology. It seems to have been popular for a time while the church was based in Judea, but passed into abeyance in later writings as the church spread into the Greek world. Interestingly enough, in Acts 3:13,26 and 4:27,30, where Peter is the speaker, Jesus is actually called "God's servant" παῖς Θεοῦ and in Acts 8:32-33 Philip cites Is 53:7-8 to explain His person and His death. Paul, on the other hand, does not exploit this image, though we can find possible traces of it in early tradition which he hands down in Phlp 2:5-11, where he refers to Jesus as a servant (δοῦλος) in v 7. Thus in his review of the interpretation of the "Ebed" passages, Jeremias comes to the conclusion that, "the christological interpretation of these passages derives from the Palestinian, pre-Hellenistic stage of the primitive Church"[41], thereby demonstrating the author's close association with the Judean church, whose interpretation

---

[38] W. Munro, *Authority in Paul and Peter. The identification of a pastoral stratum in the Pauline corpus and 1 Peter.* NTSMS 45, Cambridge: Cambridge University Press, 1982:2.

[39] For arguments for its Judean origin seen E. Lohmeyer, *KYRIOS JESUS: Eine Untersuchung zu Phlp 2:5-11*, Darmstadt: WBG, 1961; R. P. Martin, *An early Christian confession*, London: Tyndale, 1960.

[40] See J. Jeremias, *TDNT* V:682-717.

[41] Ibid., 709. Cf C. H. Dodd, *According to the Scriptures*, Welwyn: Nisbet, 1952:94.

of the Passion in the framework of the Suffering Servant was probably its greatest achievement in the evolution of its christology.

1 Peter 3:18-22

1 Peter 3:18-22 has been the subject of much discussion and special study[42]. It too begins with the particle ὅτι which suggests that a quotation is being introduced as in 1:18 and 2:21. The style is very concise and the passage introduces ideas which, although not strictly pertinent to the argument, are part of the primitive kerygma. The most common conclusion, to date, appears to be that it opens and closes with a portion of an early christian hymn[43], while verses 19-21 are part of a baptismal catechism[44]. In attempting to establish the background to the thought of Christ preaching to the disobedient spirits, it has generally been accepted that the most direct influence must have come from 1 Enoch 6 and the Book of Jubilees 5, which is based on Genesis 6:1-8. While we cannot be absolutely sure of the dates of composition of the various parts of 1 Enoch, it is clear from the Aramaic portions of it which have been found amongst the Qumran Scrolls, that it was already in circulation at the time 1 Peter was written[45]. It is even quoted in Jude 14, while the reference to the imprisonment of the disobedient spirits until judgment, in 1 Enoch 10.11-14, is echoed in Jude 6 and 2 Pt 2.4. Moreover, in the Jewish apocalyptic tradition, the story of the נפלים [46] was closely associated with the flood in the time of Noah[47]. These apocalyptic accounts also continue the tradition that Noah was righteous[48], for their Jewish writers draw a contrast between Noah as a righteous person and the "fallen angels" or disobedient spirits. Only by taking this Jewish background into account, can this complicated passage in 1 Peter be understood.

As the author closes the passage, he refers once more to the hymnic material he echoed in the opening verse. It too uses technical terms from

---

[42] See M.-E. Boismard, *Quatre hymnes baptismales dans la première Epître de Pierre*, LD 30, Paris: Cerf, 1961; R. Bultmann, Bekenntnis- und Liedfragmente im ersten Petrusbrief, *ConNT* 11:1-14, Lund, 1947; F. L. Cross, *1 Peter, A paschal liturgy*, London: Mowbray, 1954; W. J. Dalton, *Christ's proclamation to the Spirits*, AnBib 23, Rome: PBI, 1965; Bo Reicke, *The disobedient spirits and christian baptism*, ANSU 13, Kobenhaven: Munksgaard, 1949; J. T. Sanders, *The New Testament christological hymns: their historical religious background*, Cambridge: Cambridge University Press, 1971.

[43] Cf 1 Tm 2:16.

[44] See W. J. Dalton, op. cit., 13-14.

[45] See M. A. Knibb, *The Ethiopic book of Enoch*, Oxford: Clarendon, 1978, II, 6-8, who dates 1 Enoch 6 to the first century B.C.

[46] "Nephilim" - the sons of God who were regarded as fallen angels. See Gn 6:1-4.

[47] See 1 Enoch 6:65; Jub 5; T Napht 3:5; CD 2:18-20.

[48] See Gn 6:9. Cf Hb 11:7.

the Jewish apocalyptic tradition with its references to angels, authorities and powers. Parallels to its main theme of the victory of Christ over the evil powers occur in 1 Cor 15:24; Eph 1:21; Phlp 2:10; Col 2:15 and Hb 1:13 which all use imagery inspired by Ps 110:1, "The Lord said to my Lord, 'Sit at my right hand until I make your enemies your footstool'". Not only was this verse in the psalm given a Messianic interpretation in rabbinical circles[49], it was also "one of the fundamental texts of the kerygma, underlying all the various developments of it..."[50]. Consequently, in a recent article, Matthew Black can argue that the terminology formed part of an early hymnic tradition which Peter and Paul cite independently[51].

Within the context of verse 18 ὁ δίχαιος, "the righteous", is manifestly a title for Jesus. Passages like Acts 3:14; 7:52; 1 Jn 2:1,29; 3:7[52] show that it was used in this way in the early church. If Ja 5:6 could be interpreted in the same way, it would be another indication of close links between these two writers. While some christian fathers like Oecumenius, Cassiodorus and at a later stage, Bede[53] have interpreted the verse in James as referring specifically to Jesus' unjust condemnation and execution, that view is not favourably regarded today. Thus even J. B. Mayor[54], who is inclined to find a reference to the cross here, admits that "the righteous man" is primarily a generic term, whose reference is not exhausted in one individual. Greeven, in editing Dibelius' commentary, suggests that if the letter is indeed pseudonymous, it might be taken as a veiled melancholy allusion to the death of James who was called "the Just"[55]. Yet these modern arguments are not very persuasive. The *past tense* in Ja 5:6, χατεδιχάσατε, ἐφονεύσατε and the definite article τὸν δίχαιον indicate a sequence of actions in the *past* which fit a specific person. If "the Just" were to be understood as a generic term, a present tense and not an aorist would have been required for these verbs. The great complaint of the primitive Judean church against "the Rich" (i.e. the powerful amongst the priesthood and those in the government) was constantly: "You have condemned and killed 'the Righteous One'". When in Acts Peter addressed the people in the Temple, he specifically named Jesus as

---

[49] See Str-B IV, 1:452-465.

[50] C. H. Dodd, *According to the Scriptures*. Welwyn: Nisbet, 1952:35.

[51] M. Black, Πᾶσαι ἐξουσίαι αὐτῷ ὑποταγήσονται, in *Paul and Paulinism. Essays in honour of C. K. Barret*, edited by M. D. Hooker and S. G. Wilson, London: SPCK, 1982:74-82.

[52] See G. Schrenk, *TDNT* II:186-189.

[53] See S. Laws, *A commentary on the Epistle of James*, BNTC, London: Black, 1980, ad. loc.

[54] J. B. Mayor, *The Epistle of St James*, 2. ed. London: MacMillan, 1897:155.

[55] M. Dibelius, *A commentary on the Epistle of James*, Rev. H. Greeven, Philadelphia: Fortress Press, 1976:240, n. 58.

"the Righteous One"[56]. Stephen did the same in Acts 7:51-52[57]. For the primitive Judean church, therefore, Jesus was the Righteous One *par excellence* and they explained His suffering and death by projecting into them the image of *the* suffering, righteous one, the עבד of Is 53:3-9,11. Their interpretation may also have been influenced by similar charges against the rich and powerful in the Prophetic[58] and the Wisdom literature[59] particularly Wis 2:18-20[60], which already echoes Is 52:13-53:12 and is also very close to James. Since Jesus did indeed suffer such a fate in a most significant way, we may conclude that in the tradition of the primitive Judean church, both James and 1 Peter ascribe the title ὁ δίκαιος to Him.

Verse 22 at the end of this passage closely reflects Peter's sermon in Acts 2:33-36, in which he claims that Jesus has fulfilled the promise of Psalm 110:1. In rabbinical circles that psalm was traditionally given a Messianic interpretation, an interpretation which the New Testament writers adopted as well[61]. Peter again makes the same claim in Acts 5:31, while in Acts 7:56-57 it is yet again repeated in the account of Stephen's martyrdom. In fact evidence for this belief can be found throughout the New Testament, and it subsequently became part of the Apostles' Creed. All this evidence suggests that the statement of the exaltation is a precious fragment of the baptismal confession of faith of the Apostolic church, reaching back to its very roots in Jerusalem, like the Judean Christ hymn quoted by Paul in Phlp 2:6-11.

1 Peter 4:1

The aphorism "whoever has suffered in the flesh has ceased from sin" in 1 Peter 4:1 is also introduced by ὅτι. This quotation heads another passage, 1 Pt 4:1-11 in which the author is offering a renewed application of his earlier exhortations to ἀγαθοποιῶν by stressing that the prime motive behind the injunction is to do the will of God, just as "doing *tsedaqa*" implied fulfilling the Torah for the rabbis. James 4:13-15 gives a practical exposition of the same teaching in which he characterizes

---

[56] See Acts 3:13-18 and note especially v 14, "you denied the Holy and Righteous One and asked for a murderer to be granted to you".

[57] "...As your father did, so do you ... they killed those who announced beforehand the coming of the Righteous One, whom you have now betrayed and murdered."

[58] See Am 5:11f; 8:4; Is 3:10 (LXX), 14f; 5:23; Mi 2:1.

[59] See Pr 1:10ff; Ps 37:14, 32.

[60] "If the righteous man is God's son, he will help him, and will deliver him from the hand of his adversaries. Let us test him with insult and torture ... Let us condemn him to a shameful death."

[61] See W. Grundmann, *TDNT* II:37-40.

βούλημα as planning a business or a pleasure trip and similarly contrasts it with ἐάν ὁ κύριος θελήσῃ. The presentation of such parallel rabbinic-like teaching with James is an added argument in favour of the existence of a common Jerusalem catechism from which both writers drew.

1 Peter 4:7

Finally, in 1 Peter 4:12-19 the author uses ὅτι to introduce a phrase emphasizing the nearness of the *parousia*[62] as he connects the sufferings of Christ with the future glory in God's great scheme of redemption. Like the writer to the Hebrews[63], 1 Peter warns against the dangers of apostasy and resentment at suffering unjust injury, as he braces his readers to endure impending persecution which heralds the "end", insisting that God will vindicate His own. Indeed, the eschatological woe expressed in the passage as a whole reflects the heightened expectations in Judaism leading to the revolt of 66 A.D.[64].

This short investigation shows, therefore, that in 1 Peter ὅτι is used as an introductory formula for material which is very often common to James and the other New Testament epistles. Where it does not consist of adaptations or variants of Old Testament texts, it nevertheless betrays such typical traits of Jewish thought and expression, that it too must have passed through a Jewish or Jewish Christian stage in its formulation. The teaching in these passages appears to have been so highly respected, that in many instances its original verbal formulation has been kept intact, even if it is used in a different context, and sometimes it is even allowed to interrupt the flow of thought, as in 1 Pt 1:18-21. Such esteem can only be explained if the material originated in the very early Judean church and was endowed with Apostolic authority. From the history of the early church it is evident that such paraenetic material could only emanate from the church at Jerusalem, which was controlled and directed by Peter, James and John, the so-called "pillars of the church"[65], prior to James' death in 62 A.D. Hence this influential body of teaching, for which 1 Peter has reserved ὅτι as an introductory formula, may most appropriately be termed a Primitive Jerusalem Catechism.

---

[62] 1 Peter 4:17, "For the time has come for judgment to begin with the household of God; and if it begins with us, what will be the end of those who do not obey the gospel of God?"

[63] Hb 10:37.

[64] See Str-B III:336.

[65] See Gl 2:9.

CONTRIBUTORS

University of Durban-Westville
Dr Pieter J. Maartens   – Dept. of New Testament

Johannesburg Diocesan Bible College
Rev Dr J. H. L. Dijkman   – Dept. of New Testament

University of the Orange Free State
Dr Kobus (J.) van W. Cronjé   – Greek dept.
Prof Dr Jan A. du Rand   – Dept. of New Testament
Prof Dr Andries H. Snyman   – Greek dept.

Potchefstroom University for Christian Higher Education
Mr Jan Botha   – Greek dept.
Prof Dr J. Christi Coetzee   – Dept. of New Testament
Prof Dr Fika (J.) J. Janse van Rensburg   – Greek dept.
Mr Kobus (J.) H. Petzer   – Greek dept.

University of Pretoria
Prof Dr Andrie B. du Toit   – Dept. of New Testament
Prof Dr Jannie P. Louw   – Greek dept.
Prof Dr Andries G. van Aarde   – Dept. of New Testament

Rand Afrikaans University
Prof Dr Paul J. du Plessis   – Dept. of Biblical Studies

Rhodes University
Prof Dr John N. Suggit   – Dept. of New Testament

University of Stellenbosch
Prof Dr H. J. Bernard Combrink   – Dept. of New Testament

University of South Africa
Prof Dr Izak J. du Plessis   – Dept. of New Testament
Prof Dr Johnnie H. Roberts   – Dept. of New Testament
Prof Dr Willem S. Vorster   – Institute for Theological Research

University of the Witwatersrand
Dr Patrick J. Hartin   – Dept. of Divinity

Not attached to a university or college
Rev Dr G. Jorrie C. Jordaan